Introdu

Rabat
MOROCCO
Algiers
Tunis
TUNISIA
Tripoli
Benghazi
Cairo
Canary Is.
ALGERIA
LIBYA
EGYPT
MAURITANIA
Nouakchott
MALI
NIGER
TCHAD
SUDAN
Khartoum
Cape Verde Is.
Praia
SENEGAL
Dakar
GAMBIA
Bangui
GUINEA-BISSAU
Bissau
Conakry
Freetown
SIERRA LEONE
Monrovia
LIBERIA
GUINEA
Bamako
UPPER VOLTA
Niamey
Ouagadougou
IVORY COAST
GHANA
Abidjan
Accra
Lome
TOGO
Porto Novo
BENIN
Lagos
NIGERIA
Njamena
CAMEROUN
Yaounde
CENTR. AFR. REP.
Bangui
TERR. OF AFARS & ISSAS
Djibouti
Addis Ababa
ETHIOPIA
SOMALIA
Mogadishu
UGANDA
Kampala
KENYA
Nairobi
EQUATORIAL GUINEA
Malabo
Libreville
GABON
SAO TOME & PRINCIPE
CONGO
ZAIRE
RWANDA
Kigali
BURUNDI
Bujumbura
Brazzaville
Kinshasa
TANZANIA
Dar es Salaam
Zanzibar
Seychelles Is.
Victoria
Comoro Is.
Moroni
Luanda
ANGOLA
ZAMBIA
Lusaka
MALAWI
Lilongwe
Salisbury
RHODESIA
MOZAMBIQUE
Tananarive
Mauritius
MALAGASY
Réunion
NAMIBIA
Windhoek
BOTSWANA
Gaborone
Mbabane
Pretoria
Maputo
SWAZILAND
SOUTH AFRICA
LESOTHO
Maseru

Introduction to African Politics

A Continental Approach

Second Edition

LESLIE RUBIN
Howard University

BRIAN WEINSTEIN
Howard University

HOLT, RINEHART AND WINSTON
New York   Chicago   San Francisco   Atlanta
Dallas   Montreal   Toronto

Published in the United States of America in 1977 by
Praeger Publishers
A Division of Holt, Rinehart & Winston

This is the second edition of a book originally published in
1974 by Praeger Publishers, Inc.

© 1974, 1977 by Praeger Publishers,
All rights reserved

89 074 9 8 7 6 5 4 3 2

Library of Congress Cataloging in Publication Data

Rubin, Leslie.
  Introduction to African politics.

  Bibliography: p.
  Includes index.
  1. Africa—Politics and government. I. Weinstein, Brian, joint author. II. Title.
JQ1872.R8 1977   320.9′6′03   76-41968
ISBN 0-275-64700-5 pbk.
ISBN 0-275-24160-2

Printed in the United States of America

For
Neville and Martin Rubin
Dick and Irene Spero

Contents

Preface ix

1 INTRODUCTION 3

2 POLITICAL SYSTEMS IN AFRICA 8
What Is a Political System? 8 • "Traditional Political Systems 11 • Centralized Authority 13 • Decentralized Authority 19 • Traditional Political Systems and Contemporary Government 22

3 COLONIALISM AND AFRICAN POLITICS 28
The Colonial Situation: A Shared Experience, 1885–1960 33 • Colonialism and African Authority: The Dual Polity 35 • Colonialism and African Authority: New Elites 42 • Ethnic Differentiation and Ethnic Politicization 46 • Organization of the Contemporary State 50 • Colonialism and Production: A Dual Economy 59 • A New Framework for Politics 63

4 THE END OF COLONIALISM 66
Perception of Interest: Some Cases 68 • Leaders with a Mobilizing Idea 75 • Organization for Unity and Continuity 82

5 INDEPENDENCE 90
Independence Perceived 90 • Independence and Violence 98

6 SOUTHERN AFRICA 109
The White Redoubt 109 • The Republic of South Africa 111 • The Origins of Apartheid 111 • Apartheid in Practice 113 • Enforced Racial Separation 113 • Control of Movement and Employment 114 • Separate Development 115 • The Police-State Apparatus 123 • A Rigid Caste Society 125 • Black Opposition 126 • South Africa's Response to Resistance 129 • International Reaction to Apartheid 132 •

Nambia (South-West Africa) 134 • Rhodesia (Zimbabwe) 136
• The Future of Southern Africa 144

7 "MODERNIZATION" IN INDEPENDENT AFRICA 148
Nation-Building: Concepts 148 • Nation-Building: Process 152
• Barriers to Nation-Building 168 • Development: Concepts
177 • Development and Growth 179 • Barriers to
Development 180

8 ATTEMPTED SOLUTIONS 185
The One-Party State 185 • Party Organization 190 •
Elections 192 • Coups 193 • African Socialism 196 •
Single Parties, Socialism, and Revolution 199 •
Centralization 201 • Disappointments: "Not Yet
Madadiliko" 204

9 ADAPTATION OF INSTITUTIONS, CONCEPTS, AND
METHODS 211
Traditional Values in a Modern State 211 • Education 212 •
Language 215 • Chieftaincy 217 • Customary Law 223

10 COOPERATION AMONG THE INDEPENDENT
AFRICAN STATES 230
Roots of Pan-Africanism 230 • West Africa 232 • North
Africa 234 • East, Central, and Southern Africa 235 •
Toward African Unity—1958–63 237 • African Trade Unionism
243 • The Organization of African Unity 244 • The OAU
Charter 246 • The Organization of African Unity:
Achievements and Failures 251 • Regional Pan-African
Groupings 258 • Federalism 260 • The Future of African
Unity 263

11 AFRICA IN THE WORLD CONTEXT 265
Africa and the International Community 265 • The United
Nations 266 • Neo-Colonialism 271 • Anglophone and
Francophone Africa 274 • The Commonwealth 276 •
Nonalignment 283 • Africa and the United States 286 •
Africa and the Soviet Union 290 • Africa and the People's
Republic of China 294 • Africa and the Arab World 298 •
The Impact of World Economics 298 • The Dynamism of
African Politics 302

Appendix 305

Readings 317

Index 331

Preface

The idea for this book resulted from our feeling that, although there are many excellent monographs on particular African countries, parties, and movements of various kinds, and a number of valuable books of readings, no one suitable book exists for use in an introductory course which examines African politics as a study of the continent as a whole. The focus of previous books has been on specific areas of Africa—never on Africa as a whole.

The hesitancy of contemporary scholars to deal with the continent is explained by their belief that not enough has been written about politics in individual countries to provide the bases for synthesis; that the countries have not been independent long enough for definite patterns to emerge; that no man or woman is capable of absorbing enough material and information about this huge continent safely to make valid generalizations about the whole of Africa; and, finally, that regional differences are more important than similarities.

Although we may be the proverbial fools entering where intellectual angels fear to tread, our own research leaves us with a conviction that continental African politics can indeed be fruitfully studied within the framework of analysis applied to other societies. It is also important to note that African elites for years have insisted on the political similarities among their countries. Although we see no scientific reason to accept their contention *a priori*, we see no scientific reason to reject it *a priori* either. We dare not ignore the way in which people we are studying define themselves.

Therefore, despite the fact that each author of this work has a specialty, we attempt to bring in examples from all regions and most countries in Africa to support the generalizations we make. We thus risk criticism from colleagues with other specialties who will notice the gaps that necessarily exist in this book. On the other hand, we offer areas for discussion within a broader framework than heretofore employed, and, more important, we hope we have written a useful book for beginning students.

For helping us develop our ideas through discussion and challenge we are grateful to students and colleagues at the University of Cape Town, the University of Ghana, the former Ecole Nationale d'Administration of the Republic of Guinea, the School of African and Oriental Studies, University of London, and Howard University. We are also indebted to

African, European, and American scholars who have done the field research that is the basis of any attempt to synthesize and to Africans we have interviewed in connection with our past research projects. Brian Weinstein thanks Dr. Dorothy Porter, Mrs. Stokes, Mrs. Ellis, Mr. Johnson, and Mr. Nkrumah of the Moorland-Spingarn Research Foundation of Howard University; Mesdemoiselles Sudre, Lorrain, and Chaumais of the Centre Universitaire International of the University of Paris; Professor Donald E. Herdeck; and Mr. Nathaniel Anyaogu Okafor. Leslie Rubin thanks, in particular, his son Neville for a number of helpful criticisms on the planning of the book, Professor David Apter for his encouragement, Professor David Brokensha for his helpful comments, Dr. Peter Garlick for invaluable advice and assistance, Dr. Francis Awogu and Mr. Jones Ayo Akinbobola for their help with the bibliography, and Dr. J. E. Okolo for the appendix, a most useful collection of "vital statistics" on the independent states and dependencies of Africa.

We are most grateful to Denise Rathbun of Praeger Publishers for her many helpful suggestions and her invaluable editorial services.

The success of the first edition of this book reinforces our belief that a continental approach to the politics of Africa can contribute to a real understanding of the complex developments in that part of the world.

September, 1976

L.R.
B.W.

Introduction to African Politics

1 Introduction

Africa is not politically united, but similarities in the African political experience are significant. An attempt to deal with these common experiences is therefore as justified as a political study of Europe, a continent even less clearly defined geographically than Africa. Past refusals to take this approach to Africa were largely due to a lack of sufficient data, but in some cases they were based on American and European racial, economic, and political interests that are outmoded and dangerous.

Before World War II the ways in which many writers dealt with Africa corresponded to the way in which foreign governments and businessmen viewed Africa, namely, as a reservoir of small groups of beings and resources to be used for the benefit of non-Africans. Except for anthropologists, most scholars ignored the continent. Those who wrote about it often implicitly or explicitly defined Africa as narrowly as possible.

It is surprising that there might be any question about what Africa is or that Africa might be considered a rather small continent. Africa is more clearly defined geographically than is Europe; it is a huge land mass, more than twice the size of the United States, and almost completely separate from other land masses. In spite of this, there has always been a strong tendency to regard parts of the African continent as belonging to other continents or regions.

An example is North Africa. The countries from Morocco to Egypt have been included in the Middle East, and pharaonic Egypt has until recently been considered culturally *sui generis*. Sometimes the Sudan, Ethiopia, and Somalia have been included in the Middle East because of the Semitic languages spoken by some peoples in those three countries. No one would question the historical ties between Tunisia and Saudi Arabia or Turkey. The three countries might be considered in a discussion of the Middle East, but there is no reason to exclude Tunisia from Africa, of which it is a part and with which it also has ancient historical, cultural, and political ties.

In the past, the dissection of Africa went even farther. Peoples living in the savanna region south of the Sahara, for example, were considered not to be "true Africans" or "true Negroes." They were the so-called Hamites of European or Asian stock, who had supposedly brought "civilization" to Africa. One people so considered are the Fulani, who live in the broad area stretching from Senegal and Mauritania to the Central African Republic; they have earned the title Hamites because of their complex political system, rich poetic tradition, language influenced by Arabic, and physical features, all apparently related to Semitic peoples of the East. Other peoples often denied classification as Africans were the Baganda and the Tutsi. Again, those who built great Zimbabwe in Rhodesia were not believed to be "real" or "indigenous" Africans.

With the exclusion of white-dominated Southern Africa (from the Cape of Good Hope to the Zambezi River) and of the Arabic north and the northeast, there was left only a little that could be considered the African continent. It consisted of a forest zone from Guinea through the Ivory Coast, Ghana, Nigeria, then south to Zaïre and Angola. Coincidentally, this expanse corresponded with the area from which most slaves had been taken across the Atlantic. But even in this area non-African peoples were discovered. All it took to be called non-African was an intelligence or culture judged superior by the Europeans or Americans. It was even better if one were tall, had a narrow nose, and could say "Salaam."

Africa's diversity is not to be questioned, and some peoples not considered "true Africans" indeed believe that they are somehow not part of the continent. North Africans traveling south write about going "to Africa" as if they were not already there, for example. Other groups, black and brown in color, such as the Ethiopians and Somalis, also have identified themselves with other continents.

It is true that peoples of northern Africa took darker colored Africans into slavery, but this indisputable fact is sometimes disingenuously used by non-Africans to encourage division or to challenge efforts between the Arabic and non-Arabic portions of the continent at unification. It is also a fact that many dark-skinned groups, such as the Efik and Ashanti, dealt in slaves, but this has nothing to do with what is or what is not African. How people treat or treated each other is not a criterion for deciding that they do or do not belong to the same continent. Germany and Poland are neighbors in Europe, and many of their people look alike; many Germans and French are descendants of the same tribes, and yet often do not look alike. Both Poles and French have suffered at the hands of the Germans in this century. Still, the three countries are all part of Europe.

One of the first efforts to counteract the supposed divisions of Africa was the Pan-African movement, which claimed a basic unity for Africans and peoples anywhere of African descent who were dark in color. Its first effort was to bring to Afro-Americans, Caribbeans, and Africans an awareness of shared experience and need for action. Dr. W. E. B. Du Bois, one of its leaders, said that the movement was based first on the recognition of a "common racial fount" and that he believed in the necessity of action to free and unite the black race. The purpose was to ensure that black men could live like other men and develop their

INTRODUCTION

human potential as well as their territory. Pan-Africanism was therefore a political, social, and economic movement, but cultural and racial factors also came into it. Afro-American, Caribbean, and African poets later said there was a cultural core linking all blacks and that it seemed to be racial. They said that blacks shared certain sensitivities to rhythm, sight, and sound. Léopold Sédar Senghor, poet of this *négritude*, wrote of the supposedly higher sensual and emotional capacity of blacks. White racists had been saying much the same for years. Now that a few blacks have been writing the same thing, such ideas currently seem acceptable to some blacks.

The definition of Africa and "Africanité" then expanded to include the nonblack Arabs and Berbers in northern Africa. Although the Arabs moved into Africa only after the seventh century, they must now, after thirteen centuries, be considered part of Africa. Senghor has said that the Arabs and blacks are subgroups of the African people. Their languages form a continuous "chain" from north to south; their cultures converge around a similar view of the role of man and God. Negro Africa has absorbed the method and logic of Arab thinking: Arab Africa has absorbed emotion from the south. Differences will remain, but all Africans will work together, Senghor hopes.[1]

Perception of identity of purpose and struggle became political. In the very late 1950's and early 1960's, independent countries formed African organizations without much regard to color or language. The so-called Casablanca group included white Morocco and black Ghana. The Monrovia group included English-speaking Nigeria, French-speaking Senegal, and the offshore island of Madagascar. Then, in 1963, a continent-wide organization, the Organization of African Unity (OAU) was created in Addis Ababa, Ethiopia, to "promote the unity and solidarity of African states." Countries joined as they gained independence, and their leaders said they belonged to the continent, proclaiming their Africanness. Such an assertion by a country like Libya, for instance, does not exclude it from the Arab world or the Middle East, nor does such an assertion exclude Senegal from a worldwide Francophone grouping. It is an attempt to counteract and contradict those who said that there was no Africa or who had divided Africa for their own purposes. It is an attempt to work together for the pursuit of shared interests. Africa insists that it has the right to define its identity just as others do.

For us, the continent of Africa comprises the geographical Africa, from the Mediterranean Sea to the Cape of Good Hope, and from the western bulge (Senegal) to the eastern horn (Somalia), together with the offshore islands of Cape Verde, Madagascar, Mauritius, Zanzibar, Sao Tomé and Principe, the Comoros, and others. We shall attempt to

[1] Léopold Sédar Senghor, *Les fondements de l'Africanité ou Négritude et Arabité* (Paris: Présence Africaine, 1967). Although Senghor believes the two groups are African, he evidently sees important cultural differences. Senegal has opposed Arab participation in worldwide black festivals, for example.

justify ten generalizations about the politics of the whole continent as so defined.

Our first generalization, made in the next chapter, is that complex political patterns existed in Africa before the arrival of the non-African and that the patterns of those precolonial systems influence politics today. We indicate that one of the basic problems of precolonial systems was lack of centralization of power, and this is a key problem in independent states today. We also contend that older patterns of authority and loyalty have by no means disappeared.

Second, we assert that the arrival of Europeans and their efforts to establish a colonial system radically affected African politics and is a continuing influence today. The colonial situation was a shared experience all over the continent, and the colonial state, a European-fashioned administration overlying precolonial systems, was inherited by today's leaders.

Third, the colonial period was relatively brief in most areas because Africans opposed foreign control and because most of the colonial powers themselves changed their minds about their empires. African elites and masses opposed foreign control when they perceived their interests were being adversely affected, and after World War II the majority of Europeans also perceived that their interests would not be served by continuing political control over Africa.

Our fourth generalization is that most countries became politically independent relatively quickly and peacefully after African leaders demanded independence. Liberation wars were necessary in only a small minority of states. African leaders, most of whom owed their elite status to the colonial state, accepted the structures of the new states but opposed the continuing presence of Europeans who controlled it. They articulated the felt needs and grievances of the masses to strengthen their opposition and threat to the Europeans. The needs of the elite and the needs of the masses were not always the same, however.

Fifth, not all of Africa is politically independent. It is the goal of African nationalism to liberate the remaining colonies from foreign rule and to achieve majority rule in southern Africa. Settlers of European descent kept control of the Republic of South Africa, Namibia (South-West Africa), and Rhodesia (Zimbabwe). Independent African countries are unanimous in their condemnation of this situation, and many of them have actively worked for change in southern Africa.

Our sixth generalization is that two major problems facing all independent states are material development and nation-building. In addition to the difficulty inherent in definitions of these goals, there is often a considerable difference in the perception of these goals by the elites and the masses. Elites sometimes seem to be more interested in unity, whereas the masses are more interested in material development.

Seventh, in an attempt to solve these problems, independent Africa has experimented with the one-party state and socialist ideology, both designed to centralize and maintain power. These developments have been perceived in some countries as contrary to the interests of some groups and have consequently been directly related to the instability of most independent African governments and to the rise of military dictatorships.

Eighth, independent Africa has also attempted to adapt alien institutions, concepts, and methods to its own needs. Leaders have asserted an African way of doing things and have claimed new legitimacy for African languages and an educational system adapted to perceived needs.

Our ninth generalization is that the African governments recognize African unity as an ultimate goal but continue to base their programs and politics on national needs rather than on the interests of independent Africa as a whole. Unity is a goal for political and economic reasons, that is, for increased power in international affairs and for enlarged internal markets for locally produced goods and services. But no one has an easy formula for achieving unity, particularly when the masses demand satisfaction of their narrower local needs at the same time.

Tenth and last, we say that African politics cannot be taken out of the world context. It is influenced by and has influence upon world politics. Despite Africa's increasing role in world affairs, politics in Africa continues to be dominated by world politics and world economics. By that we mean that international relations affect what goes on among African states and within them; that neo-colonialism, for example, is an important force; that prices for minerals and agricultural products cannot be divorced from the non-African political and economic influences.

Justifying these generalizations does not imply failure to recognize differences. We have indicated above that there is discordance between elites and masses, as well as divergences, contrasts, and disagreements among the peoples of the various regions of Africa. Language, climate, topography, and vegetation also make for diversity.

Politics in one African country influences another; colonialism was a common experience, and shared experience has continued in its aftermath because of the inherited communication routes, the relatively similar nature of precolonial systems, the way in which independence was achieved, and the problems faced by most of these countries today. These common characteristics and shared political experience support our ten generalizations.

2 Political Systems in Africa

Complex political patterns existed in Africa before the arrival of the non-African, and the patterns of these precolonial systems influence politics today.

The realization that politics existed in Africa before the establishment of colonialism has come out of the change in the way we define a political system. The realization that contemporary politics did not begin in a vacuum also prompted us to look at the nature of precolonial systems to estimate their possible influence on politics today.

Before recent changes in the approach to the study of government, Western political scientists, looking at non-Western nations, spent their time describing institutions that resemble the intellectual models they constructed from observing their own societies. More frequently, they refused to study the non-Western societies altogether because they did not discover Western-type concepts and institutions, such as the separation of powers in America or the parliaments in Europe. In addition, they did not consider that important political systems might exist in most areas of the world outside Europe and America because those areas were colonies, subject to Europe and hence without control of their own affairs. They were considered not powerful or intellectually interesting and thus not worth studying.

What Is a Political System?

Under the influence of sociology and a behaviorist approach to politics, on the one hand, and the assertion of independence and power by formerly colonized areas, on the other, the political scientist's view has changed. He has increasingly developed more universal and more accurate terms in an attempt to deal with power and its use. In his recent introduction to political science, Karl W. Deutsch, one of the leading social scientists of our time, deals with Third World countries in the context of general politics more than other authors have in similar works.[1] Instead of describing institutions, Deutsch tries to see how the

---

[1] Karl W. Deutsch, *Politics and Government: How People Decide Their Fate* (Boston: Houghton Mifflin, 1970.)

system really functions. Instead of trying to examine fixed categories of institutions, he asks the question: How does a society work to survive and to satisfy needs? Such a basic question may be asked about any society.

Other political scientists have also told us that we can compare any political systems on the basis, for example, of their relative "capabilities" to extract or obtain resources; to regulate the "behavior of individuals and groups"; to distribute "goods, services, honors, statuses, and opportunities of various kinds from the political system to individuals and groups in the society"; to have people adopt and accept symbols of the country; and to respond to the interests of groups. Finally, we can ask, How well does the system maintain its identity?[2]

To analyze systems in any of these ways, the political scientist is now going into the field to collect empirical data: what people think, how decisions made by leadership groups or elites at the macro-level affect people in a village, the micro-political level. How does the personality of a leader affect decisions taken? How do population movements and growth and age grouping affect power and voting patterns? How does communication affect national cohesion and social conflict? A change in attitude and progress in technology, permitting the gathering of new types of information, is leading more political scientists to work with demographers, historians, psychologists, economists, linguists—in sum, the other social scientists interested in human behavior.[3]

The modern political scientist now realizes that he is using the same basic data as his colleagues but is sorting out his facts differently and is focusing on different aspects of the human experience. He is looking for the "political aspect" and the "political process" in a society. In this context, the political aspect may be regarded as that "organization oriented to the attainment of collective goals," and the political system may be considered "an agency for mobilizing resources . . . and utilizing them to implement its policies."[4] These policies have as their basic purposes the maintenance of order within the society and the protection of the distinctiveness or independence of the society by solving problems.

The specific goals and the procedures for reaching them, to say nothing of the degree of success, are determined by the values or cultures of the society, the exigencies of the times, the resources available, the authority and legitimacy of decision-makers, and the power of decision-makers or their ability to bind members of the system to their decisions.

---

[2] Gabriel A. Almond and G. Bingham Powell, Jr., *Comparative Politics: A Developmental Approach* (Boston: Little, Brown, 1966), pp. 190–203.

[3] See Karl W. Deutsch, "Recent Trends in Research Methods in Political Science," in James C. Charlesworth (ed.), *A Design for Political Science: Scope, Objectives, and Methods* (Philadelphia: American Academy of Political and Social Science, December, 1966), pp. 149–178.

[4] Talcott Parsons, "The Political Aspect of Social Structure and Process," in David Easton (ed.), *Varieties of Political Theory* (Englewood Cliffs, N. J.: Prentice-Hall, 1966), p. 93.

On the basis of these definitions every human society—humans living together in a distinctive group with known rules governing interactions—has a political aspect that can be examined by a political scientist.

The expression of the political aspect—the form that it takes—varies greatly, however. Not every society has a clearly defined state or government, for example. The state is a more or less permanent matrix of institutions and structures that can be geographically located. It is like the skeleton of the human body. The government is an institutionalized, centralized, identifiable, differentiated authority with specialized power for the enforcement of decisions it makes regarding order and the distribution of limited resources.

The form the political aspect takes can also change over time. A society that has no government can develop one, or people can try to impose one on it from the outside. Government changes, but older forms do not automatically disappear; they continue to influence people, and the concerns of earlier political systems do not necessarily change either, even with economic change because of the influence of geography, climate, and culture: "The style of authority in a given society has a way of being partly independent of the social and economic structure of that society: patterns that have been forged during a preindustrial phase live on, and indeed shape, in turn, the pattern of industrialization."[5] This means, to give another example, that the relationship between Soviet leadership and the people of the U.S.S.R. may not be very different from the relationship between the Russian tsars and their subjects. People's perceptions of and expectations of their leaders may not be different, for example, no matter what the ostensible goals or ideologies of leaders are. No contemporary political system can be isolated from previous political systems—not even that of America.

In the case of Africa, it is still difficult to determine the continuities among the three categories of political system that have existed in most countries of that continent—the indigenous or so-called traditional system that existed during the precolonial period; the colonial system imposed by European powers; and independent political systems, within the frontiers established during the colonial period. Each of these categories could be analyzed as can any European government, although it is more difficult to obtain some of the necessary data, and language barriers still prevent much basic research from being done. What we know, however, is that there are still representatives of the traditional system who have power, and that patterns of colonial government remain. Both must, therefore, be considered, even though we know that attempted conclusions about their present influence on the actual political realities of the new states must be very tentative.

---

[5] Stanley Hoffman, "Heroic Leadership: The Case of Modern France," in Lewis J. Edinger (ed.), *Political Leadership in Industrialized Societies: Studies in Comparative Analysis* (New York: Wiley, 1967), p. 112.

"Traditional" Political Systems (indigenous)

The paucity of studies about the traditional influence on contemporary politics prevents generalization, but from what we know it is safe to say that in all societies patterns of authority and the ways in which people perceive power are deeply ingrained in their culture. They do not change rapidly, and the student who is not aware of this fact risks superficiality in his view.

What made it seem that there was no political system in Africa before European colonialism was that it was not always easily discernible to the outsider. The American and European looked for houses of parliament or pillared marble supreme court buildings, and there were no *Congressional Record*, *Hansard*, or *Journal Officiel*. The political scientist usually shared the prejudices of his own society that may have participated in the conquest of colonies in Africa or taken slaves from that continent. And by denying that there could be any indigenous political systems in Africa, he helped the colonial process and helped justify the sometimes inhuman treatment to which Africans and their descendants in the Diaspora were subjected.

An important corrective to this tendency was provided by Fortes and Evans-Pritchard, two anthropologists whose studies of African societies led them to the conclusion that there were two categories of African political system—one with government and one without. There can be political systems with a state, and there can be political systems without a state. The states had governments and the stateless societies did not.

Political systems with government had fairly well-defined centralized authority, with force at their disposal to carry out decisions and allocations of resources. At some point in history, the Ashanti of Ghana, the Kingdom of Morocco, Egypt, the Toucouleur, the Wolof of Tekrur, the Merina of Madagascar, the Balozi of Zambia, the Fulani of Guinea, and the Chagga of Tanzania have exemplified this type of political system. In political systems without government, kinship groups or age groups and secret societies performed the functions of centralized authority. The Nuer of Sudan, the Fang of Gabon, the Kikuyu of Kenya, the Banda of the Central African Republic, the Igbo of Nigeria, and the Amba of Uganda are a few examples of stateless systems.[6]

Some other anthropologists, however, instead of studying *Man* became ethnographers, describing "primitive" African societies in isolation. They failed to compare African political systems with basic concepts of human organization or with other political systems and thus contributed to a tendency to treat Africa as a special part of the planet. Their terms came to haunt us. This terminology, which calls up special feelings, has been used to describe Africa at least since the start of the colonial period.

[6] For a description of the two types of systems, see M. Fortes and E. E. Evans-Pritchard (eds.), *African Political Systems* (London: Oxford University Press, 1940), particularly their introduction, pp. 5–6.

There could be a king of England, but the head of an African political system must be a "chief." There could be a form of "pure democracy" in the New England town meeting, but a similar gathering in Africa was called "primitive." The "natives" came to mean the "Africans" in people's minds, although there is no difference between a "native" of New York City and a "native" of Ibadan, Nigeria. There are tribes in Africa, just as there were twelve tribes of Israel, and just as there are forms of tribe today in Europe; but one tended to use "tribe" only in referring to Africa, although some of these "tribes" were larger than some "ethnic groups" and "nations" in Europe. Of course, there are dialects in Africa, just as there are dialects in Europe. The Yorkshireman speaks a dialect or a variation of the English language, just as the Owerri man in Nigeria speaks a dialect of the Igbo language; but one tended to use the word "dialect" for African languages in order to demote or degrade them. Words like "native," "primitive," "tribe," and "dialect" can be used, if they are defined and if they are used impartially without respect to race or continent. The failure by many scholars to explain the universal applicability of terminology was a political act, and they thus played a political role in colonization and discrimination, no matter what their intentions may have been.

In this book we use "tribe" occasionally, although "ethnic group" has been increasingly accepted as the most value-free description of many African and European groups. "Tribe" refers in a vague way to shared kinship, culture, and territory. Above the family is often a lineage or group of four or five generations, probably of male descendants of a common ancestor who actually lived in the recent past. Lineages might be grouped into clans, all of whose members also trace their descent to a common ancestor, although he was probably mythical. The tribe might be considered a collection of clans and lineages speaking at least the same dialect of the same language and whose members are descended from a common mythical ancestor. "Ethnic group" might be all people who speak the same language within a larger group speaking a different language or who identify themselves with a certain language and a certain area within a larger one. When an ethnic group becomes coterminous with an independent entity, it is a nation. How one identifies one's self and how one is accepted are the most important factors in determining tribal or ethnic identity.[7] If, therefore, one chooses to speak of the Flemish people of Belgium as a "people," or an "ethnic group," or a "tribe," one must use the same terms for the Yoruba people of Nigeria. Both groups are identified with a certain region, even though many members now live elsewhere, and both are identified with a given culture best expressed by a language. Assertion of identity and possible conflict about that identity is "tribalism" or "ethnic nationalism" in Belgium and Northern Ireland, just as much as it is in the Congo.

[7] Cf. P. H. Gulliver, "Introduction," in *idem*, (ed.), *Tradition and Transition in East Africa: Studies of the Tribal Element in the Modern Era* (Berkeley and Los Angeles: University of California, 1969), p. 24.

The anthropologist introduced us to the study of African political systems, even though we might criticize the terms he used to describe them. But he performed another crucial service for the study of African politics that we are only more recently beginning to appreciate—his methodology. Working far from the urban areas, he showed other scholars that the city was not the only place where politics existed, and that sometimes the most important politics in the long run was in the rural areas where the great majority of Africans still live. The anthropologist suggested that to attempt to understand a society, one should try to become a part of it—to participate while observing. He pointed out the richness of oral traditions, political poetry, and the political nature of social structure. Field research would get the observer closer to his subject and possibly, although not necessarily, closer to the truth. He encouraged the political scientist to undertake the micro-political study that has become much more important in recent years in all fields of political science research.

Field research draws the political scientist closer to the so-called traditional political systems. He observes that one basic similarity in these precolonial systems seems to be a persistent limit on the capabilities of centralized authority when such authority exists. A second is that central authority was primarily interested in tax collection, internal order, and recruitment for work or war. A third appears to be the strength of kinship. A fourth is the continuing strength of caste identity within ethnic groups and political systems.

Centralized Authority

An example of the limits of central authority comes from North Africa. Until the arrival of the Arabs in the seventh century, the Berber peoples lived in nomadic societies with very decentralized authority based on kinship ties. The Arabs organized a confederation of these groups and attempted to unify them by conquest. They established a capital at Fez in what is Morocco today, but their confederation did not last.

In the eleventh century, more Arabs moved into Morocco. Another kingdom then developed, but it was highly fragmented. A "sultan" headed the government in Fez and ruled through governors or nobles. Claiming to be a legitimate ruler because of descent from Muhammad, he constantly attempted to build centralized authority around himself at Fez.

A complex hierarchy of loyalty groups based largely on kinship characterized this developing kingdom. Although there were developing cities with a measure of municipal government linked with the central government, more important were religious organizations and craft guilds. According to Clement Moore, beyond the area of Fez "feuding tribal segments" were constantly dividing and uniting outside any control from central government.[8] Religion, a basis for unity, gave special powers and authority to religious leaders who, along with leaders of kinship groups, played the most important role in problem-solving.

In the mid-seventeenth century, a single dynamic leader began seriously to build a unified kingdom. In 1666, Moulay-er-Rachid founded the Alawite dynasty and, by conquering some local religious and kinship leaders, consolidated his authority. He built what Moore called a "core kingdom" around Fez that was fairly well under his control, and with outlying areas he established links and ties of loyalty.

He exercised force, sending his increasingly large army to the area of a tribe and threatening to make war on it unless it submitted to his kingdom. Negotiation then probably took place with the leaders. If an agreement was reached peacefully, the king appointed a *caid* from among the respected leaders of the tribe. The *caid* both represented the king and acted as a type of ruler of the tribe—a viceroy, in a sense. He collected taxes or tribute, recruited soldiers for the king, and kept order. In the resolution of everyday conflicts, tribes remained autonomous; customary law was applied by kinship and religious leaders. The latter owed special fealty to the king because of his claim of descent from the prophet Muhammad. The religious leaders also had special powers, because it was they who chose the successor to the king. Islam was an important legitimizing force, not just birth into the family of the king. The idea of an heir apparent or crown prince, so common and ancient in Europe, is a very recent development in the process of centralization of power in Morocco.

By the nineteenth century, an increasingly specialized bureaucracy developed, with the *caids* the most important bureaucrats. The king also developed ministries with specialized functions, although the kingdom did not have the degree of centralization that characterized the European powers of the time, and local kinship or religious authorities always seemed to be waiting their chance to reassert authority, something they did at the beginning of this century.

South of Morocco, a Fulani state also based on Islam was formed by the eighteenth century in the Fouta-Djalon region in central Guinea. After moving into this area as nomadic groups with decentralized political authority, the peoples coalesced into nine groupings, becoming more sedentary. Each group had a leader whose basis for authority was his religious expertise. He was a *karamoko*, or teacher (in a very broad sense), and, when he became leader, had the title *alfa*. Each of the nine groupings was divided into *missidi*, or parishes, organized around a mosque and then headed by another *karamoko*, or at least someone with recognized religious authority.

In time the nine *alfas* decided to unite in a confederation to make war against the non-Muslims. To insure necessary military unity, they named one of their number their leader. He was the *alfa* of Timbo area and had

---

[8] Clement Henry Moore, *Politics in North Africa: Algeria, Morocco, Tunisia* (Boston: Little, Brown, 1970), pp. 12–22.

a reputation for piety and military skill. The *alfas* took him to the large mosque of a place called Fougoumba to proclaim him leader and to unite their provinces.

For years, Karamoko Alfa, as he was called, led the Fulani in battle against their neighbors until—after one defeat—he went mad. The *alfas* met again to choose another leader, the former leader's nephew, because Karamoko Alfa's son was too young. Leadership then gradually became institutionalized, and the leader was called the Almamy. But present still were the *alfas*, who needed unified leadership—they feared that their own prerogatives in the provinces might be affected. Therefore, they tried to check the power of the new institution they had created by later insisting that the nephew of their first leader share power with the son of their first leader when he came of age. They created two competing families for the monarchy and thus succeeded in preventing the development of a strong, highly centralized monarchy.

The *alfas* and other notables, such as village chiefs, chose a council of elders that supposedly decided questions of war and consecrated the new king at Fougoumba after another council formally elected him at Timbo.

Day-to-day administration in the kingdom was mainly in the hands of the *alfas* of the provinces. The king, however, built client families around himself to take care of the developing symbols of the kingdom— a royal drum and his standard, for example—to be judges and religious men who took care of the mosques and made preparations for Muslim festivals. From these client families, the king chose representatives whom he sent on missions to the provinces.

A constant tension appears to have existed between the Almamy and *alfa*. The Almamy did not have direct contact with the people; he communicated through the *alfa* by letter. The *alfa* received the letter and then read it to the populace in the mosque. Presumably, the *alfa* might refuse to read the letter. Such a letter might authorize the *alfa* to undertake military action on his own against some non-Muslim group.

Once action was decided—like making war or collecting taxes—the *alfa* sent messages to each head of *missidi* to recruit soldiers or collect taxes. In the case of taxes, most of them were sent by the head of *missidi* to the *alfa*, who in turn sent "presents" to the Almamy.

According to some accounts, judges were chosen by the head of the *missidi*. The lowest court existed at the level of the *missidi*. A court of appeal, whose judges were also named by political heads, existed at the provincial level.[9]

To the east of the Fouta Djalon, the Ashanti people lived in a kingdom not based on Islam. As far as historians know, the Ashanti people

[9] The account of the Fouta Djalon comes primarily from Alfâ Ibrâhîm Sow, *Chroniques et récits du Foûta Djalon*, (Paris: Klincksieck, 1968), pp. 3–10, and from A. Demougeot, *Notes sur l'organisation politique et administrative du Labé avant et depuis l'occupation française*, Mémoire de l'IFAN, no. 6 (Paris: Larose, 1944).

arrived in small groups shortly after 1200 in the area of what is today Ghana. Over the next several centuries, a confederacy was formed by conquest and alliance of these groups. The discovery of gold and the tribute paid to the confederacy by non-Ashanti peoples increased its wealth. This enabled the confederacy to continue to build an ever stronger army.

The king headed the army of the confederacy; he symbolized the history of the Ashanti because of his guardianship of the golden stool and therefore had a supernatural aura about himself, much like the Muslim king of Morocco and the Almamy of the Fouta Djalon. Like his counterparts, he was also supreme judge and guardian of the laws. But decentralization was a characteristic, in that the king could not interfere in the affairs of the states on a day-to-day basis except to help maintain order. The court at Kumasi in the nineteenth century surpassed in opulence that of all the states.

More austere was the Zulu Kingdom in southern Africa. According to Gluckman, the Zulu people used to be organized into various segmenting and coalescing tribes that battled each other in the eighteenth century.[10] As in the case of Morocco, the Fouta Djalon, and the Ashanti kingdom, one leader emerged, not because of his putative religious legitimacy or ability to lead people against a common enemy, but quite simply because he was able to subject other Zulu by "his personal character and military strategy." Shaka united the Zulu and built a powerful army.

With the advent of Shaka the usual hierarchy of households, lineages, clans, and tribes—groups in which political allegiance corresponded with kinship allegiances—did not disappear. But the people shifted some of their allegiance to the king.

The Zulu, under the great military leader Shaka and his successor, Dingane, considered themselves the possessions of the king in the same way children might be considered possessions of their father. All land belonged to him too. Shaka accumulated governmental functions in his person and also considered himself the religious and medical leader of his country, an area, according to Gluckman, of about 80,000 square miles. Indeed, the religious aura that developed about Shaka recalls that about the kings of the medieval states of West Africa or about the emperor of Japan, whose physical state was said to reflect or influence the condition of the kingdom as a whole. Perhaps Shaka centralized power around himself more effectively than did the Ashanti king or the Fulani. He began his career as a military leader and kept tight control of the army on a day-to-day basis. Regiment heads were chiefs of kinship groups, and he kept them in his capital except during military operations.

The Zulu had a hierarchy of courts culminating in the king. The judges in the king's court were widely known as chiefs of tribes, rela-

[10] Max Gluckman, "The Kingdom of the Zulu of South Africa," in Fortes and Evans-Pritchard (eds.), *African Political Systems*, pp. 25–55.

tives of the king, or wise men. They served more than just a judicial function. One relative was commander of the army and one nonrelative was something akin to a prime minister of the advisory council of judges. Local rulers far from the capital were all named by the king, and they owed their own legitimacy to him.

The king did not, however, communicate directly with the people. He sent messages through his named rulers, who sent the message to ward heads, then to kinship leaders who, as in other societies, were responsible for day-to-day order and problem-solving.

The Zulu kingdom under Shaka was a federation with considerable power in the hands of the king, but it did not last long, and the evolution that might have taken place toward more centralization or bureaucratization and institutionalization was stopped by the advent of the European.

More successfully, on the island of Madagascar in the late eighteenth century, a king united the Merina people. Chiefs like the Moroccan caids became administrators responsible to the king but with considerable power of their own. The king promulgated one penal code for the kingdom, however, and more important, built roads linking parts of the kingdom with the capital to ensure control. Decentralized features remained because village councils and notables kept order and solved most problems.[11]

The Mossi of Upper Volta had one of the most interesting African states. Their king ruled over 30,000 square miles and a population of well over one million before the European conquest, and this kingdom was one of the oldest of Africa at the beginning of the colonial period.

According to Mossi tradition, a man called Ouedrago and another called Oubri founded the kingdom, and the ruling group consisted of their descendants. These descendants all belonged to specified lineages and were called Nanamse. There were actually four Mossi kingdoms, but the kingdom of Ouagadougou, around the present capital of Upper Volta, predominated. Like the Ashanti king at Kumasi, the court of the Mogho Naba, or king of Ouagadougou, was the most opulent and influenced the style and conduct of the other three courts.

The kingdom of Ouagadougou had five provinces composed of three hundred districts, and more than four thousand villages. At the head of each province was a man who served both as regional governor and as minister in the king's cabinet. Members of each governor's own lineage were then appointed administrators within the province.

Each of the three hundred districts had a head or sub-governor related to the king. This man was responsible for the administration of the district and had to report to the king through the governors, who were supposed, in their turn, to report daily to the Mogho Naba. In spite of his subordinate status, he generally ruled without interference from above, as long as he kept order and sent tribute to Ouagadougou.

[11] Virginia Thompson and Richard Adloff, *The Malagasy Republic: Madagascar Today* (Stanford, Calif.: Stanford University Press, 1965), pp. 4–5.

The relationship between governors and district heads could
because the latter, although the administrative inferiors of the
were their social superiors as members of the royal family.

District heads had councils, comprised of relatives for the most p..
to discuss important matters. They also had a type of prime minister
similar to the Ouidi Naba, the king's prime minister, and administrators
who communicated directly with village chiefs at the bottom of the
pyramid.

The most common problems and crimes were expected to be dealt
with, not at the level of the kingdom, the province, or the district, but
rather at the village level or within a kinship group. Usually, however,
serious crimes like murder were brought to the district court headed by
the sub-governor. Like many other African peoples, the Mossi regarded
courts as places where order and harmony within the community could
be re-established. If the district court could not satisfactorily resolve a
problem, litigants could appeal to the king.[12]

Possibly the most interesting precolonial kingdom was that of Rwanda.
Before the monarchy was overthrown in 1961, one dynasty, the Abanyi-
ginya, had ruled for three to four centuries.[13] The king, or Mwami, who
belonged to the Tutsi group, personified Rwanda, whose population in
1900, before colonial control, was about 1,700,000. If he were ill or
weak, the people feared the kingdom would be ill or weak. Everyone
also feared the Mwami, and the last thing a man wanted was to be
considered an "enemy of the king," who could then take his property,
exile him, or kill him.[14]

The cattle-herding Tutsi, who moved into Rwanda to conquer the
earlier arrived Hutu, controlled the monarchy and all high positions,
even though they were a small minority. Under Tutsi rule, Rwanda
expanded by European or Arab influence until early in the twentieth
century. The central government they established consisted of the king
and the queen mother; the latter in ordinary times had no real power.
The king theoretically had absolute power, but the "dignitaries," or
biru, preserved ritual knowledge and knew the various complicated ceremonies of the kingship. When the Mwami chose a successor from
among his sons, he told only the *biru*, and they kept the information
until the death of the Mwami. He also had an advisory council.

Around 1900, the kingdom was divided into seventy to ninety districts, each ruled by two officials appointed by the Mwami. Districts
were divided into "hills" with one official each. "Neighborhoods" made
up each hill and were headed by one leader of the various kin groups
that made up the "neighborhood."

It appears that the most important function of these men was to

[12] Elliott P. Skinner, *The Mossi of the Upper Volta: The Political Development of a Sudanese People* (Stanford, Calif.: Stanford University Press, 1964).

[13] Jacques J. Maquet, *The Premise of Inequality in Ruanda: A Study of Political Relations in a Central African Kingdom* (London: Oxford University Press, 1961), p. 12.

[14] *Ibid.*, p. 25.

collect tribute and pass it up to the Mwami. The tribute was not sent to the capital but rather to a royal residence in each district, the officials keeping a percentage as they passed it along.

At the base of the system was the *inzu*, composed of six generations of male descendants of the same ancestor and their respective families. Like most other African political systems the most important day-to-day political activities revolved around the *inzu*. The head of this unit acted as judge and limited legislator. He settled disputes, could levy fines, and could make new rules concerning marriage. The *inzu* head could turn over to higher authority the most serious crimes and problems.

The importance of this small unit goes beyond political relationships, too. Economic relations were most intense within it. Although the Mwami had the right to survey and even to seize the property of his subjects, poorly developed communications in the hills meant a considerable economic autonomy for the kinship groups.

Decentralized Authority

So far, we have dealt with political systems that included central governments. It is true that none of these systems had as much centralization and differentiation of function by the end of the nineteenth century as their European counterparts, but, had they not come under the control of Europeans, they might have continued to evolve toward more concentration of power and administration. They had differentiated institutionalized government: A man not considered a blood relative was accepted as leader by a large group of people, which he or a predecessor had unified. This man got his office through a regular accepted procedure. His basis for legitimacy was coming to office on the accepted procedure and through the symbols that he then manipulated. The kingdom could be located geographically, and it achieved a certain stability of size, although wars added new territory.

Local or kinship leaders made many decisions affecting the day-to-day lives of the people; central authority had the court of highest appeal; it made decisions about war and peace; it received taxes and tribute from lower authorities to maintain itself; and it guarded symbols that represented the whole people. In sum, it maintained internal order and undertook to protect the whole, whose identity it guarded. The day-to-day problems of people were dealt with at the kinship level just as in societies without government.

Groups without government had to mobilize resources and carry out policies too. The Amba people of western Uganda show how it was done. According to Winter, the Amba were and are a sedentary people who raised enough food for their own needs and remained somewhat isolated from their neighbors until the end of the nineteenth century.[15]

[15] Edward Winter, "The Aboriginal Political Structure of Bwamba," in John Middleton and David Tait (eds.), *Tribes Without Rulers: Studies in African Segmentary Systems* (London: Routledge and Kegan Paul, 1958), pp. 136–66.

The village was an "independent political unit," well defined geographically and with from 50 to 400 people, most of whom belonged to one exogamous lineage—exogamous because members of it were required to marry outside it. Although the people recognized that they belonged to a larger ethnic group, they were unable to form lasting alliances with other villages, even when threatened by what could be considered a common enemy. Rules based on kinship governed relations within the village but without creating strong bonds with other lineages and villages.

Within the village, every man shared a common ancestor of a few generations past—a man who was probably remembered by the oldest people. Elders had control over their children and grandchildren whether they were married or not. Old men had primarily a judicial role and maintained order. The maintenance of internal order received high priority—everyone was related to everyone else, and tradition refused to admit the possibility of living with nonrelatives in the same unit. Great efforts were made in disputes or even in murder cases to re-establish order. Because the unit was quite small and everyone was related, the unit as a whole would not punish one of its members with death, even though he might have been guilty of killing someone else.

There was no central figure in a village except for the dead founder of the lineage. Instead, there were groups of family heads. But there were shared ceremonies glorifying everyone's common descent from the ancestor. Land belonged to the lineage-village as a whole, but an individual accustomed to using a particular piece of land would give it to his descendants. Others recognized his right to use the land.

Beyond the village, some feuding took place between lineages within the frame of reference of the ethnic group, Amba. Above the lineage-village was a recognized clan embracing several lineages. The clan was weaker—members could not intermarry, but they were expected to help each other in case of war.

Other ties beyond the village existed because people were required to marry outside their lineage and outside their clan, and new family relationships thus formed determined political alliances. The rules were clear: A woman left her family to marry into another lineage-village. Her subsequent son, who belonged to his own father's lineage, felt some obligation toward the lineage from which his mother had come. If his mother's brothers went to war, for example, with some third lineage, he was obliged to assist them. But her brothers were not obliged to help their nephew's lineage when he went to war, unless, of course, there were some similar connection between them and the village at war. The kinship relationship determined actions that had to be taken in war and determined other relationships within and outside the village. Custom and tradition were known, and it was unnecessary to receive orders from one leader.

Interestingly enough, at the end of the nineteenth century one lineage suddenly claimed to be related to the kings of the neighboring and very powerful Bunyoro kingdom. Because of this supposed basis for claiming power, they said that one of their number should be king of the Amba. The coming of the European then stopped a movement that might eventually have led—as in the case of the Zulu—to the establishment of an Amba kingdom.

Another example is that of the Igbo-speaking peoples of southeastern Nigeria, who had had for the most part no centralized government in memory. The absence of centralized government does not mean a society cannot be complex. Gailey has written that prior to British control, there were "four viable political divisions among the Igbo. These were the extended family, then the *umunna* or localized patrilineage, the village, and the town or group of villages."[16]

The extended family with at least twenty households had a leader, but he was surrounded by other men of influence and authority, such as those who had distinguished themselves in some way and older men. Women too had their leaders, whose opinions were listened to. Extended families belonging to one lineage formed a grouping of several hundred members. This group was headed by the eldest male.

Umunnas grouped together and formed a village with a possible population of 2,000. The village leader was the eldest man of the *umunna*, considered senior to the other *umunnas*. This was the most important political unit, although it often formed a group with other villages. The group was united around a shared dialect of the Igbo language and the idea the group of villages or town had been founded by a "common ancestor, usually of divine origin."[17] In this unit the most important institution was a "council of elders or a council of titleholders."[18] Titleholders were usually men who had been successful and had achieved status through important deeds and accomplishments.

In a single village, all free men—there were also slaves—participated in the political system. Age sets, title societies, secret societies, and other cooperative organizations within which an egalitarian spirit predominated also had roles to play. In the interplay of these organizations, kin-group elders maintained order without higher authority, although the Aro-Igbo people had some dominance economically.[19] Perhaps they would have gained more power in time had the British not come.

A last force considered here, more or less traditional or indigenous, is that of the Muslim brotherhoods. The Tijaniyya, for example, began in Morocco in the eighteenth century and spread south to Mauritania and Senegal and west to Nigeria, like the Qadiriyya. Later came the Mourides, particularly among the Wolof of Senegal, who, having ex-

---

[16] Harry A. Gailey, *The Road to Aba: A Study of British Administrative Policy in Eastern Nigeria* (New York: New York University Press, 1970), p. 22.
[17] *Ibid.*, p. 24.
[18] *Ibid.*
[19] *Ibid.*, p. 29.

perienced the defeat of their leaders at the hands of the French, sought "a means of reconstituting the old social order on a new religious basis."[20]

From Libya through Tchad and into the Central African Republic, the Senoussiya played an important role as a form of organization. In fact, one leader became king of Libya, and another controlled the border region between Tchad and the Central African Republic to about 1911. In Egypt, the Muslim Brotherhood was a type of political system, and in the Sudan the followers of the Mahdi formed a political as well as a religious system. Followers were devoted to their leader in most of those brotherhoods because he promised salvation through his own intercession with God. On all matters, disciples were expected to follow the leader, which made the brotherhood a rather centralized political organization: "At a gathering of the brotherhood, members are informed of their leaders' policy decisions."[21] Brotherhood leaders had judicial, military, and economic power, just as did kin-group leaders in other types of political systems.

In spite of the changes brought by colonialism and independence, these brotherhoods persist, as do localized kinship-political systems.

Traditional Political Systems and Contemporary Government

Ask the average American where he comes from, and the city or state he indicates will generally be the place he was born—or it might be where he has lived for many years. Ask most Africans and Europeans what town or region they come from, and it will generally be the birthplace or home of their ancestors. Few Africans think of the urban area where they were born as "home," even though their fathers may have been born there too. Home is where recent ancestors came from, and ties with that home are recognized. Most urban Africans thus maintain connections with some rural home area, ethnic base, and traditional political system at the local level. If they have been successful in business and politics at the central level of government, it is likely they will have some power when they visit or return to this rural community where they have their roots. In spite of the influence of some prodigal sons, the home community exercises considerable power over its sons and daughters, even those who have left it. The tie, tenuous as it may appear, remains, and this means that the majority of Africans are still subject to at least some sanctions of the traditional political system, even though they vary greatly in importance. An individual's fear of being damned by the ancestors is important enough to stimulate

---

[20] Donal B. O'Brien, *The Mourides of Senegal: The Political and Economic Organization of an Islamic Brotherhood* (Oxford: Clarendon Press, 1971), p. 15.

[21] Lucy C. Behrman, *Muslim Brotherhoods and Politics in Senegal* (Cambridge, Mass.: Harvard University Press, 1970), pp. 9–10.

the obedience desired by the home community and those who speak in its name.[22]

For Africans living in rural areas, traditional political systems have even more importance because they embody religious ethnic identity and because they continue to assert power over the solution of everyday human problems through application of customary law. This assertion of traditional authority creates tension with the independent central government, which is constantly trying to assert its own authority and prove its own legitimacy.

Status is also at least partly determined by tradition. Although the Almamy of the Fouta Djalon disappeared many years ago, organization at the lineage level among the Fulani has not. Alliances, status, and deference patterns are still observed, but we don't know enough about the relationship between the position of a man in the traditional system and his position in the contemporary central system. In a recent brilliant study a Senegalese scholar, Majhemout Diop, asserts that the slavery of the precolonial Mali and Songhai empires in West Africa never really ended. The status of slave was merely transformed into a caste, which continues to exist to this day in independent Mali, for example.[23]

It may make a difference that a man is born of a low caste in the traditional system even if he has power in the contemporary central state system. One can be fairly sure that people know a lot about a man's position in traditional society. They know, for example, if he should be paying deference to someone else. In Guinea the son of a chief at present working in a rather low position explained to one of the authors that, in spite of his poverty compared with the wealth of a former slave of his father, there were certain demands he might make on the other man. It is difficult for an outsider to know how this deference will continue. It is also difficult to know how domestic policies are influenced by it. We know there are certain areas in which a leader in a contemporary system cannot act or in which action is practically meaningless. For example, attempts of modernizing leaders to abolish the dowry system and polygyny by very specific laws have been largely ignored.

In recent history one of the most frequently mentioned examples of intrusion by the strength of traditional relationships into the modern state is the relationship between the first Prime Minister of Nigeria, Al Hadj Sir Abubakar Tafawa Balewa, and the Prime Minister of the northern region of the country, Al Hadj Sir Amadu Bello. Politically speaking, Balewa was superior, but Bello was a spiritual head of the north from which both men had come. Bello also traced his ancestry through the Fulani conquerors of northern Nigeria to Muham-

[22] Jacques Macquet, *Pouvoir et société en Afrique*, L'Univers des Connaissances (Paris: Hachette, 1970), pp. 35–36.
[23] Majhemout Diop, *Historie des classes sociales dans l'Afrique de l'Ouest*, I, *Le Mali* (Paris: François Maspero, 1971): 34–35.

mad himself. Balewa, a more highly educated man, was of lower status in the traditional system because of the profession of his father, an artisan, and his non-Fulani identity, and everyone knew it. Bello emphasized it by claiming he himself did not want to go to the supposedly heathen south to run the affairs of Nigeria and had sent his lieutenant instead.

In the east, President Julius Nyerere of Tanzania comes from an ethnic group in the northwest of the country that has been generally looked down upon by some neighboring groups, but this fact did not prevent him from becoming a popular leader and from removing kings of more prestigious peoples once he got power. The apparently low status of Dr. Kwame Nkrumah of Ghana did not prevent him from acting against traditional authority.

In Africa there are, in any case, certain clear examples of continuity of authority from the precolonial period to the present. First, some precolonial political systems survived and even strengthened themselves under colonial rule and continued into the period of independence to become the government of the new state. Their survival depended more on the perspicacity of the monarch than on anything else.

In Morocco, King Muhammad V of the Alawite dynasty identified himself with anticolonialist forces. In 1953, the French exiled him and thus made him a national hero. A year after his return to the country in 1955, Morocco became independent, and he kept his position as head of state. In 1961, Hassan, son of Muhammad, became King Hassan II after his father's death through automatic inheritance. He maintained the kingdom and monarchy, although there were attempts to overthrow him, and he centralized power in the palace.

Tunisia's monarch, less lucky than Muhammad V or his successor, was removed in 1957 by Habib Bourguiba, who embodied Tunisia's national ambitions more than the monarch. Egypt's corrupt and despised King Farouk ruled until he was overthrown in 1952. Libya's king, Idris I, took his country to independence but was overthrown by army officers who claimed they wanted a more dynamic government. The kings of both Rwanda and Burundi survived the colonial period, but both were overthrown. The Sultan of Zanzibar fled at the time of independence. The King of Lesotho in southern Africa was temporarily removed from power after a conflict with the prime minister, himself a chief. He returned to his kingdom after a short exile to become head of state in an independent Lesotho.

Swaziland's king, Sobhuza II, has ruled his country since 1921, when it was under British control. The dynasty to which he belongs has ruled the Swazi people as long as the Alawite dynasty has ruled Morocco. When the country gained independence, he continued to reign until the military coup of 1974. Ethiopia was also an example of the survival of traditional systems at the state level.

In the above cases, the precolonial kingdom or empire evolved into a contemporary state without a sharp break with the past. The monarchical type government evolved into contemporary government.

In other instances, heads of traditional political systems became heads of new political systems that absorbed the systems from which the monarchs came. In Uganda, for example, King Mutesa II, the Kabaka of Buganda, the largest and strongest of the kingdoms in the southern part of the country, became president of an independent Uganda. This was a way of vitiating the separatist tendencies of the Baganda. However, Milton Obote, the prime minister, of a different ethnic group, overthrew the king and became president himself. The Baganda did not forget their king, even after he died in exile in Britain. One tried to assassinate Obote, and the Baganda were pleased when a military coup overthrew him in 1971. The new military government of General Amin, in deference to Baganda sensitivities and in recognition of the strength of traditional politics, brought back the remains of the king and put Baganda into high positions, at least temporarily.

In Botswana the president, Sir Seretse Khama, was the chief of the Bamangwato people, the largest ethnic group. As the country moved toward independence, he voluntarily renounced claims to the chieftaincy but went directly into politics and became president when the country achieved independence in 1966. It is certain that most Bamangwato make no distinction between Sir Seretse as president and as king.

In Uganda and Botswana, two men became president because of prestige based on their positions in traditional political systems, even though their kingdoms did not evolve into the contemporary state, as in Morocco or Burundi.

In a third variation, men who have claims of belonging to a royal family of one ethnic group became heads of state and government. President Moktar Ould Dadda of the Islamic Republic of Mauritania is a nephew of one of the three main leaders of the Moorish peoples, and everyone in that country knows it. Modibo Keita, first president of Mali, said he belonged to a royal lineage of the Malinke people. Justin Ahomadegbe, a Dahomean leader, is from a family that ruled the Kingdom of Abomey in central Dahomey. Sékou Touré said he was a descendant of the West African leader Samory Touré, and this assertion added to his popularity in pre-independence Guinea. Moïse Tshombe, head of the secessionist province of Katanga and then Prime Minister of Zaïre, and his collaborator Godefroid Munongo were closely related to royal families in southeastern Congo.

In the cabinets of many governments, and in legislatures, one finds members of royal families. Martin Kilson has called chiefs who participate in contemporary politics the "neo-traditional elites." They have legitimacy from the precolonial systems but are adapting to postindependence politics and are participating in it. In the Ivory Coast, the year before independence, 43 per cent of the members of the legislative assembly "were related to traditional ruling families."[24] Nigeria and

[24] Martin Kilson, "The Emergent Elites of Black Africa, 1900 to 1960," in L. H. Gann and Peter Duignan (eds.), *Colonialism in Africa 1870–1960*, II, *The History*

Sierra Leone recognized the chiefs by creating Houses of Chiefs as part of their legislatures.

Even if monarchs and their relatives did not or do not participate directly in contemporary politics, they have seldom been neutral. They have given their support to candidates and parties, and their backing can be crucial. Sir Milton Margai, first prime minister of Sierra Leone, had established close ties with chiefs during the many years he worked as a physician in the rural areas of his country, and their support helped him when he needed it. Léopold Sédar Senghor, Kwame Nkrumah, and Sékou Touré were known to have consulted traditional religious leaders and to have their support. Nkrumah was reported to be a disciple, for example, of the Tijani marabou, Al-Hadj Ibrahima Niass of Senegal. Niass openly condemned other leaders, like Habib Bourguiba.[25] In southern Africa, precolonial-type leaders have proved formidable adversaries for white regimes in unexpected ways. Rekayi Tangwena, chief of the Tangwena of Rhodesia, led resistance to resettlement schemes. In the Republic of South Africa, the highly educated Zulu chief Gatsha Buthelezi has become an effective spokesman against many government policies.

A last variant of the power of precolonial leaders results from government decisions to abolish traditional political systems by abolishing chieftaincy. In order not to create antagonism with such a move, former chiefs were usually integrated into high and well-paying positions in the civil service.

Whether or not the kings and chiefs remain after independence has depended most often on the leader's power needs rather than on more abstract ideas of chieftaincy in the twentieth century. If rulers support the new leader, and if they do not threaten his position, they may be kept. And even when chieftaincy is abolished, chiefs turn up in unexpected places. This is true in Guinea and Tanzania.

In Guinea, for example, most Fulani chiefs opposed Touré and his party before independence, so that when he took power his move to abolish chiefs was partly an effort to settle old scores and prevent opposition from developing. But members of one Fulani family of the old ruling group that supported him were appointed to high positions in the civil service and often placed in positions of authority in the Fouta Djalon, where they had previously ruled.

In Tanzania, the king of the Chagga, the Mangi Mkuu, a successful and popular ruler, at least from 1952 to 1957, supported the nationalist party of Dr. Nyerere, TANU, at first. For several reasons, he broke with TANU and was deposed, even before the general abolition of chiefs in

and Politics of Colonialism 1914–1960 (Cambridge, England: Cambridge University Press, 1970): 374–75.

[25] Behrman, *Muslim Brotherhoods*, pp. 119–120.

1962.[26] But, the Mangi Mkuu was named to a high post representing Tanzania in Europe. By contrast, three out of nine chiefs of the Zigua people still had power after the official abolition. One became a "divisional executive officer, in charge of a division that includes his former chiefdom." He told a visitor that "he did much the same work as he had as a chief, except for court cases."[27] Some chiefs moved laterally into business or even the church, so they still have some influence. In times of disorder and insecurity they could have even more influence.

There are probably no countries where there is not some trace of traditional political systems, although in Algeria, Guinea-Bissau, Angola, and Mozambique the traditional systems were crushed by the French and Portuguese during their relatively long periods of rule.

In summary, we have dealt briefly with political systems existing in Africa just prior to European colonialism in the nineteenth century because those systems persisted in some form to the present day and there is considerable firsthand information about them. Nevertheless, we also recognize that there were earlier political systems that formed, evolved, and collapsed, like political systems elsewhere in the world: pharaonic Egypt, the medieval empires and states of West Africa, the kingdom of the Bateké in equatorial Africa, Monomotapa. As long as humans have been living in groups, there has been a political aspect of their relationships—in Africa, in China, among the Aztecs, the Sioux, the Basques, the Israelites, the French, and the English.

No systems have remained static, but what one might tentatively say about African systems is that the kinship element and the force of decentralization were stronger than in Europe, for reasons that are not immediately apparent to us. (It is important to note this, because it is a source of continuing concern to independent governments.)

Traditional political systems governed Africa before the coming of the Europeans. They are basically tied to kinship and often to the religious beliefs of Africans. These systems have been affected by changes, but they have not disappeared. They are an essential part of African culture, and one must be aware of them to be aware of one of the most important problems of African politics.

[26] Kathleen M. Stahl, "The Chagga," in Gulliver (ed.), *Tradition and Transition in East Africa*, pp. 209–22.

[27] David Brokensha, "Handeni Revisited," in *African Affairs* (April, 1970), pp. 166–67.

3 Colonialism and African Politics

The arrival of Europeans and their efforts to establish a colonial system radically affected African politics and is a continuing influence today.

Almost everyone condemns colonialism or imperialism today. Both terms refer generally to the conquest and exercise of sovereignty over one political system by another without integrating the subjugated system and assimilating its people. Even though some traditional African leaders gave their initial consent to a form of external control, settlement, or protection, they did not freely consent to the type of colonial state that eventually developed. A basic aspect of that state was a relationship in which a human being from one political system had control over the life of a human being in another; the fact that he often could use this control capriciously was evil. It was no less evil just because the same capricious control could exist within independent states as well.

These moral judgments can be made about every characteristic of the colonial political system, just as they can be made about independent states. But they do not help us much to understand how the system worked and how it influenced contemporary politics, which is the focus of this book. In other words, our attitude toward a historical phenomenon should not obscure its complexity or dissuade us from looking at its effects.

A priori, one can say that colonialism is bound to have had some effects on contemporary Africa, because for a period of about seventy-five years European-imposed political systems dominated all of Africa, with the exception of Liberia and Ethiopia. In the context of human history, this is not much time—three score and fifteen. Many readers will be surprised by this figure and will disagree. Colonialism in Africa will seem to have lasted a longer time.

We contend that for most of the period from 1885 to 1960, six European countries—Great Britain, France, Belgium, Spain, Portugal, and Italy—made a concerted effort to conquer, administer, and hold on to Africa. (Germany was a member of the colonial club only until the end of World War I, and Portugal continued the effort to hold on into the mid-1970's.) And, for about twenty-five years, from the end of World War II to the end of World War II, it seemed they would be quite successful. These countries claimed sovereignty, or uninhibited control, over all of each African territory. Their colonial state consisted of control over peoples belonging to other pre-existing political systems which did not disappear. They codified administrative rules and set up judicial systems; they collected taxes and maintained a certain minimal order for a time; they established new political frontiers that determined the limits of contemporary states; and they established a new economic sector, orienting it toward their own. All this was done primarily to serve European interests.

Before the institutionalization of European sovereignty, Europeans had influence. After the institutionalization, the control was not so great as the European thought or wished. The seventy-five-year time span should therefore be modified in two directions.

First, it must be lengthened. Well before 1885 there were trading stations run by Europeans on the African coast, and there were small coastal colonies and posts, as well.[1] Trade between these posts and the rest of the world changed diet and economic systems to some extent in Europe, America, and Africa. The banana and manioc were introduced into Africa; Africans, gold, and ivory left Africa. Beginning in the sixteenth century, the Atlantic slave trade led coastal peoples to orient their economic activities toward the procurement of human beings for export. This horrible trade attracted many European, American, and African traders, who became wealthy. Because of this form of labor, the United States became a major producer of cotton, and it was a factor in the Civil War.

Among the European traders, the Portuguese were most active. In the kingdom of the Bakongo, located in an area that is part of three countries today—Congo-Brazzaville, Zaïre, and Angola—they established relations with the Manicongo, or king, in the 1480's. The king received material assistance and missionaries. He did not contemplate giving up his sovereignty, and not much changed in his kingdom until Portuguese advisers and priests tried to influence succession to the throne. By about 1700, European influence was such that the Portuguese could establish a small colony of Angola with a governor and an administration. The king remained, but his kingdom was weakened and ultimately destroyed.

Other European powers were also on the coast. In 1652, the Dutch established a trading and refueling station at the southern tip of Africa; in 1659, the French established a station at what is today Saint Louis in Senegal. The British made a small area around what is today Freetown the Sierra Leone colony in 1808. Non-European Turks made northern Africa part of the Ottoman Empire; Arab influence in east Africa is old, and so is Indonesian trading influence in Madagascar.

[1] If we were to consider the Arabs as colonizers or imperialists, we would, of course, be obliged to say that colonialism began in the seventh century.

Although people far from the sea were not subject to an alien-imposed political system for a long time, the need of coastal traders to supply human beings for export often created in these areas a chaotic situation of wars and movements of population. Even the most recent calculation of numbers of slaves imported to the Americas, 9,400,000,[2] is much lower than the actual number of Africans taken from their homes, because it does not count those who died in the struggle to obtain slaves, the wait in stockades on the coast, and the indescribable middle passage to the New World. The consequences to Africa have been disputed: Professor Curtin asserted that "consequences of the slave trade to African societies . . . would not necessarily vary directly with the number exported."[3] Du Bois, on the other hand, said that it "ruined" African culture, at least on the coast.[4]

It is nonetheless true that there were structural changes in precolonial political systems because of the slave trade. According to Vansina, new offices, such as minister of trade, had to be created in African governments selling slaves. Perhaps more important, the trade provided a new source of wealth, and status, and power with the subsequent appearance of new elites. In some cases, a monarch's position might be threatened by organized bands of men profiting from the trade. A man of low status could, by association with European traders and the accumulation of wealth and followers, challenge existing authority. A new foyer of power could weaken centralized authority, such as it was, or it could begin to form a government where none existed previously.[5]

In North Africa, other types of trade could also alter a political system. The French and Spanish contributed to a weakening of the Moroccan government by their so-called protégé system thirty years before the establishment of a French protectorate. As in China at the end of the nineteenth century, foreign trading countries had some rights of extraterritoriality, and Moroccans who worked for them could share in some of these rights. For example, many Moroccans did not pay taxes to the king, serve in his army, or appear before his courts because of their protection by Europeans.

Under the system, a French or Spanish businessman applied to his own country's legation in Morocco for so-called protégé certificates to be given to his employees. Because of the rights such certificates bestowed, wealthy Moroccans were interested in obtaining them. Some were inevitably sold to them. A second group, lower-ranking government officials, seemed able to obtain the certificates, creating double

---

[2] Philip D. Curtin, *The Atlantic Slave Trade: A Census* (Madison: University of Wisconsin Press, 1969), p. 268.
[3] *Ibid.*, p. 269.
[4] W. E. Burghardt Du Bois, *The World and Africa* (New York: International Publishers, 1965), p. 162.
[5] See Jan Vansina, *Kingdoms of the Savanna* (Madison: University of Wisconsin Press, 1966), pp. 196-97.

loyalties. In some areas, officials apparently preferred to spend their time working with foreign business interests rather than carrying out their assigned administrative or political functions. "As a result, central government control declined, especially in the northeastern and western provinces of Morocco."[6]

Other forces of division and subversion were encouraged by the sale of arms. European traders managed to sell arms to any group that wished to revolt against the king. Even though a French or Spanish trader may have had no reason to oppose the central government or wish for its demise, the money to be made from the sale of firearms would cause him to encourage groups opposed to the central government. Even before institutionalized colonialism, European influence was such that it "helped to bring about the collapse of the Moroccan government and, *ipso facto*, facilitated the arrival of the French."[7]

The protégés of Morocco were a political force. Elsewhere, there were other politically relevant groups that owed their existence to European influence. For example, early in the nineteenth century, returned slaves allied themselves with Europeans and had an important role to play in West African politics: The Creoles of Sierra Leone, the Aku of Gambia, the Americo-Liberians or Pioneers of Liberia, and the Brazilians or Sierra Leoneans of Dahomey, Togo, and Nigeria influenced politics before 1885.

The year 1885 marked the beginning of the institutionalization of European control because of the Berlin Conference. At the conference, which began in 1884 and ended in 1885, the Europeans set the rules for the claims of sovereignty, because they had decided they needed control over all of Africa for their political and economic interests.

Basutoland (Lesotho) was claimed in 1868, Tunisia in 1881, Egypt in 1882, and Bechuanaland (Botswana) in 1885. A protectorate over Morocco was proclaimed in 1912. Ivory Coast became a colony in 1893. British control in Nigeria dated from 1902; Zaïre was annexed to Belgium in 1908, although prior to that time it was, more or less, the property of the king. In Northern Rhodesia (Zambia) the British established an administration over two separate areas in 1899 and 1900 and amalgamated them in 1911. Jurisdiction was formally extended over Uganda in 1902. Although the Accra coastal area had been a British colony since 1821, the Gold Coast (now Ghana) was established in 1901. In Sierra Leone, the British government extended its sovereignty inland until, by about 1895, it had what is today the Republic of Sierra Leone. In Gambia, a small coastal area was transferred to Britain in 1821 and administered along with Sierra Leone. It became a separate colony in 1888, and a protectorate over the interior was proclaimed in 1893. In 1935, the two areas were amalgamated into the present-day

[6] Leland Bowie, *The Impact of the Protégé System in Morocco, 1880–1912*, Ohio University Center for International Studies, Papers in International Studies, Africa Series, no. 11 (Athens, Ohio, 1970), p. 7.
[7] *Ibid.*, p. 16.

Gambia. Although the Portuguese started their conquest of Angola in the 1570's, the military campaigns beginning in 1890 were decisive in assuring European control. In 1892, the French conquered Dahomey. They declared a protectorate over Madagascar in 1885 but did not officially occupy and annex it until 1895–96. It took the French at least from 1907 to 1909 to conquer Tchad. In 1891, the Kaiser's government took over the position of the German East African Company in Tanganyika (present-day Tanzania) and by 1898 extended its rule.

These European states extended their rule significantly after 1885, but the colonial state was not fully developed by that year. The time span could, therefore, be shortened.

Resistance to the imposition of a colonial state was much more vigorous and sustained than the Europeans had first anticipated. Europeans found that, although it was not particularly difficult to sign a vague treaty with an African leader and then color an area on the map red or blue, it was very difficult to extend real authority to control and exploit an area in the way they wanted. Second, European colonial administration—handicapped until the end of World War II by shortages of personnel, lack of money, and indecisive colonial policies—was quite unstable. This weak but by no means benevolent administration depended on local authority no matter what official policy toward it was. Last, even when colonies and protectorates were formally established and organized, a population might suddenly attempt to extricate itself from foreign control.

The Germans, who claimed sovereignty over most of what is today mainland Tanzania, could not overcome resistance until about 1900. The French completed their invasion of the central or Sudanic region of West Africa about 1902, but significant resistance continued for decades. Further east, in Equatorial Africa, the French were relatively sure of their power only after 1910, twenty years after the first treaties giving them control had been signed. The Italians in Libya attempted to assert their sovereignty in 1911, but the country knew no peace until about 1917, and that did not last long. The Portuguese were both first and last in colonial history; they did not subdue Angola until 1920.

A few scattered posts in a country linked by a rudimentary communication system that could be cut at will; mobile, military-type occupation forcing Africans to collect ivory or rubber to be sold to European traders, whose payment for the products went immediately to the administration to pay European salaries; occasional raids to recruit porters and workers from fleeing or resisting populations; collection of taxes by force—all this cannot be considered a stable political system. Gradually, however, the new state expanded its control until most Africans were living in a "colonial situation."

The Colonial Situation: A Shared Experience, 1885–1960

The French social anthropoligist Georges Balandier has called the colonial situation "The domination imposed by a foreign minority, racially (or ethnically) and culturally different, acting in the name of a racial (or ethnic) and cultural superiority dogmatically affirmed, and imposing itself on an indigenous population constituting a numerical majority but inferior to the dominant group from a material point of view."[8]

In Africa, a European minority ruled with an ideology and the threat of force based on the machine gun. The ideology proclaimed that Africans were inferior culturally, mentally, and physically, because they were less developed materially and technologically. The fact that most African peoples did not write their languages was chosen as one mark of inferiority. The use of Arabic characters by other African peoples to write their languages was discounted; the use of Amharic, Vai, and Bamun, other written languages, was derided or ignored. Africans were called uniformly "preliterate" even though in the nineteenth century a high percentage of Europeans was preliterate also.

Scholars admitted the richness of the Egyptian and Arab past, but colonial forces said contemporary Egyptians were not the descendants of the pharaohs and that Arabs were corrupted. They invented names for colonized peoples like "native," "wog," or "nègre" to try to remove them from the human race. Proof that Europeans believed it necessary quite early to assume a superior posture is not difficult to find in their own accounts. The Frenchman Louis Binger, traveling in what is today Upper Volta, was sensitive about his own role as a white:

I feel that a white man traveling in this country, whoever he may be, should not prostrate himself before a black king, however powerful the latter may be. It is necessary that a white man should inspire respect and consideration wherever he goes; for if the Europeans should ever come here, they should come as masters, as the superior class of the society, and not have to bow their heads before indigenous chiefs to whom they are definitely superior in all respects.[9]

Africans who had intensive contact with the colonial political system shared experience of humiliation, manipulation, and exploitation. Race prejudice was freely expressed, often in the most vulgar ways. The degree of humiliation depended less on which colonial power was claiming sovereignty than on whether the African lived in a rural or urban area, on the coast or inland, and whether or not there was a

---

[8] Georges Balandier, "The Colonial Situation: A Theoretical Approach," in Immanuel Wallerstein (ed.), *Social Change: The Colonial Situation* (New York: Wiley, 1966), pp. 34–57.
[9] Cited by Elliott P. Skinner, *The Mossi of the Upper Volta: The Political Development of a Sudanese People* (Stanford, Calif.: Stanford University Press, 1964), p 143.

significant European population of administrators, settlers, and bureaucrats. The later expression of African nationalist feeling was strongly influenced by race prejudice in the colonial situation.

The colonial experience was most intense in countries with a significant white settler population. Europeans tended to make their homes in South Africa, Algeria, Angola, Mozambique, Rhodesia, Kenya, and Senegal. By 1960 the proportion of Europeans to Africans in South Africa was 1 to 4; in Algeria the same year, 1 to 9; Rhodesia and Angola, 1 to 16; Mozambique, 1 to 32; Senegal, 1 to 80; and Kenya, 1 to 100. There were concentrations of whites elsewhere, too. Europeans settled in northern Tanzania and numbered 1 for every 450 Africans. Nigeria, which did not have what would be considered a significant settler population, had in 1952 (the year of the last reliable census) 1 European for every 2,000 Africans.[10] Since 1960, the white population of the Ivory Coast has increased, as has that of Gabon, and Malawi.

The great majority of these whites came from low-status origins in Europe. During the colonial period and after, they competed with Africans for economic rewards and guarded their so-called racial rights, which permitted them to raise their status and prestige. No matter what the national origins of the Europeans, they made appeals on the basis of race to the colonial government for protection of their narrow interests. If they had friends in parliament in Europe, they were in an even better position to get what they wanted, usually at the expense of the Africans. In Algeria, the Europeans by the mid-twentieth century controlled 27 per cent of all the arable land and could use the colonial administration to get more if need be.[11]

Europeans were not, however, the only settlers in a position to exploit the colonial situation. In 1948, there were 44,560 Arabs in Zanzibar and 15,211 Indians, compared with 199,860 Africans.[12] The Arabs in Zanzibar, West Africa, and Mombasa in Kenya; and the Indians here and there; and some Chinese in Madagascar did not generally own land, engaging rather in commerce. But their attitudes toward the Africans and their prejudice were similar. They, like the Europeans, tried to prevent change, and they benefited from the colonial situation.

In spite of the colonial situation, and sometimes even in the presence of the settlers, African political systems survived. They survived because the masses considered them more legitimate than the colonial structure and because the colonial structure could not completely replace the precolonial structures. The colonial state thus really contained a dual polity. This is the first important political effect of the colonial period from 1885 to 1960.

[10] Most data from Philip Mason, *Patterns of Dominance*, 2d ed., Institute of Race Relations Series (London: Oxford University Press, 1970), p. 64.

[11] Clement Henry Moore, *Politics in North Africa: Algeria, Morocco, Tunisia*, The Little, Brown Series in Comparative Politics (Boston: Little, Brown, 1970), p. 38.

[12] Lord Hailey, *An African Survey*, rev. ed. (London: Oxford University Press, 1957), p. 410.

Colonialism and African Authority: The Dual Polity

Each European country in Africa imposed a political system over the pre-existing political systems and consciously attempted in most cases to alter them. Generally, however, these African systems survived in one form or another.

Looking at the central administration and studying colonial writings, one might conclude that the colonial systems were quite different from each other in this regard. In a well-known book, Thomas Hodgkin labeled British administration "pragmatic" and the French "Cartesian"; he said the British adapted their administration to local conditions, making it therefore "more African," whereas the French, basing their activities on universal and logical principles, set up the same form of administration everywhere. Because Britain and France claimed nineteen and eighteen territories respectively, their influence is much greater than that of any other European country. We shall, therefore, deal with this supposed pragmatism and Cartesianism; rather than focus on European policy, however, it is better to try to look at the colonial system from the standpoint of the African political systems—those with governments and states on the one hand and those without these institutions on the other.

Foreign Rule and African States. The key to British pragmatism was said to be ruling "indirectly" through African institutions. Indirect rule came about, as later British writers said, because there were not enough administrators to rule otherwise, not because of any particularly ideological commitment to preserve African institutions. British weakness necessitated dependence on and manipulation of existing institutions. This worked to some extent, as long as there were visible institutions. That is, indirect rule worked when there was a pre-existing state, but it could not avoid changing the state.

In northern Nigeria, the British recognized thirty-eight emirates or kingdoms and created the so-called Native Administration around them. The emirates were not left exactly as found; they were reorganized around the emir. Sir Frederick Lugard (later Lord Lugard), architect of this system, established a "native treasury" to receive taxes. Some of the revenue then went to the European administration, and the rest to the king. A "budget provided for the salary of the emir himself and for the salaries of his office holders, the alkalai or native court judges, the treasury and central office Malams and other clerical staff, and for police and for prison warders."[13] Courts were also reorganized.

The emirate or province was divided into districts with one African heading each one; below the districts were the villages each with a headman. The British had a parallel structure: For each emirate a

---

[13] Sir Bryan Sharwood Smith, *Recollections of British Administration in The Cameroons and Northern Nigeria 1921–1957: "But Always as Friends"* (Durham, N.C.: Duke University Press, 1969), pp. 45–46.

British "resident" consulted and advised the emir at least on a weekly basis. One former resident wrote: "We were taught that at all times the prestige and authority of the chief and his administration must be upheld. . . . We were taught, too, that a government officer must on no account issue a direct order. Orders must always come from the chief or his representative."[14] Below the resident, district officers advised and followed the activities of the African heads of district. No British official was stationed in villages. Consequently, the proportion of foreign functionaries to local population was very low.

The emir, who might have as many as 2 million people in his province, as did Kano during the 1930's, had some rule-making powers. He could establish traffic regulations, for example, but this hardly interested him. His most important power remained judicial and fiscal, just as it had been before the arrival of the British. The authority to decide disputes, particularly those over land, and the authority to collect taxes are very important in Africa because of the discretionary power available. Through family ties, the emir also knew much better than the Europeans what was going on in the province. Close relatives were appointed to key positions in the cities, and others headed the districts. Village heads were more or less chosen by villagers, but they were paid out of the king's treasury and thus under some control.[15]

The native administration under the emir supposedly also had charge of technical services like road construction, prisons, agriculture, forestry, and so forth. Because trained personnel was European, whites had real control of these services.

The presence of whites in these technical services did not adversely affect the emir's power. Indeed, it is likely that many Africans perceived white technicians as working for him. Their presence, on the contrary, probably increased his prestige and authority. British presence in general was protection for the monarch. Nonetheless, one should not assume that indirect rule meant benevolent watching over legitimate traditional systems centuries old.

The emirs were, for the most part, Fulani, a minority people in northern Nigeria, who had invaded the country and conquered the majority Hausa people at the beginning of the nineteenth century. We have no evidence that the Hausa were about to revolt against their Fulani lords when the British arrived, but it is certain the British backing strengthened Fulani control. They would have protected the emirs against attempts to overthrow them. No wonder the Sardauna of Sokoto, the leading figure of northern Nigeria before 1966, said that God had sent the British.[16]

[14] *Ibid.*, p. 54.
[15] Margery Perham, *Native Administration in Nigeria* (London: Oxford University Press, 1937), pp. 81–98. We depend on her description and that of Sharwood Smith here.
[16] See Sir Ahmadu Bello, *My Life* (Cambridge, England: Cambridge University Press, 1962).

Colonialism and African Politics

The Hausa still had elements of their political systems, predating Fulani conquest, at least at the village level. There was thus a triple polity in northern Nigeria: Hausa at the village level, Fulani at the provincial and urban levels, and British at the regional and state levels. Hausa consciousness was such, despite their long subordination, that they organized their own political party (NEPU) later against the Fulani-dominated Northern Peoples Congress when politics within the colonial framework began.

Elsewhere in Africa, the British followed a similar pattern when they found an African state. They protected and strengthened the powers of men already in power who otherwise might have been replaced by the normal workings of the precolonial political system, if the British had not been there or if foreign rule had been truly indirect. In Ghana, or the Gold Coast, the Asantehene, or king of the Ashanti state, could be removed by a recognized method if he were unjust, incompetent, or corrupt, in the days before British control. British protection nullified traditional sanctions; the outsiders helped the king centralize power to a greater extent than before the colonial period. The Litunga, or king, of the Balozi in Zambia; the Kabaka of Buganda, in Uganda; the Sultan of Zanzibar, and the King of Egypt profited from British support in similar ways. Opposition sometimes stopped them. The attempts of the British to strengthen the Yoruba obas, or kings, on the model of the emirs met with great resistance and hostility in western Nigeria, for example.

African states and leaders fared less well under the French, but the latter also had their proponents of indirect rule. Marshal Lyautey, France's first head of Morocco, wrote that his subordinates must respect the Alawite dynasty and local authority. He said the French must rule indirectly through local "mandarins" and use them to advantage. African institutions must remain in place, he wrote. He then proceeded to help in the centralization of a new Moroccan state under himself and the sultan, or king, who continued to rule. Not all French writers agreed with Lyautey, some proposing that African kings be removed, on ideological, republican, grounds. Nonetheless, there are many instances where the French maintained or even strengthened African states. In Upper Volta, the Mogho Naba, or king, of the Mossi kept his kingdom, and so did Hetman in Oubangui-Chari.

Hetman, the Sultan of Rafai from 1900 to his death in 1939, had considerable power under French rule in the Central African Republic. Like the Nigerian emirs, he was a descendant of invaders (Zandé) who had created a new political system not long before the arrival of the Europeans. Hetman cooperated and helped the French and Belgians when they were establishing their administrations in what were then called Oubangui-Chari and the Congo. In return, they permitted him to remain in power—or perhaps they were obliged to accept him as a local ruler. Hetman had so much power and respect that one governor general preferred to support him in a dispute with a French administrator. A scarcity of personnel and a constant turnover of administrators meant that the French depended on him to keep order, conduct a census, render justice, and collect taxes. Once, he even tried to increase the area under his control and had the support of an administrator, no doubt captivated by his charm and logic.

French policy often depended on this man on the spot, and this is also true of British and Belgian administration.

The Belgian parliament was supposedly supreme over colonial matters, but it left the control to the king, who left it to his minister for colonies, who left it to the governor general of the Congo. Until 1933, the governor general delegated most authority to heads of the provinces into which the colony was divided. It was the heads of provinces and their subordinates who really made policy about African authority and almost everything else.[17]

Difficulty in communications made day-to-day control by governors— to say nothing of the colonial offices or ministries of colonies—impossible. One of the most famous Frenchmen on the spot who encouraged African political authority and maintenance of African states was Félix Eboué, Governor General of French Equatorial Africa during World War II.

Eboué began his career in the present-day Central African Republic. Shortly after his arrival in 1909, he showed his attitude by disobeying orders from his governor to seize an African leader who had been harassing European traders. Eboué preferred to negotiate with the man, establishing a *modus vivendi* if not an alliance. Because he was without European subordinates, Eboué found he could not bring areas under the control of France—and this meant the ability to collect taxes in peace— without African assistance. To win African assistance, he and others had to permit African leaders some autonomy. He pursued this policy in what today are Mali and Tchad.

As Governor General of French Equatorial Africa, in 1941 he wrote a famous circular or directive to his subordinates concerning African authority. In *Nouvelle Politique Indigène*, he said the French had been wrong to attempt to suppress leaders of African political systems and that they must be restored to their true place of power and prestige. Eboué admired the organization of the emirates of northern Nigeria and thought a similar system might be instituted in parts of the French colonies.[18]

In spite of Lyautey and Eboué, there was considerable disorder and uncertainty with regard to African authority. In Senegal, the French destroyed the Kingdom of Tekrur. In Algeria, the French rather systematically destroyed local authority with the help of the settlers who wanted African land and cheap African labor. They desecrated

[17] Pierre Ryckmans, *La Politique coloniale* (Brussels: Les Editions Rex, Collection d'Etudes de Doctrine Politique Catholique, publiée sous les auspices de la Fédération des Associations et Cercles Catholiques, 1933), pp. 19–28.
[18] See Brian Weinstein, *Eboué* (New York: Oxford University Press, 1972).

holy places, moved people from their land, and suppressed political organization above the village level. They had a generally more intensive and possibly more expensive administration than the British. In 1933, Robert Delavignette found there were 1,315 European officials for an estimated population of 20,000,000 in Nigeria, compared with 4,547 European officials for an estimated total of 18,200,000 in French West Africa and French Equatorial Africa. This meant one administrator in Nigeria for every 15,200 people, compared with one administrator in a French-controlled area for every 4,000 people.[19] The territories are quite different, however, the French-controlled ones being much larger in area and having dispersed populations.

A rather striking example of French uncertainty comes from Tchad. After the British gained control of neighboring Sudan, they kept what they called the sultanates, similar to the emirates in Nigeria. The Sultan of Massalit on the border with Tchad kept his position and had considerable power.

Just across the border in Tchad is the area of Ouaddai, whose people consider themselves related to the people of Massalit. Early in the twentieth century, the French abolished the monarchy of Ouaddai, but they restored it again in 1934 with a leader from the original ruling family. He, Muhammad Ourada, had gone to the French school for chiefs in Senegal and had become a clerk in the colonial administration. Once he was named sultan, his relations with the French fluctuated greatly. Eboué, governor of Tchad in 1939 and 1940, supported him and increased his power. One individual French administrator, a "man on the spot," did not have much respect for him, however.

After warning Ourada that there was no real country called Ouaddai, merely an administrative division within a French colony, the European official told Ourada that he had been named to his post because he had been a good clerk and because he belonged to the former ruling family. Don't forget who is really in charge here, the Frenchman warned, contradicting Governor General Eboué's policies:

[The restoration of the Sultanate] did not give you any sovereignty, and in this respect your situation is completely different from that of your neighbor the Sultan of Massalit whose territory was occupied by mutual agreement with the British who signed a treaty according to which the [British] Resident . . . is simply a councillor to the Sultan. Here, you collaborate in the administration of the subdivision, but the man who has responsibility to the Head of the Colony is I, and I am responsible for you. That gives me the right to give you orders, and that gives you the duty to follow them.[20]

It is only when one finds a detail such as this about the relationship between African authority and the colonial administrator that one can

[19] Robert Delavignette, *Freedom and Authority in French West Africa*, International African Institute (London: Oxford University Press, 1968), p. 18.
[20] Letter to Ourada, December 25, 1940, Archives of Tchad, Dossier Sultanate of Ouaddai.

understand what was happening during the colonial period in a given state. In the case of Tchad, it is safe to say that French rule created a great deal of uncertainty and instability in African society because of its own uncertainty and instability.

Nearby in Cameroun, the Germans tended to maintain the leaders of African states such as those of the Douala people, the Bamoum, and the northern Fulani. Like the British, the Germans claimed to be acting in an advisory capacity to local rulers.[21]

In their East African colony of Tanganyika, the Germans allowed the Sukuma leaders to remain in power. This affected fifty principal leaders, who headed the approximately fifty autonomous units into which this people had settled.[22] When the Germans met hierarchized societies in Rwanda and Burundi, they kept the Tutsi-dominated government. They kept the kings, or mwamis, and, like the British in northern Nigeria, placed a German "resident" near them.[23]

In the Katanga region of Zaïre, the Belgians respected African leadership. Mwata Yamvo Ditende Yawa Nawezi II, King of the Balunda, kept his position under the Belgians.[24] Some others, however, became clerks.

Quite different were the Portuguese, who systematically tried to destroy African government. They removed all leaders and then forced people to settle civil disputes according to Portuguese law instead of allowing some room for African law, as the French and British had done.[25]

Foreign Rule and Stateless Political Systems. The similarities in the colonial approach to stateless systems were greater than in the case of state systems, no matter what European ideas about direct or indirect rule were. For example, in the Igbo-speaking areas of Nigeria the British, supposedly so sensitive to the customs of the peoples, created chiefs where there had never been any and gave them fiscal and judicial powers. In Uganda, where the British supported the states like Buganda in the south, they found no governments in the north. Undaunted, they created chieftaincies and named men who had no traditional claim to leadership.[26] They did the same thing in Tanzania after driving out the Germans.

[21] Harry Rudin, *Germans in the Cameroons 1884–1914*, (1938; reprint ed., New York: Greenwood Press, 1969), pp. 111, 214.

[22] G. Andrew Maguire, *Toward "Uhuru" in Tanzania: The Politics of Participation* (Cambridge, England: Cambridge University Press, 1969), pp. 2, 6.

[23] Henri Brunschwig, "Un récent bilan historique de la colonisation allemande au Cameroun et en Afrique orientale," in *Revue Francaise d'Historie d'Outre-Mer*, LVIII, no. 210 (1971): 116–24.

[24] Crawford Young, *Politics in the Congo: Decolonization and Independence* (Princeton, N.J.: Princeton University Press, 1965), p. 194.

[25] Robert I. Rotberg, *A Political History of Tropical Africa* (New York: Harcourt, Brace and World, 1965), p. 317.

[26] M. S. M. Kiwanuka, "Uganda Under the British," in B. A. Ogot and J. A. Kieran (eds.) *Zamani: A Survey of East African History* (Nairobi: East African Publishing House and Longmans, 1968), p. 316.

The French divided the colonies of French West Africa and French Equatorial Africa into circumscriptions and then into subdivisions, or *cercles*, headed by Frenchmen. Subdivisions were then divided into cantons headed by appointed Africans. In Senegal, the French chose "canton chiefs . . . from among those with traditional claims to authority."[27] Almost everywhere, however, the French chose men who had been loyal to them: cooks, soldiers, and village chiefs were appointed, creating a confusion in authority, for many of the new "elites" lacked status in their home areas.

These new chiefs undermined the authority of kinship leaders in stateless political systems. People were also told they owed their loyalty and identity to a geographic expression like a canton, whose frontiers cut across kinship lines and at the head of which might be a man for whom no one had any respect. The new chief might have low status in traditional society, and he might have come from another ethnic or kinship group. The canton chiefs and warrant chiefs, unrestrained by tradition and backed by the colonialists, soon had a reputation for harsh and rapacious rule.

In spite of this confusion and corruption of African political systems by the superposition of a new state, the village and kinship basis of politics did not disappear. The Europeans could not know everything that was going on, and local administrators, except in the Portuguese system, recognized some African judicial authority anyway. An individual administrator might permit considerable judicial autonomy to a kinship group without the governor's or ministry's being aware of it. In the French system, however, the *indigénat* system gave the administrator permission to sentence Africans to two-week prison terms without trial, and he often used it.

Africans naturally tried to avoid dealing with the colonial administration. At the village and kinship-group level, judicial authority in many matters remained in the hands of those who had exercised it in the precolonial era. Councils of elders continued to meet—at night or in secret if necessary—and many important problems involving marriage, children, inheritance, and even land ownership were still resolved without calling on the colonial state and its agents. African states continued to exist, desired or not by the colonial powers, and the stateless political systems also survived. Though obviously forced to change, a duality of European-imposed and traditional African systems continued.

Contemporary African politics in French-tradition countries and in British-tradition countries shows the effects of the dual polity of the colonial state. Although we have said that neither the British nor the French ruled in a truly indirect fashion, and that the French also kept some African states during the colonial period, a rather important dif-

[27] Martin A. Klein, "Chiefship in Sine-Saloum (Senegal), 1887–1914," in Victor Turner (ed.), *Colonialism in Africa 1870–1960*, III: *Profiles of Change: African Society and Colonial Rule* (Cambridge, England: Cambridge University Press, 1971): 63.

ference resulted in areas ruled by the two European powers: For example, the British developed institutions of local government on the basis of the precolonial African government, while the French generally did not, until near the end of the colonial period. The Portuguese colonial administration was staffed by the military who directed the affairs of the colony like an occupying army allowing little or no room for local government.

The British developed institutions like a treasury and a native authority with a local civil service. The local government structures set up by the British corresponded with ethnic groups. Although the French experimented with so-called province chiefs, or paramount chiefs, to head one ethnic group, their program was not systematic, and the resulting confusion did not allow for the development of a strong vested interest in local ethnic government. The ethnic differences were and are present in the French areas, but they were not reinforced by institutions of colonial government as they were in most British-controlled areas. For example, the Baganda people of Uganda kept their king as well as a separate legislature, the Lukiko, and other institutions.

With the development of local ethnic institutions in the British system, there were possibilities for secession, once demands for self-determination were made and the states became independent. Ethnic leaders could easily ask: "What are the limits of self-determination?" If there is an independent Uganda, why not an independent Buganda? Therefore, secessionist movements based on ethnicity have been more prominent in English-speaking independent countries than elsewhere. The most striking example of such secession is, of course, Biafra, but there have been others in the English-speaking countries: Barotseland in Zambia, Buganda in Uganda, Southern Sudan, Ashanti in Ghana, Northern Nigeria, and the Masai of Kenya.

There has been talk of secession in French-speaking countries, but it has never been as serious or as overt as in English-speaking countries: In Guinea, the Fulani thought about breaking away when the country became independent, and the Fang in Gabon have talked about linking up with Fang in southern Cameroun. There have been conflicts in Morocco and Tchad, but they have not been as serious as in English-speaking areas. Similarly, in the former Portuguese areas such as Angda all liberation movements agreed to maintain the territorial integrity of the state despite their intense differences in other matters.

Colonialism and African Authority: New Elites

While the British were writing about their colonial policy in terms of direct or indirect rule, the French were thinking about their own primarily in terms of assimilation or association. The question of direct-indirect relates to the superposition of one political structure over another and the effects on old elites and structures; the question of assimilation-association relates to the rise of new leadership groups or elites who have been able to use the new structure to achieve their position. One cannot make a rigid distinction between the European powers on the basis of assimilation-association influences, any more than on the basis of direct or indirect. In other words, each system had elements of both. The general effects must be discussed.

In the twenty-year period between 1889 and 1910 colonial circles in France discussed the possibility of integrating Africa into the French nation "with its society and population made over—to whatever extent possible—in her image."[28] The idea that people born and living outside the European metropole could become French citizens was not new. All residents of France's old Caribbean colonies became citizens in 1848 and were further integrated in 1946. Senegalese born in the four towns or communes of the colony were also made French citizens. West Indians from Guadeloupe, Martinique, and French Guyane and the Senegalese later supported the extension of citizenship from their own to other areas—Algeria first and then the rest of Africa.

The doctrine of association was more important for most of French history in Africa, however, and corresponds to some extent with the idea of indirect rule. With the focus put on economic development, it was believed that local institutions must be kept intact even though the colonial administrator on the spot disagreed: "The economic betterment of the region was to be undertaken by natives and Frenchmen within the general framework of native institutions. It was a policy based on the acceptance of mutual interests and on a sort of fraternity, but not of equality."[29]

No matter whether the highest officials in the ministry were proclaiming assimilation or association as the doctrine of the moment, both were occurring in British-, French-, Belgian-, Portuguese-, and Spanish-controlled areas. What the French and, to a lesser extent, the Portuguese did more than anyone else was to encourage the belief that the most advantaged elite would be the one the most closely associated with Europe and divorced from tradition, region, and ethnic group, whether or not there had been a precolonial state. Because of the great strength of local institutions in British-controlled areas, young Africans understood that, although association with Britain and assimilation of some British ways would help bring elite status, they ought to keep close contact with African political systems. The most striking symbolic difference between the two emphases was, of course, the question of citizenship.

By law, an African could become a French citizen if he were judged to have absorbed a sufficient "quantity" of French civilization. This quantity would be measured by his religion, job, education, military

---

[28] Raymond C. Betts, *Assimilation and Association in French Colonial Theory 1890–1914* (New York: Columbia University Press, 1961), p. 8.
[29] *Ibid.*, p. 120.

service, style of life, dress, and so forth. The door to equality was apparently open through assimilation. Assimilation and citizenship would permit Africans to get better, higher-paying jobs within business, the administration, or the church. They would also have access to power and a way to escape from racial humiliation. In Angola, Mozambique, and Guinea-Bissau, the Portuguese promised citizenship and equality. Many of the more than 100,000 mulattoes of Angola did become citizens, but the vast majority was treated by Portuguese settlers and administrators in discriminatory brutal fashion.

In reality, the French did not have a systematic assimilationist policy in Africa any more than did the Portuguese or British for most of the seventy-five-year colonial period. Only after World War II were all people made citizens. Prior attempts to extend citizenship in North Africa, during the Popular Front government of 1936, failed because of organized opposition of French settlers and low-ranking civil servants. Both groups feared the loss of their tenuously held status and possibly their jobs. In the British empire, there was no explicitly articulated or official attempt to permit equality with metropolitan Englishmen and create black Englishmen. But humans everywhere tend to copy the elites, and as some of the elites in the colonial state were British, educated Africans tended to model their life-styles on those of colonial officers or metropolitan Britishers. The assimilation process can best be seen in education, where Africans learned British, French, Belgian, Spanish, and Portuguese ways.

In the French-controlled areas, Senegal had the first French schools. A government elementary school opened in 1816, and 100 years later a normal school took the name William Ponty and became a training institute for all of French West Africa. The Ponty school would come to train more than 1,000 physicians, teachers, and civil servants, a tiny but energetic new elite that would make its voice heard in unexpected ways after World War II. In equatorial Africa, the first school was set up in 1863 in Gabon and grew at a much slower rate than others in West Africa. Education of a European sort was most developed in Algeria, which had the first European-type university. Tunisia and Morocco kept many of their precolonial schools, but some were transformed by the French, like the Sadiki College in Tunisia, where French and Arabic studies were taught together.

In the British-controlled areas, schools opened in southern Nigeria in 1845 at Badagri, and in 1848 at Calabar. In Ghana, the Dutch had established their first school in 1644, but the British established the more permanent institutions on the coast early in the nineteenth century.[30] In Portuguese colonies government schools opened for the first time in the 1960's, although the Catholics had had some schools since the sixteenth century.

[30] See Lucy Mair, "New Elites in East and West Africa," in Turner, *Colonialism in Africa*, III: 167–92.

Africans with access to education by Europeans partially assimilated themselves to a European model that they saw at close hand or studied about. The Europeans they saw were not, of course, always strictly representative of the elites of the metropolitan European country, and many Africans constructed in their own minds an ideal type. Among themselves, they often developed close exclusive ties that separated them from the African masses as much as from the Europeans. Old school ties like Achimota in Ghana, William Ponty in Senegal, Sadiki College in Tunisia, and Fort Hare in South Africa were as important as those of the British public schools, Oxbridge, or the Ecole Coloniale. Africans in Portuguese colonies had no such institutions outside of a few in Lisbon itself.

What the growing African elite in all countries feared most was an educational system supposedly "adapted to their needs." Whenever colonial officials attempted to promote vocational education, agriculture training, and teaching in African languages, the Africans protested. For example, Achimota School was founded in Ghana as an "African" school—in other words, to teach young Africans about West African history and local problems of development, and generally prepare them for leadership roles in rural development. Opposition came from their parents, chiefs, and those who had been educated already. As a result, African-related subjects decreased in importance in the school's curriculum: "It was no more a school rooted in African conditions than were ... the other secondary schools, rather was it a secondary institution modelled on English lines but with vastly superior resources."[31]

Achimota school provided the door to higher jobs in the administration and to universities in the United Kingdom, then to even higher jobs and well-paying professions like medicine and the law. This is what a developing "administrative bourgeoisie" or a developing "colonial elite" wanted.[32]

The new elite in British-dominated colonial states generally kept one foot in traditional ethnic politics, where the British were developing institutions of local government. New elites in Tunisia and Morocco did the same. In Algeria, new elites were convinced by the assimilationist appeal until European-settler barriers to it changed their view. At first, therefore, they cut themselves off from tradition. They looked toward France, identifying their aspirations with reforms that would make them citizens equal with metropolitan Frenchmen. Members of the earliest group of politically active men, like Ferhat Abbas, were born about

---

[31] Philip Foster, *Education and Social Change in Ghana* (Chicago: University of Chicago Press, 1965), p. 168.

[32] Balandier, cited in Martin Kilson, "The Emergent Elites of Black Africa, 1900 to 1960," in L. H. Gann and Peter Duignan (eds.), *Colonialism in Africa 1870–1960*, II: *The History and Politics of Colonialism 1914–1960* (Cambridge, England: Cambridge University Press, 1970): 391; and Paul Mercier, "Evolution of Senegalese Elites", in Pierre L. Van den Berghe (ed.), *Social Problems of Change and Conflict* (San Francisco: Chandler, 1965), pp. 167–68.

1907. The route to educational opportunity had been opened by the French, and a small group became lawyers and physicians.

These men learned about the ideal of liberty, equality, and fraternity in French schools and from French books. Believing that equality and fraternity were possible within the French nation, they formed *Jeune Algérie*, their first organization, which called for reforms: "Assimilation, then, became the key to their hopes, and for this goal they became actively involved in politics in the 1930's."[33] After their desires were thwarted by French settlers, a disillusioned elite and younger men turned to a more radical and revolutionary movement, which eventually brought Algeria to independence.

Perhaps if desired reforms, including the early extension of citizenship, had taken place, the Algerians, like the Senegalese elite, would have remained more closely tied with France. They had gained their elite status through the colonial system and through increased assimilation of French culture. They looked outward toward France for direction and inspiration. The newer elites in English-speaking countries looked inward. Their sphere of activity was a region in a colony or the colony as a whole; they seldom belonged to metropolitan-based organizations or parties, and much of their support was ethnic. This pattern has affected contemporary African politics and African relations with the former colonial powers. Partly as a result of the colonial experience of the elite in French-dominated countries, these men tend to associate themselves much more with France and French culture than do elites in English-speaking countries. Because of the long war of liberation and Portugal's own weakness, elites in the former Portuguese colonies do not identify themselves in the same way with European culture. Ethnic consciousness and ethnic politicization seem to be somewhat more characteristic of the former British- and Belgian-dominated states. Ethnic awareness is now an important factor in African politics everywhere.

Ethnic Differentiation and Ethnic Politicization

Within the dual polity, and as new elites grew, some ethnic groups gained a comparative advantage over others: One African state survived better than another, for example, or people from one ethnic group entered more easily into the ranks of the new elite. Often geography played the most important role, or the perspicacity of a leader who quickly saw the way to take advantage of the colonial state for himself and for his people. Some groups had the earliest access to schools, then the first posts in the colonial administration, which gave them knowledge about how it could be manipulated. Their cooperation and position could create a favorable impression among the colonizers who, with a "soft spot" for such and such a group, might favor it, thus continuing

[33] William B. Quandt, *Revolution and Political Leadership: Algeria 1954–1968* (Cambridge, Mass.: MIT Press, 1969), p. 34.

the cycle. Members of this group might have the skills required to organize a trade union, a movement, or a political party before others, and then be in a better position to run the independent state.

Generally, those who had a comparative advantage were coastal peoples, river-dwellers, and lake-dwellers. They met the European first as traders, before the colonial period, and were the first to get his goods in exchange for ivory, gold, slaves, and other products. These goods included guns, which gave them an advantage in war with other ethnic groups. Some got the chance to go to Europe. With the establishment of colonies they often helped the European as guides and interpreters, and they began to form a new elite of clerks, teachers, traders, and priests within the new political framework. In some cases they had a very important stake in learning new ways from the European and forming alliances with him. The small coastal ethnic groups were threatened by larger ethnic groups in the interior, from whom they had perhaps fled. Jealously guarding their favored position as intermediaries, they feared that without an alliance with the European they might be inundated and overwhelmed.

Some of the early stories about cannibalism originated with the ethnic groups on the coast, who wanted to frighten the Europeans, or at least inhibit their desire to establish trading relations with the interior. In Gabon, the Myènè, a small group on the coast, signed the first treaties with the French after a long history of trade in slaves with Europeans. The Myènè let the French set up posts on the land in exchange for protection and guns. They tried to discourage direct French contact with the Fang people in the interior with stories about the so-called savages. Later, they went to the first schools, which were established on their land. Because they were literate in French, they became the first Gabonese clerks, and their women bore the first Eur-African children, a few of whom were cared for and educated by the European fathers. Later, they played a more active role than their numbers would suggest in the formation of political parties and trade unions.

In the Central African Republic, two small groups living along rivers met the French before the much more numerically important Banda group. These were the Ngbaka and the Banziri who, it appears, feared the Banda and may have been driven to the rivers by them. When missionaries set up schools, they attended them. The first African priest was an Ngbaka, and he became the first head of government as the country evolved toward independence. The second head of government was an Ngbaka, the third an Ngbaka. The Banziri, numbering no more than a few thousand, have many clerks and usually one cabinet minister, while the Banda and the Baya, who are poorly organized but who probably account for more than half the population in the whole country, are poorly represented in the administration and in the government.

In Tchad, the southern Sara became Christians and went to school. One of them, a former civil servant, François Tombalbaye, became the first president of the country. In Congo, the few Bavili of the coast took advantage of French education and played a preponderant role in the beginning of politics in that country. In Sierra Leone, the Creoles; in Gambia, the Aku; in Liberia, the Americo-Liberians were most important. In Ghana, the coastal Fanti got control of trade with Europeans before the colonial period; these traders helped support the schools.[34] The Fanti had a more important role in the beginnings of a modern Ghana than their numbers would suggest. In Nigeria, first the Yoruba and Efik on the ocean got education. In Tanzania, the residents of Lake Victoria went to the first mission schools and then played an important role in administrative and political development. In Guinea-Bissau mixed Eur-Africans and inhabitants of Cape Verde islands received the first opportunities, and they later led the liberation movement.

An interesting example of two ethnic groups' differentiation and politicization because of the colonial experience has been described recently by Dr. Obaro Ikime in his book *Niger Delta Rivalry*.[35] The Itsekiri and Urhobo peoples in Nigeria live along the mouth of the River Niger. The Itsekiri on the coast numbered somewhat more than 32,000 in 1952, while the Urhobo in the interior numbered 436,000. The Itsekiri position on the coast ensured earlier contact with the Europeans. They were also fairly well organized into a state with a king, or olu, and had a sense of common identity. The Urhobo political system had no government, and the average Urhobo identified with his clan, which was ruled by a council.

As early as the fifteenth century, Itsekiri appear to have had contact with the Portuguese. They traded with the Europeans and began to sell Urhobo slaves, who had been sold to them by Urhobo of different clans. (Urhobo clans fought among themselves, but the Itsekiri, doubtless conscious of their small numbers and having a somewhat centralized political system ensuring the peaceful settlement of disputes, would not sell any Itsekiri into slavery.) The European had no direct contact with the Urhobo, who remained in the interior, and soon got the idea they were "less civilized" than the Itsekiri, perhaps because of Itsekiri stories about them.

The first missionaries in the area naturally also met the Itsekiri first; they gained converts to their faith and set up schools. The Itsekiri thus assimilated some European ways, spoke English, and strengthened their position. They considered themselves "more civilized" than their Urhobo neighbors, according to Dr. Ikime.

In 1884, the British signed a treaty of protectorate with an Itsekiri leader, Chief Nana. The British helped him expand his influence because he was their ally. Itsekiri economic roles grew with the diversification of trade activities and then entry of new companies, who still

---

[34] Foster, *Education and Social Change in Ghana*, pp. 49–50.
[35] Obaro Ikime, *Niger Delta Rivalry: Itsekiri-Urhobo Relations and the European Presence 1884–1936*, Ibadan History Series (New York: Humanities Press, 1969).

remained on the coast: "As late as 1905 the firms were still content to [remain on the coast]."[86]

Relations between the Itsekiri and the Urhobo were not bad at the end of the nineteenth century. They both gained from the trading activities, and the Urhobo respected the Itsekiri leader Nana, whose mother was Urhobo. They also respected the Itsekiri traders who set up posts among them or who regularly traveled into Urhobo territory. These traders spoke Urhobo and had married Urhobo women. The inlanders also had a great deal of respect for the Itsekiri alliance with the British, about which they had heard from the Itsekiri themselves.

This situation changed when, in order to increase their trade, the British decided to set up trading posts in Urhobo country, thus jumping over the Itsekiri middlemen. In 1892 and 1893, they signed treaties with the inlanders, and the Itsekiri middleman role began to decline. The Urhobo saw they could have direct contact with the powerful foreigners, and they began to have access to British schools.

Schools were opened for the Urhobo in 1902 and 1903, but it was not until the 1920's that the Urhobo could compete for jobs. In the meanwhile, the Itsekiri who had accompanied the British traders and missionaries into Urhoboland as interpreters and guides kept their favored position, boasting of their role in "opening up" Urhoboland. The British also continued to favor the Itsekiri, and this favoritism must have been obvious to the Urhobo.

In 1900, the British began to institutionalize a court system and set up local government. That aggravated a growing tension between the Itsekiri and the Urhobo and created great uneasiness among the latter. The Urhobo, with their decentralized political system, had had village councils and clan councils to settle disputes, while the Itsekiri were accustomed to centralized institutions. British-created institutions were thus more congenial to the Itsekiri than to the Urhobo. The British outlawed the Urhobo clan and village courts and set up centralized Native Councils with Itsekiri judges and Urhobo judges from only some of the clans. Itsekiri traders and educated men were appointed to these courts. Because courts were few in number, the Urhobo often had to travel some distance to get to them and then had to submit their disputes to Urhobo from other clans or to Itsekiri.

To make matters worse, the British had a strong desire to create chiefs where they had not existed. They created a paramount chieftaincy and a hierarchy of warrant chiefs to collect taxes for the whole Itsekiri-Urhobo area, which was made into one administrative division. They named an Itsekiri, Dogho Numa, to the post. This was an unfortunate choice because, from the point of view of the Urhobo, he abused his authority by the capricious appointment of unpopular men as warrant chiefs. The British supported this unpopular man, and matters became worse. The earlier *modus vivendi* between the Itsekiri and Urhobo was

[86] *Ibid.*, p. 99.

eroded as suspicions of discrimination grew among the Urhobo. The latter may have begun to realize they were more numerous than the Itsekiri.

In 1927, the Urhobo rioted against the chiefs and the tax system. In the face of this conflict, the British realized they had to reorganize their government. They maintained the two ethnic groups in one administrative division, but they abolished the central courts, letting the Urhobo return to their clan and village judicial system. The hated Dogho conveniently died, and more schools were opened for the Urhobo.

About 1934, the Itsekiri requested the re-establishment of their leader, the olu. The Urhobo feared that if the Itsekiri had one leader again, they might be in a better position to dominate them. They protested, and some Itsekiri reacted, creating tensions. The British went along with Urhobo objections. In 1944, however, the Itsekiri began once again to agitate for one ruler, whose name, they said, should be "Olu of Warri," Warri being the administrative division in which both the Itsekiri and Urhobo lived. The Urhobo protested that this would mean the olu was their leader, too. The Itsekiri retaliated by saying that the olu should be the Urhobo ruler, because traditionally the Urhobo were slaves of the Itsekiri. Such assertions led to further deterioration in ethnic relations and consciousness.

By 1952, politics had begun at the regional level—the Western Region of Nigeria, within which the area was at that time incorporated. Itsekiri voices were loudest, because some Itsekiri had higher positions than the Urhobo. Nigerian political leaders granted their request for the appointment of an olu. The Urhobo reacted by rioting, and the two groups fought. The Itsekiris' favored position grew, and one of them, Okotie Eboh, became Nigerian Minister of Finance after independence in 1960. The Urhobo became quite aware of their numerical predominance and relative lack of representation in the highest offices of government. Tensions continue to the present.

In almost every state of Africa, similar cases of ethnic differentiation and subsequent politicization took place during the colonial period. Europeans had "favorites" among the different ethnic groups, and this led to difficulties between the favored and the unfavored. The Europeans contributed to divisions in other ways as well. They did not always set out to create such interethnic tensions. Because of geography and ethnic attitudes toward European education, some tensions were inevitable as the framework for the contemporary African state came into existence.

Organization of the Contemporary State

Europeans drew frontiers for about forty-five states enclosing thousands of precolonial political systems entirely or partially. Boundaries were often carelessly drawn, and this fact will have important effects on interstate relations within Africa for many years.

The Europeans also made internal administrative divisions like provinces, regions, and circumscriptions, which are still generally used, albeit with different names. These divisions, set up to facilitate governance, recruitment of workers, and unified control over communications, sometimes corresponded with previous divisions between African political systems, but often they did not. Upsetting traditional patterns of communication and loyalty again was to have long-range effects.

Finally, the Europeans developed administrative laws, procedures, and styles strongly influenced by their own models at home. These are difficult to discard. The colonialists formed a local armed force for the purpose of maintaining order over the newly defined political system and to carry out the judgments of courts and administration. And they established patterns of centralization and decentralization of power that still contribute to differences between English-speaking, French-speaking, and Portuguese-speaking states.

State Boundaries. Although African leaders complained that Europeans had drawn artificial interstate boundaries during the colonial period, they have accepted them as "natural" since independence despite some important exceptions. The idea of natural frontiers is an expediency, however, to avoid conflict or to make claims on neighboring states. No country—not even an island state—has God-given or natural frontiers. Circumstance, mistake, guile, power, and "who got there first" play as great a role as geography, ethnicity, or logic in determining the frontiers of most countries. Santo Domingo, an island in the Caribbean, has two independent states, Haiti and the Dominican Republic, while Madagascar, a larger island in the Indian Ocean, has one independent state, the Malagasy Republic.

The Mississippi River in the middle of one country does not divide it, and the Niger and Benue do not divide Nigeria into different countries, either. The Rhine, a smaller geographic feature, is used as a frontier between France and Germany. The Pyrenees separate France from Spain, but the Urals do not now separate or divide the Soviet Union any more than the Rockies divide the United States. Ethnic groups on both sides of international frontiers can be found in almost every country: the Magyars in Hungary and Rumania, Basques in France and Spain, Kurds in Iraq, Turkey, and Iran, Fulani in Senegal and Guinea, Bakongo in Zaïre, Congo and Angola. In some countries the desire for a change in frontier to unite a group or return sacred soil is deeply felt, but in most cases it is a political leader or small group that uses the issue to further particularistic goals while justifying the claim on the basis of "natural frontiers."

This is not to say, however, that one frontier is as good as any other, or that Africa is exactly the same as any other continent. Frontiers can affect a country's system of communication, for example, by cutting it off from the sea. A landlocked country must be on good terms with or conquer other countries between it and the sea. Frontiers may also be drawn in such a way as to favor one country with natural resources over the neighbor. After World War II, for example, the French hoped to be able to hold on to the mineral-rich Saar area, even though the people there are German-speaking. The people voted for reunification with Germany thus giving that country valuable resources. Problems in communication and great disparity in resources caused by the way in which frontiers were drawn are sources of possible conflict between countries because they may frustrate minimal development in one country.

A frontier should thus be judged on the basis of whether or not it permits the development of a viable political and economic system— one that has a fair chance of maintaining a minimum level of security and identity, of communicating with its people and with the outside worlds with some minimum of efficiency and authority, allowing for centralization of power, permitting a minimum satisfaction of local needs on the basis of local resources, and expanding economically by such resources or through trade and negotiation. Frontiers are, of course, elements of state power, and they influence the exercise of authority in elongated Chile, surrounded Switzerland, and the once-divided Pakistan.

Some peoples in history have had more control over the drawing of their frontiers than others. The Swiss had more to say about the matter than the Pakistanis and the people of Czechoslovakia. The frontiers of most African states were drawn by outsiders consciously serving their own interests. The exceptions are Ethiopia, Morocco, and Egypt, plus a few other small states like Swaziland, where strong precolonial kingdoms were able to include their frontiers within the new colonial political system. Some others were less successful. The King of the Balozi of Zambia, for example, tried to include all of what he regarded as his kingdom when it was taken by the British. The Portuguese claimed it was part of their colony of Angola. The King of Italy arbitrated and divided the disputed territory into two parts in 1905.[37]

The example shows that the African states probably had a slight advantage over the stateless political systems. The groups with governments had centralized leadership that signed treaties with the Europeans incorporating most or all of their kingdoms in the colonial state; or a king's forces were conquered, and the Europeans made a claim to all his state. No one could speak for the peoples without government.

The Akan group in West Africa was split between Ghana and the Ivory Coast. There was no Akan government, but sections of the group, like the Ashanti, had their own highly structured states. The Ashanti kingdom was incorporated within Ghana. Similarly, although the Fulani are a large group extending from Senegal and Mauritania all the way

---

[37] Gerald L. Caplan, *The Elites of Barotseland 1878–1969: A Political History of Zambia's Western Province* (Berkeley and Los Angeles: University of California Press, 1970), p. 88.

Colonialism and African Politics 53

across West Africa to the Sudan, they had no single government at the end of the nineteenth century. The Fulani government of the Fouta Djalon was incorporated within Guinea, and the individual emirates in Kano and Zaria were incorporated within Nigeria. The British and French agreed in 1890 that the whole Fulani Kingdom of Sokoto should be under British control although it proved difficult to determine all Usman dan Fodio's frontiers.[38] The Mossi Kingdom was absorbed within Upper Volta, while the stateless Berbers of North Africa, the stateless Fang of Equatorial Africa, the Masai of East Africa, as well as the Manlinke, Somalis, and Ewe were split between two or more colonial states. With the coming of independence, some of these groups have been interested in unity and some not. The Ewe are often pointed to as an example of a divided people, but they have not been as interested in living together in one state as certain politicians. The Somalis, on the other hand, appear to be very interested in living in one independent state.

Division or unity of a precolonial African political system did not play a very important role in European frontier-drawing. It is difficult to understand how frontiers were drawn, in any case. Many look so careless, and they were incomplete at independence. Even when Europeans were in a position to settle boundaries through delimitation and, finally, through definite demarcation, they often did not.

One of the most peculiar frontiers in Africa is that between Gambia and Senegal. It is an example of one type of boundary drawing, namely, placing a frontier "at a constant distance from an irregular topographical feature." In 1889, the British, with trading posts along the Gambia River, which flows through the heart of today's Senegal, and the French, who were controlling Senegal, set the boundary of Gambia as follows: "Part of this boundary ran on each side of the Gambia River at a distance of ten kilometers from the river bank. The map attached to the agreement shows the course of the Gambia to be extremely tortuous and the delineated boundary on each side of the river is portrayed as a series of intersecting arcs of circles, each having an apparent radius of ten kilometers."[39] Gambia now has the same ethnic groups as Senegal, and the latter is almost cut in two because of the frontier delineation.

In spite of the fact that France had control over both Morocco and Algeria, they only demarcated the frontier for a distance of about 100 miles inland from the Mediterranean, thus leaving important problems for the two states to settle after independence. They also confused the matter by permitting border areas to be administered from Morocco, even though they were part of Algeria. After independence the two countries fought over the area of Tindouf in the extreme southwest of

[38] Derrick J. Thom, "The Niger-Nigeria Boundary 1890–1906: A Study of Ethnic Frontiers and a Colonial Boundary," *Papers in International Studies, Africa Series* no. 23 (Athens: Ohio University Center for International Studies, 1975), p. 19.

[39] A. C. McEwen, *International Boundaries of East Africa*, Oxford Studies in African Affairs (Oxford: The Clarendon Press, 1971), p. 47.

Algeria.[40] Similarly, the British had control over both Sudan and Egypt. In spite of this, the question of the frontier between the two countries was not completely settled, and Sudan administered an area that was formerly considered part of Egypt. In 1958, the Egyptians claimed this area of about 10,000 square miles, but Sudan was able to keep it.[41] Libyan frontiers with Tunisia and Algeria were not settled until the 1950's.

The French, Germans, and Spanish tried to agree on frontiers between Cameroun, Gabon, and Equatorial Guinea. They worked at the problem intermittently between about 1885 and the 1920's—more than thirty-five years. They attempted to follow the course of rivers for the most part, although the Fang people—without any centralized government—lived on both sides of the rivers chosen as frontiers. Reports of missions that chose these rivers were not approved immediately by the governments back in Europe, as was necessary; difficulties in communication with colonial administrative centers like Libreville, Yaoundé, and Bata meant that territory changed hands depending on the dynamism of some local colonial official and the nationality of the European traders present. It also meant the Europeans fought among themselves before agreements were finally made and ratified.[42]

Even worse were trade-offs decided in European capitals. They looked peculiar on maps and in some cases were destined to create unviable states and to confuse African populations. In 1911, for example, the French gave the Germans a slice of Gabon, the French Congo, and Oubangui-Chari that had nothing to do with rivers, mountains, or ethnic groups. The Germans had recognized French control over Morocco but wanted some property in return, to permit communication with the River Congo from Cameroun. Added to their possession in Southwest Africa, they got a small piece of land going east to Zambia and also a bit of land to add to northern Cameroun, called the "duck's beak" because of its shape. All this was done for services rendered elsewhere in Africa.

The British did no better in East Africa. For example, they never were able to delimit the frontier between Kenya and Italian-controlled Somalia or between Tanganyika and Nyasaland (now Malawi). In 1891, the British of Kenya and the Italians of Somalia agreed that the River Juba would separate their spheres of influence. This river frontier split the Somali-speaking people. The Somalis, a nomadic people, continued to cross the Juba into Kenya. By the time the countries became independent, about 240,000 Somalis were living in Kenya and demanding

---

[40] See Anthony S. Reyner, "Morocco's International Boundaries: A Factual Background," in *Journal of Modern African Studies*, I, no. 3 (1963): 313–16.

[41] John A. Cookson *et al.*, *U.S. Army Area Handbook for the Republic of the Sudan*, 2d. ed. Department of the Army (Washington, D.C.: 1964), p. 336.

[42] See André Mangongo-Nzambi, "La délimitation des frontières du Gabon (1885–1911)," *Cahiers d'Etudes Africaines*, IX, no. 33 (1969): 5–53.

that the area be attached to Somalia. The government of Somalia has used this demand as a basis for irredentist claims on Kenya.[43]

The frontier between Malawi and Tanzania has been a problem because of British failure to settle the question of Lake Nyasa as a frontier. The two countries are separated by this large body of water. Before 1929, the colonial reports for Nyasaland showed no lake at all despite its size. (McEwen says it is large enough to cover all of England to a depth of a hundred feet.) In 1929, the lake was shown with the boundary in the middle of it. Maps in 1942 and 1947 left the lake boundary out entirely. In 1948, the British drew the boundary on the eastern shore, giving the whole lake to Malawi. The confusion has continued to the present.[44] This and other problems will continue to plague Africa, but demands for border changes because of the discovery of valuable resources—as in the case of the claims Mali began making in 1974 for Upper Volta territory—cannot be blamed on the colonialists.

Administrative Divisions Within States. Other boundary problems that do not get much publicity are those within individual African states. The Europeans used the same criteria for establishing intrastate administrative divisions as they had used for interstate frontiers, but they were more unstable. Internal boundaries could become state boundaries and vice versa; one division could be attached to or detached from another without the concerned population's understanding why.

From 1906 to 1913, Nigeria was divided into the Colony (Lagos) and Protectorate of Southern Nigeria, on the one hand, and the Protectorate of Northern Nigeria, on the other. In 1914, Sir Frederick Lugard amalgamated the two areas into one unit called the Colony and Protectorate of Nigeria, and he became its governor general. By 1952, the country had three distinct regions, the north, the west, and the east (plus the Cameroons Trust Territory). After independence the government created a fourth region, the midwest. In 1967, the easterners tried to set up their region as an independent state on the basis of the boundaries drawn by the British. In the same year, the central government redrew all internal boundaries, creating twelve states; in 1975, it redrew them once again, making a total of nineteen states.

The Nigerians were left with a large federation, just like the Canadians, the Americans, and the Australians. The British had continued in Africa their traditional desire to federate colonial territories, making possible interstate divisions into intrastate divisions. For example, when they gained control of part of Cameroun after World War I, they attached it to Nigeria, and they attached their part of German Togo to Ghana. In East Africa, they attached Buganda to Uganda and Barotseland to Zambia, but kept these two areas separate administrative divisions within the new state. They tried to federate Kenya, Tanzania, and

[43] McEwen, *International Boundaries of East Africa*, pp. 113-15.
[44] See *ibid.*, p. 182.

Uganda and succeeded for a time in uniting Zambia (then Northern Rhodesia), Malawi (then Nyasaland), and Southern Rhodesia. The unification of the Republic of South Africa, made out of Cape Province, Natal, the Orange Free State, and Transvaal, is also in part due to British federalizing tendencies. After 1933, the Belgians did the same thing in Zaïre by concentrating power in the capital in the hands of governors general rather than in the provincial administration.

French policy was quite different. Instead of attaching Cameroun and Togo to contiguous French colonies after World War I, the French ruled them separately. In French West Africa and French Equatorial Africa, internal divisions between Guinea and Senegal, for example, became interstate divisions. Upper Volta was cut out of the Ivory Coast, and Mauritania was created in 1920. Tchad was part of the Central African Republic until 1920. In the 1930's, the four states of French Equatorial Africa were ruled as one state with internal administrative divisions corresponding to the four present-day states.

Algeria, considered an integral part of France, was, however, more similar to the British states. The French united a coastal area with a vast hinterland, but as the country approached independence they tried to separate the oil- and gas-rich desert from Algeria. They had earlier tried to separate the Fezzan region of Libya from the rest of that state. Morocco and Tunisia, governed by the Ministry of Foreign Affairs, were kept separate from Algeria, governed by the Ministry of the Interior. The French did not seek to unite the three states, although there have been at times strong desires expressed by the people for Mahgrebian unity. If the British had ruled the region, they probably would have tried to federate the three states; if the French had ruled Nigeria, they would doubtless have created three or four countries out of it.

Some Frenchmen thought French control would be more effective and enduring if small countries were kept separate. With time, local African vested interests opposed federation. The commercial-minded British were more interested in large free-trade zones with a unified command over communications, labor, and taxation. They, too, wanted to maintain control. Their method was not to break up territories into small countries but to draw internal boundaries and make voting arrangements in such a way that white minorities (in East and Central Africa) or conservative pro-British African elites would be politically dominant. In Kenya, the British divided the eastern lake region into two provinces. They arranged the boundaries of one so that there was only a small African population, thus facilitating European settlement.[45] In Nigeria, they insured Fulani dominance by dividing the south into two regions and keeping the north united, so that in elections northern parties would get more seats in parliament.

The British also respected previous administrative divisions of African

[45] G. H. Mungeam, *British Rule in Kenya 1895–1912: The Establishment of Administration in the East Africa Protectorate* (Oxford: The Clarendon Press, 1966), pp. 91–92.

states. When they took their part of Cameroun and attached it to Nigeria, the British resident of Bornu in northern Nigeria took charge of one of the four Cameroun divisions left by the Germans, and this corresponded with a precolonial pattern. The division "in precolonial times had owed allegiance to the rulers of Bornu."[46]

Although the French tended to respect previous administrative divisions in Madagascar and Morocco and in a few other areas with well-organized precolonial states, in a general way their cantons, subdivisions, and *cercles* were set up to suit their own needs. And there was considerable shifting about of administrative boundaries, probably more than in British-controlled areas. The Portuguese incorporated Mbunda states into Angola and restructured the administration of the area. Because of the usual tendency in American scholarship to praise the British for their colonial methods and to condemn the French for theirs, one might be tempted to see British respect for and reinforcement of precolonial systems through boundary manipulation as useful to later African leaders. In the long run, however, the French approach (and the Portuguese as well) was probably more useful to the centralizing tendencies of elites in independent African states.

European methods and organization have also been highly respected even by those Africans most critical of colonialism. Some African students returned to Africa with the idea that if their own countries were *more* like the metropolitan country they would be better off. This was perhaps truer of elites from Francophone countries than of those from British-controlled areas.

For example, when Guinea became independent in 1958, the Ministry of Foreign Affairs, hastily organized, had large African-oriented offices, one for the United Nations, and one for Europe. After the first Guinean received his doctorate in international law in a French university and returned home to take a high post in the Ministry of Foreign Affairs, the ministry was reorganized strictly along French lines.

After the Ivory Coast colony was officially established in 1893, the French divided it into nineteen *cercles* dominated generally by one ethnic group. The nineteen were divided into about fifty subdivisions and then into about 516 cantons by 1939.[47]

When the Ivory Coast became independent in 1960, the new government kept the original nineteen *cercles*, although the designation was changed to subprefecture, the name given to similar administrative divisions in France. They were then grouped into four departments or

[46] David Gardinier, "The British in the Cameroons," in Prosser Gifford and William Roger Louis (eds.), *Britain and Germany in Africa: Imperial Rivalry and Colonial Rule* (New Haven, Conn.: Yale University Press, 1967), p. 526.

[47] We are basing this discussion on Martin Staniland's articles, "Colonial Government and Populist Reform: The Case of the Ivory Coast—Part I," *Journal of Administration Overseas*, X, no. 1 (January, 1971): 33–42, and "Part II: Local Administration at Independence and After," *Journal of Administration Overseas*, X, no. 2 (April, 1971): 113–26.

prefectures following the French system. Political leaders explicitly stated that one of the basic principles of reform must be to institute a truly French system of administration and education to replace the "second-rate" system they had under the colonial state. One deputy said in 1959: "We should get rid of the redundant colonial structure. I hope that our new departments will be identical . . . to those of metropolitan France. . . . I want to see the replacement of the colonialist titles like *cercles* and *subdivisions* by the titles of prefecture, subprefecture, and *arrondissement*."[48] The Ivory Coast has replaced the French administrator, but the African often has the same idea about his work and the same training in administration as his European predecessor.

Administrative Traditions. The European colonial administrator—the *commandant de cercle*, the resident, the DO—was an elitist and a generalist with a relatively high salary and generous perquisites. He was mostly interested in maintaining control and order for the purpose of collecting taxes and facilitating European enterprise; once these goals were accomplished he worked to develop education and some social services, often, in the early days according to his own plan. The African administrator in independent states tends to have the same characteristics and to work for these goals in similar style.

The French colonial officials at the top of the administrative hierarchy were trained in two- or three-year programs at the Ecole Coloniale. "Colo," as it was called, had trained a few West Indian and Asian officials from its inception and later began accepting Africans. After World War II, it changed its name to the Ecole Nationale de la France d'Outre-Mer. Portuguese representatives had military training. The British, by contrast, did not have the same extended formal training program; they sent their men for lectures at Oxford but expected them to learn most on the job. The absence of a tradition of training in public administration did not, however, prevent the British from establishing specialized institutes in Africa.

These European generalist administrators had the most power, and they openly disdained technicians. The commandant had control over the activities of the irrigation specialist and made more money than he; he lived in the largest house, for which he did not have to pay. He was the head of the local administration and, particularly in the French system, was the most important judge. He had power of recruitment; taxation was his responsibility. He made many rules or applied general rules according to his own ideas to the area. He was the symbol of authority.

The European administrator outside the urban areas was chief of police and military commander. He used as troops Europeans and Africans from other colonies or from other regions, usually nearer the coast. Africans recruited from coastal populations that had once sold

[48] From *Journal Officiel de la Côte d'Ivoire*, cited in Staniland, Part II, p. 115.

inland peoples into slavery could not be expected to have much respect for them. There are many stories of mistreatment by coastal African soldiers and policemen used by European administrators to maintain order, collect taxes, and recruit workers inland. No outside invaders threatened the security of the colonial state.

From the beginning of the colonial state, African clerks worked alongside the administrator, carrying his commands to the soldiers or chiefs. The African clerks were paid a much lower salary than the European, and they had few of the perquisites. As Africans rose in rank, they began to agitate for higher salaries and the same perquisites as Europeans; they strove for equality with Europeans. Eventually they got it.

African administrators have been strongly influenced by European administrative traditions, either because they worked for many years with the Europeans or because they attended European-run schools and institutes. They are generalist and elitist and cumulate different functions, just as their predecessors have done. They are also paid more than technicians, which Africa needs very badly, and disdain them. Their main function is to maintain order and high rates of production of export crops, recruit workers for industry, and generally oversee the administration. Development projects are most often started by foreign technicians.

One of the results is that the independent administration may be seen by the African masses to be as exploitative as the colonial administration. Posts formerly occupied by Europeans are called "European positions," even though they are now filled by Africans; some blacks are referred to as "black white men" when they have the same large house and salary.

A major difference between the European and the African administrator is that the latter has greater control over the African masses because of better-developed communication, because he understands the language, perhaps, and because he has more tools at his disposal—such as the single-party apparatus. In spite of the fact that he is an African, he may associate himself more with his professional group within and outside his country than with the masses of people. Like his European predecessor, he may also work most closely with the European-oriented enterprise that brought a dual economy to Africa.

Colonialism and Production: A Dual Economy

European-oriented pockets within colonial states produced crops or minerals for export; they were largely divorced from the surrounding economies of African political systems, but they diverted labor and encouraged population movement and a change in communication patterns. Neither the older political systems nor their internally oriented economies disappeared. Consequently, dual economies were another result of colonialism.

Africa produced some varieties of peanut or groundnut, cotton, and other products before the coming of the European, but the demands of the European market led to the introduction of new crops or varieties. Coffee, cocoa, bananas, oranges, peanuts, palm products, jute, tea, cotton, vanilla, cloves, and grapes were introduced, and Africans were forced or attracted to their production. A goal of the Europeans was to introduce what they called rational production of industrial crops for export and for taxes in place of the mere collection of wild products like rubber and ivory. But, Walter Rodney accused the colonialists of bringing disease, famine, and of creating patterns of economic and human exploitation that persist.[49]

Even though Europeans were in a position to set up a rational production system, they generally did not do so. Because many Africans were taken away from food cultivation, there were periods of famine; today most states cannot provide enough food for all inhabitants, particularly in urban areas. In addition, many of the same crops were introduced in several countries, thus putting them into competition, made all the worse because each colony produced one major crop instead of several.

The cotton or coffee was produced on European-run plantations. Africans were not permitted to engage in the transformation of the products, which were sent to the coast in European-owned trucks and then to Britain or France in European ships. Gradually, the colonial state became quite dependent on the European market: An increasing part of the "country's fortunes [was] bound up with the export of a small number of primary products, the price for which [was] determined much more by events elsewhere—by changes in demand or in the supply from other countries—than by any action or decision of the country itself."[50] In 1930, for example, the price for East African–produced coffee suddenly plummeted from 120 to 70 pounds per ton, because of changes that had nothing to do with East Africa.[51] About the same time, Africans were encouraged or forced to produce potatoes in the Central African Republic, only to see them rot for lack of transport. Algerian grapes rotted on the vine when France had a surplus production of its own.

Extractive industries have more recently encouraged duality. Although gold and iron ore were mined and used in Africa long before the Europeans set foot there, the Europeans increased the dimensions of production and set up industrial communities and even cities separated

---

[49] Walter Rodney, *How Europe Underdeveloped Africa* (London: Bogle-L'Ouverture, 1972), pp. 223–310.

[50] C. C. Wrigley, "Economics and Social Development," in J. F. Ade Ajayi and Ian Espie, eds., *A Thousand Years of West African History: A Handbook for Teachers and Students* (Ibadan, Nigeria: Ibadan University Press and Nelson, 1965), p. 423.

[51] Cyril Ehrlich, "Economic and Social Developments Before Independence," in Ogot and Kieran, eds., *Zamani*, p. 335.

Colonialism and African Politics   61

from the surrounding country and economy. Out flowed the gold of Ghana and South Africa, the petroleum of Angola, Algeria, Nigeria, Congo-Brazzaville, Gabon, and Libya; the uranium of Gabon, the Central African Republic, Zaïre, and Niger; the copper of Zambia and Zaïre; the bauxite of Guinea, Gabon, Cameroun, and Ghana; the manganese of Gabon; the chromium of Southern Rhodesia; the diamonds of Guinea, Sierra Leone, Liberia, and South Africa; the iron of Liberia, Nigeria, Guinea, Gabon, and Mauritania; the potash of Senegal; and the lumber of Ivory Coast and Gabon. Most of the minerals were shipped out of Africa after minimal processing.

In order to get these products to Europe and America, roads, railroads, and a telecommunication system had to be built. The new infrastructure was thus oriented toward the coast instead of inward along river basins and across the Sahara, formerly a "highway for trade and culture,"[52] but then a barrier as Africa turned toward the sea, where the European ships waited.

In 1898, the railroad line from Kinshasa (Léopoldville) to Matadi port opened in Zaïre, and lines from the inland areas farther from the coast opened in the next twenty years. In 1911, Cameroun had a railway; Senegal in 1885. The same year, Ghana began to export cacao, and the railroad was therefore soon begun to facilitate transport linking the agricultural area of Kumasi with the sea in 1903.[53] In 1906 the British completed a railway to mining centers in Zambia.[54] In Nigeria, the railway moved north from the coast in 1898, reaching Kano in 1912 and expanding to Enugu in the east in 1916.[55] In 1917, a railroad line extended from Addis Ababa in Ethiopia to Djibouti, the French port and capital of French Somaliland (today's French territory of the Afars and the Issas). In 1931 the Benguela Railroad from Southern Zaïre through Angola to the Atlantic was completed, and Zaïre's copper flowed out. The French did not finish their Congo-Ocean line from Brazzaville to the Atlantic until 1939. In South Africa, Cape Town was linked with Johannesburg, and Lourenço Marques in Mozambique with Zambia.

Communication patterns and mineral production, as well as the location of the headquarters of the colonial states, contributed to the founding and development of cities. Urban areas existed in Africa long before colonialism, but new centers were created. According to the geographer William Hance, the first cities in Africa were founded by Africans about 3,000 B.C. Alexandria has existed since 332 B.C. Tripoli and Constantine since A.D. 313. Aksum in Ethiopia dates from the first century of this era; Mali's Gao, Somalia's Mogadishu, and Kenya's port of Mombasa date from the seventh century. From the eighth to the

---
[52] I. William Zartman, "The Sahara—Bridge or Barrier?" *International Conciliation*, no. 541 (January, 1963), p. 11.
[53] Rotberg, *Political History of Tropical Africa*, p. 291.
[54] *Ibid.*, p. 310.
[55] Wrigley, "Economic and Social Development," p. 427.

tenth centuries, Fez in Morocco, Algiers, Meknis, Cairo, and probably Great Zimbabwe in Rhodesia were founded. In the tenth and eleventh centuries, Kano, Zaria, and Katsina in northern Nigeria, as well as Ife and Benin in southern Nigeria and Tombouctou in Mali, were established. The Bakongo founded their capital at San Salvador before the fifteenth century. From the sixteenth through the nineteenth centuries, Africans created Labé in Guinea, Segou in Mali, Bobo-Dioulasso and Ouagadougou in Upper Volta, Abéché in Tchad, and Mopti in Mali. Kumasi was built in 1663 in Ghana, and Tananarive was founded in 1625 on the island of Madagascar by the Merina people. The great city of Ibadan was established by the Yoruba in 1829.[56]

The Europeans created new cities on the coast and along their railroad lines. Nairobi, the capital of Kenya, "was born as a railway base in 1899, providing employment, a market for local produce, and general economic stimulus."[57] Europeans began Dar es Salaam in 1862, Maseru in Lesotho in 1869, Kinshasa in 1881, Bamako in 1883, Johannesburg in 1886, and Abidjan in 1903.[58] The Portuguese formally established Luanda in 1575.

Because urbanization is increasing all over the world, one can assume that it would have happened at a quick rate in Africa without colonialism. But colonialism provided the spark in Africa and created the outward-oriented cities that eventually became more important than the old African cities. Between 1900 and 1967 the percentage of Moroccans living in towns and cities rose from between 5 per cent and 10 per cent to 30.7 per cent. Algeria rose from 13.9 per cent in 1886 to 32.5 per cent in 1967; and Egypt, 19.1 per cent in 1879 to 41 per cent in 1967, making it, along with South Africa (45 per cent in 1967), the most highly urbanized country on the continent. In West Africa, Mauritania has only 6.1 per cent of its population urbanized, while neighboring Senegal had 29.2 in 1967. Inland states like Mali, Upper Volta, Niger, and Tchad have less than 10 per cent of their populations in urban areas, but the drought and famine of 1973 doubtless drove many more people to the cities. Ghana had 8 per cent in 1921 and 26 per cent in 1967; Cameroun, 5.8 per cent in 1950 and 17 per cent in 1967; Tanganyika, 1.2 per cent in 1931 and 5.4 per cent in 1967; Rhodesia, 12.8 per cent in 1950 and 19.2 per cent in 1961–62; and Madagascar had 5 per cent in 1913 and about 15 per cent in the mid-1960's.[59]

With a general increase in urbanization during the colonial period and after came a concentration of facilities and services in one or two outward-oriented cities. The contiguous cities in Sudan, Khartoum, Omdurman, and North Khartoum "employ nearly all of the educated Sudanese, contain half of the public utilities and most of the nation's

[56] William A. Hance, *Population, Migration, and Urbanization in Africa* (New York and London: Columbia University Press, 1970), p. 210.
[57] Ehrlich, "Developments Before Independence," p. 337.
[58] Hance, *Population, Migration, and Urbanization*, pp. 215–16.
[59] *Ibid.*, pp. 223, 238.

industry, the main commercial and financial establishments, the only university, and the national government offices; they account for 90 per cent of the vehicles registered in the country."[60] In other countries the concentration is equally impressive. With such centralization, political and economic control of a country depends on the control of a very small area.

Rural economies have not been completely oriented toward these cities and industrial areas. Many continue to produce for their own needs and trade. Although in 1972 officially recorded trade among African states amounted to only 7 per cent of a total African trade,[61] much unofficial trade continues. Carried on along old trade routes, which do not respect contemporary administrative boundaries, it is called smuggling. To see and understand it, one must be on the spot. Only in some inland town along the old trade routes can one realize that official trade figures, airline and train schedules, and road maps show only part of the communication picture. In fact, one can travel anywhere in Africa by land or water along the old routes, even though they are not officially recognized. For many Africans, these routes and means of communication are the most important ones. This system of communication, as well as traditional production and consumption patterns, is separate from the outward-oriented economy.

A New Framework for Politics

For all the duality within the colonial state, a new framework for politics and economics was provided toward which all political systems are slowly orienting themselves. New identities—about fifty states; new bases for legitimacy; and new instruments of power developed within the colonial state. The colonial state provided government for African political systems that had none; it provided means to try to absorb African political systems with governments; and, most of all, it provided the beginnings and tools of highly centralized political systems in Africa.

In Algeria, the French set up municipal councils in the 1840's in towns and, a decade later, general councils for the departments into which they divided the country. In 1947, they created "an Algerian Assembly of 120 members, 60 of whom would be Muslims."[62] Parties were therefore formed, and some people gained political experience within a larger cadre than the precolonial one. Most of Algeria's older leaders had some experience in one or more councils and in trade unions. They also learned how to use weapons while soldiers in the French Army.

In a typical English-controlled state, Sierra Leone, the governor, with his own officials, ruled as executive and legislative authority from 1808,

[60] *Ibid.*, p. 210.
[61] *West Africa*, February 18, 1972, p. 172.
[62] Quandt, *Revolution and Political Leadership*, p. 55.

the year it was declared a Crown Colony, to 1863. In 1863, two separate councils, an executive council and a legislative council, replaced the former arrangement, and the governor appointed coastal Africans to the latter.

In 1895, the government established the Freetown Municipal Council, to which Africans could be elected. In 1924, a constitution enlarged the legislative council to twelve official members and ten unofficial members. Eight of the unofficials were African, and three of those were elected. Voting districts were set up for these very limited elections. Kilson has written that the 1924 constitution "did provide a new framework for the development of African interests."[63] He says this because elected officials—with a constituency to please—began to agitate for change within the context of Sierra Leone. In 1938, a standing finance committee of the legislature was created with an African majority, and in 1943 two Africans were appointed for the first time to the executive council. Two years later, another assembly was created for the hinterland; prior to that time the coastal elites controlled all political life. Constitutional proposals in 1947 led to an African majority in the councils, and after the 1951 constitution Africans held the majority of seats on the legislative and executive councils. A year later Sierra Leone had its first African ministers, and in 1953 a chief minister, in the person of Sir Milton Margai, who became the Premier in 1956 and led the country to independence in 1961. As in Algeria, trade unions began to operate within the Sierra Leone context rather than within the context of one ethnic group. Lawyers established a bar association in 1919, civil servants began their association about 1907, the carpenters their "Carpenters' Defensive Union" in 1895. Railway workers established their Mutual Aid Union in 1920.

The pace was slower in France's west and middle African territories. Prior to World War II, Senegal had representative institutions in the four communes and could elect a representative to the French parliament. There were elements of communal government elsewhere and some advisory *conseils d'administration,* with African members but with little or no power. Governor General Eboué attempted to promote more autonomy for the colonies during World War II and to bring more Africans into the administrative structure.

Beginning with the Brazzaville Conference of 1944, changes took place. High-ranking officials decided there must be a colonial parliament and local assemblies. Trade unions were also authorized, and metropolitan groups as well as parties began to organize in every colony. In October, 1945, elections were held on a territorial basis throughout the empire. The constitution of October, 1946, which established the Fourth Republic, provided for a weak French Union with institutions provid-

---

[63] Martin Kilson, *Political Change in a West African State: A Study of the Modernization Process in Sierra Leone,* Center for International Affairs Series (Cambridge, Mass.: Harvard University Press, 1966), p. 139.

COLONIALISM AND AFRICAN POLITICS 65

ing a "training ground for junior politicians."[64] Most important were elections to the French parliament and the establishment of local territorial assemblies and regional Grand Councils. Local assemblies gradually increased their representativeness and power. With the reforms of the *loi-cadre* in 1956–57, each territory got an African executive authority, then a full government, with the establishment of the Fifth French Republic the following year. The evolution went much faster from 1958 to 1960, when the countries became independent. Changes in the Portuguese were prevented by a government as repressive in Portugal itself as in Africa. Incredible as it may seem, the legislative elections the Portuguese allowed in Mozambique in 1973 provided for only 8 of 53 seats for Africans. And, thirteen years after most countries became independent Mozambique had only 60,000 registered voters out of a population of almost 8,000,000 that year.[65]

The development of representative institutions was not designed generally to bring about independence, although the British claim it was. Most of these institutions were viewed as exploitative by the African masses, but a growing elite gained experience with them and began to articulate demands through them.

In most instances, change came about because of growing African demands for change, not because of some colonial plan. In spite of differing perceptions of the colonial situation, the growing African elites wanted change. They soon demanded independence for the colonial state created by the foreigner.

---

[64] Edward Mortimer, *France and the Africans 1944–1960: A Political History* (New York: Walker, 1970), p. 101.

[65] On July 7, 1971, the Constitution was amended to grant greater autonomy to the overseas provinces, but subject to administration, direction, as well as economic and political control, continuing to be vested in the government of Portugal. An "Organic Law for the Overseas Territories" was enacted in 1972, designating Angola and Mozambique as States with elected legislative assemblies subject to a veto by the Lisbon-nominated governor-general.

4 The End of Colonialism

The colonial period was relatively brief in most areas because Africans opposed foreign control and because colonial powers themselves changed their minds about their empires.

African opposition to the claims of alien political systems over their own political systems never ceased from the beginning to the end of the colonial period, even though some peoples or groups accepted European presence and benefited from it. Movements of opposition took different forms at different times; their goals changed and interests varied. But if there had been no African initiative, the whole continent would still be under foreign or minority domination, as the Republic of South Africa, Rhodesia (Zimbabwe), and Namibia (South-West Africa) are as late as 1976.

For a long time, Europeans misunderstood or ignored African resistance. Their views of African opposition were influenced by an erroneous belief in their supposed racial superiority and by methods used by the colonialists to justify colonialism to their fellow Europeans. European public opinion did not always support colonialism, and governments, too, had to be convinced that it was politic to keep up the flow of funds. The colonial lobby of businessmen, the military, the bureaucracy, and the church feared European criticism of overseas expansion, and they wanted increased aid from public funds.

As a result, the colonial forces minimized news about African opposition or distorted the form it took. Language tricks were useful. For example, the Europeans were said to have sent "armies" under "officers" to fight the African "bands" of "tribesmen" led by "rebels" and "witchdoctors." The Europeans were pictured as "police" and "military" in clean white uniforms, establishing "peace and order" out of supposed "chaos," moving against African "terrorists" and "bandits." European armies reputedly used "civilized" methods of conquest that they called "pacification"; they were reported to be well organized and disciplined while fighting for a higher cause, as contrasted with Africans, who took "uncivilized oaths," did not have clothes, and carried "spears" and "poisoned arrows." Popular accounts showed the Europeans separated from their loved ones. These "brave" men, outnumbered by the "hordes," had to survive the numerous "exotic tropical diseases," too. Convinced that some support would bring permanent victory, governments and organizations sent money, although never in the quantities desired.

The End of Colonialism

African perceptions of the Europeans and their motives were not always correct, either. In some areas, before the end of the slave trade, Africans thought the whites were cannibals; otherwise, why would they be taking people away? In other places, Africans saw the whites in their areas as employees of some African king or saw them as allies of traditional enemies. It was certainly in the interest of some kings and governments to leave the impression with other kings and governments that they had an alliance with the foreigners who could supply them with effective weapons. The weapons could then be used to settle old scores that the European knew nothing about or misunderstood.

In the Central African Republic, for example, the French kept Sultan Bangassou in power. They considered it expedient to have an intermediary who could keep peace and collect taxes, but they definitely considered him "their man," whose territory they were willing to defend. They did not realize, of course, that the people thought the whites were employees of the sultan. Many Africans considered the whites mercenaries, whom the king had hired to keep his kingdom intact.[1]

Thus, perception of danger and perception of interest influence peoples' reactions to a developing colonial state. If people do not perceive that their interests are being hurt, how can they act? And if they do not perceive where the real threat is coming from, any action they decide to take will be useless.

Opposition depends on a leader, who can either embody traditional legitimacy, represent the precolonial political system, or articulate the interests of the people in the form of a new mobilizing explanation of why action is necessary.

Opposition also depends on an organization to ensure unity and continuity. At the most basic level, that of a specialized fighting force, some hierarchy of command, system of communication, method, and direction are obviously necessary. At another level, that of the political system itself, there must be some organization to ensure replacement of leaders, maintenance of loyalty, assurance of logistic support, and recruitment of troops.

Perception of interest by a group, the type of leader and his mobilizing idea, and the form of organization used by Africans varied from political system to political system, and again at three different points in the establishment of the colonial state. Political systems without centralized authority opposed the imposition of the colonial state in ways different from those used by the centralized state. Small, divided groups did not all at the same time perceive the same interest; they did not recognize one leader; and they had no unifying organization. Political systems with governments had the advantage in this respect; they resisted more quickly and overtly than decentralized systems in the first of the three stages of opposition, what we call the period of rejection of alien claims to sovereignty. On the other hand, once the central governments sur-

[1] E. de Dampierre, *Un ancien royaume du Haut-Oubangui* (Paris: Plon, 1967), p. 465.

rendered, all resistance came to an end. A decentralized political system might keep up initial resistance longer because there was no leader to surrender for everyone. Defeat was piecemeal and protracted.

After an over-all defeat, however, the differences between the types of political system seem less important. Africans regrouped their forces if they chose to oppose colonialism, followed new leaders with new ideas, and experimented with organization. In this second, or what might be considered "exploratory," period they opposed specific colonial policies with leaders and organizations that did not immediately appear to be political because they seemed like remnants or survivors of old religions or other traditional groups, or because they seemed to arise so spontaneously without any precedents. Impressed by the power of the Europeans, moreover, Africans in this period also employed some European as well as African organizations or techniques to make their will felt.

In a third period, which we may call the acceptance of the colonial state framework, grudging or not, new elites who were the very creation of the colonial state realized they could use the new structures to pursue their own interests, which might or might not be those of the masses. This small group perceived the European as a barrier to the realization of their interests. To succeed in removing that barrier, however, the European's methods of organization, his style of leadership, and his techniques of control and organization were perceived as useful. Precolonial systems and techniques were often strongly rejected. By using European organizations and methods, this African elite eventually gained power. All forms of African opposition to foreign rule may be examined, we believe, in this rubric.

Perception of Interest: Some Cases

Period of Rejection of Alien Claims to Sovereignty. The Kikuyu, who had no centralized system of government, did not react in sustained fashion to the imposition of foreign control, partly because they did not immediately perceive the danger to their interests from European presence on their land. For example, a Kenyan recalls in his autobiography that one day his family noticed a European "had quietly slipped on to our land. We did not know he was coming to stay, since he had just built a little mud and grass house. . . . The Kikuyu gave him the nickname Kibara, for he was always beating people, but he did not seem to do much actual planting; he did not plant any crops or coffee, and did not come into any Kikuyu village—I think because he was afraid probably. . . . No one thought that Kibara had come permanently." Suddenly, they heard that the land occupied by this European had apparently been "sold" by him to another European, rather curious since he never owned it. But, "then our people, including Waweru, the chief, were asked to move a little further west. Of course it was government policy to sell land without telling the occupiers. Then later the new 'owner' would come along and say, 'This land is mine; I bought it from the government.' "[2]

The Ethiopians, in contrast, however, acted against the Italians without hesitation. After signing a treaty of friendship with the Italians, they discovered that the foreigners were claiming the emperor had signed a treaty of protectorate. The Ethiopian state immediately rejected the claim. In a forthright and dynamic statement to Europe in 1891, Emperor Menelik II said that Ethiopia was an independent political system and intended to remain so. Italy sent troops to support its claim. Growing conflicts led to face-to-face battles. In 1896, Menelik, with 100,000 men under his command in a well-organized, well-trained force, crushed the Italians.

The difference between the two cases, Kikuyu and Ethiopians, aside from the fact that the first lost and the second won, was that the Kikuyu perceived no harm to their interests from European presence and claims. The Ethiopians immediately perceived that one state wanted to control another state. They acted, realizing full well what sovereignty meant and what they could lose.

Other examples show that there was widespread rejection of European claims to sovereignty in Africa. The Germans demanded the surrender of the Yao in southwest Tanzania. Macemba, or Machemba, their leader, wrote in Swahili that he would rather die than agree to obey the Europeans, because obedience is what the Yao perceived the Germans to be after: "If it should be friendship that you desire, then I am ready for it, today and always; but to be your subject, that I cannot be.... If it should be war you desire, then I am ready but never to be your subject."[3] For years the Yao resisted, but the invaders used machine guns against them and against the Hehe, who fought from 1891 to 1898 in the south-central part of the country when Mkwawa, their leader, preferred to commit suicide rather than surrender.[4]

In southern Angola, the Portuguese decided to expand their claim south from the very small area they had controlled since the fifteenth century. In 1839, they founded a town along the southern coast and in 1850 began to move inland, where they settled at Huila. Africans attacked them, but apparently the settlers agreed to pay tribute or taxes to the Soba, the ruler of the area, to buy off African pressure.

Peace apparently continued until the 1880's, when the Europeans began to refuse to pay taxes to the Africans. Battles began in about 1885, and in 1904 there was a full-scale war between the Portuguese who were

---

[2] Harry Thuku and Kenneth King, *Harry Thuku: An Autobiography* (Nairobi: Oxford University Press, 1970), p. 2.

[3] Cited by Basil Davidson in *The African Past: Chronicles from Antiquity to Modern Times* (London: Longmans, 1964), pp. 357–58.

[4] Robert I. Rotberg, "Resistance and Rebellion in British Nyasaland and German East Africa, 1888–1915: A Tentative Comparison," in Prosser Gifford and William Roger Louis, eds., *Britain and Germany in Africa* (New Haven, Conn.: Yale University Press, 1967), pp. 671–72.

moving farther inland and the Cuamato and Cuanhama peoples. The Portuguese losses: "Out of 500 men 16 officers, 12 NCO's, 109 European soldiers and 168 native soldiers were killed" by the Africans.[5] Skirmishes continued for the next ten years until the Portuguese suffered a disastrous defeat near the border of then German-controlled Southwest Africa or Namibia. Misunderstandings between the Germans and Portuguese led to a German attack on Portuguese positions. After the Germans attacked, the Ovambos attacked and pushed the Portuguese from their military camps and settlements. The southern part of Angola was therefore independent at the end of 1914 and the beginning of 1915. But independence was short-lived. The years of war had upset the planting cycle, and a famine began. Thus weakened, the Africans were in no position to face the army of 11,000 men the Portuguese sent. By the end of 1915, the southern part of Angola had been attached to the rest of the colony.[6]

In present-day Ghana, the Ashanti early perceived a threat to their economy when the British took control of the Elmina trading center from the Dutch. The change of European control meant that the Ashanti middlemen would no longer be able to sell their slaves on the coast because of British efforts to suppress the trade. Therefore, they sent their armies south to attempt to protect their interests and, at first, defeated the enemy.[7]

In Algeria, a confederation under Abd-el-Kader fought French claims to that country from 1830 to 1847. In Morocco, people living in the Atlas Mountains rejected French claims to sovereignty, even though the king had submitted. The last surrenders to the French came as late as 1934.[8] The Zulu fought European movement inland in 1779, and they won more battles than they lost for the next thirty years. The European claims to land for cultivation and cattle conflicted with Zulu claims to land for their cattle. It was not until 1906 that the Zulu were finally defeated.

Bloodied in battle or not, Africans were shocked by European power, which was based on superior weapons and organization. Some also thought that God must be on the whites' side because of their successes. European rule and power were accepted then and studied by the conquered peoples of Africa. This did not prevent opposition to specific policies, coupled with a growing awareness on the part of the Africans

---

[5] René Pélissier, "Campagnes militaires au sud-Angola (1885-1915)," in *Cahiers d'Etudes Africaines* IX, no. 33 (1969): 80. My account of these wars comes entirely from Pélissier.

[6] See James Duffy, *Portuguese Africa* (Cambridge, Mass.: Harvard University Press, 1959), p. 227.

[7] W. W. Claridge, "British Advance in Ghana Halted by Ashanti, 1873," in Wilfred Cartey and Martin Kilson (eds.), *The Africa Reader: Colonial Africa* (New York: Random House, 1970), pp. 7–14.

[8] Clement Henry Moore, *Politics in North Africa: Algeria, Morocco, Tunisia*, The Little, Brown Series in Comparative Politics (Boston: Little, Brown, 1970), pp. 33, 44.

of the need to learn more about the Europeans and their ways and machines.

Period of Rejection of Specific Colonial Policies. It did not take long for the Africans to begin different forms of opposition after the Europeans made good their initial claim to sovereignty. Groups did not necessarily oppose the whole colonial state, but they acted when they perceived that specific colonial policies hurt their vital interests. They acted where possible to oppose "unwelcome changes of a kind that upset traditional social, economic and political systems."[9] Frequently, this opposition took the form of tax riots, flight from and revolt against recruitment as workers and soldiers, action against the establishment of harmful frontiers, resistance to attempts to change customs, reactions to humiliation and racism, and boycotts of new legal systems and European economic practices.

In southeastern Nigeria, an important tax riot took place. Resentment had been building up because of the establishment by the British of chiefs over the Igbo-speaking people who had no tradition of chiefs. Anger reached the surface when the British decided that the so-called warrant chiefs would levy a tax on men. This led to some riots in 1927, but the most serious action came two years later.

In 1929, in the area of Aba, one of the warrant chiefs named by the British gave the impression that women might be taxed as well as men. The women of Aba and Owerri organized themselves along precolonial lines in age societies. They attacked chiefs and British property in Aba, Owerri, Calabar, and Opabo. In one riot, thirty-two Africans were killed by British fire, which eventually succeeded in suppressing the movement. Although the British clearly won, they made some reforms to prevent further trouble.[10] Revolts against taxation also took place in Sierra Leone in 1898, and among the Zulu in 1906.

In the Central African Republic in 1929, the Baya revolted against the recruitment of their men for the construction of the Congo-Ocean railway, and in Madagascar, young Merina in about 1912 organized a movement, Vy Vato Sakelika, to fight the French. In Senegal and Mali railroad workers struck after World War II, inspiring Ousmane Sembène to write a great novel about the event, *God's Bits of Wood*.

The Fulani of the area of Labé began to organize against the French when colonial authorities altered the frontiers of the province headed by Alfa Yaya. When they established frontiers between the colony of Senegal and Guinea and then with Portuguese Guinea, the French cut away from Alfa Yaya some of his territory. The Fulani prepared for revolt, but the French seized the leader and exiled him to Dahomey.

---

[9] Robert I. Rotberg, "Introduction," in Robert I. Rotberg and Ali A. Mazrui (eds.), *Protest and Power in Black Africa* (New York: Oxford University Press, 1970), p. xxiii.
[10] Michael Crowder, *A Short History of Nigeria* (New York: Praeger, 1966), pp. 259–60.

To prevent further organization, they broke up the Fulani province into three administrative districts with three clerks as chiefs.[11]

In Geman-controlled Tanganyika, a famous rebellion began in 1905, after the Germans had introduced cotton cultivation and forced labor, which "seriously interfered with subsistence farming."[12] People must have feared they would not be able to cultivate enough food for their needs if they were forced to plant, cultivate, and harvest the cotton for the Europeans or the European-imposed chiefs. Africans therefore attacked German planters and such other foreigners as Arabs and Indians. The uprising spread rapidly and lasted from about July, 1905, to August, 1907. The revolt, called the "Maji-Maji," was ruthlessly suppressed by the Germans.

These European attacks on the society were seen as a threat to the survival of the society. In Kenya too the Africans reacted to this threat with violence. A general climate of insecurity began in Kenya with the seizure of land by whites.[13] The insecurity grew after the Europeans from Britain and South Africa wanted to lower wages in 1921 and introduced an identity card system like the passbook in South Africa. The Europeans, especially missionaries, also began active campaigns against such basic Kikuyu customs as female circumcision. The Kikuyu reacted violently, attacking some missionaries.

All these attempts to oppose specific policies of the colonialists failed or brought only slight reforms. Destruction of the colonial state was impossible. New elites perceived this fact best and began to consider new avenues for resistance or amelioration of their own status within the colonial states.

Acceptance of, and Participation in, the Colonial Framework. Some groups had from the beginning accepted participation in the colonial state, because they saw they had something to gain from it, usually a favored position with regard to a traditional rival. With the establishment of the colonial state, new elites were also created whose very existence depended on the new system. They accepted the institutions the Europeans established, but they wanted control of them through increased participation. They competed with the old elites, whether the latter cooperated with the Europeans or not, and they competed with the Europeans themselves.

This new elite has been called an "administrative bourgeoisie" or a "colonial elite." Members were civil servants, teachers, soldiers, professionals, and intellectuals. Those who belonged to small African political systems or who had relatively low status in the precolonial state

[11] A. Demougeot, *Notes sur l'organisation politique et administrative du Labé avant et depuis l'occupation française*, Mémoire de l'IFAN, no. 6 (Paris: Larose, 1944), pp. 47-59.

[12] John Iliffe, *Tanganyika Under German Rule, 1905–1912* (Cambridge, England: Cambridge University Press, 1969), pp. 18–29.

[13] Carl G. Rosberg, Jr., and John Nottingham, *The Myth of the Mau Mau: Nationalism in Kenya* (New York: Praeger, 1966) p. 74.

may even have viewed colonialism as a form of liberation or protection. They attempted to better themselves through the new political system. With the introduction of schools, and then a few opportunities to study in European or American universities, their level of education improved to the level of the European or above. The Europeans who sensed the competition prevented the educated Africans from moving to the highest levels, and the Africans came to the conclusion that the Europeans must be removed.

In Egypt, for example, a middle class of educated men, landowners, and soldiers grew at the end of the nineteenth century because the government permitted Egyptians to own land, expanded educational opportunities, and raised some to officer status in the army. These groups wanted to move farther, and they opposed some of the powers of the British-supported king.[14] They thus organized the Nationalist Party in 1907 and demanded an end to British occupation. Although the group did not succeed in its goal, it began to spread the idea of an independent Egyptian nation and gave its sympathizers self-confidence.[15]

In Cameroun, by contrast, there was no large group of landowners, businessmen, or military of indigenous origin, but there were civil servants, clerks, teachers, and some professionals. They had been created through the schools of the colonial state. Their interests were tied to a new state, but they wanted better jobs commensurate with their abilities. At the same time, a young elite among the Bamiléké people in particular opposed the old chiefly elite and the European-named chiefs. The groups combined to oppose the French.[16]

In Senegal, where the Africans of the cities of Dakar, Rufisque, Gorée, and Saint Louis had French citizenship before 1848, they participated in the electoral process of the colony. They elected municipal councilors and a deputy to the French parliament. However, for a long period, metropolitan or white Frenchmen and the Eur-African Creoles controlled the position of deputy. As the African elite group increased in size and educational level, its members expected better jobs. The fact that they did not get them came as a surprise, and they perceived a direct threat to their interests when, after 1900, an influx of Europeans "came to their country and impeded the advance of young Africans in business and administration."[17]

The Senegalese reacted by accepting the existing system. In 1914, they united behind an African running for the post of deputy, in the

[14] See Mahmud Zayid, "The Origins of the Liberal Constitutionalist Party in Modern Egypt," in P. M. Holt (ed.), *Political and Social Change in Modern Egypt* (London: Oxford University Press, 1968), pp. 334–35.
[15] Arthur Goldschmidt, Jr., "The Egyptian Nationalist Party: 1892–1919," in Holt (ed.), *Political and Social Change in Modern Egypt, passim*, especially p. 333.
[16] Victor T. Le Vine, *The Cameroon Federal Republic* (Ithaca, N.Y.: Cornell University Press, 1971), *passim*, especially p. 17.
[17] G. Wesley Johnson, Jr., *The Emergence of Black Politics in Senegal: The Struggle for Power in the Four Communes, 1900–1920* (Stanford, Calif.: Stanford University Press, 1971), p. 124.

hope that he might raise wages of civil servants, provide retirement pay for ex-servicemen, and generally help to combat discrimination. The election of Blaise Diagne, the first black deputy, was not enough to bring about the desired changes: "A single Senegalese deputy in the Paris Chamber, among more than five hundred others, could hardly hope to modify general French policy. He could hope only for more modest satisfactions, special treatment at official events, personal enrichment or concessions to faithful followers."[18]

The pattern was similar elsewhere. The small legislative councils set up in English-controlled countries could not represent the opinion of the growing elite and could not bring about an end to grievances. In Ghana, the ex-servicemen who had served in British armies were dissatisfied with their lot after World War II. They knew they had been paid less than British soldiers for risking their lives for Britain, and they were unhappy about the lack of remuneration once the war was over. Educated Africans also perceived that they would always have to take orders from Europeans who were no better educated than they; they "saw no way of ever experiencing political power under the existing regime."[19]

With the beginning of some development and the growth of urban areas, a new group, the industrial workers, grew and began to perceive group interests. They naturally wanted higher wages, particularly to be able to purchase European goods in shops. They depended on European shops and imported goods because they could not cultivate crops themselves, and because their tastes changed. Housing in increasingly crowded urban areas was also expensive. Like all workers around the world, they began to ask for a shorter work week and an increased minimum wage. In the French countries, a labor code was adopted in December, 1952; but it did not include the desired raise in wages, and Europeans resisted its implementation. In Guinea workers struck for two months beginning in September, 1953, until their demands were met.[20]

In southern Africa and Kenya, where discrimination against Africans was most blatant, workers protested. In Malawi in 1944, civil servants and even some chiefs demanded an end to discrimination. At a meeting speakers "condemned the color bar, deplored the restriction that reduced Africans to a state of social inferiority, and humbly requested the government to permit Africans to enter movie theaters, to purchase goods from European-owned stores without being forced to ask for them through a hatchway."[21] These civil servants wanted to see European films; they did not want to destroy the theater in which they were being

[18] Ruth Schachter Morgenthau, *Political Parties in French-Speaking West Africa* (Oxford: Clarendon Press, 1964), p. 34.
[19] Kwame Nkrumah, *Ghana: The Autobiography of Kwame Nkrumah* (New York: International Publishers, 1957), p. 74.
[20] Morgenthau, *Political Parties*, pp. 228–29.
[21] Cited by Robert I. Rotberg, *A Political History of Tropical Africa* (New York: Harcourt, Brace and World, 1965), p. 349.

The End of Colonialism

shown. In other words, the theaters, like the institutions of the colonial state, were basically acceptable to the elite. Africans merely wanted their civil rights, which meant equal participation within the colonial state alongside the Europeans. When Europeans stood in their way, Africans perceived that the only way they could satisfy their interests was to remove the Europeans from the colonial state. To do this they needed leadership and organization.

Leaders with a Mobilizing Idea

Without acceptable, that is, legitimate leadership, no group could effectively oppose alien rule. Without a mobilizing idea that explains to people their relationship to each other as followers, their collective relationship with the leader, and the reasons for action put in terms of interests, a leader cannot stimulate and maintain loyalty, nor the discipline and sustained action necessary to force change.

Three types of leader appeared during the three stages of opposition to colonialism. The first type included those who had already led Africans in war against other African states; they were the military specialists and precolonial leaders who did not have to say very much to their followers in order to mobilize them. If the United States, for example, an established political system with institutions considered legitimate, were suddenly invaded, American leaders would not be required to explain very much to mobilize the people. The same, of course, was true in Africa when traditional leaders were still in charge.

The second type included men who accepted in part, at least, the need to bring about some changes in Africa. Some were precolonial leaders. Most were not; they were partially educated in European schools; they were part of some European organization, particularly the church, and often made an appeal to the supernatural for support. The third group comprised men with considerably more European education who were the most alienated from precolonial African political systems. They participated in and could manipulate the symbols of the colonial state and articulate interest in terms of the new framework. A small group, they also had to try to articulate the interests of other, less Westernized groups to persuade them to give them support. Some people, perhaps the majority, were never mobilized in these efforts.

Period of Rejection of Alien Claims to Sovereignty: Some Cases. The Wolof under Lat Dor, the king, fought the French moving inland in Senegal. The invaders defeated the king and destroyed his kingdom. They continued inland, where they met more resistance from Samory, who fought them for fifteen years.

Samory began his career as a peddler, then was a soldier in two different armies. He set out on his own about 1867 and began to conquer territory with a group of soldiers loyal to him personally. By the mid-1870's, he had built an empire in the general area of present-day

Mali, Guinea, and Sierra Leone. He used Islam to cement his empire and ensure loyalty.

In the course of his expansion, he met the French moving inland north from Senegal toward Bamako. Inevitably, the two interests clashed, and they fought. Then the French and Samory signed a treaty of friendship and commerce. The African leader, as interested in expanding his domain as the French, but wary of them, began thereafter to extend his empire east to Sikasso in today's Upper Volta. The French watched him, and once the people of Sikasso, who did not regard Samory as acceptable, broke away from him, the Europeans saw their opportunity. They encouraged revolts against him by subject peoples and signed a treaty with one of his enemies. After these revolts, Samory tried to rebuild his empire and by 1891 had modernized his army with the purchase of British guns. He was able to claim many victories over the French, but in the process he lost an excessive number of his men.

Samory then moved east in a weakened condition, closely followed by the French. Realizing he might be defeated in a head-on confrontation, he avoided the pursuer. During 1892 and 1893 he built a new empire, mainly in the northern part of today's Ivory Coast. By 1895 the French in the Ivory Coast, however, were themselves moving north. They attacked Samory in 1895, but he defeated them, and moved into Ghana. In 1896 he fought the British moving north and won again, capturing three pieces of artillery, which he added to his sizable arsenal of rapid-fire rifles.

Samory fought the French again and decided to give up his empire in the Ivory Coast because of the European advance. This time he moved west. The French attacked from the rear and succeeded in capturing him. Samory, defiant to the end, tried to commit suicide, but the French saved his life, tried him, and sentenced him to exile in Gabon, where he died in 1900.[22]

Samory had felt himself less bound by tradition than other rulers, such as Lat Dor, and could experiment with new methods and weapons. He was also quick to move his geographic base when necessary. Not choosing to defend a specific homeland but merely a provisional "empire," he had a flexibility of space and maneuver denied to states attempting to hold anciently occupied territories. Perhaps these were some of the reasons for his great ability to resist.

Less effective were leaders of small precolonial groups. In Lesotho in southern Africa, Moorosi led the Phuthi people, who numbered about 5,000. When the whites invaded his territory in 1865, Moorosi fled and watched the British assert their sovereignty over his domain in 1868 and 1871. He returned to confront the British.

[22] The best account of Samory's career is Yves Person, "Samori and the Resistance to the French," in Rotberg and Mazrui, (eds.), *Protest and Power in Black Africa*, pp. 80–112; and Yves Person, *Samori: Une révolution dyula*, Memoire no. 80, 2 vols. (Ifan-Dakar: Institut Fondamental d'Afrique Noire, 1968).

THE END OF COLONIALISM 77

His opposition started after he learned a British official had intervened in a dispute trying to apply British standards to a situation clearly governed by rules of African society. Moorosi asserted tradition to his disputants, warning them not to obey the British. He confronted British officials, and after some confusion an African was killed.

Moorosi then claimed the British were actually his subordinates, although in a tactical retreat he agreed to submit to them. Quietly he advised his people to resist the imposition of alien authority and custom. In 1877 Moorosi began to organize his men against the British, and in January, 1878, the leader instructed his people not to pay a tax on women. The British seized his son, but Moorosi sent men to break him out of jail.

The son fled to the mountains, and Moorosi joined him. The British laid seige to the mountainous retreat for eight months, and eventually they won after killing Moorosi. They imprisoned some of his people and dispersed them in Cape Colony, thus effectively destroying their political system.[23]

Muslim leaders along the Mediterranean attempted to use their religion as a mobilizing idea against the French. The Moroccans had seen the French invasion of Algeria and feared the worst. As more Frenchmen came to Morocco to trade, and as the Europeans put pressure on King Hassan I to accept their advisers, the monarch countered by attempting to get assistance from Egypt and Turkey on the basis of shared religion.

Moroccans residing in Egypt petitioned for assistance for their king, and some Egyptians and Turks traveled to Morocco as advisers. One Moroccan, Ahmad al-Hiba, led his countrymen in battle against the French. Turks and Egyptians reportedly supplied him with some money, arms, and men, but the French defeated him at the battle of Sidi Bou Outhman in September, 1912.[24]

In conclusion, leaders of precolonial systems and precolonial organizations, no matter what their courage and intelligence, were inadequate to meet the European challenge, and Africans soon realized it. They knew a different type of leader was necessary but were unsure what talents he would need to mobilize people to follow him.

Period of Rejection of Specific Colonial Policies. Separatist church movements are an example of rejection of certain colonial policies or agents, rather than of the entire colonial system. The term "Ethiopian" or "Ethiopianism" has been applied to some of them. Their leaders seldom led Africans to open revolt except in one famous case, that of the Providence Industrial Mission (PIM) Church and John Chilembwe.

Chilembwe was born into the Yao group in Malawi. That country,

---

[23] See Anthony Atmore, "The Moorosi Rebellion: Lesotho 1879," in Rotberg and Mazrui, eds., *Protest and Power in Black Africa*, pp. 3–35.

[24] Edmund Burke, "Pan-Islam and Moroccan Resistance to French Colonial Penetration 1900–1912," in *Journal of African History*, XIII, no. 1 (1972): p. 114.

then called Nyasaland, was under British control after 1891. The Yao had been defeated by the Europeans, and a great malaise afflicted the country because of seizure of land by the whites, the preaching of missionaries, and the slave trade.[25]

Chilembwe got a job with Joseph Booth, a European missionary with radical views about politics, economics, and religion. He thus learned about race relations, taxes, and government on a worldwide scale, and he studied European church organization.

In 1900, after returning to Malawi from a trip to America with Booth, he founded the Providence Industrial Mission, and gained additional popularity by traveling to Portuguese-controlled areas, where he requested prison reform. Chilembwe's churches thus grew and spread in a context of general ferment. People had begun to complain about the loss of their land, low wages, discrimination, and new taxes imposed by the British. Recruitment of soldiers for World War I and a famine added to the general disorder brought by the Europeans. In retaliation some European owners of coffee plantations burned the small PIM churches built by workers. Chilembwe decided he must lead a revolt against the colonial state. He may have wanted to drive the British out completely, but more probably he wanted reform and an end to recruitment and discrimination. He also wanted to show the Europeans that they could not continue to treat the Africans as something other than men, to make a "symbolic gesture to show that Africans . . . would not always accept passively the spate of changes and discrimination which the rush of European rule was heaping on them."[26] His revolt itself lasted a very short time, from January 23 to February 4, 1915, and did not accomplish much. Three Europeans were attacked and killed, including the manager of the coffee estate where PIM churches had been burned. Not all Africans supported the revolt, and African soldiers remained loyal to their British commanders. Chilembwe himself was killed, and the British suppressed his church and movement harshly. But the colonial administration did undertake a few reforms by trying to stablize land and by encouraging the settlers to show more respect toward Africans.

The use of religion by a leader was not the only way to mobilize followers to oppose the colonial regime. Leaders like Harry Thuku began to experiment with European-style organizations to combat Europeans.

Thuku, a Kikuyu leader, was born in 1895 in Kenya, a descendant of earlier Kikuyu leaders. As a youngster he worked at a Protestant mission, the Gospel Mission Society run by Europeans, and went to their church school.

After associating with Europeans in the mission for a few years, he

---

[25] Our account depends on that of George Shepperson and Thomas Rice, *Independent African: John Chilembwe and the Origins, Setting and Significance of the Nyasaland Rising of 1915* (Edinburgh: Edinburgh University Press, 1958), p. 400.
[26] *Ibid.*, p. 255.

The End of Colonialism

went to Nairobi to work in a European bank, and then for a newspaper. Next, he became a telephone operator at the government treasury in Nairobi.

By working with churchmen and the civil service, he made up for his lack of formal education. He purchased a bicycle with his earnings, which permitted him to meet and visit many people in the area of Pangani, an African suburb of Nairobi, where a growing group of Africans discussed the ways in which the colonial state hurt African interests.

Because of the many abuses, humiliation, and continued loss of land, Thuku and his friends formed the Young Kikuyu Association in 1921. Realizing they needed the support of the non-Kikuyu for any action they might undertake, they changed the name to the East African Association, but most members were still Kikuyu. Up to about 1920, Thuku became increasingly involved in protest.

More people began to look to him as a leader as he articulated their grievances. In 1922, he spoke against forced labor and told women to stop work and return to their homes. The British arrested him, and demonstrations, particularly by women, led to several deaths at the jail where he was kept. The British deported him from Nairobi to prevent further disturbances and detained him from 1922 to 1930.[27] Without Thuku, his organization declined, but the British failed to make the necessary reforms that might have prevented the rise of another organization. Settlers' holdings continued to expand; humiliations and insecurity did not abate, resulting in a more violent movement later.

All these movements failed to achieve their immediate objectives, but they provided a link between the first leaders of resistance and the leaders who eventually brought the countries to independence. The last group had ideas that had nothing at all to do with God or religion. They worked totally within the secular order and were able to mobilize a larger group of people from several different precolonial systems.

Period of Acceptance of the Colonial Framework. With time, more individual Africans who attained higher levels of European or colonial education traveled outside their countries, generally developed their intellects through reading and observation, and became aware of events in Asia, Europe, and America. Ali Mazuri, an African political scientist has pointed to the Atlantic Charter, the United Nations Charter, and the Bandung Conference of 1955 as important influences on such men. In meetings at Bandung, Indonesia, April 18 to 24, 1955, the principle of self-determination was expounded. Asian states like India and Burma had become independent, and they urged others to follow them. China had undergone a revolution and desired to promote revolution elsewhere.

A total of twenty-nine countries sent representatives to Bandung,

---

[27] This account comes from *Harry Thuku: An Autobiography*.

including Ghana, Egypt, Ethiopia, Liberia, Libya, Sudan, and Tunisia from Africa. Nehru of India and, particularly, Chou En-lai of China dominated the meetings. Participants agreed to promote Afro-Asian economic and cultural cooperation. They condemned racism and called for self-determination. The Africans were encouraged by this meeting and others that followed.[28]

Individual African leaders were also encouraged by meetings with anti-colonial leaders elsewhere, who helped them articulate an anti-colonial idea and probably made suggestions about organization.

Forces within the colonial state also encouraged a challenge to European Supremacy. European schools and bureaucracies were inevitably the most important of these forces. LeVine has found that out of 46 "founding fathers" of African states 30 per cent were teachers and 20 per cent were civil servants.[29]

Albert Luthuli of the Republic of South Africa summarized his experiences in European-run Adams College, which produced many members of the new African elite: "I was fascinated by the horizons which my own education opened up, and eager to be instrumental in educating others."[30] Men like Luthuli, a third-generation Christian, a teacher, and an elected modernizing chief, began to understand the European-created and European-dominated state from the inside. They accepted the idea of modernization, which generally meant a high degree of Europeanization, and they opposed previous leadership, even that of the separatist church. Like Luthuli, Kenneth Kaunda of Zambia, the son of an African missionary, called for extension of the franchise in 1955, a struggle against the color bar, "for getting higher posts for Africans in the . . . Civil Services, and in military and police forces according to merit and not according to their colour."[31] Luthuli and Kaunda accepted the colonial state framework. So did the Sudanese leaders of the civil servants in 1943, when they demanded self-determination for their country. They planned no return to the Madhist Islamic state or to the Funj sultanate of the precolonial era. They wanted self-determination for a new Sudan, which the foreigners they wanted to remove had created. As bloody as the anti-European wars in Algeria, Guinea-Bissau, Angola, and Mozambique were, the modernizing leaders still looked to Europe, America, and China for new organizations and technologies.

In 1956, Sylvanus Olympio, fluent in English, French, German, Ewe, and other African languages, equipped with a degree from the London

[28] See Paul F. Smets, *De Bandoeng à Moshi: Contribution à l'étude des conférences afro-asiatiques, 1955–1963* (Brussels: Université Libre, 1964), pp. 6–26.

[29] Victor T. LeVine, *Leadership Transition in Black Africa: Elite Generations and Political Succession*, Munger Africana Library Notes, no. 30 (Pasadena: California Institute of Technology, 1975), p. 15.

[30] Albert Luthuli, *Let My People Go* (New York: McGraw–Hill, 1962), p. 34.

[31] Kenneth D. Kaunda, *Zambia Shall Be Free: An Autobiography* (London: Heinemann, 1962), p. 65.

School of Economics and experience as an agent for one of the largest European trading firms in West Africa, demanded independence for a new state called Togo.

Another civil servant–teacher, Julius Nyerere, chose a nonviolent approach in the trust territory in East Africa, Tanganyika. His political awakening began at Makerere University, where he and friends discussed the extension of rights to African civil servants within the colonial state. They sought equality with the Europeans at first and used the Tanganyika African Association as a vehicle, even though it had originally been founded by the British.

In 1949 Nyerere went to Great Britain to continue his studies at the University of Edinburgh, where while in the freer atmosphere of a metropolitan university he continued his study of philosophy, history, and economics. There he began to write essays about colonialism, condemning its abuses. Although it is not certain that Nyerere got the idea his country must be independent while studying at Edinburgh, he did decide during his sojourn there to devote himself to politics.

Three years later he received his university degree and returned home, where he became active in the Tanganyika African Association and led its transformation into the Tanganyika African National Union, or TANU, in 1954. By that time he was talking about independence.

Nyerere tried to mobilize people during the next few years by saying the country must be self-governing and multiracial, and that a timetable must be set for change. He preached nonviolence and attacked specific colonial abuses that people in different areas were concerned about. For accusing colonial officials in the party newspaper of wrongdoing, he was put on trial for libel. He paid a fine instead of going to prison, because elections were being held and he wanted to participate.

The franchise was extended gradually to more and more Africans, with TANU winning elections in 1958 and 1960. After the latter election, the colonial government allowed for the creation of an executive controlled by Africans. In 1961 the country became independent, and Dr. Nyerere became its first prime minister and then its first president.

The earliest generation of Algerian leaders, born into families of some means, were university graduates and such professionals as lawyers and physicians. They asked for equality, adopting as their message the motto of the French Revolution, "Liberty, Equality, and Fraternity." Ferhat Abbas was the most outstanding of these men. He had been educated in French universities and spoke better French than Arabic. He had faith that the French would extend citizenship in Algeria and hoped for modernization and industrialization under French leadership.

He and others of similar persuasion founded a movement called Young Algerians. It agitated for reform of the colonial state, which it accepted. The introduction of some elected bodies in Algeria gave the impression reform was coming. In 1936, for example, the socialist-led

Popular Front government in France proposed an extension of citizenship, but because of settler opposition the reform failed.

A younger group watched this failure. Many came from poorer, more rural backgrounds than Ferhat Abbas, and the great majority had no university education. Ahmed Ben Bella, for example, did not successfully complete his secondary school education. But apparently Ben Bella realized that having fought for France gave him no reason to expect any gratitude from the settlers, who continued to discriminate, humiliate, and prevent the advancement of Algerians after World War II as before. In spite of this sense of discrimination, he ran for office in his town and was elected. He also ran for the French-created Algerian Assembly.

The authorities apparently tried, in Ben Bella's view, to seize his father's farm, and he shot the man claiming the land. He then moved more or less underground, participating in the organization of secret movements culminating in the Front de Libération Nationale (FLN), which began the movement for independence in 1954 by using violence against the European settlers and the French administration. The FLN message was that assimilation was a sham, and that the only way to achieve equality was through independence. Its members, like their predecessors, had accepted the colonial state framework, and once the country achieved its independence in 1962 they did not seek to federate with any other country, choosing rather to take over the existing new state.

Most of these future leaders were part of the European-oriented aspect of the dual polity that we said characterized the colonial state. Portuguese African elites followed the pattern. Amilcar Cabral, Dr. Agostinho Neto, and Dr. Eduardo Mondlane were highly educated: one, an agronomist trained in Lisbon; the second, a poet-physician; the third, professor of anthropology at Syracuse University. Their goals were control of the new state and then insuring Africans got the benefits of the new institutions. There was a limited future for most of them in the precolonial-oriented part. They developed a sense of their own potential as men and as professionals, and they found inspiration in the tiny group of men who had already reached the heights in Africa. Kwame Nkrumah, Nnamdi Azikiwe, and Albert Luthuli indicate in their autobiographies they had been inspired by the famous African educator Dr. Aggrey, who preached individual achievement and elitism.

Organization for Unity and Continuity

Without some form of organization, movements of opposition and resistance could be no more than sporadic bursts of energy without significant results for the maintance or the restoration of sovereignty to African-controlled political systems. Leadership itself may be judged on its ability to develop an enduring organization. Many African political systems—even the most centralized—tended and tend today to be highly personal. The result is that, once the leader disappears, the organization undergoes great change. Béhanzin, King of Dahomey, embodied the spirit of the kingdom. As long as he evaded French capture, people had a sense of the continued existence of the kingdom; once the French seized him, the kingdom was officially destroyed.

Having realized that precolonial organization had been ineffective against the Europeans, the developing elite experimented with new forms of organization and symbols that they used to protest against specific colonial abuses. Africans were genuinely impressed with European power and recognized that organization is basic to power. In the third period, therefore, European organizations, like political parties and trade unions, were completely accepted and were successful in the pursuit of power and sovereignty.

Period of Rejection of Alien Claims to Sovereignty. The success of the Ethiopian resistance to Italian claims to sovereignty depended on the organization of the Ethiopian state, which absorbed several different precolonial systems, and the organization of the Ethiopian army by Menelik II.

Menelik II had studied European technology and organization and had modernized his army. He recruited for the army and trained his men in the use of modern equipment; he knew he could not isolate his country from the rest of the world, and he knew he must learn from the rest of the world. According to Richard Pankhurst, from 1882 to 1887 the emperor purchased 25,000 rifles. In the following years he obtained more equipment from European states. His Italian enemies were unable to keep their organization intact as well as Menelik. [32]

Westward, in present-day Nigeria, the Yoruba were quickly defeated by the British, because they were unable to establish larger political entities or even alliances. By the nineteenth century they were divided into more than twelve separate kingdoms, which fought among themselves. The Ijebu particularly disliked the Ibadan, who traded with Lagos, a British colony since 1861.

The Ijebu harassed traders moving between Ibadan and Lagos, and the British, who taxed the trade, lost money. They decided to send a force against the Ijebu in 1892 in order to establish "an Ijebu protectorate as the only means of ensuring uninterrupted trade." [33]

The Ijebu knew of the British plans, and they had a standing army because of previous wars with other African states. Significantly, they refused an alliance with other Yoruba kingdoms, such as Egba, and sent their army of 7,000 to 10,000 against a British-led force of fewer than 500 soldiers and 500 carriers. The British had machine guns and the Afri-

[32] See Richard Pankhurst, "Ethiopian Emperor Menelik II Repulsed Italian Invasion, 1895," reprinted in Cartey and Kilson, eds., *The Africa Reader*, pp. 33–39.
[33] Robert Smith, "Nigeria-Ijebu," in Michael Crowder (ed.), *West African Resistance* (London: Hutchinson, 1971), p. 177.

cans breech-loaders, which they had not been trained to use effectively. On May 19, 1892, the Ijebu lost 1,000 men in battle, compared with about 50 deaths on the European side.[34] The shocked Yoruba did not resist further British advances, and the British extended a protectorate over almost all of Yoruba land by 1893. The Ijebu still apparently recall with pride the bravery of their men, but they eventually realized that Ijebu organization was inadequate to the task.

Period of Rejection of Specific Colonial Policies. When the people of southern Tanzania revolted against the introduction of cotton cultivation, which, they realized, would upset the agricultural cycle, they attempted alliances that had been remarkably absent during the initial period of European claims. The Ngoni and the Yao had been enemies but tried to establish a new organization to fight more effectively. One chief wrote:' 'We received an order from God to the effect that all White Men had to quit the country. We are ready to fight them. . . . I wanted to send you cattle as a present, but I was unable to send them. This war ordered by God must come first. Send 100 men with guns. Help me in taking the Boma. . . . Let us forget now our former quarrels."

Such alliances came too late. At an earlier period, they might have been able to wear down the Europeans or convince European public opinion that colonialism was too expensive. New organization was necessary that would unite much larger groups of people above the old constraints of precolonial political systems.

The Somalis experimented. In order to surmount clan division, they founded the Somali Youth Club in 1943, and in Libya, which the Italians occupied in 1911, resistance formed around the Sanusi brotherhood, an Islamic organization.

The most innovative organizations were the movements that "imposed new regulations and new instructions on the faithful; they brought believers into the Congregation by dispensing 'medicine'; they promised immunity both from witchcraft and from bullets."[35] By dispensing such medicine in 1905, leaders of Maji-Maji had convinced Tanzanians that the dreaded bullets of the Germans (which they knew all too well) would turn to water, "maji" in Swahili.

Such movements were often institutionalized into separatist churches that, like Chilembwe's PIM, could lead a revolt, or into other churches that did not engage in open revolt. The most famous of these movements was Mau Mau.

In Kenya the Kikuyu organized a separate school system and a separate Christian church, and they asked for the establishment of a Kikuyu grand chief, even though none had existed in the memory of living man.

[34] *Ibid.*, pp. 179–81, 189, and 193.

[35] T. O. Ranger, "African Reactions to the Imposition of Colonial Rule in East and Central Africa," in L. H. Gann and Peter Duignan, eds., *Colonialism in Africa 1870–1960*, I (Cambridge: Cambridge University Press, 1969): 314–15.

Jomo Kenyatta published his book *Facing Mount Kenya* in 1938; it set down Kikuyu customs and beliefs and promoted Kikuyu unity by setting standards for this decentralized people and showing African pride in the face of European racism and discrimination. These attempts led to increased Kikuyu aggressiveness.

After the end of World War II, a larger group of Africans with experience of army organization returned to Kenya. Many had gone to India, where they saw the nationalist organization of Gandhi.

At the same time white control of Kenya's land expanded inexorably. Africans began to organize on a new basis. They took oaths to ensure unity and unswerving support for their leaders, who ordered demonstrations and resistance. Formerly, Kikuyu had moved rather docilely from the land when government agents told them to move; in the late 1940's, they began to resist because of the oaths they had taken. Although the oathing ceremony itself had variations, it used some old Kikuyu symbols to tie it with the past. It was a technique to unify people above precolonial and colonial divisions. Europeans exaggerated the nature of the oath in order to support their contention that the opposition was uncivilized. In October, 1952, a pro-British Kikuyu leader was assassinated. The British then announced they had discovered a movement they called Mau Mau, supposedly organized to kill or drive all whites from the country.

Kikuyu leaders like Jomo Kenyatta were tried and sentenced, and 100,000 Kenyans were placed in government reserves. Violence increased apace. About 15,000 Kikuyu hid in the forested area of the country and organized themselves into an army or a group of armies to fight the British, who laid siege to the area. By 1956, many thousands had been killed, and the British claimed that "law and order" had been re-established.

A somewhat similar but much shorter movement occurred in French-controlled Madagascar in 1947. French settlers had also seized land on that island, and French companies held much rich land in reserve. Malagasy civil servants were paid less than their French counterparts. In 1912 young professionals and civil servants met to study their history and Malagasy culture, which they thought should not disappear. But they also agreed that their societies must modernize. Representatives of several precolonial political systems met to form a secret group called Vy Vato.

About the same time, the French began recruiting Malagasies for service in their colonial army in the southern part of the country, where people openly resisted. Members of Vy Vato, recognizing some solidarity between themselves and the southerners decided to encourage resistance to recruitment. The French discovered the plan and arrested several members.

In 1929 student groups demonstrated for an extension of rights to the Malagasies. In 1946, professionals and civil servants founded a new movement to fight for higher salaries, the Mouvement Démocratique de la Rénovation Malgache (MDRM). The movement went farther than previous organizations, asking for "autonomy in internal affairs," and some members also asked for independence. Added to the civil servants were 15,000 Malagasy veterans of World War II, who, like veterans elsewhere, did not get the benefits they expected.[36]

In January, 1947, elections to the provincial assemblies were held, but the administration arrested MDRM members to prevent their election. MDRM representatives won anyway. The French quickly added new conditions for election to the Malagasy Assembly established after World War II such as in the other French-controlled areas. The French wanted to insure the election of pro-French representatives. The frustration of the people grew.

The night of March 29–30, 1947, groups of Malagasies who denounced existing organizations attacked military camps, where they seized modern weapons, and attacked and killed many Frenchmen.[37] The revolt was most active from the end of March to June or July, 1947, although scattered attacks on the French took place for another year. The repression was severe. Estimates of from 60,000 to 90,000 Malagasy deaths have been made.

In spite of the importance of the movement, not much is known about its organization, except that it was not based on existing organizations. It also managed by oaths or other means to unite many different peoples, and it served as a symbol to all Malagasies of their resistance and opposition to the French-controlled colonial state. On the tenth anniversary of the uprising, the Malagasy writer and political leader Jacques Rabemananjara said: "Since 1947, the date of 29 March has become sacred for us; it will remain an unerasable chapter in our history."[38]

Period of Acceptance of the Colonial Framework. After the failure of older forms of organization against initial European claims, and then the failure of experimental organizations against specific colonial abuses, the new elite studied organization and mobilizing techniques carefully in Europe, America, and even India. Although they were part of European-imposed organizations—the colonial civil service and the Christian church, for example—they suspected they were probably inferior to their counterparts in the metropole. They knew the colonial schools, for the most part, were inferior, and they were convinced that the colonial officials were less competent or even less "civilized" than their colleagues in Europe. Autobiographical and biographical data indicate an interest in European organization in its natural habitat.

Kenneth Kaunda, the leader of Zambia's independence movement, says he realized that "the white man lords it over us . . . not because he happens to be white but because he is better organized than we are; that is his secret."[39] A major weakness of African organizations was a narrow

[36] Raymond K. Kent, *From Madagascar to the Malagasy Republic* (New York: Praeger, 1962), pp. 91–92, 102.
[37] Pierre Boiteau, *Madagascar: Contribution à l'histoire de la nation.*
[38] Speech reprinted in Jacques Rabemananjara, *Nationalisme et problème malgaches* (Paris: Présence Africaine, 1958), p. 50.
[39] Kaunda, *Autobiography*, p. 152.

base of support. A small group of high-ranking African civil servants and professionals had little power and could not impress the British, French, Portuguese, or Belgians with courteous memoranda. Neither could an organization based on a single precolonial state. New leaders, therefore, organized parties, often on European models, to win elections, and trade unions to negotiate and strike; they used newspapers, often in European languages, to spread their message of reform and then independence.

In Zambia, or Northern Rhodesia, the first new organizations were so-called welfare associations, whose civil servant and teacher members discussed their own complaints about salaries and racism. Kenneth Kaunda, son of an African Christian missionary and himself a schoolteacher, and others of similar background introduced a new political party, the Northern Rhodesian African Congress, to these associations. Their goal was to politicize this elite. Then they appealed to the ex-servicemen, who, having fought to save Great Britain from the invader in World War II, were discriminated against at home. They tried to articulate the grievances of all Africans in order to get support: "The Congress organizer regarded himself honestly as a worker in the cause of freedom and a means through which the frustrations of the people could express themselves."[40] If this meant supporting cattleowners who objected to what was a beneficial inoculation of their livestock, the new party did it.

In 1952 the Congress, urban-based like other parties, tried to organize in the northern part of the country. It changed its name to the African National Congress (ANC) and set up a newspaper to spread its message all over the country. By 1955 the Congress was fighting resettlement and supporting a boycott of shops in the northeastern part of the country. Organization continued, and Europeans protested against the party. Kaunda replied that they were organizing "for exactly the same reasons as white politicians and trade unionists, to safeguard the interests of their people."[41]

In August, 1960, at a meeting of party leaders, some of whom had been in prison, their leader, Kaunda, told them that history was on the side of independence. Events in India, Egypt, and Ghana proved it. He called for an organization of the whole country, clarification of goals, and nonviolent methods. He said the party must remain in constant communication with all the people and that it "must become the trusted mouthpiece of all the people so that each and everyone would be ready to suffer if necessary, together, in the cause of freedom."[42]

How many people joined the new UNIP is not easy to know. Groups joined for different reasons, and Kaunda estimates that by 1955 the party had 105 chiefs, 500 African civil servants, and 3,000 village headmen, and a total membership of 37,000 men, women, and children.[43]

A younger group of professionals believed, like Sékou Touré, Kenneth

[40] *Ibid.*, p. 57.
[41] *Ibid.*, p. 80.
[42] *Ibid.*, p. 154.
[43] *Ibid.*, p. 66.

Kaunda, Ahmad Ben Bella, Eduardo Mondlane, Agostinho Neto, Amilcar Cabral, and Kwame Nkrumah, that the masses of people must be mobilized to joint their movement to ensure effectiveness. After a conflict with more conservative members, Bourguiba founded the Neo-Destour in Tunisia to join together the interests of all groups. Although its leaders were involved in secular activities and were, for the most part, not very devout Muslims, they used Islam for their own purposes. For example, they supported the conservative idea that Muslims who became French citizens should not be given traditional Muslim burials, and they preached in the mosques. They organized workers and coordinated their trade unions with the Neo-Destour. They organized a press to articulate their ideas and interests.

Variations of this process of national party organization took place in Zaïre and Nigeria. Not all of the elites in those very large countries were convinced that their interests lay with the states as constituted, even though they did not propose a return to the precolonial systems. Western Nigeria, where most Yoruba lived, constituted a bloc of more than 10 million people, more than most other African states, and the Bakongo constituted probably 2 million in Zaïre and Congo-Brazzaville. The Bakongo formed the Abako party to unite themselves, and the Yoruba formed the Action Group to win power in Nigeria, or lead their region should it ever become a separate state.

The Yoruba were particularly concerned about unity, because they had long fought among themselves. This was one reason why the British had no trouble defeating the Ijebu. Once colonial institutions were accepted, however, the elite became worried that continued division would prevent the Yoruba from winning sufficient seats in the first legislative assemblies established by the British, and that their customs would continue to be corrupted. Without sufficient seats, they would not be in a position to control benefits in terms of goods and services. Other groups, such as the increasingly united Igbos or Hausas, would control everything.

In 1945, therefore, young professional Yoruba in London, including Obafemi Awolowo, who had previously worked as a clerk, journalist, and businessman, and who was then studying to become a lawyer, founded the Egbe Omo Oduduwa. This cultural organization for Yoruba people acted to prevent conflict among members and encouraged solidarity for its own sake. Members of the Egbe then formed a political party in 1951, the Action Group, to contest elections organized by the British. It later attempted to become a Nigerian party and made demands for political change.[44] Because of Portuguese restrictions on political activity, the Guineans and Cape Verdians founded the PAIGC only in 1956 with headquarters later in Guinea-Conakry. MPLA was founded the same year by Angolans with headquarters later in Brazzavilla. Mondlane and

---

[44] See Richard L. Sklar, *Nigerian Political Parties: Power in an Emergent African Nation* (Princeton, N.J.: Princeton University Press, 1963), *passim*.

The End of Colonialism

his friends founded FRELIMO late in 1962 and set up headquarters in Dar es Salaam.

In face of increasing demands for change, Europeans first tried to organize counterparties. These organizations never succeeded for long, and an African elite gradually gained more power. European governments conceded rapidly, step by step, to the African organizations, because they feared violence and because a change in public opinion at home had begun once Europeans saw political parties, trade unions, African lawyers, and other professionals rather than kings and so-called witch doctors lead opposition movements. The Soviet Union and the United States were also increasingly critical of empire. By 1960, France, Great Britain, and Belgium all recognized the right to immediate independence. They understood that it was not against their own interests. Only the Afrikaner and British settlers of South Africa, the British of Rhodesia, and Portuguese refused to accept the tide of history.

In Africa north of the Zambezi River, an African elite replaced a European elite. The colonial state had become independent.

5 Independence

Most countries became politically independent relatively quickly and peacefully after African leaders demanded independence. Liberation wars were necessary in only a small minority of states.

When the colonial elite concluded that it could not hope to replace the Europeans without obtaining sovereignty for the colonially established state, it demanded independence immediately. By so doing, it seized the initiative from Europeans, a gesture that seemed to symbolize a change in the relationship between Europe and Africa, between colonizer and colonized.

For seventy-five years, most initiative had come from the Europeans. They invaded and conquered; they had established new trade networks and reoriented part of the economy; they had founded and staffed new schools to teach their languages and technology. And it was the colonizer who had created a new framework for a state that African leaders now were attempting to manipulate. Under pressure, the Europeans recognized the need for reforms, but they tried to shape and control change. Some of them admitted that Africans might have independence one day in the future but claimed the right to decide when they would be "ready" for it. Because the new African elite accepted the colonial framework, they would not claim legitimacy for the precolonial systems. At the same time they rejected the idea that Europeans could decide when they had come of age.

Independence Perceived

Prior to the independence movements of the 1950's four countries were already independent—South Africa, Liberia, Ethiopia, and Egypt. The African elite knew about these countries but, with a few exceptions, was not significantly influenced or inspired by them. It is true that African leaders had cheered the Boers fighting the British at the beginning of the century, but after South Africa became independent in 1910 they realized they had no kinship with a white minority that treated blacks worse than the colonial powers elsewhere.

Ethiopia, Egypt, and Liberia had more kinship with the rest of Africa but had little influence. Ethiopia had claimed independence for more than a thousand years and had beaten back the Italians at Adowa.

Independence

Menelik's victory did not, however, prevent Europeans from exerting influence over the country. The French and Italians controlled Ethiopia's access to the sea, and after the death of the emperor in 1913 the Italians, British, and French tried to influence his successor.

In order to protect his country, Haile Selassie, the new emperor, joined the League of Nations. Foreign influence through schools, advisers, and trade increased, although the ruler, a clever strategist, tried to play off one influence against another. In 1934 Italy renewed her claims on Ethiopia, making war on the country in 1935 and 1936. Condemnation by the League of Nations was ineffective, and the Italians occupied the country until 1941, when the British replaced them. The latter attempted to maintain their influence but recognized Ethiopian independence at the beginning of 1942. American influence partially replaced the British in the form of advisers, aid programs, and international support.

It was difficult for the new elites of other countries to find inspiration or a model in Ethiopia. They protested when the Italians invaded the country, but few found monarchy desirable, and the emperor, who claimed to be a descendant of Solomon and the Queen of Sheba, had reportedly denied his African identity. Only after the beginning of the independence movements did Ethiopia identify itself with all of Africa, and then the emperor attempted to put his country in the forefront of unity movements by inviting independent states to his capital for the meeting that led to the creation of the Organization of African Unity in 1963.

Like Ethiopia, Egypt had associated little with most of Africa. Dominated by white Semites, it identified most with such other areas as the Arab Middle East and the broad world of Islam. After the end of the British protectorate in 1922, a new constitution promulgated the following year provided for a continuation of the dynasty founded by Muhammad Ali, a prime minister, and an elected legislature, which together ruled the country for the next twenty-nine years.

During this period, many British subjects lived in Egypt, foreign companies had a monopoly over the purchase of cotton, and the British and French owned the Suez Canal Company. In spite of foreign influence and an autocratic king, some groups in neighboring Sudan and Libya looked to Egypt for inspiration. Since the establishment of a condominium over Sudan in 1899, the country was ruled by the British under the guise of joint British and Egyptian sovereignty. Groups of Sudanese hoped for independence and then union with Egypt after 1922, and Egypt sent agents south to promote this idea. An Egyptian even assassinated the governor general of Sudan in 1924.

In 1942, an organization of Sudanese civil servants demanded that the British and the Egyptians recognize Sudan's right to self-determination. Then two political parties were founded, one favoring independence and unity with Egypt and the other just independence. To support the first party Egypt appeared before the United Nations after

World War II to protest continuing British presence in Sudan, and Egyptians wrote a new constitution for the country. In response to this agitation, the British began a process to bring the country to independence, but they heartily disliked the idea of unity with Egypt and attempted to discourage it. In 1953, an agreement between the British and Egyptians provided for self-government or internal autonomy, and complete independence came on January 1, 1956.[1]

Egypt has continued to hope for union with the Sudan, and many projects have been put forward to the present day. Meanwhile, Egypt lost a war with Israel in 1947, and leaders saw the need to expand Egyptian influence all over Africa in order to win allies and discourage African relations with Israel. Under the late President Nasser, Egypt became a leader in African affairs partly for these reasons. Consequently, independence movements from Algeria to South Africa have received aid and inspiration from Egypt.

Of the four independent states, Liberia was identified most consistently with the rest of Africa. The only independent black republic in Africa was founded by and for freed slaves. It had declared itself independent in 1847 under black settler, or Americo-Liberian, rule. Unfortunately these settlers considered themselves superior to Africans and acted accordingly. As a result, in 1915 they had to call for American support to put down an uprising. America also protected the country against repeated French and British attempts to seize it, but the protection was ambiguous at best.

Since 1912, foreign advisers played an important role in decision-making in Liberia, and complicated, unfair loans tied the country to external creditors. In 1926, the government signed an agreement with the Firestone Rubber Company, permitting the latter to grow rubber in return for protection from foreign governments and a loan for $5 million, used to pay off other debts. Liberia then had to accept more American advisers, including a financial adviser named by the President of the United States. "Service charges [on the loan from Firestone] and advisers' salaries amounted to a fixed charge of nearly $270,000 a year, constituting 20 per cent of government revenues in 1928 and about 50 per cent in 1931."[2]

Firestone increased its control to include ownership of the major bank, the radio communication system, and an airline, and prospecting rights to look for minerals on the million acres of land granted them by the impoverished Liberians.[3] During World War II, American influence increased after the stationing of American troops in the country and the installation of such communication facilities as a transmitter for the Voice of America.

[1] For an account of the process, see S. C. Ukpabi, "The Independence Movement in the Sudan," in *Tarikh*, IV, no. 1 (1971): 41–53.
[2] Raymond Leslie Buell, *Liberia: A Century of Survival 1847–1947* (Philadelphia: University of Pennsylvania Press, 1947), p. 33.
[3] *Ibid.*, pp. 43, 48.

Making matters worse for Liberia's image were rumors and then European accusations of forced labor and even complicity in slavery during the 1920's and 1930's. A few members of the growing elite in other African countries protested against the criticism of Liberia, because they perceived the republic to be an integral part of black Africa and worried that unfair judgments would reflect on all blacks. In 1932, for example, Nnamdi Azikiwe, later the first President of Nigeria, wrote an article in a Negro American publication defending Liberia. He blamed Firestone Rubber Company and the Europeans for sabotaging Liberian independence and for judging Liberians more harshly than they judged themselves.[4] He called on blacks in America to help Liberia, which, in his view, "may yet be the medium of political consciousness and self-determination which forces will facilitate the establishment of a national hegemony of the black man in that mysterious and symbolic 'question marked' continent of Africa."[5]

In spite of this hope, Liberia could never serve as a symbol of independence for the rest of Africa as long as it was ruled by a minority so obviously under foreign influence. In addition, the country only began to identify its destiny with the rest of the continent when independence movements were already under way and when the government feared its own interests might be undermined if it were labeled colonialist. Since 1959 President Tubman and his successor, President Tolbert, have participated in African conferences and organizations without taking leadership roles.

For these reasons, Frantz Fanon's judgment that "the independence of a new territory, the liberation of the new people are felt by the other oppressed countries as an invitation, an encouragement, and a promise,"[6] does not apply to the independence of Egypt, South Africa, Ethiopia, Liberia, or even to Libya, the first African state to become independent in the 1950's. Libya quietly—even unobtrusively—became independent in 1951, under United Nations supervision, as a result of a compromise among the three European states that controlled regions of the country after World War II. A conservative king became head of a state noteworthy for its Western orientation and American military installations. It made no effort to inspire other states, and independence movements found no model in Libya. Models came a few years later, however, and developments all over the continent were to come surprisingly fast.

Ghana, Guinea, Togo, Cameroun, and Algeria in particular inspired Africa and offered encouragement by example beginning in the late 1950's. These countries served as examples because other Africans saw they were seizing the initiative from the Europeans, and in this forceful

---

[4] Ben N. Azikiwe, "In Defense of Liberia," in *The Journal of Negro History*, XVII: 1 (January, 1932), p. 46.
[5] *Ibid.*, p. 50.
[6] Frantz Fanon, "The Algerian War and Man's Liberation," in Frantz Fanon, *Toward the African Revolution: Political Essays* (New York: Grove Press, 1967), p. 145.

confrontation between European and African, the African, for the first time since the battlefield of Adowa, won.

On July 10, 1953, Kwame Nkrumah called for constitutional reform that would bring independence to Ghana. Less than four years later, on March 6, 1957, the new state became independent. The African masses in other states did not know the details of that evolution toward sovereignty. They did not realize that Ghana's economic strength played an important role in the decisions made, but they knew Dr. Nkrumah had dynamically demanded and won independence. They believed that a revolution of some kind had occurred.

One year after Ghanaian independence, Sékou Touré, the leader of mineral-rich Guinea, thrilled Africa on August 25, 1958, by saying in the presence of General Charles de Gaulle: "We prefer liberty with poverty to slavery with wealth." The phrase had been used before by Dr. Nkrumah and others, but now it had been thrown in the face of the leader of the second largest European empire. A black man was standing up to a white man and demanding change.

At the very moment Sékou Touré spoke, members of the Armée Nationale de Liberation (ANL) were fighting for independence in Algeria, thus showing the world that Africans would shed blood for independence if necessary. A smaller and ultimately unsuccessful military action was also taking place in Cameroun, where the Union des Populations du Cameroun demanded independence immediately and fought the French and those African leaders who seemed to be under European influence. The Togolese, a trust territory like Cameroun, were asking for independence by the end of 1957. Although they did not get it until 1960, "it was the Togo timetable that was forcing the pace" for some other French-controlled areas.[7]

In addition to actions by these individual states, an important meeting in 1958 brought leaders from twenty-eight states together to share ideas and strategies. By 1958, Kwame Nkrumah's name was known all over Africa, and when he called for the meeting in his capital, the continent watched. The All African Peoples' Conference (AAPC) opened December 5, 1958 and lasted until December 13. Most of the twenty-eight countries present were not independent and were thus represented by heads of political parties, movements, and trade unions. The chairman, Tom Mboya, dynamic young labor union official from Kenya, set the tone by saying: "The problem is not to know if we want independence, but how to get it."[8]

Delegates to the AAPC voted support for the Algerians and Camerounese and declared that violence was acceptable if it were the only effective means to bring about independence. They created a permanent secretariat and planned future meetings.

[7] Edward Mortimer, *France and the Africans: 1944–1960* (New York: Walker, 1969), p. 241.
[8] Cited by Immanuel Wallerstein, *Africa: The Politics of Unity* (New York: Random House, 1967), p. 33.

INDEPENDENCE

More important than resolutions and offices was the symbolism of sharing ideas about change and the mutual encouragement given for independence. For example, after Patrice Lumumba returned home to Zaïre from Accra, his speeches to mass meetings about his experiences and observations incited people to riot against the Belgians at the beginning of 1959. These riots contributed to the rush to independence one year later. In 1960, African demonstrators, doubtless encouraged by changes elsewhere in Africa, confronted South African police at Sharpeville to protest discrimination and were gunned down. Particularly after Congolese independence, Angolans, Guineans, and Mozambicans perceived that despite the extremely repressive colonial systems in their countries, they, too, could become independent.

The demonstrators in Zaïre and elsewhere perceived change as possible because of what they had heard about Ghana, Togo, Guinea, and Algeria. They talked in the grand language of nationalism, freedom, liberation, revolution, modernization, and sharing the wealth and technology of the twentieth century. But what these words really meant to them depended on their particular interest or grievance: a chance for schools, an end to cattle-dipping, taking back stolen land, more jobs, lower prices, security. It was a time of great expectations—and fear.

Not everyone saw independence as beneficial to their interests, and not everyone shared the thrill of speeches and confrontations in Ghana, Guinea, or Algeria. In London, Paris, Brussels, Madrid, and Lisbon, governments and merchants sat down to decide how to respond. The French and the Belgians proposed Eur-African communities, in which African states would have internal autonomy but with foreign policy, defense, and trade under European control. The Spaniards and Portuguese made the colonies into overseas provinces, pretending Africans would have the same rights as Europeans. The British organized puppet political parties around conservative leaders and groups to slow the pace of change or to ensure continued British influence. Most of these efforts failed.

With the exception of Portugal, ruled by a shortsighted reactionary government, Europeans wanted to avoid the type of long and costly war in which France had been involved in Indochina and Algeria, and they recalculated their interests just as they had done earlier in India, Burma, and the Middle East. They were also better aware than the African masses that the elites wanted continuing close ties to be able to take advantage of the larger economic aid programs being offered. They knew that the African states could not easily create their own currencies and would therefore remain for the time being in the sterling and franc zones. They recognized the insecurity of some African leaders and obtained rights to maintain military bases in these countries in return for secret agreements to protect regimes. Finally, they knew that the tax base of small countries could not support the civil services and development programs. Foreign investments, advisers paid by metropole, and even budget subventions would continue to be necessary, thus permitting considerable leverage.

Although the colonial powers could not easily predict the attitudes and actions of the United States and the Soviet Union, they knew both countries had a rather unsure posture as to dealing with newly independent states. The two world powers had few African specialists, and neither had a large pressure group trying to influence policy one way or the other. It was no secret that black Americans, though a large minority, were treated as second-class citizens in their own country and thus could not alter American policy. Great Britain, France, and Portugal had already used American Marshall Plan aid to bolster their positions in Africa after World War II; in spite of memories of Roosevelt's anti-colonialism and statements by the young Senator John F. Kennedy in 1957 that America should support demands for independence of Algeria, Europeans knew that the solidarity of the anti-Communist NATO alliance was a foundation stone for American foreign policy and could be used as leverage in meeting possible American initiatives more pro-African than pro-status quo. Statements by the American government during the 1950's concerning Africa were ambiguous at best and, in retrospect, generally tended to allow the European colonizers to work out the best terms they could with the African elites. Additionally, there was a small but growing American business investment in several African countries, which could encourage hostility to African initiatives.

Britain, France, Belgium, Portugal, and Spain obviously had much less leverage with the Soviet Union, whose Communist ideology gave Africa an important place in its view of its own worldwide role as a revolutionary anticapitalist state.

According to Communist ideology, the Soviet Union should always have been intensely interested in Africa. Lenin had written in *Imperialism, the Highest Stage of Capitalism* that "the upheaval of a Western proletariat and the struggle of colonial peoples would merge into a single revolutionary process directed against their common tormentors."[9] However, under Stalin the Soviet Union tended not to follow this idea.

During the 1920's and 1930's, colonial powers had an exaggerated view of Communist plots, although there were Communist parties in South Africa (composed mainly of whites), in Algeria, and in Egypt. In the 1940's, the RDA movement of the French colonies allied itself with the French Communist Party, and Communist study groups, offering lessons in organizational techniques, attracted future leaders. Activities of the Soviet Union itself were minimal, and by the 1950's Communist influence on leaders demanding African independence even seemed to decrease. The leaders themselves became deeply distrustful of the Communists. West Indians, for instance, such as George Padmore and Aimé Césaire, who had been close to Africans, had quit the Communist Party, and Africans often found European Communists domineering and even racist. The government of the Soviet Union seemed clumsy in

---

[9] Robert Levgold, *Soviet Policy in West Africa* (Cambridge, Mass.: Harvard University Press, 1970), p. 2.

its moves and self-serving. Only slowly did it begin to take advantage of opportunities in Africa, for example, in Egypt and Guinea. It was only later that China began playing a role in Africa. Thus, early in the 1960's the colonial powers had reason to believe they could survive loss of direct political control to the new African elite who, they suspected, would not or could not fall easily under the influence of another European country.

Within Africa, the European settlers had a less detached view of the changes. They perceived a direct and immediate threat to their material and even physical well-being. With the coming of independence, particularly in Algeria, about 850,000 Europeans fled by the end of 1962. By the end of 1976 most of the 390,000 whites in Angola and the 250,000 whites in Mozambique had fled to Portugal or South Africa. Those who left Algeria, Kenya, and some other states moved elsewhere, such as Madagascar, the Ivory Coast, Gabon, Rhodesia, and South Africa, whose government also looked with consternation at the changes. The *apartheid* regime in South Africa braced itself by new legislation in the 1950s and 1960s depriving the black and brown majority of its few rights.

In Swaziland, the king's attempt to reserve power to those who favored traditionalism angered young educated Swazi, who formed their own political party. Disagreements led to a conference in London in January, 1963. A year later, the country had a new constitution, with elections scheduled for June, 1964. The king was successful in getting his favorites elected, and he brought the country to internal self-government in 1966 and then independence in 1968, preserving the status of the chiefs.[10]

Similarly, in Uganda the elite of the Province of Buganda, which had been a separate kingdom, attempted to preserve its position, as did the Tutsi elite of Rwanda. Neither has been as successful as the king and chiefs of the Swazi. The people of Mayotte island, largely Christians, feared independence as part of Muslim Comoro and declared their desire to remain part of France in July, 1975, when the leaders of Comoro declared its independence. French support insured Mayotte's success.

Lastly, some countries were not enthusiastic about the independence of other countries and even tried to prevent it. Francophone states did not support Algerian independence as late as 1960, probably because of French influence over them and because of their own economic weakness. Morocco openly and loudly opposed independence for Mauritania, because it claimed the territory as part of Morocco. In more muted tones, the Ivory Coast proposed to absorb Upper Volta, which had once been part of its territory, and its president, for other reasons, opposed Guinean independence. Egypt wanted Sudan. South Africa tried to gain control of Lesotho, Botswana, and Swaziland.

[10] See Richard P. Stevens, *Lesotho, Botswana, and Swaziland* (New York: Praeger, 1967).

The self-proclaimed African Revolution was therefore greeted with mixed feelings in both Africa and Europe. No one quite knew what it would bring. If it were to be a real revolution, it might take unexpected turns, out of the control of those who expected to profit most from it.

Independence and Violence

Frantz Fanon claimed that real independence in Africa would require violence. In his view, revolution, which independence should bring, could only come from the most oppressed groups who must totally destroy "the colonial system, from the pre-eminence of the language of the oppressor . . . to the customs union that in reality maintains the former colonized in the meshes of the culture, of the fashion, and of the images of the colonialist."[11]

The possible appeal of such an idea notwithstanding, African as well as European history shows that the most oppressed peoples or groups do not lead movements for change, although the elites that do lead them claim to act in their name. History also shows that political, economic, and social change can never be complete, because there is always considerable carryover from one system to another, no matter if violence or nonviolence brought about the change.

Political Change in African History. Africa was not static before the arrival of the Europeans. Changes took place in African political systems well before the colonial period, and they had nothing at all to do with Europeans. For example, the Fulani holy war of Usuman dan Fodio altered the political system in what is today the northern part of Nigeria.

For years, Fulani cattle-herders had moved eastward across western Africa; among them traveled the "Torodbe Fulani" who were "a clan of scholars and clerks."[12] Inspired by a revival of Islam that had begun in North Africa, they believed firmly in theocracy. During the eighteenth century, Islamic theocracies had already been established in the Fulani homelands in present-day Guinea and Senegal, and the word spread east. The Torodbe began to hate the rulers of the seven Hausa states in northern Nigeria, where they lived, because of the latter's failure to adhere strictly to Muslim law.

A Fulani Torodbe, Usuman dan Fodio, born in one of the Hausa states in 1754, became a political force in the state of Gobir and influenced reform there. Competition with the Hausa leader of Gobir grew. In 1804, the ruler attacked one of his supporters, thus convincing Usuman dan Fodio he must proclaim a *jihad*, or holy war, against Hausa infidels. With Fulani and Hausa followers, he attacked the Hausa forces

---

[11] Frantz Fanon, "Decolonization and Independence," in Fanon, *Toward the African Revolution*, p. 105.

[12] The account of this precolonial African revolution comes from Robert W. July, *A History of the African People* (New York: Charles Scribner's Sons, 1970). The citation is from p. 186.

INDEPENDENCE

and won. He then organized a new empire in which a series of Fulani-ruled emirates "bound to Sokoto [the capital] by religious allegiance" replaced the seven Hausa kingdoms.[13] Unity was maintained to the period of independence in 1960. Usuman dan Fodio had thus changed the frontiers of the political system, creating a unified state with a religious basis.

Another, somewhat different type of military leader, Muhammad Ali, brought change to nineteenth-century Egypt. After he overthrew and massacred the Turkish Mamluks, who had ruled the country from the thirteenth to the eighteenth century, he began to modernize the Egyptian state. He introduced large-scale cotton cultivation and nationalized the land, which changed the economy of the country. He built a new army and a modern bureaucracy, unifying the state relatively peacefully.

A century and a half later, political change leading to independence from European rule was for the most part nonviolent in Egypt and elsewhere. With four or possibly five important exceptions, African states gained their independence quickly and peacefully after their leaders demanded it.

Violence and Change. Where independence was not achieved by peaceful means, it was brought about by extreme violence. Sometimes it was directed against the European colonialists, and sometimes against Africans. In Algeria, Guinea-Bissau, Mozambique, and Angola violence between African and European led directly to independence from European rule, although the collapse of the Fourth French Republic and the disappearance of the Salazar dictatorship in Portugal were important factors. In Rhodesia it is possible that all-out war between white and black or between black and black will determine that country's future government although negotiations initiated in 1976 by American Secretary of State Kissinger held out hope for peaceful change to black-majority rule.

After a century of foreign rule the Algerian Front National de Libération (FLN), whose twenty-two leaders decided military action was the only way to remove the French, began a war for independence. The FLN divided the coastal part of the country into five areas, or *willayas*. One leader was in charge of action in each of these regions, and a sixth was named to oversee operations in the sparsely populated Sahara. Uprisings began in each *willaya* and involved somewhere between 1,000 and 3,000 men, poorly armed with weapons from Egypt and possibly Morocco. The masses of people did not immediately follow the FLN, but the French reacted swiftly by jailing and killing suspected activists.

In mid-1955 violence spread widely. On August 20, 1955, for example, one hundred Frenchmen were killed in one raid, and more Algerians, impressed with the efficacity of the movement, rallied to the FLN. In 1956 the Front established a type of legislature, the Conseil National

[13] *Ibid.*, p. 194.

de la Revolution Algérienne (CNRA), and an executive, the Comité de Coordination et d'Execution (CCE). The following year, they called a general strike of Algerian workers and succeeded in encouraging students to boycott schools. Their success gained them more adherents, although a majority of the population remained, and always remained, outside the FLN. The Front then began a campaign of urban bombings and attacks on individual Europeans. The French reacted harshly with mass killings and torture to elicit information about the Front's activities.

The leaders fled to Morocco and Tunisia, and in 1958 they established a government in exile, the Gouvernement Provisoire de la République Algérienne (GPRA), which several foreign governments recognized. Armies of Algerians were trained at the same time in Tunisia and Morocco.

The war continued to drain France's resources. Criticisms in the United Nations, growing opposition in France, particularly because of the torture, the conviction that all countries should have the right to self-determination, and the threat of civil conflict brought the Fourth Republic to a state of collapse. A military coup in Algiers and a subsequent appeal by distraught political leaders in Paris brought General Charles de Gaulle, hero of World War II, out of retirement. At first he supported reforms in an effort to stop the conflict. He soon realized the war could be ended only by granting self-determination. In 1961 Algerians voted for the idea of self-determination. The French electorate in metropolitan France supported the idea, too. Negotiations with the FLN began in May, 1961, and lasted until July, without resolution of the conflict.

Adding to the difficulties were the series of bombings and assassinations in France and in Algeria carried out by the Secret Army Organization (OAS), a group of Europeans who wished to sabotage negotiations and change the French government. Nonetheless, negotiations resumed in early 1962, at the town of Evian on the Franco-Swiss frontier, and a ceasefire was signed in March. Another referendum on July 1, 1962, brought the country to independence after almost eight years of violence and several hundred thousand deaths.

Independence did not immediately guarantee great change for Algeria. De Gaulle had already announced in February, 1962, that relations of "domination" would be transformed into relations of "cooperation" in the case of Algeria, as in the case of other dependencies. The cooperation the so-called Evian agreements of March provided for was extremely favorable to French interests in General de Gaulle's view: "Close economic and monetary association . . . greater cultural and technical cooperation; privileged position for nationals of each country; . . . rights concerning our research and our extraction of petroleum of the Sahara; continuation of our atomic and space tests in the desert; use of the [naval] base at Mers-el-Kébir and of several airports for our forces for at least fifteen years; the maintenance of our army in Algeria for three years

INDEPENDENCE

where we judge it appropriate."[14] These agreements were soon altered drastically, but it is clear that basic French interests, as far as the government and business were concerned, were protected by July 1, 1962.

Liberation wars against Portugal began in 1961 in Angola under the leadership of Holden Roberto's União des Populações de Angola (UPA), which then transformed itself into the Frente Nacional de Libertação de Angola the following year. Within the next two years the Movimento Popular de Libertação (MPLA), headed by Dr. Neto and supported by the Soviet Union, began somewhat less important military operations in Cabinda and then more important efforts in the east. The União Nacional para a Independência Total de Angola (UNITA) joined the war in the east and central part of the colony in 1966. In Guinea-Bissau Amilcar Cabral's Partido Africana da l'Indepencia de Guine e Cabo Verde (PAIGC) opened a new battle front in 1962 and quickly dominated the struggle. The third anti-Portuguese liberation war was launched in 1964 in Mozambique by Dr. Mondlane's Frente de Libertação de Moçambique (FRELIMO).[15]

PAIGC survived Cabral's assassination in 1971 and had effective control of most of the country by the 1974 coup in Portugal, which hastened the end of the empire, because the new military government in Lisbon recognized the right to self-determination. FRELIMO also survived Dr. Mondlane's murder in 1969 but was less successful except in areas contiguous with Tanzania. Strife among the three movements in Angola facilitated Portuguese control, although Portugal was still obliged to station almost half of its 200,000 troops in Africa in that colony.

By October, 1974, Portuguese troops had left Guinea-Bissau, although its leaders had already declared their country independent on September 24, 1973. Mozambique followed and raised its new flag on June 25, 1975. Cape Verde islands officially won sovereignty on July 5, 1975. The island colony of Soa Tomé and Principe, off the coast of Gabon, had had its own but less active liberation movement, the Movement for the Liberation of Soa Tomé and Principe (MLSTP), and it became independent on July 12, 1975 after negotiations with the Portuguese. The agreed date for Angola's independence was November 11, 1975, and although a coalition of the three movements was supposed to run the government, a civil war that lasted until early 1976 was won by the MPLA.

Outside Algeria, Guinea-Bissau, Mozambique, and Angola, other violent struggles were not wars of liberation. The operations of the Union des Populations du Cameroun (UPC) and the Mau Mau did

---

[14] Charles de Gaulle, *Mémoires d'espoir: le renouveau 1958–1962* (Paris: Plon, 1970), p. 132.

[15] For a history of the movements through 1969 see Paul M. Whitaker, "The Revolutions in 'Portuguese' Africa," *The Journal of Modern African Studies*, VIII, no. 1 (1970): 15–35.

not lead directly to independence, although 10,000 Africans died before the end of the "emergency" in Kenya. Mau Mau definitely contributed to such changes as the opening of higher ranks in the civil service to Africans, some land distribution to Africans, and increased representation of Africans in the legislative council. It may also have convinced Europeans that they should eventually grant independence. For example, a conference in London in 1960 provided for an African majority in the legislative council and in the executive council; Kenyans then knew their country would become independent.

Mau Mau definitely contributed to such changes as the opening of higher ranks in the civil service to Africans, some land distribution to Africans, and increased representation of Africans in the legislative council. It may also have convinced Europeans that they should eventually grant independence. For example, a conference in London in 1960 provided for an African majority in the legislative council and in the executive council; Kenyans then knew their country would become independent.

In an election in February, 1961, the Kenya African National Union (KANU), headed by the alleged former Mau Mau leader, Jomo Kenyatta, won, and he was released from detention. In June, 1963, KANU formed the government and led the country peacefully to independence on December 12, 1963.

In two other countries, Rwanda and Zanzibar, violence led to internal change that had little to do with the issue of independence and did not contribute to independence, at least from a European power. Zanzibar and the Pemba Islands off the east coast of Africa had been ruled since 1830 by the Sultanate, which had come from Oman on the Arabian peninsula. Many Arabs moved to the islands, where they controlled the trade in cloves and considered themselves superior to the Africans and Shirazi of Persian descent. The British Protectorate, which began in 1890, overlay the Arab state, which overlay African communities of Swahili-speaking people.

In December, 1963, the islands peacefully gained their independence from Great Britain, but on January 12, 1964, a secret army attacked the police and Arabs. The leaders of the revolt were members of the Afro-Shirazi Party (ASP), which had lost elections to an Arab-dominated party. At least 5,000 Arabs were killed in the revolt, and the ASP took over the government of the country. Many Arabs left for the mainland, and their lands and properties were seized by the new government, composed of Africans from the mainland and the islands.[16]

Although the British appear not to have played a role in this violence, the Belgians seem to have encouraged the change that took place in Rwanda. After World War II, the Belgians instituted some reforms as stipulated in the trusteeship agreements under the United Nations. The

[16] Michael F. Lofchie, "The Zanzibari Revolution: African Protest in a Racially Plural Society," in Robert I. Rotberg and Ali. A. Mazrui (eds.), *Protest and Power in Black Africa* (New York: Oxford University Press, 1970), pp. 124–67.

Independence

Belgian-controlled church spread ideas of democracy, and the majority Hutu began to get education in church and government schools. The Hutu became increasingly aware of the possibilities for change and resented Tutsi rule.

In March, 1957, a group of Hutu issued a manifesto demanding democratization of their society. They were more interested in altering their relationship with the Tutsi than in altering that with the Belgians. The Tutsi reacted by attacking the Hutu. In June and July, 1960, the Belgians introduced elections in the various towns, with wide suffrage leading to a Hutu victory.

Beginning in 1960, the Hutu started to take revenge on the Tutsi for the violence of 1959 and for the rule of the past centuries. The Belgians did not stand in their way and apparently advised Hutu leaders on steps they could take to make their changes permanent. On January 28, 1961, for example, 3,000 town councilors met at Gitarama and voted for the abolition of the monarchy. After a period of more violence between Hutu and Tutsi, the country became independent July 1, 1962. As in the case of Zanzibar, the violence had nothing to do with independence from the Europeans but, rather, involved the desire for internal change.

Violence took place immediately in Zaïre and Equatorial Guinea as a result of intergroup tensions or competition between politicians. The Belgians, frightened by the riots of January, 1959, began to move quickly to bring about political change, although they did not at first contemplate independence for Zaïre.

A so-called Round Table Conference, convened in Brussels at the beginning of 1960, drew up a constitution called the *Loi Fondamentale*. Elections held in May, 1960, brought to power Patrice Lumumba as prime minister and Joseph Kasavubu as president when the country became independent in June. A mutiny of African troops, the secession of Katanga Province, and the settling of old scores between ethnic groups led to a period of extreme violence, necessitating the intervention of troops from the United Nations from 1960 to 1964.

The failure to begin the process of change earlier also created a violent situation in Equatorial Guinea, Sahara, and Djibouti. In 1964 Guinea became autonomous with an African legislature and executive under the supervision of a Spanish governor. On August 15, 1968, a referendum on the island of Fernando Po and the mainland, Rio Muni, approved an independence constitution with only 61.1 per cent of the vote. In September elections for the presidency and the legislative assembly took place, and on October 12, 1968, the country became independent.

Barely four months later, in February, 1969, violence broke out. Fernando Po threatened to secede, as the Bubi continued to fear for their status, and political leaders fought among themselves for control of the country. During a period of chaos, most of the Spanish left and many Africans were killed. Once again, violence occurred about the time of independence but did not lead to independence, as it had in Algeria.

In the Western Sahara the Spanish left their colony to be divided between Morocco and Mauritania, and evacuated personnel as a local movement, Polisario, claimed independence in 1976. Battles between Moroccans and the Algerian-supported Polisario began. The promise of independence for Djibouti in 1977 brought the threat of violence, too.

Nonviolence and Change. With the exception of Algeria, Kenya, Cameroun, Angola, Guinea-Bissau, Mozambique, Zaïre, and Equatorial Guinea, African states experienced little or no anti-European violence with the coming of independence. Whatever conflicts there were came from party and some ethnic competition, but even then there was no widespread, sustained violence. For example, in the period between 1954 —when Dr. Nkrumah demanded independence for his country—and Ghana's independence in 1957, the country was relatively peaceful. In April, 1954, a new constitution provided for internal self-government. On June 15, elections brought a majority for Nkrumah's Convention Peoples Party (CPP) after intense competition with other parties, such as the National Liberation Movement backed by Ashanti cocoa-producers. In 1956, the British government said that Ghana would become independent after further elections, perhaps in the hope that more conservative parties would weaken the CPP. The Ghanaians complied and went to the polls on July 12 and 17, 1956. The CPP won against the combined efforts of all other parties, which had been organized into the United Party, and kept a majority of seats in the legislature. Kwame Nkrumah was again prime minister. In September, the British set the date for independence, and on March 6, 1957 their flag came down. The Ghanaians got their independence in four years because they asked for it. The same thing happened in Guinea, although under different circumstances.

The Fourth French Republic had introduced legislative assemblies into its African territories in 1946, and reforms in 1957 created African executives. French-speaking elites observed events in Ghana. Although France did not officially recognize the African right to independence in West Africa, Equatorial Africa, Madagascar, or Somaliland, they knew the status of Togo, as well as Cameroun, must change because of their status as United Nations Trust Territories.

The United Nations had specified that Togo would one day become independent, and the British had hoped to integrate their part of the country with Ghana. In June, 1954, they asked the United Nations to supervise a referendum in the near future so that British Togo might become a region in an independent Ghana. In French Togo, a number of dynamic, educated leaders wanted change too, and, fortunately, French administrators agreed with them that the country should at least become autonomous. New legislation thus altered the status of French Togo.

The so-called Togo Statute of April 16, 1955, provided for a type of cabinet, five of whose nine members would be elected by the legislative

INDEPENDENCE

assembly. In fact, however, neither the cabinet nor the assembly had much power. Elections to the assembly in June brought a pro-French group to power, and it asked for autonomy within the existing French Union.

In 1956, the voters of British-controlled Togo voted for unification with Ghana, and French-controlled Togo received a second statute, which created the "Autonomous Republic of Togo," with its own prime minister, Nicholas Grunitsky, and a flag as a symbol of separate identity. Some Togolese asked for an end to trusteeship status, and the United Nations sent a mission there in June, 1957.

The United Nations suggested further elections with universal suffrage, and the French gave up authority over most Togolese affairs except for the crucial control over money, defense, and foreign policy. The April, 1958, elections brought Sylvanus Olympio to power. He was much more interested in change than other leaders, and declared that Togo should become completely independent: "By September [1958] Olympio was negotiating with the new French government to fix the date of complete independence in 1960."[17] The date chosen freely by Olympio was April 27, 1960. The course was set for Togo before Guinea became independent.

Guinea became independent before Togo, however, by simply voting "no" to a new constitution that would have included it and other states of French West Africa, French Equatorial Africa, and Madagascar in a so-called *Communauté*. The *Communauté* would have granted autonomy and identity to each state, but foreign affairs and defense would still have been in the hands of the French. The closeness of the ties would also have ensured economic and cultural dependence. According to the official justification for the proposal, African countries would have an equal voice with France; in fact, the institutions of the *Communauté* were so arranged that the metropole would easily have maintained control.

President de Gaulle did not recognize independence as a legitimate alternative for the African states except for Togo and Cameroun. He knew it could take place but called it "secession," and he vaguely threatened to cut off economic assistance to any country voting against the constitution and thus for independence.

Even though the constitution had been submitted to a committee of African political leaders—Senghor of Senegal, Tsiranana of Madagascar, Lisette of Tchad, Lamine Guèye of Senegal, and the Ivory Coast leader Houphouët-Boigny, a minister in de Gaulle's cabinet at the time—some leaders objected that Africans had not really been consulted. At a meeting in July in Dahomey, they recommended a vote against the constitution and thus for independence. But their commitment to independence was ambiguous. Bakary Djibo, leader of Niger, said he favored independence followed by a free confederation with France. With the exception of Bakary Djibo, the other leaders at the meeting changed their

[17] The chronology is from Mortimer, *France and the Africans*, pp. 298-99.

minds later, perhaps because they understood they could not vote "no" and still receive aid, which they needed more than Guinea. Their idea had been confederation with France after independence, but the French clearly would not accept their initiative or their idea. The President of France said to the Africans: Here is our plan. Take it or leave it.

In August, President de Gaulle toured Africa to encourage support for a "yes" vote. At Dakar, where he was greeted by demonstrators carrying signs calling for independence, he said: "If they want independence, let them take it." In Guinea, after Sékou Touré had announced with éclat that he would tell his people to vote "no," General de Gaulle, in an angry mood, said that Guinea could become independent if it so desired. He hinted, however, that the consequences of such a choice would not be favorable.

On September 28, 1958, voters in the metropole and Africa went to the polls to submit a "yes" or "no" for the constitution of the Fifth Republic. With the exception of Niger and Guinea, African leaders campaigned for a "yes." Because of pressures from the governor, outsider interference from the Ivory Coast, and a high rate of abstentions, Niger finally voted "yes." Sékou Touré's party was better organized than Bakary Djibo's Sawaba, and the country had much more self-confidence because of the richness of its soil and the promise of foreign exchange from the exploitation of mineral resources. Guinea voted "no" with the same massive majority as other states voted "yes" to the constitution.

The French moved quickly, and the country was officially granted *de facto* independence on October 2, 1958. Touré immediately wrote de Gaulle that he wanted his country to remain closely tied with France and the newly born French *Communauté*. He asked de Gaulle for *de jure* recognition of Guinea's independence, insisting that the people of Guinea wished to maintain with France "a solid friendship." To ensure such friendship, President Touré willingly signed a protocol with France in which he agreed that French would remain the official language of Guinea.

On October 15, 1958, the Guinean leader reportedly wrote to President de Gaulle saying he wanted his country to remain in the French monetary zone. At that time, remaining in the franc zone meant that Guinea would have permitted the French to coordinate its foreign trade with other French-speaking states, that exchange rates with foreign currency would be under the control of the French, and that Guinea would not be free to sign trade agreements with countries outside the franc zone without the approval of officials in Paris. Guinea remained in this monetary area until 1960, when it created its own currency.[18]

France had clearly hoped to see Guinean independence fail and immediately tried to weaken the state as much as possible. It pulled out its administrators, and many of them burned their files to disrupt the ad-

---

[18] Georges Chaffard, *Les carnets secrets de la décolonisation*, II (Paris: Calmann-Lévy, 1967): 223.

INDEPENDENCE

ministration. The French stopped the arrival of some teachers; they ceased bank credits, and French companies liquefied and exported assets; they held up rice shipments used to feed the population of Conakry in particular; and lastly, they tried to stir up trouble against Sékou Touré in the Fouta Djalon region. Later, the French government reportedly tried to encourage Guinean exiles in Senegal and the Ivory Coast to organize insurrections against President Touré.

The efforts to weaken or overthrow Touré in order to show the other states the supposed undesirability of independence failed because of Guinean support for Touré and the speedy evolution elsewhere to independence. In neighboring states like Togo, Cameroun, Ghana, and Nigeria, African elites were in power. After an attempt to alter the *Communauté*, all states became independent in 1960. The only exception was the French part of Somaliland, still a French possession.

Two-thirds of Somalia, the parts controlled by Britain and by Italy, became independent peacefully in 1960. In 1958 the inhabitants of the French part had voted for continued dependence, and in March, 1967, the people of the same area voted for a new status of autonomy under French control. The name of the country was changed to the French Territory of the Afars and the Issas. Pressures from other African countries in 1975 and 1976 convinced FTAI's leader, Mr. Ali Aref, to ask for independence. It appeared by mid-1976 that the French would maintain an important military base at Djibouti, but Somalia and Ethiopia might be tempted to invade the territory to protect their own interests.

With the exception of Algeria, North Africa moved peacefully to independence. The Neo-Destour party, founded in 1934, agitated for change. The supporters of the idea of change were mainly the middle classes of merchants and professionals, like their leader, Habib Bourguiba. Artisan groups and workers also supported the Neo-Destour's demand for change, because they hated competition with cheap imported French goods.[19]

The Neo-Destour negotiated with the French for change between 1954 and 1959. The French Prime Minister in 1954, Pierre Mendés-France, prepared the way for internal autonomy and appointed a Tunisian government "to negotiate the Conventions that would grant home rule to Tunisia."[20]

Between 1954 and 1956, the Tunisians won control over many internal affairs, but the French controlled foreign relations, police, and general questions affecting internal security. One reason for French control over internal security was that, as in Cameroun, a movement was developing that wanted to remove the French immediately from the country and to end Bourguiba's power by violent means. The so-called Youssefists who followed Salah Ben Youssef, the former General Secretary of the

[19] Charles A. Micaud, with Leon Carl Brown and Clement Henry Moore, *Tunisia: The Politics of Modernization* (New York: Praeger, 1964), pp. 81–82.
[20] Ibid., p. 89.

Neo-Destour, began a campaign of violence, but the campaign was crushed by the French with Bourguiba's cooperation.

On March 20, 1956, an agreement between the French and the Tunisian government granted what amounted to independence, with the Tunisians obtaining control over their own foreign relations and internal security. Elections took place on March 25, 1956, affirming Neo-Destour dominance. On July 25, 1957, the king was deposed by the declaration of a republic, and on June 1, 1959, the country had a new constitution.

At the other end of the continent, in Lesotho, a newly elected legislature in 1960 began debating constitutional, peaceful change toward independence. The country's leader, or paramount chief, as he was called, supported change and criticized British rule. In November, 1965, the prime minister, Chief Leabua Jonathan, announced the country would become independent. On October 4, 1966, the Kingdom of Lesotho became independent quietly while the world looked with apprehension at the growing tensions in neighboring white-ruled states.

6 Southern Africa

Not all of Africa is politically independent. It is the goal of African nationalism to liberate the remaining colonies from colonial rule and to achieve majority rule in southern Africa.

The White Redoubt

The three African countries that have not yet attained independence based on majority rule—the Republic of South Africa, Rhodesia,[1] and Namibia—are geographically at the southern tip of the continent. South Africa and Rhodesia may be classified as white-supremacist states; Namibia, formerly known as South-West Africa, is *de jure* under the control of the United Nations but in fact is under the thumb of the Republic of South Africa. In addition, nearby Lesotho, Botswana, Swaziland, Malawi, and Zambia, politically independent states, feel the weight of white minority and colonialist influence in South Africa.

Southern Africa, as a coherent, separate entity, is a recent addition to the political map of Africa. It started to take form as a new bloc in response to the movement for control of the colonial state by blacks; the growth of violent resistance by Africans within some of the countries; and the collaboration between the banned African nationalist movements of South Africa and Rhodesia. Today it is recognized as an area committed to the permanent maintenance of white domination, and therefore to the unequivocal repudiation of the principle of majority rule, which is accepted in the rest of Africa.

South Africa's policy of *apartheid* expresses the determination of a 300-year-old white group to retain its privileged social and economic status at all costs. Rhodesia, while equally committed to white domination for the foreseeable future, practices a less rigid separation of the races and permits the Africans a measure of participation in the government of the country but has moved deliberately toward the *apartheid* pattern of South Africa. Namibia is governed and administered by South Africa under the system of *apartheid*.

In these countries (1) both the white minority monopolizing political power and the black majority excluded from it appear to be agreed

---

[1] The territory that became a self-governing British colony in 1923 as Southern Rhodesia is now known as Rhodesia. Its African name is Zimbabwe.

that there is no hope of negotiated gradual change leading to majority rule; (2) the policy of white minority rule is condemned by the United Nations, which is not, however, prepared to compel the white minority governments to change their policies; and (3) the white minority in power faces violent black resistance aimed at achieving majority rule, the resistance being backed by the Organization of African Unity, approved by the United Nations, and supported directly by several African countries. In 1976 the situation underwent a significant change. The Rhodesian government agreed to black-majority rule within two years, and the South African government started moving toward negotiated independence for Namibia.

The potential danger inherent in the attempt to perpetuate white minority rule is underlined by the wide disparity between the white and nonwhite populations in the area as a whole and in each of the individual countries.

WHITE AND AFRICAN POPULATIONS IN SOUTHERN AFRICA

Country	Whites	Africans	Total
South Africa	4,160,000 (17%)	17,745,000 (71%)*	24,920,000
Rhodesia	271,000 (6%)	5,700,000 (94%)	5,971,000
Namibia (South-West Africa)	90,000 (13%)	656,000 (87%)	746,000
	4,521,000 (14%)	24,101,000 (86%)	31,637,000 (100%)

Until 1974 events served to strengthen the forces of white supremacy in Southern Africa. Economic sanctions against Rhodesia, the growth of violent resistance within the three former Portuguese colonies, and continued combined guerrilla activity by the national liberation movements of South Africa, Rhodesia, and Namibia inevitably brought South Africa, Rhodesia, and Portugal closer together. South Africa's wealth, military power, police force, diplomacy, and propaganda were all made available to its partners to help them withstand internal resistance and external pressures. South Africa's skillful use of the "carrott-and-stick" techniques had ensured that Lesotho, Botswana, and Swaziland acted (whether they liked it or not) as buffers against African hostility from the north, while the establishment of diplomatic relations with Malawi provided additional valuable protection to the white

* In addition there are two million "Coloureds" and 700,000 Asians in the Republic of South Africa.

Africans, Coloureds, and Asians in South Africa have now rejected the term "nonwhite" and adopted the term "black." This terminology is now used by the South African Institute of Race Relations and such newspapers as the *Rand Daily Mail*.

supremacist partnership. Southern Africa was thus encouraged to continue to ignore the challenge from independent black Africa and to defy the international community.

By 1976, the area of white redoubt had been greatly reduced; it faced intensified pressure from independent black Africa and the international community; and averting a disastrous race war had become a matter of considerable concern for the United States and the rest of the Western world.

The Republic of South Africa

At the center of the forces committed to the maintenance of white supremacy in the southern extremity of Africa is the Republic of South Africa with its policy of *apartheid*.

The Origins of Apartheid

Although the word *apartheid* (pronounced apart-hate) is today familiar throughout the world, it was almost unknown in the land of its birth only twenty-five years ago. An Afrikaans [2] word meaning literally "separateness," it saw the light of day as the name of the policy adopted by the Nationalist Party, which won the South African general election of May 26, 1948. But one will look in vain for the word *apartheid* in the edition of the standard Afrikaans-English dictionary published as late as 1946,[3] and used in the schools and universities of South Africa. It achieved lexical legitimacy in 1950. In the first volume of the definitive Afrikaans dictionary published by the government, *apartheid* is defined as

a political policy in South Africa based on the broad principles of (a) differentiation according to differences of race and/or colour and/or level of civilization, as opposed to *assimilation*; (b) the maintenance and perpetuation of the separate identity of the different colour groups which the population comprises and the separate development of these groups according to their own nature, tradition and aptitude, as opposed to *segregation*. In its practical application the policy comprises regulations which include, inter alia, measures designed to achieve a degree of merely local separation e.g. in respect of residence, public accommodation, transportation, entertainment, etc.; measures concerning political rights, e.g. separate voters' rolls, separate representation in Parliament and Provincial Councils; further territorial segregation e.g. the setting aside of comparatively large areas for the exclusive use of one population group e.g. the native reserves.[4]

[2] Afrikaans, by law one of the official languages of the Republic of South Africa, is a derivative of the Dutch language introduced by the settlers who came from Holland in 1652. Their descendants—those who regard Afrikaans as their mother tongue—are Afrikaners.
[3] *Tweetalige Woordeboek* (Afrikaans-English) deur Prof. D. B. Bosman, I. W. van der Merwe M. A. en ander (Nasionale Pers, Beperk, Kaapstad, Bloemfontein en Port Elizabeth, 1946).
[4] *Woordeboek van die Afrikaanse Taal* A-C (Die Staatdrukker, Pretoria, 1950).

The present usage of the word *apartheid* has acquired a connotation that goes far beyond its South African dictionary limits and has come to be universally accepted as an appropriate term to describe undesirable race relations in other parts of the world.

The South African government has become increasingly sensitive to this widespread use of the word *apartheid* in a pejorative sense. Attempts to find more palatable substitutes have met with no success. Such terms as "separate development," "parallel development," and "separate freedoms" having failed to gain acceptance during the past twenty years, the Minister of Bantu Administration and Development announced on February 15, 1970, that he had renamed South Africa's official policy. It would henceforward be called "multinational development." But all the indications are that this latest attempt to make the *apartheid* flower smell sweeter by giving it a new name has shared the fate of its predecessors. The term *apartheid* seems to be firmly entrenched as part of the international vocabulary.

When Afrikaner nationalism came to power in 1948, it inherited a system of government and administration that, through its policy of "segregation," rested firmly on the concept of white supremacy within a framework of separation of the races in all walks of life. But the policy had come to be implemented in a laissez-faire fashion; laws were not enforced as strictly as they might have been, and official eyes were frequently closed to contact, at many levels, across the color line. It remained for the new regime to act swiftly in giving to the existing pattern a rigidity, a harshness, and an over-all inhumanity that had been unknown before or elsewhere except in Nazi Germany, which many white South African leaders had viewed with admiration.

Dr. Hendrik Verwoerd, former Prime Minister and the architect of *apartheid*, supported Nazi propaganda and pro-Nazi activity during World War II. During the same period Balthazar J. Vorster, the present Prime Minister, said: "We stand for Christian Socialism which is an ally of National Socialism. You can call it the anti-democratic principle if you wish. In Italy it is called Fascism, in Germany National Socialism, and in South Africa, Christian Socialism."[5]

The new government had come to power with the aid of the *Broederbond* (Band of Brothers), which infiltrated the public service, churches, and the professions and continues at present to ensure Afrikaner dominance within the white group.

Following its success in the election of 1948, the Nationalist Party altered its fascism in one way in order to unite all whites. The newly elected government tried to establish good relations with the Jewish leadership and lifted the ban on Jewish membership of the party that had been imposed during the war. But there continued to be manifestations of anti-Semitism,[6] and antiblack measures increased under the doctrine of *apartheid*.

[5] Sarah Gertrude Millin, *The Reeling Earth* (London: Faber, 1945), pp. 66–67.
[6] Leslie Rubin, "South African Jewry and Apartheid," *Africa Report*, XV (February, 1970): 22.

Apartheid in Practice

According to the South African government, *apartheid* is a policy designed to ensure the survival of the white South African nation, while dealing justly with the Africans and the other black groups. It promises the Africans self-fullfillment and full development in their own separate homelands, and adequate provision for the separate development of the other blacks. The government maintains that it is pursuing this policy honestly and sincerely and that it is the only policy that can serve the best interests of all sections of the population, white and black alike.[7]

Apartheid comprises four elements: (1) the enforced separation of white and black; (2) the control of African movement and employment; (3) the "separate development" of the black groups; and (4) a police-state apparatus, controlled by a white minority, designed to curb resistance and opposition from the black majority comprising over 80 per cent of the population.

Enforced Racial Separation

A vast apparatus of laws and administrative procedures separates white from black in every walk of life. A population register that contains the names of all South African citizens classifies them as "White," "Bantu" (African), or "Coloured," as the case may be. The "Coloured" group is divided into seven subgroups: Cape Coloured, Malay, Griqua, Chinese, Indian, Other Asian, and Other Coloured. The Japanese, because of the importance of their trade relations with South Africa, are accorded an honorary status as whites.[8] Every person who has attained the age of sixteen must possess an identity card, which includes a photograph and describes the bearer as white, colored, or African; when the holder is an African it must, in addition, state the ethnic group or tribe to which he is assigned.

But classification in the population register is never final. Even if a person has been classified as "white" and provided with the appropriate identity card, he may at any time be reclassified as a colored person. The consequences of such reclassification for the person concerned and for his family are always very serious; in some cases they are disastrous.

The sign *White Only/Blankes Alleen* (like all other notices, usually in both official languages) appears on park benches; at the entrances to post offices, railway stations, cinemas, theaters, libraries, museums, art galleries, zoos, and sports grounds; on bridges and beaches; on buses and trains; outside hospitals and clinics. Within buildings (private and public alike), it will invariably appear above at least one of the elevators.

---

[7] For a fuller exposition of the S.A. government case, see Leonard M. Thompson, *The Republic of South Africa* (Boston: Little, Brown, 1966), pp. 3–7.

[8] *The Star*, Johannesburg, January 30, 1971.

Marriage, sexual relations, and acts of physical intimacy falling short of sexual intercourse, for example, kissing or fondling, between white and black are prohibited. There is strict residential separation of the groups in the towns, the Africans, Asians, and coloreds being required to occupy townships or areas set aside for each group several miles from the town itself, which is reserved for exclusive occupation by whites.[9] The sick are treated in separate hospitals or in strictly separated sections of the same hospital. Black victims of an accident may not be carried in the ambulance used for white victims; there are separate ambulances for white and black. The government may prevent Africans from attending services in a church where whites worship, or from participating in social activities arranged by a church for its white and black members. There are separate schools for whites, Africans, Asians, and coloreds. Blacks get their higher education at ethnic colleges established for Asians and coloreds or, in the case of Africans, at the ethnic college the student is required to attend according to his official classification; that is, if he is classified as a Zulu, he must enroll at the University of Zululand, even if his home is in another part of the country.[10]

Control of Movement and Employment

Stringent laws control the movement of Africans. The purpose of these laws (the "pass" laws) is to prevent a permanent African population in the towns and at the same time to maintain a controlled supply of migrant labor to satisfy the needs of commerce and industry. All Africans whose labor is no longer required (either because the needs of local employers are fully satisfied or because they are unfit for employment because of age or ill health) are removed to putative homelands in the areas allocated to the tribal group to which they are assigned by law. In many cases, they have never lived in the areas to which they are removed.

An African permitted to remain in a town must possess a reference book, to be carried on his person at all times and produced on demand of a policeman or any one of numerous officials in the Department of Bantu Administration and Development. The book must contain information relating to his right to be in the town and to work, such as the signature of his employer and of officials in labor bureaus, as well as receipts for the various taxes he is required to pay, such as the poll tax. According to the Commissioner of Police, for the year 1969–1970

---

[9] See Barry Higgs, *The Group Areas Act and Its Effects* (United Nations Unit on *Apartheid*, 1971).

[10] The list of prohibitions and restrictions designed to ensure separation between white and black is formidable. Some idea of the range and scope of these prohibitions, and of the penalties applicable, can be obtained from *Apartheid in Practice* (New York: United Nations OPI, 1972), statements 103, 106, 108, 118, 119, 133, 143, 169, 171, 172, 223, 224, 225, 226, 228. Rev. ed. (New York: United Nations, 1976. OPI/553).

Southern Africa

an average of 2,500 persons per day were arrested, detained in jail, and charged under the "pass" laws. For the year 1972–1973 the average had dropped to 1413 persons charged per day.

In addition to the direct manipulation of the flow of African labor into and from the towns, there are laws that prevent an African from doing skilled work; empower the government at any time to reserve specified occupations exclusively for whites; and deny to Africans the generally accepted rights of workers to strike and organize in trade unions.[11] An African worker's opportunity of acquiring skills and efficiency is limited by the grossly inferior educational facilities available to Africans. For the year 1973–1974 the per capita government expenditure on the education of white children was $677, on African children $40. Schooling for white children is free and compulsory; for Africans, it is not compulsory, and African parents have to find the money for fees, uniforms, and books. The tribal colleges Africans are required to attend for their higher education provide instruction and facilities that are inferior to those available in the white universities. In the academic year 1968–1969, degrees and diplomas were awarded to 10,740 whites; the awards to Africans totaled 277.[12]

The earnings of African workers are considerably lower than those of white workers. Recent statistics show that a white construction worker earns more than five times the amount paid to an African doing comparable work. In manufacturing, the approximate monthly earnings of white and black workers were $342 and $64 respectively; in mining, $395 and $24 (with some additional payments in kind) respectively. The inequality persists in the over-all earnings of white and black. In 1973 the average monthly household income of a white family was $720, of an African family $77.[13]

Separate Development

The promise of "separate development" for the nonwhite groups that the new government made when it came to power in 1948 had an ob-

---

[11] In September, 1970, African workers on a housing project were using garden trowels to lay building blocks, because if they used builder's trowels, their work would be classified as "skilled" in terms of the law. This took place with the full knowledge of the Department of Labor and the Department of Community Development. These government departments were thus parties to the circumvention of the South African law that reserves the occupation of bricklaying, in the area where the Africans were employed, exclusively for whites. *Race Relations News*, vol. 32, no. 9 (September 1970), p. 6.

In 1973, following widespread strikes by African workers, a new law legalized African strikes, but subject to very stringent limitations.

[12] *Industrialization, foreign capital and forced labour in South Africa* (New York, United Nations, 1970), paras. 68–73. (Serial number: ST/PSCA/Ser.A/10.) This study was prepared by Sean Gervasi, research officer in economics at the Institute of Commonwealth Studies, Oxford University, at the request of the United Nations Unit on *Apartheid*.

[13] *Ibid.*, paras. 15 and 16; *Survey of Race Relations*, 1974, p. 107.

vious appeal to the whites (particularly the Afrikaners), who had been warned so insistently during the election against the *swart gevaar* (black menace).

In 1950, the government decided to investigate the potential of the Bantu areas (formerly known as the Native Areas or the Reserves) for implementing "positive" *apartheid*. The investigation was carried out by the Commission for the Socio-Economic Development of the Bantu Areas Within the Union of South Africa under the chairmanship of Professor F. R. Tomlinson. It was known as the Tomlinson Commission, and all its members were carefully chosen for their sympathy with government policies.

The Tomlinson Report, completed in 1954 and summarized for the public two years later, was a great disappointment to the government.[14] The members of the commission did, it was true, choose separate development rather than integration as the answer to South Africa's race problem. But in doing so, they produced a forbidding documentation of the immense difficulties that stood in the way of converting the Bantu areas into viable homelands for the African people.

The commission emphasized three points: that rehabilitation of these neglected areas was a matter of the greatest urgency; that the expenditure of very large sums of money was essential; and that fundamental changes were required in the social and economic structure of the areas. It called for government expenditures of $280 million within ten years to relieve the economic backwardness of the areas, urged the introduction of white capital and industrial enterprise, and proposed that Africans be granted freehold title to land to encourage progress. The government disagreed sharply with its own hand-picked experts. It decided that the commission had exaggerated the expenditure required, and the other two proposals were rejected summarily. A total expenditure of $100 million was approved, and an initial sum of $10 million was voted. By 1961, only $22 million had been spent, and though considerable sums of money have been made available since then the grave warning of the Tomlinson Commission has not been heeded.

But the most far-reaching—and, for the government, the most disturbing—conclusion of the Tomlinson Commission related to population growth in South Africa. It was estimated that, by the year 2000, the total population would be 31 million—21 million Africans, 4.5 million whites, 4 million coloreds, and 1.5 million Asians. It was maintained that, even if the commission's economic proposals were put into effect, the Bantu areas would not be able to accommodate more than 70 per cent of the African population. Thus, the commission had come to the conclusion that, even if the policy of separate development was implemented, *under the optimal conditions prescribed by the commission*, the Africans, forty-five years later, would still substantially outnumber

[14] U. G. 61 of 1955 (Pretoria: Government Printer). The full report comprises 18 volumes, containing 51 chapters totaling 3,755 pages and includes 598 tables and an atlas of 66 large-scale maps.

SOUTHERN AFRICA 117

whites in their own areas—6.5 million Africans to 4 million whites. The government's own experts had, in effect, demonstrated that the policy of separate development could not remove the white minority's fear of being overwhelmed by a black majority.

The commission's prognostications have been justified by developments since the report was issued. The African population in the white areas has steadily increased. According to preliminary information based on the 1970 census, the number of Africans in the urban areas increased by 1,200,000 in the last ten years; 53.3 per cent of the Africans, or almost 8 million, live in the white areas with fewer than 4 million whites; and the proportion of whites to the total population, which was 19.3 per cent in 1960, has dropped to 17.8 per cent. The significant fact is that, notwithstanding more than two decades of "separate development," including extensive forcible removal of Africans from the towns, more than half the Africans are not yet living in the Bantu areas. They continue to live in "white" South Africa.[15]

Three years before the Tomlinson Report was completed, the government had enacted a law that was to lay the foundation for the future system of African tribal "homelands." The Bantu Authorities Act, passed in 1951, purported to ensure that Africans would conduct their affairs in accordance with their own traditions.

The tribal authority, consisting of a chief or headman and a number of appointed councilors, is the basic unit in a hierarchical system that extends through district and regional to territorial authorities. The Bantu Affairs Commissioner (who is, of course, white) may veto the appointment of any person appointed as a councilor by the chief or headman; the Minister of Bantu Administration and Development may, at any time, depose any chief or headman and cancel the appointment of any councilor. The minister or any one of a number of white officials may, whenever he chooses, attend any meeting of a tribal authority and take part in the deliberations. A commissioned police officer may attend such meetings whenever he pleases; a policeman may attend when he has been duly instructed to do so by a commissioned officer.[16]

The Bantu Authorities System was received by the Africans with attitudes ranging from suspicion to hostility; in some areas, chiefs who accepted the system faced violent opposition form the tribesmen. In the Transkei, from 1959 onward, chiefs and headmen were murdered, their property was destroyed, and there was widespread civil disobedience. The violent resistance continued for two years, until is was

[15] *The Star*, Johannesburg, October 3, 1970. See also Gavin Maasdorp, *Economic Development for the Homelands* (S.A.: Institute of Race Relations, Johannesburg, 1974), 28–31.

[16] Hahlo and Kahn, *The Union of South Africa: The Development of Its Laws and Constitution* (London: Stevens & Son, 1960), pp. 800–801; Leo Marquard, *Peoples and Policies of South Africa*, 4th ed. (London: Oxford University Press, 1969), pp. 119–26; Bantu Authorities Act No. 68 of 1951, sections 2–4; Proclamation No. 180 of 1956, sections 11(5), 13(2) and (4) and 16; G. N. No. 5955 dated October 11, 1957, Regulation No. 6.

suppressed by the use of extensive police powers of arrest, control of movement, and banishment, and with the aid of military forces sent into the affected areas.

Ultimately, the government succeeded in getting the new system established, using a combination of force and inducement. When it was considered necessary, influential opposition was removed; from 1955 to 1958, thirty-four chiefs and headmen were deposed.[17] In most cases the fact that chiefs are paid by the government was sufficient to ensure compliance; in some cases a chief who cooperated with the government could expect an increase in his subsidy. There were other inducements, such as increased powers of local taxation granted to a tribal authority about to be established. There were also deterrents, such as a threat to reduce or withhold funds for social services in the area. By 1968, although small pockets of opposition continued to exist, several hundred Bantu authorities (including a number at the territorial level) had been established throughout the country, and since then the system has moved steadily toward completion.[18] The extension of the retribalizing process to urban areas was begun with the enactment of the Urban Councils Act of 1961. The first council was established in 1963; by 1968, there were twelve. The councils, which are subject to arbitrary government control, like the tribal authorities, encourage the representation of ethnic units within an urban area instead of the African population as a whole. They do not offer the Africans any greater powers than those provided by the advisory boards the councils replaced.[19]

By 1959 much had been done to ensure *separation*: nothing had been done to honor the commitment to *development*. Criticism of government policies, within the country and abroad, was mounting.

The government responded by enacting the Promotion of Bantu Self-Government Act. A white paper explaining the background and the objects of the new law declared its purpose to be "provision for the gradual development of self-governing Bantu national units." The act recognizes eight national units: North-Sotho, South-Sotho, Swazi, Tsonga, Tswana, Venda, Xhosa, and Zulu. (It has since become clear that this classification is somewhat arbitrary. The October, 1968, issue of *Scope*, an official publication, lists nine named "Bantu Nations"— the Swazi omitted, West Sotho and Ndebele added—and a tenth group called "others.") The act also provides for the conferment upon territorial authorities, established under the Bantu Authorities Act, of legislative authority and the right to impose taxes and undertake works. It makes provision, too, for the appointment of five white commissioners-general "to form a direct link for consultation between the units and the government, and to give guidance to the units in order to promote

[17] *House of Assembly Debates*, 1959, col. 324.
[18] *Survey of Race Relations*, 1963, pp. 107–10; 1965, pp. 133–34; 1966, pp. 170–71; 1968, pp. 145–47; 1969, pp. 128–31.
[19] *Survey of Race Relations*, 1961, p. 119; 1965, pp. 164–65; 1966, pp. 170–71; 1968, pp. 180–82; 1969, p. 155.

their general development"; and territorial authorities are empowered to nominate Africans as their representatives in urban areas.

The act abolished the existing parliamentary representation of the Africans. Since 1936, the Africans of the Cape Province had been represented in the House of Assembly by three white members out of a total of 156; the Africans of all four provinces had been represented in the Senate by four white members out of a total of forty-eight. This complete and summary disfranchisement of four-fifths of the South African population was justified in an official statement by the twofold argument that the existing representation was "the source of European fears of being swamped by the Bantu in the political sphere" and that the "legitimate needs and desires" of the Africans would receive better attention under the new system.

In 1962 the government announced its intention to grant "self-government" to the Transkei. The Transkei Constitution Act was passed, and in 1963 the first "self-governing" African national homeland, or Bantustan, came into existence.[20]

The powers granted by the constitution do not cover the whole of the traditional area of the Transkei, and the South African government controls the Transkei Legislative Assembly. The assembly is, however, empowered to legislate with respect to a number of matters: taxation, interior courts, public works, welfare services, and "generally all matters which in the opinion of the State President and according to his written directions are of a merely local or private nature in the Transkei." Above all, the legislative competency of the assembly is subject to the overriding limitation that *no law passed by the assembly (even when it relates to a matter within its competence) may take effect unless it receives the approval of the President of the Republic of South Africa*.[21]

In the economic domain, advancement in the Transkei has been hampered by inadequate funds and South Africa's refusal to permit normal industrial development within the territory. In 1959 the Bantu Investment Corporation was established, controlled by a board of white directors appointed by the South African government. In 1965 the Xhosa Development Corporation was established. But the record of both corporations belies the claims made for them by the government. Over-all financial aid has been inadequate, providing assistance to a few small undertakings, while achievement in creating new opportunities for employment has been insignificant. Healthy industrial development is seriously inhibited by South Africa's policy of "border industries," that is, the refusal to permit white capital and initiative within the Bantu areas, accompanied by inducements to whites to set up industries

---

[20] For a more detailed description of the events preceding the enactment of the Transkei Constitution Act, see Leslie Rubin, "The Republic of South Africa: White Politics," in John A. Davis and James K. Baker (eds.), *Southern Africa in Transition* (New York: Frederick A. Praeger, 1966), pp. 20–42.

[21] For further details of the Transkei Constitution, see Carter, Karis, and Stultz, *South Africa's Transkei: The Politics of Domestic Colonialism* (Northwestern University Press, 1967), pp. 120–24, 185–88.

close to the borders, cheap labor being supplied by the inhabitants of the Bantu area.[22]

The result is that the Transkei provides employment within the territory for only a handful of its people, while hundreds work in the mines, factories, and farms of white South Africa. The problems created by inadequate employment opportunities within the territory have been increased by the repatriation of Transkei citizens employed in the Cape Province. The enforced removal of men from jobs in South Africa and their enforced return to a putative homeland that has no jobs to offer them continues, notwithstanding repeated protests by Chief Minister Matanzima.[23]

Elsewhere, in the other Bantu areas, development has also been sporadic and slow. Progress has been made in the establishment of Bantu Authorities, but in some areas (for example, Zululand), opposition to the system continued until 1969.[24] During 1967 a group of prominent businessmen, city councilors, and municipal officials was taken on a conducted tour of the future "homelands" in the Transvaal. They were critical of the slow rate of progress and did not believe that these areas could be made sufficiently attractive to reverse the increasing flow of Africans to the urban areas. Dr. J. Adendorff, general manager of the Bantu Investment Corporation, addressing a conference of SABRA (a pro-government race relations organization), said, "At the present rate of development the Bantu homelands will never be able to absorb the increases in the Bantu population and assure decent standards of living."

The Bantu Homelands Constitution Act, passed in 1971, provided for the granting of "self-government" to other national units along the lines of the provisions of the Transkei Constitution. A number of legislative assemblies were created during that year to take the place of territorial authorities already established under the Bantu Authorities Act.

---

[22] Carter, et al., *South Africa's Transkei: The Politics of Domestic Colonialism*, p. 178; *Race Relations News*, vol. 29, no. 12, (December, 1967), p. 4; *Survey of Race Relations*, 1965, pp. 125–27; 1966, pp. 136–40. In 1968, the Promotion of Economic Development of Bantu Homelands Act provided for the creation of further corporations, all under government control, and with restrictions on their activities calculated to prevent the creation of any but minimal opportunities for the economic advancement of the people. This law perpetuates declared government policy—condemned by leading South African economists—of preventing the introduction of white capital or initiative into the Bantu homelands. (*The Star*, March 16 and 23, 1968.) Economic development since the enactment of this law has been disappointing. (*Survey of Race Relations*, 1969, pp. 138-41); *Race Relations News*, vol. 29, no. 12 (December, 1967), p. 6. Since 1973 there have been some relaxations on an *ad hoc* basis of the prohibition of white capital.

[23] D. Hobart-Houghton, "Economic Development in the Reserves," *Race Relations Journal*, vol. 29, no. 1 January/March, 1962, pp. 10–19; Carter et al., *South Africa's Transkei: The Politics of Domestic Colonialism*, p. 177; *News/Check*, Johannesburg, October 27, 1967.

[24] *Survey of Race Relations*, 1969, p. 131. By 1974 eight "homelands" had become "self-governing": Transkei, Ciskei, Bophuthatswana, Lebowa, Gazankulu, Vendaland, Qwaqwa, and Kwazulu.

In June, 1971, the proposed Zulu homeland presented the government with a challenge. Chief Gatsha Buthelezi, speaking for the 4 million Zulus (the largest of the nine major African nations), declared that, while he had reservations about the policy of separate development, he was agreeable, "operating from powerlessness," to the establishment of a homeland for his people.

Buthelezi's emergence as a forthright African leader of considerable political ability led to attempts by the government to prevent his election as chief executive of the Zulu Territorial Authority. The attempts failed. And when the authority met in 1972 under Buthelezi's leadership to consider the proposed constitution for the Zulu homeland, it refused to endorse the provision requiring members of the legislative assembly to swear allegiance to the Republic of South Africa. The authority declared that it was willing only to swear allegiance to the state president and the Zulu king. Buthelezi explained that he could not support allegiance to the South African government because he disapproved of many of its laws.

The stance of the Zulu nation as expressed by its leader was a shock to white South Africa as a whole and served to reinforce the fears of many of Prime Minister Vorster's supporters that the creation of independent African homelands would undermine white authority and power.[25] In 1974 Prime Minister Vorster rejected a request by all the leaders of the eight "homelands" for an increased allocation of land to the African people, and he reaffirmed that the area available would remain what it had been, namely 13 per cent of the total land area of South Africa.

In 1975 Chief Kaiser Matanzima announced that the Transkei would become independent in 1976, pursuant to agreement reached with the South African government. (The leaders of the remaining seven "homelands" had announced earlier that they rejected the offer of "independence.") African Foreign Ministers, speaking at the United Nations, declared that the Transkei's application for membership of United Nations would be rejected, and at independence Transkei became an outcast.

Separate development also applies to the other black groups, the colored and the Asians. The Coloured group, numbering 2 million, has its origins in unions between the Dutch settlers and the seventeenth-century slave population in the Cape. The majority of them live in the Cape Province. In 1956 they were deprived of the common roll franchise that they had enjoyed for more than a century; instead, the Coloured voters of the Cape Province were placed on a separate roll

---

[25] *Survey of Race Relations,* 1971, pp. 24–29. Buthelezi has since continued his courageous stand by demanding allocation of more land and leading a call for a federal union of all "homelands." The constitution for Kwazulu, represented by Buthelezi, has not come into effect because the South African government has so far failed to announce a date for the first election. See also *Survey of Race Relations,* 1974, pp. 193–95.

and permitted to elect four representatives (white) to Parliament. In addition, the government later established a Council for Coloured Affairs, to advise the government on all matters affecting the interests of the colored people. In 1964 a new body was substituted, called the Colored Representative Council, to be replaced in 1968 by another council consisting of forty elected and ten nominated members, with power to draft laws relating to certain specified matters affecting the colored people. No law may take effect unless it has received the prior approval of the Minister of Coloured Affairs.

In 1968 two laws were enacted that completed the process of imposing on the Coloured people almost total social and political separation. One of these laws abolished colored representation in the South African parliament; the abolition took effect in 1971, when the term of office of the four white representatives of the Coloured people came to an end. The other law, the Prohibition of Improper Political Interference Act, prevents the association of Coloured persons with whites as members of the same political party or in any other related political activity. The second election to the Council, in 1975, resulted in an overwhelming victory for the Labor Party that had announced that it rejected *apartheid* and called for Coloured representation by their own people in the South African parliament. Faced with this deadlock, the government rushed a law through parliament empowering the Minister of Coloured Relations to exercise the powers and functions of the Council, and the Council voted to adjourn until 1976.

Perhaps the most eloquent comment on what separate development has meant for the Coloured people is that hundreds of them have left South Africa during the last few years and continue to do so; among them are men who have played a leading role in various professional and business fields.

The Asians, who number 614,000 and whose origins go back to immigration from India more than a century ago, have made a significant contribution to the economic development of South Africa. For them there is a department of Indian Affairs and a nominated South African Indian Council, which has advisory functions only and consists of twenty-five members appointed by the (white) Minister of Indian Affairs. The government has announced that a partly elected council will eventually be established. A recent study of the large Indian community of Johannesburg gives an idea of the effect of *apartheid* on the Indians of South Africa. It records that many long-settled Indian residents fear economic ruin as a result of their enforced removal from homes and businesses under *apartheid* laws; that there is a growing emigration of Indian teachers, doctors, and lawyers to Canada and other countries; and that a sense of insecurity is causing many Indian businessmen to seek investment outside South Africa.[26]

[26] *Survey of Race Relations*, 1969, 15–16; Peter Randall and Yusuf Desai, *From "Coolie" Location to Group Area: Johannesburg's Indian Community* (Johannesburg, South African Institute of Race Relations, August 1967).

To sum up, the policy of separate development appears to be incompatible with the facts of South African life. In relation to the Africans its feasibility is becoming increasingly doubtful because of the poverty of the "homelands" and the dependence of the South African economy on African labor. As to the Coloured people and the Asians, they simply do not fit into the pattern of "separate development." Neither group has a traditional "homeland," and the Coloured people (often called "brown Afrikaners") have laid down deep roots in white South African society through their strong ties—in language, culture, and religion—with the Afrikaner.

The Police-State Apparatus

The fourth and last element in *apartheid* is a police-state apparatus designed to curb black resistance. The black opposition to the *apartheid* laws has been met by the government with a number of increasingly ferocious laws used to stamp out all activity that aims to change the existing system. The cumulative effect of these laws and the way in which they are administered is to make a mockery of South Africa's claim that its system is based on the rule of law. While there is an independent judiciary that is appointed and functions superficially according to recognized Western standards, in fact, the court's powers (particularly in the case of Africans) to promote justice and remedy injustice are severely limited. Because of the array of laws granting to policemen and other officials widespread powers of arrest, detention, search, and interrogation, the area within which the courts are permitted to reach an independent decision is greatly circumscribed. The extent to which individuals may be deprived of fundamental rights by the arbitrary act of a Cabinet Minister, a policeman, or another official is apparent from *Apartheid in Practice*, statements 190, 264, 265, 268, 269, 270, 274, 280, 282, 284, 285, 287, 290, 299.

Some of the aspects of the administration of justice in South Africa that have caused concern are the frequent use of the death penalty, the lawless conduct of the police, and the common disparity between sentences for white and nonwhite offenders, particularly in the lower courts. South Africa accounts for nearly half the executions carried out in the whole world: in the latter half of 1966, sixty-six persons were executed — one white, nineteen colored, and forty-six African. There has been a marked increase in the number of persons executed in the last two decades. While it is the general rule for a black to be executed for the rape of a white woman, no white has ever been executed for the rape of a black woman: the usual punishment is imprisonment, which rarely exceeds five years. An example of the common practice of imposing heavier sentences on black offenders than on whites is the report that appeared in the Johannesburg *Star* on April 20, 1968, of two crimes and the respective sentences: An African man was sentenced to imprisonment for two years for entering vehicles in a public street at 3 A.M.: a white man alleged to have shot an African boy in the lip, forehead, and back with an air rifle, was fined $42 or thirty days' imprisonment.

In 1975 thirteen members of the South African Students Organization (SASO) and the Black Peoples Convention (BPC) were charged with offenses under the Terrorism Act. Professor Charles-Albert Morand, who attended the trial as an observer for the International Commission of Jurists and interviewed several of the accused, reported that they had been subjected to "various acts of violence and torture" by policemen and other officials while under detention and awaiting trial.

The South African government has extended its police-state activities to include the harassment and intimidation of South African refugees in Britain. Following disclosures by *The Observer*, the matter was raised in the House of Commons in December, 1971. The parliamentary debate disclosed that, since 1966, the South African security service had employed agents in Britain to infiltrate anti-*apartheid* organizations, recruit informers, and carry out surveillance of British persons as well as South African exiles.[27]

Within South Africa, the activities of the Special Branch of the Police and the recently established Bureau of State Security (BOSS)[28] are reinforced by a continuing process of discouraging dissent. Other governmental organs use a variety of methods to control free expression of opinion and to intimidate opponents of *apartheid*.

There is strict censorship of books and films.[29] Thousands of books—many of them accepted as literature in the Western world—are banned. Grounds for prohibition are never furnished, but the general policy (apart from prohibition of pornographic or blasphemous material) appears to be to exclude all material either critical of *apartheid* or approving of interracial association, particularly sex relations between white and black. The Publications Act, passed in 1974, increased the powers of the government to declare publications or films "undesirable." Any publication or film favoring intermarriage between white and black is deemed, without the need for further proof, to be "undesirable."

Weekly newspapers and magazines have been banned. The Liberal Party newspaper *Contact* and the anti-*apartheid* magazine *The New African* were harassed out of existence by prosecution under emergency regulations and the requirement of large cash deposits as a prerequisite to continued publication. In addition, the publication, in any form, of the writings of many South Africans now abroad is prohibited by law.[30]

[27] *The Observer*, London, November 14, December 12 and 19.
[28] See *Apartheid in Practice*, statements 295–300. See also *Apartheid in Practice* (1976), statement 200.
[29] *Ibid.*, statements 176, 177, 179.
[30] *Ibid.*, statements 198, 199.

The denial or withdrawal of a passport is one of the indirect methods used to curb dissent. South Africans in the country know that criticism of government policies will imperil their chances of getting a passport and may result in the withdrawal of a passport already issued; those abroad have every reason to fear that such criticism will have a similar result. In 1961, when the distinguished author Alan Paton returned from a visit to the United States where he had received the Freedom Award and been interviewed about South Africa, his passport was withdrawn as soon as he returned. It was not restored to him until 1971.

An African seeking a passport must deposit with his application $240 if he is traveling to Europe, $480 if he is traveling to the United States. He must also produce recommendations from two persons of standing and a report from the appropriate local authority testifying to his good character and stating that "he is considered a fit and proper person to visit countries where there is no racial segregation."[31]

The government may refuse a passport but grant the applicant an exit permit. This enables him to leave the country but subject to the condition (even though he was born in South Africa) that he will never return. The holder of an exit permit who returns to South Africa is guilty of a criminal offense punishable by imprisonment and removal from the country after he has served his sentence.[32]

In 1975 some *apartheid* prohibitions were modified as part of declared government policy to "improve race relations," that is some theaters were conditionally opened to blacks; the government called on officials to enforce the pass laws in a "more humane" manner. During the same period opponents of *apartheid*, mainly blacks and white students, were banned, held in detention, and imprisoned. The relaxation of *apartheid* was peripheral. The essential structure of the system remained unaffected.

A Rigid Caste Society

We can now attempt to describe—in the light of the foregoing discussion of *apartheid*—how *apartheid* looks to the blacks of South Africa. A quarter-century of *apartheid* has created a rigid caste society unique in the world of today. There are many countries where racial prejudice exists, and some where racial discrimination is practiced, but it is only in South Africa that discriminaton based on race or color is enforced by law and officially entrenched by the organs of political and economic power as an essential and permanent part of national policy. The overriding criterion applied to determine the place of a man in the life of his country is his race as determined by law. An arbitrary system of racial classification confines a person to membership in either the white or one of the black groups, and the groups are mutually

[31] *The Star*, Johannesburg, February 26, 1972.
[32] See *Apartheid In Practice*, statement 204.

exclusive except for association in a master-servant relationship. Law has created rigid barriers that separate the different groups. Public policy sedulously buttresses these barriers, and under combined legal and social pressures they have become virtually impassable.

Above all, to be classified as "white" is to be recognized as dominant and superior; classification as black is equated with subordination and inferiority. To maintain strict separation between groups within this caste society, it is necessary to have many officials and to arm them with wide powers. The number of officials charged with the task of ensuring compliance with the large body of race laws grows year by year. So do the powers with which these officials are vested. What are known as civil rights in the Western world tend in South Africa more and more to mean—almost completely for Africans, somewhat less for colored persons and Asians, but increasingly for whites as well—privileges accorded to the citizen at the discretion of an official, for example, a government inspector or the superintendent of an African township, or at the discretion of a member of the large and pervasive police force.

At the very core of South Africa's social structure is the stigma of racial inferiority. To be nonwhite in South Africa is to be denied the capacity for complete self-fulfillment as a human being possessed by a white person.[33]

Black Opposition

There has been opposition to *apartheid* ever since the present government came to power. It has taken various forms, and naturally the main thrust of the opposition has been provided by the Africans.

The Africans began by organizing protests and appealing to the government to call a National Convention representative of all the people. This appeal was ignored, and all subsequent attempts by the African National Congress (ANC) to bring about consultation between the government and the African people failed. Led by Chief Albert Luthuli (who was awarded the Nobel Peace Prize in 1961), the Africans moved from negotiation to defiance—the deliberate disobedience of *apartheid* laws coupled with readiness to accept the punishment provided by law—but continued to eschew violence. The government response was to enlarge, extend, and reinforce *apartheid* and to meet opposition with greater repression. Meanwhile, a desire for more militant action by many young men led to the emergence of a Pan Africanist

---

[33] For a detailed description of the *apartheid* laws and their effect, see Bunting, *Rise of the South African Reich*; *Repressive Legislation of the Republic of South Africa* (New York: United Nations, 1969. Prepared by Mrs. Elizabeth Landis at the request of the Unit on *Apartheid*), *Objective Justice* (New York: United Nations), vol. I, no. 1; vol. II, nos. 1, 2, 3, 4 (1969, 1970). See also, F. E. Auerbach, *South Africa: A Fundamentally Unjust Society?* (Johannesburg: South African Institute of Race Relations, 1970).

Congress (PAC). The repressive policies of the government were exposed to the world when, on March 21, 1960, at Sharpeville near Johannesburg, the police opened fire on a crowd of unarmed and peaceful African demonstrators protesting against the pass laws, killing 69 and wounding 178. Women and children were among the dead and wounded, and it was established that a high percentage of the victims were shot in the back while running away. The Africans reacted by organizing other demonstrations and staying away from work in a number of factories in the larger towns. The government declared a state of emergency, outlawed both the ANC and the PAC, and arrested and detained thousands of men and women, most of them Africans. These events marked the end of peaceful African opposition to *apartheid* and the beginning of violent resistance. For a few years, underground organizations—one representing the ANC, another the PAC, and a third comprising both whites and blacks, with white students in the vanguard—engaged in sabotage that resulted in significant damage to property and some loss of life. But the ruthless methods of the government, including an extensive network of spies and informers, were successful in putting an end at least to large-scale organized resistance. Today, all overt opposition to *apartheid* appears to have been stamped out. Most of the important leaders of the resistance have been tracked down; some are serving life sentences on Robben Island; others are rendered politically impotent by ban, house arrest, or banishment; and the rest have fled the country. But by the very nature of its response, the government has ensured that underground resistance will continue; with every door to negotiated change slammed in their faces, the Africans are left with no alternative but violence. In August, 1970, an explosion in the heart of Johannesburg released a number of anti-*apartheid* leaflets bearing the name of the outlawed ANC. No damage was done, and scattering leaflets cannot be classed as dangerous revolutionary activity, but the obviously implied message to the police, the government, and many perceptive whites could hardly have been missed: Regardless of widespread ruthless repression, the forces of clandestine resistance are still at least capable of obtaining explosives and are not yet sufficiently intimidated to be afraid to use them in a planned operation designed to let the African people know that resistance is not altogether dead. More important still, it had been decided to use explosives to scatter leaflets; but once explosive material is combined with the willingness and courage to use it, it can just as easily be used to destroy property or people. Since 1972 nonviolent black opposition to *apartheid* has been provided by the activities of the Black Peoples Convention (BPC) and the South African Students Organization (SASO). The government has responded by using the police state apparatus, that is banning and detention, against their leaders.

A quite different kind of threat to the *apartheid* structure is the constant risk in the large cities of spontaneous outbursts of violence by Africans. This has occurred more than once when the grossly overcrowded trains bringing African workers into Johannesburg from the townships have been involved in collisions resulting in death and injury to passengers. On one occasion, the white engine driver was done to death by a mob of infuriated passengers; on another occasion recently, the police were able to control a similar mob, intent on avenging the death of some of their friends, only by the use of large, heavily armed forces and fierce dogs.

The confrontation between white and African today must be seen within the context of the acceptance by both parties to the conflict that it can be resolved only by force. There is no longer room for negotiation. The South African government stresses repeatedly that it is not prepared to consider any compromise whatsoever involving a basic modification of *apartheid*. So the Africans, left with no alternative, are committed to guerrilla activity in order to achieve their freedom; the whites, facing the threat of attack and infiltration from beyond the country's borders, are finding it necessary to strengthen their military forces and extend their police-state apparatus, and, in addition, to undertake new measures to assure future protection for South Africa's borders.

Preparations by the ANC for armed action against South Africa began in 1960. With the establishment of the Organization of African Unity in 1963, the activities of the ANC (as well as those of the PAC) came under the direction of the National Liberation Committee of the OAU, headquartered in Dar es Salaam. Since then, both Tanzania and Zambia, under the dedicated commitment of Nyerere and Kaunda to militant action against *apartheid*, have been the mainstays of support for the liberation movements of Southern Africa, which include ZAPU (Zimbabwe African People's Union) and ZANU (Zimbabwe African National Union) of Southern Rhodesia, and SWAPO (South West African People's Organization) of Namibia. The first combined guerrilla action by the ANC and ZAPU took place in 1967 in Southern Rhodesia, where the liberation forces sustained heavy losses in an encounter with a Southern Rhodesian army contingent supported by members of the South African police and using South African equipment. Sporadic activity continues, and regular training is provided in a number of camps in Southern Africa and other African countries.

African guerrilla activity presents no immediate threat to South Africa. What does concern the South African government is a future threat that can come from developments in the guerrilla movement and in Africa as a whole.

South African guerrilla activity is part of a force whose long-term capacity to challenge white rule throughout Southern Africa should not be underestimated. The forces of the ANC and ZAPU continue to train, receive new equipment, attract recruits, and engage in sporadic activity. In Rhodesia, they have tied down a well-trained army and police force supplemented by police reinforcement from South Africa. In Namibia attacks by SWAPO are increasing. South Africa has found it necessary to introduce a system of special training of young men for "counter-terrorist" activity and to have a substantial force patroling its northern borders.

South Africa's Response to Resistance

The South African government has responded to the guerrilla threat by taking steps both within the country and beyond its borders. Within the country, there has been an enormous increase in the military forces and an extension of the police-state apparatus. The budget estimates for defense grew from $56 million in 1960 to $912 million in 1974–1975, and during that period there has been a substantial reorganization of the army, air force, and navy, all now supplied with the most up-to-date equipment. The Terrorism Act, which added to the already wide powers of detention without trial vested in the police and was retroactive, was used to arrest, detain, torture, arraign for trial, and ultimately convict and sentence to imprisonment thirty-five Namibian guerrillas.[34]

The fact that Rhodesia has similar goals and faces similar threats has led naturally to the development of close relations with South Africa. As we have seen, the cooperation between the ANC and ZAPU in guerrilla activity has resulted in reinforcements from South Africa.[35]

South Africa has developed a broad strategy in relation to independent black Africa that is designed (1) to minimize the danger of guerrilla activity on its borders, and (2) to build good relations between the independent African states and South Africa, or at least to reduce their active hostility. In the case of Lesotho, Botswana, and Swaziland (particularly vulnerable for geographical and economic reasons), the result has been a reasonable certainty that these countries will not offer any support or encouragement to guerilla activity directed against South Africa. Substantial financial assistance to Malawi and the encouragement of increased trade with other countries are tending to ensure that those countries will not support the call of the Organization of African Unity for action against *apartheid*.

---

[34] On the military forces, see Abdul S. Minty, *South Africa's Defence Strategy* (London: Anti-Apartheid Movement, 1970); *Military and Police Forces in the Republic of South Africa* (New York: United Nations, 1967). On the detention and trial of the Namibian guerrillas see *Survey of Race Relations*, 1968, pp. 53–54, 59–62, 303–305; 1969, pp. 72–73.

[35] Colin Legum and John Drysdale, *Africa Contemporary Record: Annual Survey and Documents 1968–1969* (London: Africa Research, Ltd., 1969), p. 321. The announcement by Prime Minister Vorster in September, 1970, that the South African government was prepared to enter into a nonaggression pact with any African country met with no positive response from any of the African states. The Nigerian Commissioner for External Affairs responded by telling Mr. Vorster that as long as South Africa denied political rights to her own people, she could not expect to be at peace with the rest of Africa.

Diplomatic relations have been established with Malawi (the only country in Africa to have such relations), which openly refuses to support the African boycott of South Africa. There are indications that Mauritius is seeking to develop closer ties with the Republic. In 1970 President Houphouët-Boigny of the Ivory Coast called for a meeting of African leaders to initiate a new policy toward South Africa. He urged the abandonment of such existing anti-*apartheid* measures as boycotts, guerrilla activity, and the refusal of landing rights to South African aircraft, and called for initiation of direct talks with Pretoria. There was immediate support for the proposal from Gabon. The reaction of most other African states was unfavorable. The proposed dialogue with South Africa came before the meeting of the Council of Foreign Ministers, which preceded the plenary meeting of the Organization of African Unity, in June, 1971, and was rejected by the overwhelming majority of the delegates. By the end of 1972 the South African government was conceding that the dialogue policy was in disarray.

Following the overthrow of the Caetano regime in Portugal in 1974, which resulted in independence for Mozambique and Angola, Prime Minister Vorster took the initiative in calling for negotiations aiming at peace in Southern Africa. A favorable response from Zambia led to discussions with President Kaunda and the initiation of pressure on Rhodesia to move more speedily toward majority rule. There were several discussions between Vorster and Smith, and by 1975 South Africa had withdrawn its forces from Rhodesia. Devolopments in Angola in 1975 brought a sharp increase in South Africa's vulnerability. By the end of the year the forces of the MPLA, backed by Russia and supported by Cuban troops, were in effective control of the whole country and had been recognized by the OAU and many European powers as the legitimate government. By April 1976, South African troops had been withdrawn and diplomatic contact had been made between South Africa and the MPLA government of Angola.

In the meanwhile Vorster's policy of detente in Southern Africa, announced in 1974, met with some success. Based on the use of his influence on the Smith regime to hasten black majority rule in Rhodesia and good relations with independent black Africa, it produced a response from three states. In 1975 Vorster visited Liberia and had talks with President Tolbert; and a Minister of the Central African Republic and the Information Minister of the Ivory Coast (accompanied by his white wife) visited South Africa.

South African propaganda presents *apartheid* as a sincere and genuine program of social development intended to provide all blacks with complete freedom in their own areas. A generously financed and efficient propaganda machine pours out a flood of information through the South African embassies and the Information Service of South Africa. The importance attached to propaganda by South Africa is apparent from the growth in public expenditure on it. The information budget was $140,000 in 1948; in 1970 it was at least $5 million. Radio South Africa, the shortwave external service of the South African Broadcasting Corporation, plays an important part in the dissemination of propaganda directed specifically to the countries of Africa. Using very powerful transmitters, it devotes 170 hours a week to a program called *The Voice of South Africa*, which is broadcast in nine languages and intended for Africa as a whole. A common theme in the propaganda of Radio South Africa is the advantage to be gained by the countries of Africa from good relations with the Republic. Here is an example from a broadcast in 1969:

> Now there is a new realism, arising to no small extent from black Africa's increasing experience in affairs of state. Confronted with the realities of government, the more sensible black leaders are coming to realize more and more that emotionalism is a heavy burden to bear in international relations. Similarly, confronted with unmistakable evidence that cooperation with South Africa engenders prosperity, it must have become clear to black leaders having the welfare of their people at heart that there is not much to be gained by aloofness and animosity, especially not in the face of South Africa's constant willingness to place its vast knowledge and experience at the disposal of the entire continent.[36]

By 1976 the Vorster strategy was beginning to crystallize as a pragmatic policy designed to buy time for the white *laager*. Its essential elements were disengagement from white-ruled Rhodesia, considerable flexibility in concessions to the insistent demand for an independent Namibia, and the pursuit of good relations (reinforced by the prospect of aid in various forms) with Mozambique.

Reviewing South Africa's strategy as a whole, it may have made some progress in reducing the immediate force of the drive against *apartheid* by independent Africa, but its long-term effect is likely to be minimal. Whatever success South Africa may have achieved in wooing the independent states of Africa must be balanced against the underlying forces that bind these states together in opposition to the white supremacy of Southern Africa. These bonds, which at times appear to be loose and tenuous, can give rise to tough and united action, as the reaction to the invasion of Guinea and to the proposed arms deal with South Africa has shown. Further proof of this was provided in 1975 when western-oriented African states announced their support for MPLA, despite its Soviet-backing, on the ground that the opposing liberation movements, UNITA and FNLA, were backed by South Africa. Thus, South Africa's skillful strategy notwithstanding, the degree of solidarity on *apartheid* among the majority of the African states would appear to be an inherently powerful force more likely to grow than to decline as time goes on. In June 1976, rioting in African townships throughout the country resulted in hundreds of deaths, thousands of injuries, and considerable

---

[36] Vernon McKay, "The Propaganda Battle for Zambia," *Africa Today*, January, 1971.

property damage. There was a prompt reaction by the United Nations Security Council, which condemned "massive violence against and killings of the African people, including schoolchildren and students and others opposing racial discrimination." Beginning with demonstrations by schoolchildren, the disorders appeared to mark a new stage in organized black resistance to *apartheid* that was bound to hasten the end of white-minority rule in South Africa.

International Reaction to Apartheid

The international community has been unequivocal in condemning *apartheid* and has repeatedly called on South Africa to change its policies. From 1952 to 1960 several resolutions by the U.N. General Assembly "deplored" South Africa's failure to comply with the principles of the United Nations Charter or "appealed" to the South African government to revise its policies. The South African response was, in the first place, that the United Nations was not competent to pass such resolutions because the charter precluded the discussion of the internal affairs of a member state, and, in the second place, that *apartheid*, far from being unjust to the blacks, was in fact in their best interests and in the best interests of all the people of South Africa. The Sharpeville massacre of 1960 resulted in a firmer attitude by the United Nations. For the first time, on April 11, 1960, *apartheid* came before the Security Council, which declared that the situation in South Africa might endanger international peace and security. On November 6, 1962, the General Assembly adopted a resolution calling on member states to take the following steps: Break off or refrain from establishing diplomatic relations with the Government of the Republic of South Africa; close their ports to all vessels flying the South African flag; prohibit their ships from entering South African ports; boycott all South African goods and refrain from exporting goods, including all arms and ammunition, to South Africa; refuse landing and passage facilities to all aircraft belonging to the Government of South Africa and companies registered under the laws of South Africa. On August 7, 1963, the Security Council adopted a resolution that, *inter alia*, called "upon all States to cease forthwith the sale and shipment of arms, ammunition of all types, and military vehicles to South Africa." On December 4, 1963, the Security Council called on all states "to cease forthwith the sale and shipment of equipment and materials for the manufacture and maintenance of arms and ammunition in South Africa," but also, in a final attempt to seek a negotiated solution of the conflict between South Afrcia and the international community, asked the Secretary-General to establish "a small group of recognized experts to examine methods of resolving the present situation in South Africa through full, peaceful, and orderly application of human rights and fundamental freedoms to all inhabitants of the territory as a whole, regardless of race, color or creed." The group was appointed, but the South African government refused a request that it be permitted to visit South Africa.

The report of the Group of Experts, which was published on April 20, 1964, proposed that one more attempt be made to persuade South Africa to cooperate with the United Nations, in particular by calling a National Convention fully representative of all the people, failing which, the Security Council should be asked to impose effective economic sanctions. This final appeal to the South African government, like those that had preceded it, fell on deaf ears. Since 1964 the General Assembly has continued to pass resolutions condemning *apartheid*.

The drive behind the United Nations resolutions on *apartheid* from 1960 onward came from the newly independent African states. Their condemnation of South Africa's "main trading partners"—directed at the United Kingdom and the United States—expressed a growing sense of frustration as they observed the contrast between words and action in the behavior of the Western powers at the United Nations. On the one hand there was the calculated and deliberate defiance by South Africa of the pleas, the appeals, and, ultimately, the threats of the international community by entrenching and intensifying *apartheid* even while it was being condemned in the strongest terms. On the other hand there was the spectacle of the United States and the United Kingdom leading the chorus of condemnation while at the same time increasing trade and investment in South Africa; readily supporting resolutions that condemned *apartheid* while consistently abstaining on resolutions that called for economic boycott.

In February, 1970, two high-level statements purported to describe United States policy on Southern Africa. A report presented to the President by Secretary of State William Rogers, at the conclusion of his visit to ten African countries, included the following passage: "We will continue to make clear that our limited governmental activities in South Africa do not represent any acceptance or condoning of its discriminatory system." President Richard Nixon, in his *State of the World* report, said:

> Though we abhor the racial policies of the white regimes, we cannot agree that progressive change in southern Africa is furthered by force. The history of the area shows all too starkly that violence and the counterviolence it inevitably provokes will only make more difficult the task of those on both sides working for progress on the racial question. The United States warmly welcomes, therefore, the recent Lusaka Manifesto, a declaration by African leaders calling for a peaceful settlement of the tensions in southern Africa. That statesmanlike document combines a commitment to human dignity with a perceptive understanding of the depth and complexity of the racial problem in the area—a combination which we hope will guide the policies of Africa and her friends as they seek practical policies to deal with this anguishing question.

The phrase "limited governmental activities" in Secretary of State Rogers's statement is, to say the least, a somewhat disingenuous description of United States economic involvement in South Africa. Direct support by the U.S. government may be limited, but American investment is almost a billion dollars and represents about 11 per cent of the total foreign investment in South Africa. Eighteen per cent of South Africa's exports are to the United States, and about the same percentage of its imports come from the United States. American oil and motor companies are heavily involved in major industries in South Africa. Under a quota system, the U.S. government subsidizes South African sugar producers. The subsidy, which has increased during the past few years, exceeded $5 million for the year 1968.[37] (For a full discussion of United States policy on southern Africa, see Chapter 11.)

The statement from President Nixon's report is also open to serious criticism. To describe the Lusaka Manifesto as "calling for a peaceful settlement" in Southern Africa is to misrepresent its essential nature. The authors of the manifesto in fact said they would give their full support to peaceful change in Southern Africa *if it were possible*. But they went on to make it quite clear that, because the existing situation made peaceful change impossible, they were committed to the support of guerrilla activity by the national liberation movements. The essence of the declaration by the fourteen African states that signed the manifesto is their unequivocal commitment to the liberation of southern Africa by force at the present time.

In 1974, South Africa was excluded from the current session of the General Assembly, and a Security Council resolution calling for her expulsion from the United Nations was vetoed by Britain, the United States, and France, each reiterating condemnation of *apartheid* while asserting belief in the possibility of voluntary change. By 1976, the United Nations could look back over some two decades during which repeated condemnation of *apartheid* coupled with warnings that the patience of the international community was running out had met with South Africa's defiant refusal to make any fundamental change in the white power structure.

We turn now to a brief discussion of each of the remaining countries of South Africa.

Namibia (South-West Africa)

After the conclusion of World War I, the administration of South-West Africa was entrusted by the League of Nations to South Africa as a "mandated territory," subject to South Africa's solemn obligation to "promote to the utmost the material and moral well-being and social progress of the inhabitants of the territory." With establishment of the United Nations after World War II, South Africa was requested to

---

[37] For further information on United States economic involvement in South Africa, and for varying views on United States policy, see *Hearings before the Subcommittee on Africa of the Committee on Foreign Affairs, House of Representatives, 89th Congress, 2nd Session.* (U. S. Government Printing Office. 1966). For further information on the South African sugar quota, see *United States Subsidy to South Africa: The Sugar Quota* (American Committee on Africa, undated).

place South-West Africa under the new trusteeship system set up the United Nations. Unlike all other mandate powers, South Africa refused to do so but undertook to "continue to administer the territory scrupulously in accordance with the obligations of the Mandate."

After the Nationalist Party came to power in 1948, the South African government refused to cooperate with the United Nations on the ground that it had no authority to supervise South-West Africa's administration, because the mandate had terminated automatically when the League of Nations went out of existence.

In 1960 Ethiopia and Liberia instituted proceedings before the International Court of Justice to determine the rights of the United Nations and the obligations of South Africa. In 1966, the court decided—to the amazement of international lawyers throughout the world—that it was not competent to give a decision on the question raised because the applicants lacked a legal interest in the subject matter of the claim.

Encouraged by the failure of Ethiopia and Liberia to obtain a decision from the court, the South African government went ahead with the speedy extension of *apartheid* to the territory and the complete subjection of South-West Africa to its control. The General Assembly of the United Nations responded to South Africa's action by resolving on October 27, 1966, that "the Mandate is terminated, that South Africa has no other right to administer the Territory, and that henceforth South-West Africa comes under the direct responsibility of the United Nations," and on May 19, 1967, a United Nations Council on South-West Africa was established, to administer the territory until independence was achieved. On June 12, 1968, the General Assembly proclaimed that the territory would, "in accordance with the desires of its people, henceforth be known as Namibia," and on March 20, 1969, it called upon South Africa to withdraw its administration immediately from Namibia.

Throughout the period 1966 to 1969, the South African government repudiated the United Nations' right to intervene and refused to cooperate in any way with the council on Namibia. The council was prevented from entering Namibia to perform its functions pursuant to the decision of the United Nations. On July 29, 1970, the U.N. Security Council adopted two resolutions concerning Namibia. The first called on all states, *inter alia*, to ensure cessation of commercial relations concerning Namibia, to withhold loans or credits or other financial support that might be used in trade or commerce with Namibia, to discourage investment in Namibia, and to "withhold protection of such investment against claims of a future lawful government of Namibia." The second resolution asked the International Court of Justice for an advisory opinion on the question: "What are the legal consequences for States of the continued presence of South Africa in Namibia notwithstanding Security Council Resolution 276 (1970)?" (Resolution 276 had declared the continued presence of "the South African authorities" in Namibia to be illegal, and everything done by the South African government concerning Namibia after the termination of the mandate to be illegal and invalid.)

The United States announced on May 20, 1970, that it would actively discourage American investment in Namibia, would encourage other nations to take similar steps, and that it was "consulting with other governments on possible further moves." While this decision is a welcome indication of a somewhat firmer attitude by the United States, its effect is minimal as compared with the substantial American trade and investment within South Africa, and it is therefore most unlikely to have any significant impact on South Africa's attitude.

On June 21, 1971, the International Court of Justice declared:

> The continued presence of South Africa in South West Africa being illegal, South Africa is under an obligation to withdraw its administration from Namibia immediately and thus put an end to its occupation of the territory.

South Africa's immediate response was a public broadcast by Prime Minister Vorster rejecting the decision as "an international political vendetta" against South Africa. As an advisory ruling, the court's decision has no binding legal effect, but it could conceivably lead to an intensification of international pressure against South Africa.

During March, 1972, Kurt Waldheim, the newly appointed Secretary-General of the United Nations, visited Namibia, where he was met by protests against continued South African control from the Ovambo people. He also had discussions with Prime Minister Vorster. At the conclusion of his visit, he expressed the hope that South Africa would "grant self-determination to Namibia." Proposals made for further negotiations with South Africa proved unacceptable to SWAPO and were criticized by several African states. By the end of 1973 a negotiated solution seemed unlikely. During 1973 South Africa encountered vigorous opposition from the Ovambo to the establishment of a homeland for this ethnic group, the largest in Namibia. The Security Council decided unanimously that the Secretary-General should terminate negotiations with South Africa. Sean McBride was appointed U.N. Commissioner for Namibia in 1973, and since then there has been a marked increase in African pressure and an international demand for early independence. A Security Council decree issued in 1974 authorized the seizure of goods shipped out of Namibia without United Nations permission. In 1976, at a conference in Dakar, President Senghor, an early supporter of dialogue with South Africa, pledged Senegal's full support for the campaign to end South Africa's control of Namibia. Increased SWAPO guerilla activity combined with the new threat presented by the MPLA victory in adjoining Angola placed unprecedented pressure on South Africa to move toward an early withdrawal.

Rhodesia (Zimbabwe)

In 1910 it was envisaged that Southern Rhodesia, which then belonged to the British Africa Company under charter granted by the British Crown, might in due course become part of South Africa. In

1923, a referendum was held to determine the wishes of the white inhabitants. By 9,000 votes to 6,000, the white settlers rejected incorporation by South Africa, the charter lapsed, and Southern Rhodesia was formally annexed by Britain as a "self-governing colony."

Most of the white population had originated in South Africa, and South African cultural and economic influence on Southern Rhodesia was a significant factor in its development. It was not surprising, therefore, that the new British colony, from the beginning, developed social and political patterns marked by separation of the races and white supremacy, which closely resembled the South African structure. In 1931 the Land Apportionment Act established separate areas in the colony for ownership by whites and Africans respectively, and in 1934 the Industrial Conciliation Act deprived African workers of the right to bargain through trade unions, and entrenched a system under which they were confined to unskilled labor, with the skilled white worker earning fifteen times the wages of the unskilled black worker.

In the two neighboring colonial territories, the protectorate of Northern Rhodesia and Nyasaland, the pattern was broadly similar. However, because of the British policy of encouraging cooperation between the white settlers and the indigenous African population, neither white domination nor the color bar in industry took the rigid form that developed in Southern Rhodesia.

In response to pressure from the white settlers and to British opinion, which supported the idea on economic and administrative grounds, the British government took steps to combine the three territories, and in October, 1953, following a series of conferences, the Federation of Rhodesia and Nyasaland (Central African Federation) came into existence. There were thirty-five seats in the federal legislature (seventeen for Southern Rhodesia and eighteen for the other two territories together), including nine to which each of the three territories elected two Africans and one white, with the specific function of guarding African interests. Thus, the white minority in the three territories had twenty-six representatives in the federal parliament, the black majority nine.

African suspicion of the initial proposals for federation soon grew into overt opposition, culminating in violent resistance during the period 1958 to 1960. The earliest and strongest reaction came in Nyasaland, where the young nationalist leaders persuaded Dr. Hastings Kamuzu Banda, who had moved to Ghana after many years of residence and medical practice in England, to return and become leader of the Nyasaland National Congress. His militant leadership resulted in outbreaks of violence, followed by the declaration of a state of emergency, the banning of the congress, and the imprisonment of Banda and other nationalist leaders. In Northern Rhodesia too there was organized African resistance, which had been consolidated by 1960 with the establishment of the United National Independence Party (UNIP) under the leadership of Kenneth Kaunda. In 1960 the Monckton Commission reported that there was strong opposition to federation among the African population and recommended that territories wishing to secede should be permitted to do so. The demands for secession by Nyasaland were asserted with increasing intensity, and in 1962 Britain recognized its right to secede. The secession of Nyasaland took place in 1963, and the Central African Federation thereupon ceased to exist.

In Southern Rhodesia, events took a different course. There, African nationalism, faced by a more numerous and powerful white-settler community, was late in developing as an organized force. The Southern Rhodesia African Nationalist Congress, led by Joshua Nkomo, was encouraged to increase its demands by the example of events in Nyasaland and Northern Rhodesia, and in 1959 it was banned by the government. It reappeared under other names, and finally, in 1962, as the Zimbabwe African People's Union (ZAPU), with Joshua Nkomo as president.

The official policy of partnership in Southern Rhodesia, as in the Federation as a whole, envisaged gradually increased African participation in the exercise of political power. The leading protagonists of this policy, Sir Godfrey Huggins (later Lord Malvern), the first Federal Prime Minister, and his successor, Sir Roy Welensky, placed considerable emphasis on the gradualness of the process and (in private anyhow) left no one in doubt that they intended white domination to continue for the foreseeable future. Sir Godfrey Huggins was notorious for a number of public statements in which he declared his belief in the inherent inferiority of the African. Clearly, genuine partnership between white and African was not contemplated.

But even the limited political advancement offered to Africans was seen by some whites as a threat to their interests, and the first election in Southern Rhodesia after federation saw the emergence of the Dominion Party, which opposed the policy of partnership. The Dominion Party was later to become the Rhodesian Front, which in due course, under the leadership of Ian Smith, issued the Unilateral Declaration of Independence.

The first Prime Minister of Southern Rhodesia after federation, Garfield Todd, had moved toward a cautiously liberal orientation of policy in the direction of genuine multiracialism. This was sufficient to create opposition within his own party, and in 1958 he was replaced by Sir Edgar Whitehead. Under Whitehead's leadership, the government declared the African National Congress unlawful and detained a number of its leaders, but it did introduce some reforms designed to lessen the economic hardships and the social discrimination suffered by the Africans. Also, the constitution was amended to increase African representation in the legislature. But the increase still left the whites with an overwhelming parliamentary majority, and the Africans decided to boycott the election that followed. It was at this election, in 1962, that the white voters turned against the United Federal Party of Sir Edgar Whitehead and voted the right-wing Rhodesian Front into power. Political advancement rejected by the Africans as totally inadequate was seen by the white electorate as a dangerous concession to African demands.

The ban on the African National Congress was lifted, and Nkomo and other detainees were released. Opposition by ZAPU was intensified, but a growing body of African opinion considered Nkomo's policy insufficiently militant. The result was the formation of the Zimbabwe African National Union (ZANU), led by the Reverend Ndabaningi Sithole; a split in the forces of African nationalism; the beginnings of a wasteful and often bitter conflict between the rival parties; and the dissipation of the force of resistance to white rule that continued until 1972, when the Front for the Liberation of Zimbabwe (FROLIZI), with a leadership including representatives of ZAPU and ZANU, came into existence. Violent acts committed by these organizations brought an immediate response from the new government. Stringent laws were enacted that penalized opposition.

Pressing Britain to grant independence, the Smith regime announced its intention to consult the electorate and also ascertain the wishes of the African population. In October, 1964, a referendum of the voters (90,000 whites and 13,000 Africans), 61 per cent of whom voted, resulted in a 90 per cent vote for independence. Almost all the Africans abstained. The promised consultation with the African people took the form of a traditional meeting of chiefs *(Indaba)*, the senior chief declaring that they wanted Britain to grant independence and requesting representation of the chiefs in the legislature. Lord Malvern called the *Indaba* "a swindle." This was an accurate description. As a seasoned practitioner of the art of maintaining white supremacy, he knew only too well that Southern Rhodesian chiefs are appointed by the government, paid by the government, and may be removed from office by the government at any time. However, although the British government refused to be taken in by this "swindle," the combined effect of the repressive legislation, the division in the ranks of the African nationalists, and wooing of the chiefs was to render African resistance to the regime largely ineffectual.

The British response to the request for independence was that it would not be granted unless there was satisfactory proof of genuine African support and an adequate guarantee of reasonable progress toward majority rule. A series of discussions between the two governments failed to produce agreement, and on November 11, 1965, Prime Minister Smith announced the Unilateral Declaration of Independence (UDI). Only six days earlier his government had declared a state of emergency, which was allegedly needed to deal with threats of sabotage. The Minister of Law and Order and his officials were vested with extremely wide powers of arrest, search, interrogation, censorship, prohibition of association and assembly, and detention without trial. The state of emergency, originally announced for a period of ninety days, has been extended repeatedly since then.

Britain declared the UDI unlawful and proceeded to treat Southern Rhodesia as a colony in rebellion, but it was unwilling to put the rebellion down by military force despite strong pressure from many African states, led by Tanzania, to do so. Instead, Britain applied selective economic sanctions. Nine African states—Tanzania, Ghana, Algeria, the People's Republic of the Congo (Congo-Brazzaville), Guinea, Mali, Mauritania, Sudan, and the United Arab Republic—broke off diplomatic relations with Britain. After the failure of renewed discussions, the matter came before the United Nations, which, at Britain's request, imposed economic sanctions in 1966. The expectation that economic pressures could bring down or at least significantly weaken the rebel regime has not been fulfilled. Action by the United Nations from 1966 onward, including a resolution calling for a complete ban on all trade and travel, had little effect at first. Aided by South Africa, the rebel regime was able to overcome the effect of the oil embargo, and the world demand for such commodities as minerals and tobacco ensured the continuance of clandestine trade, which appeared to leave the economy substantially unharmed. But by the end of 1970, while there were no grounds for anticipating the early collapse of the regime, it clearly faced serious economic problems. Sanctions had prevented an increase in foreign-exchange earnings, and it had become impossible to finance the expansion of industrial development on which the country depends. Income from the external sale of tobacco and from the export of minerals was too small to relieve the situation. The government faced demands from the white farmers for increased assistance, financial aid from South Africa was less readily available than it had been, and the public debt had almost doubled since UDI.[38]

On March 3, 1970, Southern Rhodesia became a Republic, and the international isolation of the rebel regime was reaffirmed. Eleven of the thirteen countries that had, until then, maintained some form of consular representation in Rhodesia withdrew their representation. Among them was the United States, which closed the consulate-general in Salisbury and announced that it "has regarded and continues to regard the United Kingdom as the lawful sovereign."

On March 17, 1970, the Security Council, having met at the urgent request of Britain, adopted a resolution that called on all member states to

> immediately sever all diplomatic, consular, trade, military and other relations that they may have with the illegal regime in Southern Rhodesia, terminate any representation that they may retain in the territory, and immediately interrupt any existing means of transportation to and from Southern Rhodesia [and] increase moral and material assistance to the people of Southern Rhodesia in their legitimate struggle to achieve freedom and independence.

This was followed by a resolution on November 18, 1970, which reaffirmed past resolutions calling for a trade embargo and other economic measures and also called on "the United Kingdom as the administering power, to take urgent and effective measures to bring to an end the illegal rebellion in Southern Rhodesia and enable the people to exercise

---

[38] *The Observer*, London, October 11, 1970.

their right to self-determination in accordance with the Charter of the United Nations." Britain supported the resolution.

The new Conservative government in Britain had meanwhile announced its intention to reopen negotiations with the rebel regime but made it clear that the application of sanctions would continue. Discussions were initiated, and Prime Minister Ian Smith declared his willingness to do everything possible to seek a solution. But shortly thereafter his government introduced a law that left no one in doubt that Southern Rhodesia intended deliberately and swiftly to develop a system modeled on *apartheid*. This law, the Residential Property Owners (Protection) Act, provides for the separation of whites from Asians and coloreds (people of mixed race), and requires the forcible removal of Asians and coloreds from their homes.

Meanwhile, the regime's repressive treatment of African opposition, combined with British vacillation and the ineffectiveness of economic sanctions, drove the African nationalist leaders to the use of armed force. Some members of ZAPU and ZANU had been trained as guerrillas, and in 1968 a number of guerrilla bands entered Rhodesia from Zambia. Action against Rhodesian security forces, assisted by a contingent of the South African police, continued for several weeks before the raids ceased. The guerrillas sustained considerable losses in a campaign conducted against them with land and air forces, but they inflicted some losses on the Southern Rhodesian forces. There were renewed guerrilla incursions into Southern Rhodesia from 1970 to 1976, and the South-African police continued to cooperate with the local forces in dealing with the raids, which, though sporadic, appeared to be part of a planned strategy for the future.

The new republican constitution that came into force in 1970 provides for a legislature of sixty-six members, fifty white and sixteen African. African representation will increase according to the increase in the total amount paid in income tax by the African population. When the African tax contribution equals the white tax contribution, the Africans will be entitled to the same representation as the whites, namely fifty members. The maximum number of African seats for all time is fixed at fifty.

Early in 1971 the British government took the initiative in reopening negotiations with the Smith regime. Following discussions in Rhodesia between a British team, led by Lord Goodman, and Prime Minister Ian Smith and members of his government, agreement was reached between the two governments on proposals for a settlement of the dispute. The proposals were presented to the House of Commons in November, 1971.[39] They provided for amendments to the 1970 Constitution, leading to African majority rule within a reasonable period, steps to end

---

[39] *Rhodesia, Proposals for a Settlement.* Presented to Parliament by the Secretary of State for Foreign and Commonwealth Affairs by Command of Her Majesty, November, 1971. Cmnd. 4835 (London: Her Majesty's Stationery Office).

racial discrimination, and a ten-year development program, to which both governments would make equal contributions. The British government claimed that the proposals constituted "a just and sensible solution to the Rhodesian problem in accordance with the Five Principles."[40] But they were made conditional "upon the British government being satisfied that they are acceptable to the people of Rhodesia as a whole." However, an authoritative study of the proposals by Professor Claire Palley concluded that "African majority rule seems to be postponed almost indefinitely." The study estimated that the earliest date when the Africans could expect to achieve a parliamentary majority was the year 2035; and even this estimate rested on the assumption (seriously questioned in many quarters) that the Smith regime could be depended upon to adhere strictly to the proposals and not alter the new constitution once independence had been granted.

An unexpected development within Rhodesia was organized opposition to the proposals. This came from a new body, the African National Council, headed by Bishop Abel Muzorewa of the United Methodist Church. The council claimed to be nonpolitical and to have been established with the sole purpose of opposing the proposed settlement. It succeeded in building up widespread opposition among all sections of the African population. In the course of his activities Bishop Muzorewa visited the United States, where he appeared on national television.

To determine whether the settlement was acceptable "to the people of Rhodesia as a whole," the British government appointed the Pearce Commission, which spent several weeks in Southern Rhodesia interviewing African leaders and addressing meetings of Africans in the towns and the rural areas. The result appeared to be overwhelming African rejection of the settlement and demand for immediate majority rule, even by the chiefs who had been expected (partly because of their alleged conservatism, partly because of their vulnerability to pressure by the Smith regime) to support the settlement. In March, 1972, the commission returned to Britain. Its report was issued in May, 1972. It concluded that "the people of Rhodesia as a whole do not regard the proposals as acceptable as a basis for independence." There is no doubt that the African position was considerably strengthened by the commission's activities. The Smith regime's claim to have the support of the African population, particularly the chiefs, was exposed as un-

[40] They are:
1. The principle and intention of unimpeded progress to majority rule, already enshrined in the 1961 Constitution, would have to be maintained and guaranteed.
2. There would also have to be guarantees against retrogressive amendment of the Constitution.
3. There would have to be immediate improvement in the political status of the African population.
4. There would have to be progress toward ending racial discrimination.
5. The British government would need to be satisfied that any basis proposed for independence was acceptable to the people of Rhodesia as a whole.

founded, while African nationalism was revived and invigorated.

The British government announced that it would continue the sanctions ordered by the United Nations. The Smith regime stepped up *apartheid* legislation while engaging in discussions with leaders of the African National Council. In August, 1973, the Commonwealth Heads of Government expressed "intensive concern" over the Rhodesian situation, agreed to seek a peaceful settlement with the objective of majority rule, and decided to make sanctions more effective.

But there was an unexpected change in the situation. In 1973 Rhodesia closed its border with Zambia, except for the export of copper, alleging Zambian responsibility for guerrilla activity in Rhodesia. Zambia responded by suspending copper exports by rail through Rhodesia. When the Smith regime then announced the reopening of the border, Zambia persisted in its refusal to use former trade routes through Rhodesia. Zambia's stand attracted immediate sympathy and support from Africa and at the United Nations, and it continued with financial and other support from the United Nations and a number of African states, to use alternate routes through Zaïre, Malawi, and Mozambique for its external trade.

Following intensified guerilla activity the Rhodesian government was, by 1975, taking brutal action against the Africans. Persons suspected of concealing information about guerillas were tortured, and 100,000 tribesmen were forcibly removed from their homes to crowded "protected villages" under strict army and security surveillance. The Indemnity and Compensation Act, passed in 1975, indemnified members of the armed and security forces against all claims in respect of ill-treatment of persons arrested or removed.[41] In 1975, responding to persistent pressure from South Africa, which consulted closely with Zambia and periodically with Tanzania and Botswana, the Smith regime commenced discussions on steps towards majority rule with Joshua Nkomo, who had emerged as a spokesman for the seriously split African National Council. By 1976 these talks had made little progress, guerilla activity was increasing, and the MPLA victory in Angola created the prospect of Russian arms and Cuban troops being moved into Mozambique for action against Rhodesia. In March 1976 a critical situation developed with the announcement by the Mozambique government that its border with Rhodesia had been closed (thus denying Rhodesia vital access to the sea), and that "a state of war existed." The Commonwealth secretariat announced that Mozambique would receive financial aid to compensate for losses suffered, and the British government announced consideration of a contribution. U.S. Secretary of State Kissinger warned that the white minority faced "its last opportunity for a peaceful settlement." Clearly time was running out fast for the Smith regime. Majority rule now appeared to be inevitable and very close indeed.

[41] International Commission of Jurists, *The Review*, no. 15 (December, 1975).

In September 1976, following diplomatic initiatives by Kissinger that led to decisive pressures from South Africa, the Smith regime announced its agreement to majority rule within two years. The announcement was followed by a conference of black and white Rhodesian leaders in Geneva to agree on an interim government until then.

The white population (270,000 in 1976) has increased by only 34,000 since 1962, notwithstanding strenuous efforts to encourage immigration, and young whites continue to leave Rhodesia. The African population during the same period increased from 3,600,000 to 6,000,000.

The Future of Southern Africa

Let us try now to formulate the important issues likely to affect the prospects of majority rule for the people of Southern Africa.

1. Despite appearances to the contrary, Southern Africa is inherently unstable. It is one of the areas in the world where peaceful progress is constantly threatened with disruption, because the application of *apartheid* and white minority rule in any form is irreconcilable with African determination to achieve majority rule. The fast pace of developments in Namibia, Rhodesia, Mozambique, and Angola since 1974 has emphasized the increased vulnerability of South Africa, and has renewed the prospect of the black majority's active resistance to *apartheid*. The 1976 riots could well be the beginning of a progressive escalation of such resistance on a scale hitherto unknown in South Africa.

2. *Apartheid* is, by its very nature, the ultimate insult, not only to every African but to every black man wherever he may be, because it rests clearly on the concepts that race or color is the sole determinant of a man's right to participate in the life of his country and that, in every walk of life, being white connotes superiority and dominance—being black connotes inferiority and subordination.

3. The confrontation between the forces of white supremacy in Southern Africa and the forces of liberation in independent black Africa is likely to result in armed conflict. This view is held not only by African leaders, who are often suspected of excessive emotionalism, but also in responsible and influential quarters of the Western world. An editorial in *The Times* of London (October 15, 1970), dealing with the new Conservative government's announced intention to supply arms to South Africa, included the following paragraph:

Among the facts of the southern African position now is the impact which the conservative election pledge has had on public opinion and political attitudes in many African countries, which the African leaders cannot ignore. This has indeed helped to reveal *how grave is the threat of ultimate armed confrontation between black and white—of outright race war—in Africa.* [Emphasis added.]

Southern Africa

On January 30, 1972, Edward du Cann, MP, a member of the Conservative Party prominent in the British business world, addressing the House of Commons on his return from Southern Africa, reported that the Africans were more determined than ever to rule themselves. He said, "The risk of savage racial war in Southern Africa is real . . . not some distant amorphous thing but almost imminent."

4. The world powers could hardly avoid being involved in such a race war. In the event of such involvement, the Communist powers would probably support the blacks, thus making alignment of the Western powers with the whites almost inevitable. Already the guerrillas of the national liberation movements are being equipped, trained, and financed by Soviet Russia and Communist China. Not because the liberation movements sought Communist support, but because the unwillingness of the Western powers to provide assistance (based on the decision that they could not condone the use of force) left the liberation movements with no alternative.

5. The United States and the other Western powers should take immediate steps to arrest the process in southern Africa threatening a race war with a grave risk of conflict between the leading world powers. Western leaders should aim at early preventive action rather than intervening after the race war has begun.

6. A policy of economic disengagement from South Africa by the United States could seriously challenge continued white minority rule. A real threat to the material interests of the whites with the ending of American trade and investment would make them responsive to black demands for negotiated change.

Such a policy—other trading powers would follow America's lead— would serve notice on the Vorster regime that the Western world has decided to substitute action for rhetoric in its fight against *apartheid*. It would greatly enhance goodwill for the United States among the 300 million of independent black Africa.

Since 1971, a number of American corporations have been under pressure—mounted by student bodies, the churches, and a number of black organizations—to cease their activities in southern Africa. None of them has yet done so. The Polaroid Corporation responded by undertaking a program of improved pay and working conditions for its African workers and establishing an African educational fund out of its profits. General Motors has taken similar steps. During 1972 the Americans for Democratic Action called for a boycott of the products of the Gulf Oil Corporation because of its activities in Angola and Mozambique.

7. The belief that eradicating *apartheid* is relevant to black America's own fight for complete equality (a correlation first articulated by Martin Luther King) is gaining increasing acceptance. Since 1971 there has been a marked growth in awareness of South African problems, and in identification with the victims of *apartheid*. The initiative has come mainly from the Black Caucus of the U.S. Congress and black student orga-

nizations at many universities. The Black Convention held in Gary, Indiana, in March, 1972, and reflecting all shadings of black political opinion, committed itself to support for the liberation of southern Africa. African Liberation Day in 1972—May 27—was commemorated by many black organizations and was the occasion for a demonstration in Washington, D.C., attended by thousands of black Americans.

8. The Christian churches of the United States have begun to question the propriety of having investments that support *apartheid*. In 1967 the Methodist Board of Missions withdrew an investment of $10 million from the First National City Bank of New York because the bank had refused to terminate some of its own investments in South Africa. In 1971 the Episcopal Church, with a substantial shareholding in the General Motors Corporation, demanded that the corporation cease manufacturing in South Africa. The National Council of the Churches of Christ, describing this demand as "only the tip of the iceberg," announced that at least six major Protestant denominations were studying the question of ensuring that investments conformed to social policy. Changes in investment policies by these denominations could affect securities worth $4 billion.

The letter from the Presiding Bishop of the Episcopal Church to the Chairman of the Board of General Motors said that *apartheid* would lead to "great instability and turmoil in South Africa." It added, "We are further convinced that this turmoil will inevitably result in the destruction of the foreign capital invested in South Africa."

9. The South African government could not ignore organized large-scale economic pressures from the outside world. The familiar saying, so beloved of Afrikaner politicians—"rather poor and white, than rich and mixed"—has yet to be tested in the hard light of fact. Until now, all that the white has had to suffer for maintaining *apartheid* is a mass of rhetoric—criticism, condemnation, warnings, threats. But the flow of money into his country, which sustains the present system and thus ensures the continuance of his privileges as a white, is uninterrupted. And it increases year by year.

If the price the white had to pay for continuing *apartheid* were action by the United States and the other trading powers, withdrawing investment and ceasing trade, he might well conclude that the price is too high and that the time has come to consider an alternative course based on negotiations with the African majority.

No one can be certain that this will be the white's response. The best way to find out is to face him with the choice. There is a growing belief throughout the Western world that such economic pressures constitute the only reasonable alternative to unchecked progression toward a destructive race war and that it should at least be tried before it is too late.[42]

[42] For an excellent comprehensive discussion of the problems involved in economic pressure on South Africa, see Charles Harvey and Others, *Foreign Investment in South Africa: The Policy Debate* (Study Project on External Investment in South Africa and Namibia, Africa Publications Trust, Uppsala, 1975).

The urgency of the southern African challenge to the United States as a world superpower was expressed in moving terms by President Julius Nyerere in an address to the United Nations on October 15, 1970:

As far as the peoples of southern Africa are concerned, therefore, the choice is now clear. They can acquiesce in their own humiliation and accept their position as third-class subjects of an alien ruling power, or they can fight for their own manhood. They are now making that choice. And they are doing it for themselves. They are choosing future life at the cost of physical death and suffering for many. What nation, or what free people, dares to tell the masses of South Africa, of Rhodesia, of Namibia and of the Portuguese colonies that they are wrong? Who is it that can tell these people that they should acquiesce in the daily humiliation of themselves and their children?

Events since 1974 have served to underline the gravity of Nyerere's warning.

7 "Modernization" In Independent Africa

Two major problems facing all states are material development and nation-building.

Independence promised change from the humiliation President Nyerere referred to in southern Africa as cited in the previous chapter. Beyond the desire for an end to suffering from discrimination, onerous taxation, forced labor, high prices, and blocked social mobility during the colonial period, most Africans, elites as well as masses, saw a need for some material or structural evolution along the lines set by countries in Western Europe and by China, Japan, the Soviet Union, and the United States. Viewed from afar, life seemed better in those powerful countries. By whatever means a country like the United States had amassed its wealth and power, African leaders promised their followers movement toward that level by a process they called "modernization."

Even though modernization means different things to different people, it is usually viewed in two general ways: unity and development. The aspiration for unity, particularly on the part of the elites, signifies a wish for an African form of nationhood within the frontiers established by the colonial state, in a region, or, occasionally, over all of Africa. The aspiration for development, particularly on the part of the masses, means the desire for an increase in material well-being, increased earning power, liberation from the constraints of poor communications, adequate institutionalization, and African control of all new structures. The difficulties in reaching these goals have been overestimated by some European observers and underestimated by some African leaders.

Nation-Building: Concepts

Ethnicity. For a century, whites have exaggerated the importance of the cultural-regional groups they labeled "tribes" or ethnic groups as barriers to unity.

All ethnic groups were once independent political systems or parts of independent political systems. In the United States, where until recently the importance of ethnic divisions has been underestimated, groups like the Italians, Irish, blacks, and Jews once belonged to other political systems in which their own culture was dominant or national. By moving to a larger society strongly influenced by Anglo-Saxon culture, and by living side by side with different cultural groups within one political system, such groups became ethnic minorities or cultural enclaves within an alien culture group.

This general process was going on in Africa before the arrival of the Europeans, and the colonial state also transformed independent political systems into ethnic groups. An example of precolonial nation-building is that of Rwanda and Burundi, where, starting in the eighteenth century, Tutsi invaders began to build new state institutions absorbing the Hutu people who already lived there. "The universalistic norms of the Tutsi invaders (that is, universalistic in relation to themselves) were substituted for the parochial, inward-looking familial orientations of the indigenous Hutu societies; a 'national' monarchical structure was instituted where only clan solidarities previously existed."[1] In Rwanda, as we have seen, the Hutu have overthrown the Tutsi, but they accepted the political framework established by the Tutsi and the Europeans.

In North Africa, beginning in the seventh century, Arab invaders converted the Berbers to Islam, spread the use of their language, and began to build large new communities. The Merina people of Madagascar, ruled by a strong centralizing monarch, began to unify all peoples on the island after 1787. In both cases one language became dominant.

These examples bring us to a second important point, that is, that different languages spoken by different ethnic groups within one country are less of a barrier to national unity than is commonly believed. Many independent states already have one dominant African language, even though they have chosen a European tongue as the official language of the country and even though other languages have not disappeared. Madagascar, Morocco, Algeria, Tunisia, Libya, and Egypt have national languages, spoken by almost everyone, even though Berber is also still spoken by large minorities in northern Africa. Tanzania has Swahili, the country's official and national tongue; the Central African Republic has Sango, spoken everywhere in the country but not used in official documents. In southern Africa, where the populations of the three African states are culturally rather homogeneous, Swaziland has its own language, and so do Botswana and Lesotho. The people of Somalia possess one language, although there are important dialectical differences in the spoken and written forms. Increasing numbers of people in Senegal and Gambia speak Wolof, even though they may belong to different ethnic groups. Most black Rhodesians speak Shona. Other states, like Kenya, Uganda, and Zaïre, make use of lingua franca, such as Swahili, spoken over large areas, or Lingala, used in an important region; in West Africa and Mauritius, Creole and pidgin English are widely spoken.

[1] René Lemarchand, *Rwanda and Burundi* (New York: Praeger, 1970), p. 491.

In the absence of a dominant language in a country, linguists have observed that people will find a way to communicate if they anticipate benefits from communication. Even though Spanish and Italian are different languages, they have a common base—Latin—and with some effort those who speak one can understand the other in a general way. Within many African countries, different languages are similarly related—like the Bantu group, for example—and some communication is therefore possible within this linguistic circle. In addition, in many countries where numerous small groups are living in close proximity, Africans, like East Europeans, tend to learn and speak several languages, and they can communicate with each other by using words and phrases from different languages at the same time. They mix their languages in the course of one conversation without knowing it. The observer who is making a survey of languages spoken will be unable to find out the extent of communication unless he himself is knowledgeable in the languages concerned and is able to observe the interchange and to hear many conversations.[2]

Africans are justly proud of their own languages, but this feeling does not prevent them from learning and using other languages. Similarly, there is nothing sacrosanct about the ethnic group with which each language is associated. Of course, each group has basic values treasured by its members, but these need not disappear with absorption into larger groups. Human beings may have multiple loyalties, although, it is true, such loyalties may conflict one with the other.

Ethnic group divisions may or may not coincide with other divisions in an African country. There are divisions between men and women, old and young, herders and farmers, Protestants and Catholics, and there are pyramids of patron-client relations and classes. The Muslim brotherhoods and some trade networks are examples of clientelism; no matter what the ethnic identity of patron and client, they work together for mutual benefit and form groups of loyal members. Developing classes will also probably be more important than ethnic divisions. High-ranking civil servants, for example, find that mutual interests may outweigh language or ethnic differences.

No country has an absolutely culturally homogeneous and monolithic population. Although France, for example, is called the first modern nation, the country still has divisions. As a result, all political systems are always in the process of trying to integrate their peoples, and this process is basic to nation-building.

Integration. France, Switzerland, the Soviet Union, Canada, Germany, Great Britain, and the United States must keep above a threshold level of integration or internal unity to maintain their status as large, unified states. Some would claim that it is only the ruling elite that benefits

---

[2] For an interesting study of language use in the city of Kampala, Uganda, see Carol Myers Scotton, *Choosing a Lingua Franca in an African Capital* (Edmonton, Alberta: Linguistic Research, 1972).

from this integration, because by subordinating internal conflict in the name of unity the ruling class can more easily exploit the masses and pursue its own narrow interests. This view is, however, too simplistic. The masses can benefit from a large, integrated community because only it can bring order, security, and even a stronger sense of identity they may need:

integration is that minimal consensus which permits the maintenance of social order, the functioning of a system of public and private institutions for the production and distribution of services regarded as essential, recognition of minimal rights of all groups in the population, enforcement of those obligations necessary to maintain the system, and the provision of those services necessary to maintain the system and permit its normal growth and change.[3]

An integrated group can provide acceptable ways to resolve disputes peacefully among its members who have come to share the same basic rules of behavior. Because people have lived together, sharing their experiences and developing a common culture that forms a basis for mutual understanding, they also begin to communicate better among themselves than with other groups. Peaceful settlement of disputes, ease of communication, mutual trust, sharing of values, and living together under the same institution are what "community" means.

Today, the nation is the highest level of independent community that can be located geographically:

It is a community of order which, by the intermediary of its institutions, symbols, and leaders now have the power to be efficacious in the maintenance of norms of behavior and internal peace; it is a social and cultural system whose norms for behavior are widely accepted and shared in a given territory. It is the highest level of loyalty group now—the supreme loyalty group—for which members who are not kin are expected to be willing to give their lives.[4]

The nation-state includes the political institutions and framework that direct the activities of the community. Nationalism is the desire to free the national community and to build and maintain its integration; it is an effort to strengthen it so that it might better maintain internal order, solve problems, and protect itself from outside threats.

[3] Philip E. Jacob and Henry Teune, "The Integrative Process: Guidelines for Analysis of the Bases of Political Community," in Philip E. Jacob and Henry Teune (eds.), *The Integration of Political Communities* (Philadelphia and New York: Lippincott, 1964), p. 136.
[4] Brian Weinstein, *Gabon: Nation-Building on the Ogooué* (Cambridge, Mass.: MIT Press, 1967), p. 5. A somewhat different definition of nation may be found in Carl J. Friedrich, "Nation-Building?" in Karl W. Deutsch and William J. Foltz (eds.), *Nation Building* (New York: Atherton, 1963), p. 31: "any cohesive group possessing 'independence' within the confines of the international order as provided by the United Nations, which provides a constituency for a government effectively ruling such a group and receiving from that group the acclamation which legitimizes the government as part of the world order."

Extreme forms of nationalism have, of course, led to destructive wars and the suppression of freedom; lack of nationalism has led to the disintegration of the group. A balance between national integration on the one hand and individual and ethnic freedom on the other must therefore be reached. This means that governments should not fear a certain level of internal conflict, which may be creative. Outside observers are too quick to predict doom and destruction when there is some ethnic conflict in Africa. It is true it may be terribly destructive and lead to secession, but it may also be constructive. Fighting for control of national institutions through elections shows acceptance of those institutions, for example.

There may be more ethnic conflict and tension in most African states than in most European states, but national integration is partly a question of degree everywhere. Yugoslavia, the Soviet Union, Iraq, India, Nigeria, Malaysia, and Guyana have ethnic groups that claim the loyalty of most people. Sweden, Japan, and Egypt, with more homogeneous populations, are much more integrated and claim the loyalty of their citizens much more easily. Most African states are below the threshold of integration, and all over the continent attempts are being made by ruling groups to integrate all ethnic fractions within the frontiers perceived as national. In some places, efforts are made to enlarge the national community by uniting two or more states or parts of states, and elsewhere there are attempts to make it smaller through secession or by liberating what is perceived to be the "true nation." These processes may be seen in three parts. First, every nation must have a motive force and core nationality; second, its people must have shared experiences that consolidate their loyalties and make them more similar; and third, decision-makers must help draw ethnic groups together through politics designed to increase integration.

Nation-Building: Process

Motive Force and Core Nationality. Every nation must have a group of people who wish to free, build, and strengthen the community. Their motives and interests may vary, and they may or may not impart their own ethnic culture to the nation. The motive force of German unity in 1870 was Prussia under the leadership of Bismarck, although earlier in history groups of liberals and intellectuals attempted the same goal. The movement for independence and unity in India was led by lawyers and the upper class, or castes, from which Gandhi and Nehru had come. In Middle Eastern countries, the impetus for change came first from religious leaders, middle-class elements, and intellectuals, then the military. The Zionists who fought for a political Israel were primarily from Eastern Europe. In Africa, the same group of intellectuals and civil servants who wanted independence for the colonial state also wanted to integrate national communities. Coming for the most part from different ethnic groups, they could not supply the core nationality.

By core nationality we mean that ethnic group which imparts its culture to the growing national culture more than others do.[5] In France, the people of the Ile de France, surrounding the city of Paris, filled this role, and the language spoken there became the language of the whole country. The White Russians of the Soviet Union had the same importance, and so did the English of Great Britain, who more or less absorbed the Scots in the north and the Welsh in the west but who had much less success with the Irish, who had their own island and religion. The reasons they were able to predominate had perhaps to do with their location, their control over the important cities, their trade monopoly, their aggressiveness, and their institutions and organization.

In European countries without such core nationalities, a new culture might develop or there may be continuing conflict, leading to violent suppression of peoples, or new forms of association, such as a confederation or even secession of one group from the others. In Belgium, the Flemish-speaking people and the French-speaking people now form two mutually hostile communities prepared at times to split the country in two parts to preserve their identity and what they perceive to be their paramount interests. This is also true to some extent in Yugoslavia, where Serbs and Croats strive for dominance or separation. It is increasingly true in Canada, where the French-speaking people are becoming separatist after years of discrimination by the Anglo-Saxon majority.

In Africa, the Arabs served the function of a core nationality from Morocco to Egypt. In Senegal, the Wolof have played the same role, and the Amharic people living around the capital city of Addis Ababa in Ethiopia tried. In the Central African Republic, small riverine groups, perhaps fearful of ethnic conflict with larger inland communities, have promoted a riverine language, Sango, throughout the country, and have thus set the direction of cultural development. In Gabon, the Fang and, perhaps, the coastal Omyènè have been the most important ethnic groups, dominating the schools and the civil service, and providing a cultural focus for the developing nation by presenting their own culture as representative of the whole country. The Baganda of Uganda had such a function in the past, but there is hostility toward them today and possible rejection of their language by the northerners in power. In Upper Volta, the Mossi dominate. The Kikuyu tend to influence the development of a Kenyan culture. Mali has a core Mandingo culture that influences other language groups.

The Ivory Coast, Tanzania, Nigeria, and Zaïre have no one dominant ethnic group that could serve as a core nationality. The Ivory Coast and Tanzania have a number of very small groups, and Tanzania appears to be developing a national culture free from dominance by any particular ethnic group. Both Nigeria and Zaïre have very large groups that

---

[5] See Rupert Emerson, "Nation-Building in Africa," in Deutsch and Foltz, *Nation Building*, pp. 95–116, and Rupert Emerson, *From Empire to Nation* (Cambridge, Mass.: Harvard University Press, 1960.)

have fought each other in recent years, nearly tearing apart their respective countries. Since the overthrow of Emperor Hailie Selassie the challenges to Amhara supremacy and national unity have multiplied in Ethiopia.

The consolidating process by which these different and sometimes antagonistic ethnic communities form around a core nationality or build a new nationality may be measured quantitatively.

By living in one territory, under the same institutions, facing the same enemies, developing the same resources, coming to terms with the same environment, peoples share the same experiences. They become relevant to one another, and the possibilities increase that they will develop a sense of common identity and community. It is true that the sense of community sometimes develops before the establishment of the state, but many countries, including the United States, have developed a sense of nationhood because people lived together under the same institutions. In Africa institutions are similarly trying to build a sense of community and nationhood by increasing contact among ethnic groups. We suggest that this process may be measured quantitatively.

There must first be "physical contact" between different people or groups of people. People who have communications with each other are "mobilized" for shared experiences and are "mobilized" into a current of communications that may eventually change a physical relationship into an effective relationship. To measure how intensive communication is, one must use such criteria as location of markets, settlement patterns, population movements, mass media or communication facilities, road construction, movement of vehicles, mail, and so forth.[6]

The second stage is a change in the sentiments and attitudes of poeple; it is "assimilation." People find that on the basis of shared experience they communicate with increasing effectiveness with certain members of a particular system more than with others. People of one group might become assimilated by another, or several groups might be assimilated into something new. When what Deutsch has called the "communication habits" of a population become increasingly standardized, assimilation is occurring.

Intensity of communication is more easily observed than is attitude change. People who ride on the same bus together and listen to the same radio are subject to the same outside communications, but the intensity of their interactions is slight. People who live in the same village are bound to share many of the same experiences and, depending on the size of the community, are bound to have some contacts that influence their opinions about each other. The intensity of their interactions is greater. Opinions may be judged only by knowing about his-

---

[6] Weinstein, *Gabon: Nation-Building*, pp. 13–15. The basic methodology is inspired by Karl W. Deutsch, *Nationalism and Social Communication: An Inquiry Into The Foundations of Nationality*, 2d ed. (Cambridge, Mass.: MIT Press, 1962), and Karl W. Deutsch, "Social Mobilization and Political Development," *American Political Science Review*, 55 (September, 1961): 493–514.

tories of conflicts between people, by extensive travel in the country. History is used to explain the present by the past; when it is oral, it is more flexible. It is useful to know the place neighbors have in the oral histories and stories of people.

With increased mobilization and assimilation, a national culture develops, along with a national history and what we call a national belief system. They, in turn, contribute to further consolidation. Without mobilization, people remain divided, and if peoples mobilize on a regional basis, the chances for conflict increase.

Through the use of census data and studies by demographers, we can begin to study mobilization, lack of mobilization, and regional or ethnic mobilization. By studying histories of areas, perhaps taking attitude surveys, observing ethnic alliances and conflicts, we can get an idea of growth of a community or division between communities. For example, a population-density map of the Republic of Sudan shows a relatively empty zone along the frontier with Egypt, then a rather densely inhabited area in the form of a band extending from east to west from the sea to the Tchad Republic, about 248 miles wide. South of this settled area is another relatively empty zone extending from east to west and 30 or more miles wide. There are more populated areas south of this zone, but they are not as solid as the northern settlements.[7] The map also shows that the railroad does not extend very deeply into the southern region.

We know from other sources that the peoples of the north are Muslim, speak Arabic, are generally fair in color, and have a reputation for having captured and sold into slavery southern inhabitants such as the Nuer, who are non-Muslim, speak other languages, and are generally darker in color. We know from colonial history that, when the British gained control over the Sudan in the late nineteenth century, they effectively stopped the spread south of Islam and the Arabic language. They encouraged Christian missionaries in the south and prompted English as the official language. Thus, added to the distance and lack of beneficial communications between populations were a history of some antagonism between north and south because of the slave trade and the encouragement of differentiation by the British colonial authorities. Those three factors contributed to a division of the two regions and provided the demographic and historical background to the conflict that eventually developed.

North-south differences may also be seen in West Africa. A population map for Ghana shows that density is greatest along the coast and that people live for a distance of about 200 miles inland. Then there is a zone, about 150 miles wide, practically empty of population. In the northern part of the country population is about as dense as that along

---

[7] Observed on a map supplied by K. M. Barbour, "Population Mapping in Sudan," in K. M. Barbour and R. M. Prothero (eds.), *Essays on African Population* (New York: Praeger, 1961), p. 113.

the coast.[8] The northern part of the country has received fewer material benefits than the south, and some northerners feel discriminated against. But Ghana is smaller than Sudan and has a better communications system, and thus has enough contact and control to prevent the same type of conflict from developing. Density of population and a good communications system doubtless permitted Angolans to keep Cabinda while neighbors and a local elite tried to separate it from Angola in late 1975.

In Togo, northerners were isolated from the south because of poorly developed communications. The French colonial authorities decided to put northerners into important posts because they feared that southerners, who had gone to European schools, would try to bring about radical political change. They, rather than southerners, were thus recruited into the colonial army. In elections in the 1950's, the southerners gained the upper hand and formed a government under a southerner, Sylvanus Olympio. To punish northern collaboration with the French, Olympio gave a minimum of posts to the northerners and refused to give northern soldiers jobs in the new Togolese army. Little money went for northern development. As a result, northern regional consciousness increased, and in 1963 soldiers from that region assassinated Olympio. Since that time the northerners have been in control of the government.[9] Whether or not the mobilization of northerners for contact with southerners will tend to diminish differences between north and south remains to be seen. A systematic study of consolidation through shared experience would be necessary.

Consolidation Through Shared Experience: Mobilization. Communications may be bringing the whole population of Togo together, if other government policies do not divide them into groups that may be mutually antagonistic. An example of the possibilities of consolidation is Gabon, where one of the authors has done field work.

Gabon, a relatively small country with about 550,000 inhabitants belonging to about eight major ethnic groups, may be crudely divided into three general zones of mobilization: places where people are relatively nonmobilized, where they are partially mobilized, and where they are mobilized for intensive contact with people of different ethnic groups. We have called these zones Heartland, Contact, and Nationalizing.[10]

The Heartland Zone is a group of contiguous cantons, the smallest administrative division in the country above villages, in which one

---

[8] See map, T. E. Hilton, "Population Mapping in Ghana," in Barbour and Prothero, *African Population*, pp. 96–97.

[9] Ernest Milcent, "Tribalisme et vie politique dans les états du Bénin," in *Revue Française d'Etudes Politiques Africaines*, no. 18 (June, 1967), pp. 37–53.

[10] This study appeared in somewhat different form in Brian Weinstein, "Social Communication Methodology in the Study of Nation-Building," in *Cahiers d'Etudes Africaines*, no. 16 (1964), pp. 569–89, and idem, *Gabon: Nation-Building on the Ogooué*. © 1967 by the MIT Press. Reprinted by permission of the MIT Press.

ethnic group clearly predominates, with at least 80 per cent of the total population. Internal communication is fairly good and is better than means that link the area with other parts of the country. Contact Zones are on the edges of Heartland Zones; from about 50 per cent to 80 per cent of the people belong to one group. Such zones are cantons in which people of different ethnic groups live in adjoining villages or in the same village or are centers of attraction, such as administrative posts and markets to which people from different Heartlands travel regularly. They are most likely along roads and rivers, which provide a link between Heartland Zones.

Nationalizing Zones are groups of contiguous cantons and centers of attraction such as cities and industrial camps, in which no ethnic group accounts for 50 per cent of the total population. The internal means of communication are best here: They are public, mechanical, and regular. It is usually the place where the most important decisions affecting the country are made.

Heartlands: The largest Heartland in Gabon is that of the Fang, who account for one-third of the total population of the country. The center of this Heartland corresponds with the administrative region of Woleu-Ntem in the northern half of the country along the Cameroun frontier. It is similar to the Fulani Heartland in Guinea, the Berber stronghold in the Atlas Mountains of Morocco, and the concentration of Banda around Ippy in the Central African Republic.

Until recently, this region has been relatively isolated from the rest of Gabon, but it has had long and intensive contact with Cameroun and Equatorial Guinea by land and by water. In recent years, a new road to Libreville has opened, facilitating communications, but communication has been more intense with Cameroun and Equatorial Guinea. Radio Cameroun is a popular source of information and entertainment.

For fourteen of the sixteen cantons of Woleu-Ntem, there is a regular service of autocars that link the administrative centers of the region. Another means of internal communication was a regional newspaper formerly published by Fang teachers. This newspaper was ethnically oriented, and the government in recent years has discouraged such publications.

According to a census taken ten years ago, 98 per cent of the population in this region were Fang. Non Fang live in well-defined quarters in the towns, but these men and women are largely Bulu, who are related to the Fang, from Cameroun, or they are Bakota who moved from a neighboring region to work as servants or attend a Roman Catholic secondary school.

While these "foreigners" move into the Woleu-Ntem, the present Fang residents do not move much. The census indicates that 80 per cent of the men between the ages of fifteen and fifty-nine were born in the place where the census-taker found them. However, only 12 per cent of the women were born in the place where they were counted.[11] These data do not mean that the Fang have not moved out from their Heartland—in fact, they have done so. What it means is that the present residents are fairly stationary, except for the women. According to Fang custom, men and women must marry outside their clan, and women must live with the husbands' families. This means that most women come from outside the immediate area of present residence.

The sixteen cantons of Woleu-Ntem, plus eight cantons in adjacent regions where the Fang are also 80 per cent of the population or more, constitute the Heartland. There were 70,000 Fang out of a total Fang population fourteen and older in Gabon of 106,000 in this region. On the basis of settlement patterns, therefore, 66 per cent of the Fang are nonmobilized. That is to say, their contacts are almost exclusively with other Fang. Using this procedure, we found that, if the whole population of Gabon is taken into account, 56 per cent live in Heartlands and are thus nonmobilized, while 44 per cent are mobilized to some extent because they live in Contact Zones or Nationalizing Zones.

Contact Zones: Many Fang come into contact with other groups around the town of Makokou. It is situated in the eastern part of the country on a main road and on two rivers used by the people to travel to what they still call the "poste." They come to deal with the administration, to go to the market on Saturday, to buy sugar or cloth at one of the European-owned shops, to go to school or to church. The people travel by canoe or by the trucks used by the administration to collect coffee beans for the small factory where they are sorted and roasted for export. Buses go to Libreville, the capital.

At night, Makokou disappears. Everyone except the merchants and civil servants goes home to the surrounding villages. The Bakwélé live up the Ivindo River, which extends northeast from Makokou toward the Congolese frontier; the Bakota and Shaké live up the road to the east and along the Liboumba River, which extends toward the southeast; the Fang live to the west and northwest along the road to Libreville and near the Mvoung River, which comes into the region from Woleu-Ntem.

Two of the four cantons around Makokou are mainly Bakota and Shaké, who account for 5,000 out of a total population of 5,800. One of the cantons is Fang—they number 4,400 out of 4,900—and the fourth canton is Bakwélé, with 1,700 out of 2,300 of the population of the canton. All these people have tended to move toward Makokou or have been regrouped in villages closer to Makokou, where they meet at the market or where some of them work during the day.

Census data indicate that very few people are moving into areas of

---

[11] *Recensement et enquête démographiques, 1960–1961: Résultats provisoires ensemble du Gabon*, Service de Coopération de l'Institut National de la Statistique et des Etudes économiques (Paris, 1963), p. 24.

ethnic groups different from their own. There are examples of intermarriage, but they appear to follow patterns. For example, in a village of a hundred people, there may be five or six mixed marriages, but all the men are Fang and the women are Bakwélé or Bakota. There are no examples of Fang women married to Bakota or Bakwélé men.

Residents listen to Radio Gabon and powerful Radio Brazzaville. Gabon newspapers arrive late, but people do not appear to read these government-controlled publications anyway. Many men have worked in the neighboring Congo, and older people remember that cloth and sugar used to come from the Congo before the road to Libreville was improved.

Adding this area to other Contact Zones in Gabon, we find that if the total population of the country is taken into account, 21 per cent of the Gabonese are partially mobilized.

A *Nationalizing Zone:* A large Nationalizing Zone of Gabon is in the shape of a triangle formed by eighteen cantons and the three cities of Libreville, Lambaréné, and Port-Gentil. There is a regular system of land and water communication in this area. Libreville and Lambaréné are connected by a paved road, on which regular transportation is assured by buses. Lambaréné is linked with Port-Gentil and the Atlantic Ocean by a navigable section of the Ogooué River. Ships and boats move regularly between Libreville and Port-Gentil and between Port-Gentil and Lambaréné. Merchandise is brought to Lambaréné from Port-Gentil and Libreville. Government publications are more likely to be found in this triangle than elsewhere, and the national radio broadcasting company is heard more frequently than other stations. The television station is mainly restricted to Libreville.

In this zone, there were about 84,400 people fourteen years and older; the Fang, the largest single group there, account for only 22,600, or 27 per cent of the total. Few of these people were born in this zone: in the age group fifteen to fifty-nine, only 25 per cent of the men were born in the place where they were counted during the census, and only 20 per cent of the women were born in the place where they were counted.[12]

In the Gabonese Nationalizing Zone, no ethnic group occupies a single solid zone and most cantons are not contiguous with a Heartland Zone. Villages are interspersed ethnically, and within each village several ethnic groups are represented. In canton "Lac Nord," for example, there are 1,800 people: 500 are Fang, 400 Bapounou, 190 Omyènè, 140 Eshira, 50 Bakwélé, and 520 others from almost every group in the country. The twenty-eight villages are all mixed, and intermarriage is frequent. In the village called Guelimoni, for example, there are twenty-five married couples of which fourteen marriages are unmixed and eleven are mixed. Contrary to the patterns in Contact Zones, there are examples of people from any given group in this canton marrying people from any other group.

[12] *Ibid.*, p. 24.

Libreville, the largest city in Gabon (with a population that must be about fifty thousand in 1973) is divided into five "groups," each with four or five quarters that have had a chief. Some "groups" used to be predominantly Omyènè, who have lived longest in the city, but now members of other groups, such as the Fang, have moved into every part of the city. The Fang accounted for 40.5 per cent of the total Gabonese population. The other large groups are the Omyènè with 15.1 per cent of the population, and the Bapounou with 10.9 per cent.[18]

Naturally, the major educational and religious institutions and some of the major economic institutions are in this zone. Most intensive interethnic contact is possible here, although there is still a tendency toward ethnic regroupment. Churches, schools, and other institutions tend to have ethnic labels attached to them. For example, the oldest churches are generally associated with the Omyènè; others are Fang and Bapounou. In the city, Fang, who back in Woleu-Ntem think of themselves as belonging to a certain clan, consider themselves Fang mainly. The smaller divisions disappear, and there is a process of recalculation of identity.

According to our calculations, about 23 per cent of all Gabonese live in this zone, where intensive contact with different peoples is probable. These people cannot avoid contact with other groups. The percentage would be higher if we could add the industrial workers at the uranium and manganese mines, but there are not many workers at these sites, and they tend to return home after their contracts are finished,

The ethnic breakdown in the Nationalizing Zone corresponds with certain political patterns. The largest groups are the Fang, the Omyènè, the Bapounou, the Eshira, and the Bandjabi, and the most important political leaders after 1957 came from these groups. The three most important leaders during the decade from 1957 to 1967 were Léon Mba, a Fang, the first president, Paul Gondjout, an Omyènè, who organized the dominant party, and Jean-Hilaire Aubame, a Fang, the country's deputy to the French National Assembly and then leader of the opposition when the country became independent. An Eshira was an important colleague of President Mba. Since the death of the first president in 1967, a new man, Albert Bongo, a Téké from the far southeast, has been head of state. Very few members of his ethnic group have migrated to the Nationalizing Zone, but he was not elected in a popular election and probably would not have become president without outside influence.

Consolidation Through Shared Experience: Assimilation. A process of attitude change accompanies the process of mobilization described above. The problem is to discern what the changes are by trying to investigate people's perceptions of the nation and of their neighbors, according to the zone they live in.

[18] *Ibid.*, p. 26.

Heartland Zones: People remember their own particular histories best in Heartlands, and they are the ones most concerned about speaking and preserving the language and customs of the group. In every village someone can always be found who remembers The Beginning, and he can usually relate several generations of his own ancestors. The Fang of Woleu-Ntem remember their history very well. They also have an advantage over other Gabonese in that they have a written version of their history.

The history of the Fang called the "story of the migration of the children of Afrikara," appears in small pamphlets published in the southern Cameroun.[14] It is accepted by most Fang of Woleu-Ntem as their standard history, and it has helped maintain some Fang sense of identity as well as increased Fang ethnic unity as opposed to narrower clan or regional unity.[15]

The people of this region also say they only speak Fang or French, even though many have lived in other areas where they were probably obliged to learn other languages, so cross-ethnic communication has possibilities despite Fang pride. Civil servants and teachers assigned to this region try to learn the Fang language, and if they marry Fang they are rather quickly accepted as kin.

Contact Zones: People may also remember their histories in Contact Zones, but these histories resemble remarkably those of the ethnic groups with which they have the most contact. Those other groups are given a role more important than that given to them in the Heartland; the part they play appears to be strongly influenced by what the present relations between the two groups are.

For example, Nze in the Contact Zone near the town of Makokou is a regrouped village that used to be five villages—one Shaké and four Bakota. There are three clearly defined neighborhoods: two of them, Shaké and Bakota, live more or less juxtaposed, with one-third of the marriages mixed. The third section was about fifteen or twenty minutes on foot up the road. Only Bakota were living there. They used to live with other Bakota and Shaké but recently moved out, even though the administration considers them to be part of Nze. They moved out because a Shaké shot one of their sheep that was destroying a cocoa tree; they are quite angry about it and say that they have their own chief. In effect, these Bakota have become demobilized and differentiated from the Shaké and the other Bakota. Their history reflects these relationships.

In the histories of the Bakota and Shaké, who were still living together, each group has an important place for the other; they had been allies in wars; they had almost always lived together; they were close relatives descended from the same ancestors. In contrast, the Bakota who were living by themselves, first announced proudly that *they* were

[14] Ondoua Engute, *Dulu Bon be Afrikara* (Elat, Ebolowa, Cameroun: Mission Presbytérienne, 1954).

[15] James W. Fernandez, "Folklore as an Agent of Nationalism," in *African Studies Bulletin*, May, 1962, p. 5.

the "pure" Bakota. They said they could not understand the Shaké accent very well. They claimed they were never allied with the Shaké and were not descended from the same ancestors. The Shaké were, in fact, not mentioned in their history.

People are more conscious of ethnic differences in Contact Zones than in Heartlands, as the investigation in Nze shows. The Bakota and Shaké living together were conscious of differences but tried to minimize them. The Bakota living apart tried to maximize differences. In time of peace and prosperity people do not talk much about the differences; but when coffee prices go down, and they have less income, or when taxes go up, they start complaining in ethnic terms. For example, they might say that they are unable to sell their coffee at good prices because the Fang officials favor their relatives.

In ordinary times they accept civil servants and teachers from other groups. The latter are not required to learn local languages. People tend to claim they speak other peoples' languages or French. Intermarriage patterns indicated in census data are confirmed by attitudes. The Fang say that a Fang woman would never marry a Bakota man because Bakota are supposedly "inferior"; they accept marriages between Fang men and Bakota women. There appear to be no rules with regard to Bakota-Shaké marriages, although Bakota leaders indicate they would prefer to see Bakota men marry Shaké women rather than Shaké men marry Bakota women. Because these groups calculate descent along the male line, their rules about intermarriage ensure that the children will identify themselves with their fathers' families.

Nationalizing Zones: Patterns of attitudes are somewhat different in Nationalizing Zones. Some people appear to have completely forgotten their particular histories there, but they are not alarmed about it. People from other groups are most visible, and everyone is most conscious of differences, but in times of general peace and prosperity there appears to be a desire to get along. People seem to adopt different customs most rapidly in this area; they speak many languages and readily accept teachers in their villages from any group in the country.

The village of Dakar, with some 200 people, is located not far from the city of Lambaréné. Séké, Nkomi (Omyènè), Fang, Bapounou, Bapindji and Mitsogo live there, but in different contiguous neighborhoods. The Mitsogo live in two different neighborhoods, according to where they came from. These various groups have not been living together very long (except for the Séké and Nkomi), and intermarriage is still rare, except for the Séké and Nkomi.

The Séké came here first, followed by the Nkomi and the others, after the nearby logging camps for which they had originally been recruited as laborers closed down. The Séké are gradually becoming part of the Omyènè ethnic group, even though they are not originally of that group. Their chief denies there is any particular Séké history, and he is not concerned about it; it is the same as that of the "rest of the Omyènè," a group with considerable prestige. These people speak the Omyènè tongue, but their neighbors claim that when the Séké are by themselves, they speak "Séké." Almost everyone in the zone speaks Fang and/or Omyènè.

There is intermarriage in the village, but the Fang tend to stay off to one side. They arrived last and tend to disdain the non-Fang, although they make an effort to get along with them on a day-to-day basis.

In nearby industrial enterprises, such as the logging camps, the factories in Port-Gentil, and the mines, workers are conscious of ethnic differences, but surveys have found there is a conscious desire to get along with other workers, with whom one must have daily contact. Everywhere in the world, as "industrialization increases, the degree to which the individual must confront and work with members of different [ethnic groups] increases, as does the potential for association-based groups such as trade unions."[16] The Gabonese sociologist Laurent Biffot found, in a sample taken from three different enterprises, that 27 per cent of the workers interviewed thought workers tended to group themselves according to ethno-geographic affinities; 65.2 per cent said workers tried to build an *esprit de corps and* to sympathize with other workers regardless of ethnic group.[17] In so far as these industries provide some of the benefits offered by ethnic groups, they may contribute to a weakening of ethnic loyalties: "Certain progressive industries offer substantial social security benefits, such as medical care, housing, education, and retirement pensions, which may increase the individual's commitment to urban life by decreasing his dependence on traditional ties."[18]

This zone of high contact is a nucleus for a change in attitudes. Shared experience is most possible and most intense. It is in everyone's interest to build a larger community, because everyone is far from the Heartlands and would be threatened by interethnic violence, which, of course, is more possible in this zone than elsewhere.

Developing National Cultures and Belief Systems. With the development of a larger community must come the growth of a national culture and a national belief system. By national culture, we mean a core of values, ways of doing things, level of technology, and shared historical memories for people within a defined community and state. By national belief systems, we mean that this same group of people shares a core of ideas about their relationship to the new community and its institutions. They share beliefs about the purposes of the institutions and their own obligations.

[16] Richard Vengroff, "Urban Government and Nation-Building in East Africa," in *The Journal of Modern African Studies*, IX, no 4. (1971): 589.
[17] Laurent Biffot, *Facteurs d'intégration et de désintégration du travailleur gabonais à son entreprise* (Paris: Office de la Recherche Scientifique et Technique Outre-Mer, 1960), p. 96.
[18] Vengroff, "Urban Government," p. 589.

An African national belief system has most of the same functions as a belief system anywhere else; it must tell people who the Africans are in general, and who the Nigerians, Togolese and Kenyans are in particular. The national belief system explains internal and external policies to the people within the nation and to the people without the nation.[19]

Side by side with a more or less official belief system promoted by the government to explain its policies and actions is an unofficial belief system, or systems, among the people. They have certain ideas about the reasons for government actions based on their experiences and prejudices. These beliefs change with the times, but there is a core of beliefs that remains in people's minds and also as part of the official line.

One example of a core belief is found in the Ivory Coast and in Gabon, where the people and government both believe that before independence their two countries paid more money into the treasury of the French West Africa and French Equatorial Africa groups than the other members. The people agree that these two rather rich countries should stay out of pan-African unification programs. Another core belief shared by most Africans is that colonialism is bad but that it had its good points, too, such as introducing schools and road construction.

Official and unofficial beliefs tend to coincide best on issues of foreign policy. In a situation of conflict between Algeria and Morocco, most people supported their respective governments. With regard to internal policies, the very optimistic, often rhetorical, messages of leaders concerning unity and progress are often met with considerable scepticism by people who have not enough teachers, schools, or jobs.

The development of national culture is more difficult to observe except through the gradual spread of language. An interesting example comes from Ethiopia, where the Amharic language is being spread among the Galla and others because of commercial links, alliances, and Christianity, which "integrated [people] into a nationwide calendar of ritual activities, a far-flung decentralized system of religious instruction, carried on in specialized centers of learning."[20]

The people of Uganda, unlike the people of Ethiopia, seem to be adopting Swahili, a language unassociated with any particular ethnic group. Even though the language is often associated with low social status, people don't seem to realize how much they use it rather than the language of the Baganda people, who have considerable prestige and who dominate the civil service and professions. The results of a recent survey show that English-speaking and Luganda-speaking people of high status change to Swahili in conversation with lower-status people because they desire to communicate. People of lower status who speak Swahili thus impose their language choice on people of high status, be-

[19] Weinstein, *Gabon: Nation-Building*, p. 137.
[20] Donald Levine, "The Roots of Ethiopia's Nationhood," in *Africa Report*, May, 1971, pp. 12–13.

cause the latter perceive some benefit to themselves in being able to speak with everyone. In the sample taken, Ugandans use English quite often in office situations, but "at home with neighbors, 83 per cent choose some Swahili as a lingua franca."[21] The extensive use of this neutral language permits each ethnic group to maintain whatever level of identity it wants to keep and may provide an important unifying force in the country. Government nation-building policies support or weaken such elements of unity.

Consolidation Through Decision-Making. Conscious decision-making by leaders can facilitate consolidation or promote disintegration. First, the president and his ministers make decisions affecting the extension of communication facilities. They may want to favor the regions they come from or make the extraction and shipment of some mineral resource easier. Whatever the motives, the extension of these roads and railroads has an effect on consolidation of the population. For example, the construction of the Tan-Zam railway from Dar es Salaam to Zambia will help communication between western Tanzania and the coast. The transfer of the capital of Tanzania to the inland town of Dodoma, begun in 1974, is another attempt to facilitate access to government and to increase government influence. The extension of the Trans-Cameroun railway north will bring more northerners into contact with southerners.

Second, governments give benefits like schools to areas where they have previously been very limited. The federal government of Nigeria is spending more money on education in the northern part of the country, where people have a lower educational standard than in the south, and like Tanzania began to introduce universal free primary education throughout the country during the academic year 1976-77. The Cameroun government has been trying to integrate English-speaking populations into French-speaking populations by encouraging them to attend schools in eastern Cameroun. Because resources are limited and political leaders careful to favor their own constituencies, there is a tendency in many countries for leaders to favor their own regions excessively. These policies will obviously tend to maintain present divisions or divide peoples in the long run. For example, it appears that in Kenya the Kikuyu are getting more than their share of benefits. They have the highest school enrollments; they get the most government loans; they have the highest per capita incomes. Leaders of other groups have complained about the alleged "Kikuyuization" of the civil service.[22]

Division is, of course, the conscious policy of the government of the Republic of South Africa and to a lesser extent that of the white-controlled government of Rhodesia, as we have already pointed out. By creating separate Bantustans for each ethnic group, the contacts and communications between Xhosa and Zulu can be decreased, for example.

[21] Carol Myers Scotton, *Choosing a Lingua Franca in an African Capital* (Edmonton, Alberta: Linguistic Research, 1972), p. 66.

[22] Donald Rothchild, "Ethnic Inequalities in Kenya," in *The Journal of Modern African Studies*, VII, no. 4 (1969): 689-711.

This will tend to divide them in spite of their shared experience of suffering under the white minority governments.

Elsewhere, for purposes of unity, a third policy is that of ethnic balance. Presidents of some countries, like the leaders of the Democratic Party in the United States, try to make sure that different ethnic groups are represented in their cabinets, in the high ranks of the civil service, and in the legislative assemblies. They know that such representation, which must be based on region as well as on ethnic group, might instill in some populations the confidence that their interests will be represented in the central government and that they will not be discriminated against in the distribution of benefits. Representation also has a symbolic value, building pride in people when they see one of their sons or daughters in high places.

Every time a high appointment is made, Africans scrutinize the name to find out what group the appointee belongs to, in much the way Americans examine Supreme Court and cabinet appointments. In a debate in the Ghanaian parliament in 1970, several speakers complained that after the coup d'état that removed President Nkrumah from power the Ewes began to fill the most important positions in the army because of the important position of the Ewe military man, Kotoka. When Ankrah was the major leader, the Ga group to which he belongs became more important; then, when Afrifa, the Ashanti man, took over the Ashanti became more numerous in high posts. An MP admitted that ethnic groups engage in "ethnic arithmetic": "A person begins to feel very much about his tribe when he looks around him and he does not see some of his tribesmen in the public services."[23]

One or two Christian Copts usually find their way into Egyptian cabinets, and one or two Berbers into Algerian and Moroccan cabinets. On the other hand, very few Fulani occupy high posts in Guinea, even though everyone knows they are the largest single ethnic group in the country; and few Luo find their way into high positions in Kenya, even though they are second only to Kikuyu in numbers. General Amin increasingly in 1975 and 1976 reserved the most lucrative posts in Uganda for certain northern ethnic groups and even for foreigners from Sudan. It is true that the colonial powers preferred to give education to some ethnic groups rather than to others or favored certain groups in army recruitment, such as the Tiv in Nigeria and the northerners in Uganda, but independent governments cannot completely blame colonial authorities for imbalance when they themselves favor one group or another.

Exclusion of members of a particular ethnic group from high government or army posts is a more important matter in African countries than in the United States, because the size of the United States provides more possibilities for upward mobility, wealth, and prestige than is the case

---

[23] "Tribalism in Ghana," *Legon Observer*, May 22, 1970, reprinted in Colin Legum (ed.), *African Contemporary Record: Annual Survey and Documents, 1970–1971* (London: Rex Collings, 1971), p. C 168.

in the smaller African states. In America and Western Europe a man can become rich and improve his status through his own business, the churches, trade unions, charitable organizations, foundations, and universities, as well as through government and civil services. In Africa the government, civil service (including education), and army are usually the only hierarchies that give benefits, because industry is under the control of foreigners and other institutions have been absorbed by the state.

A fourth conscious policy of the government to build solidarity is the civic education program. All countries have programs to teach the young and the adults about their duties to the nation, why it is important to suppress ethnic feeling, and why they must be loyal to the government and institutions.

One of the most conscious civic education programs in Europe has been in France. The French have not had the ethnic problem of Africa, in spite of separatist tendencies of Bretons and Basques. What they have had, however, are very different forms of government that still have their partisans. Even though the country has been a republic for most of the past century, there are some Bonapartists and monarchists, and some who savor the memory of Marshal Pétain's Etat Français, the quasi-Fascist puppet regime during World War II. Therefore, the French republic instituted civic education to foster love of country and to encourage support for a republican form of government and democracy.

In Africa there is a conscious attempt to teach a new attitude toward government as representative and nonexploitive—in other words, to change the image more or less established by the colonial regime. In Africa, more than in most non-African programs of civic education, students are also taught to be loyal to the individual holding the office of head of state. Children are supposed to learn to suppress particularistic ethnic feeling insofar as that feeling conflicts with loyalty to the state and nation; they are also supposed to learn about desirable change in work habits, the idea of freeing women from the bonds of tradition, and other innovations useful to the state and often opposed to the customs of precolonial groups. The importance of schools in promoting loyalty to the new community is therefore particularly great in Africa.

A fifth, and related, policy of government to promote consolidation is through the articulation of an ideology as part of the official belief system. In this area, African governments have been very unproductive and unoriginal. Most governments offer little in the way of direction and goals for their people, although they have tried. Two or three efforts in this direction, however, might be discussed.

The President of Tanzania has articulated a direction for Tanzania in the famous Arusha Declaration. The President of Senegal did the same in his book *Nation et voie africaine du socialisme*,[24] in which he explains that the Senegalese nation transcends what he calls the various

[24] Léopold Sédar Senghor, *Nation et voie africaine du socialisme* (Paris: Présence Africaine, 1961).

"homelands" of Senegal, meaning, of course, the Heartland ethnic areas like the Fouta Toro of the Fulani. He says that the Nation is a result of "reconstruction," and the State is the means to restructure. The Nation is superior to the homeland, because it frees the individual from his primordial loyalties.[25]

In Egypt, during the period just after the military replaced the monarchy, everyone felt the need for a guiding ideology. In 1954, therefore, President Nasser published his small book *Philosophy of the Revolution*, which gave Egyptians an idea where he intended to lead the country.[26] Nasser also helped create the Islam Congress; he went to Bandung in 1955; and he articulated a doctrine of neutralism, Arabism, and Socialism, which made him a hero of the Arab world.

More recently, Guinea-Bissau has developed a dynamic civic education program. Even before independence the PAIGC's Center for Political and Military Instruction conducted education programs for returning refugees and party cadres.[27] A dynamic literacy campaign (in Portuguese) has been expanded since independence, and it, too, contains an important dose of civics. Mozambique opened a new party school for what it calls political reeducation in 1975.

Other ways in which decision-making contributes to consolidation are through everyday actions of the government: the establishment of rules and procedures for writing contracts, for example, if the colonial method is not acceptable, or improvement of social services to provide benefits to the needy and extension of services to all people, not just an urban bourgeoisie. It must also have a way to force people to obey if they do not have the habit already. Thus, a government uses a police force and even an army to ensure compliance and order. Excessive use of such methods to help bring about consolidation may have the reverse effect, of course, and lead to troubles and more barriers to consolidation and nation-building.

Barriers to Nation-Building

Any ethnic group may be organized and consolidated around new or old symbols and then act as a barrier to consolidation of a larger community. Differences in educational opportunity, jobs held, population movement, policies of colonial or independent governments, opportunism of ethnic leaders, or economic interest can lead to the development of a separatist ethnic-group consciousness. Leaders of such a movement define their group to include enough people to make it a viable threat and exclude enough people to provide a target for future action. The size can be flexible: "Group size in most cases depends on the

---

[25] *Ibid.*, pp. 24, 23.
[26] Gamal Abdel Nasser, *Egypt's Liberation: The Philosophy of the Revolution* (Washington: Public Affairs Press, 1955).
[27] Lars Rudebeck, "Political Mobilisation for Development in Guinea-Bissau," *The Journal of Modern African Studies*, X, no. 1 (1972): 1–18.

ability of subgroups to form a common identity. This, in turn, depends heavily on perceived similarities among the subgroups taken together vis-à-vis the other groups they confront in the society."[28]

They articulate real or imagined grievances, fears, and interests in order to mobilize the masses, just as the earlier nationalist leaders articulated grievances against the European. Then they propose a program for action.

The sense of uncertainty about the future that accompanied independence is a source of the need that ethnic leaders feel to mobilize ethnic groups. They are afraid that, in the competition for jobs left by the Europeans, they will be left out. This is one reason for the brutal conflict among Africans in Angola before the victory of MPLA in early 1976. Bakongo supported FNLA; Mbundu backed the MPLA; and Ovimbunda joined UNITA. They are also afraid of the resurgence of historical conflicts and patterns of dominance that existed before the arrival of the Europeans. The old competition between the coastal-dwellers and the peoples of the inland, or the worldwide tension between the cultivator of the soil and the herdsman, could be revived with independence.

One of the most violent conflicts between ethnic groups at the time of independence was that between the Baluba and the Lulua in Kasai Province in south-central Zaïre. During the colonial period, Europeans brought Baluba workers into Lulua country when the Lulua refused to work for them, although some were already there. The Baluba thus had the benefit of schools, and the Europeans began to unify them as a group by organizing chiefs, whereas they had had none before. In order to reward Baluba collaboration with them, the Belgians also gave the Africans land the Lulua claimed as their own.

Reacting against this set of circumstances, the Lulua began to organize themselves after their leaders called for Lulua solidarity. In 1953, for example, they set up an organization called "Lulua-Frères," and they asked the Belgians to recognize one grand chief to symbolize their unity, even though there had been no such monarch in history. In 1959 Lulua leaders met to organize a party; they also asked the Baluba to return to their original area. The Baluba also organized themselves into an ethnic organization, the Nkonga Muluba, but they said Lulua could also be members. They claimed the two groups were really one people.

Zaïre writers, in agreement with this view, claim that the conflict that erupted into attacks by the Lulua against the Baluba in 1960 had its origins in the colonial period, which helped divide the two peoples. Because of migrations and separation, the Lulua began using the name "Lulua," whereas, according to Mabika Kalanda, they were originally Baluba.[29] In other words, some Africans, fearing conflict, defined the

[28] Donald L. Horowitz, "Three Dimensions of Ethnic Politics," in *World Politics* (January, 1971), p. 239.
[29] Mabika Kalanda, *Baluba et Lulua: Une ethnie à la récherche d'un nouvel équilibre*, Etudes Congolaises, no. 2 (Brussels: Editions de Remarques Congolaises, 1959).

ethnic group in terms of one Baluba-Lulua community, while others, with different interests, defined it as two separate groups. The triumph of the latter view led to the deaths of thousands of people. Ethnicity may thus be manipulated in different ways: to unify people or to divide people.

Ethnic Manipulation for Unity. In independent states, ethnic leaders realized that their positions would be strengthened if their own ethnic groups were well organized in order to supply the votes needed in the coming struggle to win power in assemblies. They engaged in a process called "retribalization," "a process by which a group from one ethnic category, whose members are involved in a struggle for power and privilege with the members of a group from another ethnic category, within the framework of a *formal* political system, manipulate some customs, values, myths, symbols, and ceremonials from their cultural traditions in order to articulate an *informal* political organization which is used as a weapon in that struggle."[30] In order to accomplish this goal, some leaders try to establish a kingship and then try to become the king or influence the choice of the king, and then try to make the group as large as possible by convincing certain peoples that they really belonged to the ethnic group.

In 1947, for example, just after the new French Union allowed for elections, the Fang called for the creation of a chieftaincy, and Léon Mba, who had political ambitions, tried to be named king, or chief. Such a king or chief might have been able to unite the Fang of the Heartland and the coast had he been named, thus ensuring control over one-third of the country's population. About the same time an attempt was made to unite the larger Pahouin group of Gabon, Equatorial Guinea, and Cameroun, of which the Fang are one part. Such a large group would have been able to influence elections in Cameroun, where the far more united northerners threatened to gain control of the country.

Division of the Ewe between Ghana and Togo was used as a justification by the Ghanaian government for an effort to unite the two countries, and it is now the basis of some Ewe attempts to secede from Ghana and unite with Togo. The separation of the Bakongo people between Congo-Brazzaville, Zaïre, and Angola has tempted political leaders such as Joseph Kasavubu, first President of the Republic of Zaïre (when it was called the Congo), to unify his group into a new state.

Ethnic ties between Cameroun and small Equatorial Guinea have also provided an excuse for claims. In 1962, after Cameroun had become independent and united with the British-controlled southern Cameroons, claims were made on Equatorial Guinea, which was still under Spanish control. A Camerounese leader claimed that territory had been taken

[30] Abner Cohen, *Custom and Politics in Urban Africa: A Study of Hausa Migrants in Yoruba Towns* (Berkeley and Los Angeles: University of California Press, 1969), p. 2.

away from Cameroun by the colonialists but that, in any case, Rio Muni, the mainland part of Equatorial Guinea, was the "natural and ethnic prolongation of a Cameroun, the continuation of the Fang-Ntumu people." Cocoa-rich Fernando Po was also claimed because of ethnic identification based on a very vague connection.[31] Some Camerounese hope to re-establish the somewhat mythical state of Kamerun, the German colony whose frontiers varied and for a very brief period included parts of Gabon, the Central African Republic, and Congo-Brazzaville.

Attempts to unify the Somali people have had disruptive effects in the relations between Ethopia, Somalia, and Kenya. In 1959 Somalis in what was to become the Republic of Somalia formed the Pan-Somalian National Movement at Mogadiscio. Their goal was unity of the Somali-speaking people. Both Ethiopia and Kenya have resisted attempts to cut away any of their territory in the name of ethnic unity, and conflict has simmered among the three states.

The most disruption and conflict have come, however, from attempts to make an ethnic group into a nation by secession.

Ethnic Manipulation for Secession. The most famous examples of the assertion of ethnic identity are those that have endeavored to transform ethnic groups into nations by establishing their own separate states. Some of these assertions of separatism have been extremely violent, particularly when the interest of the elites seemed to correspond with the interests of the ethnic masses.

Our first example, that of the Sanwi, did not produce much violence, because separatism was largely an affair of elites. The 40,000 Sanwi of the Ivory Coast belong to the Agni grouping and are related to the Ashanti in neighboring Ghana. They had a separate state government and king before the arrival of the Europeans.

The French recognized the separate identity of this people when they established a protectorate over them in 1843 by keeping the kingship intact. In reaction to a secession attempt at the time of World War I, the French abolished the state. The people agitated for re-establishment of the political system within the Ivory Coast in the next decades, with the result that the French restored the king in 1943.

The Sanwi king and some of his people felt threatened in the next few years by the migration of other ethnic groups into their territory and, as democratic reforms were instituted, felt that some vassal peoples might get their freedom from them. Making matters worse, from the point of view of the elite and the king, was Félix Houphouët-Boigny's rise to prominence. This leader of the Democratic Party of the Ivory Coast had proclaimed that he would not let chiefs stand in the way of

---

[31] Paul Soppo Priso, "Face à l'harmonisation de l'Afrique: le Cameroun et la Guinée Espagnole," in *Communauté France-Eurafrique*, no. 134 (September, 1962), pp. 6–8.

his programs. Fearful of his status in an evolving Ivory Coast, the ruler of Sanwi requested an autonomous status in 1959.

France rejected this separatist request, and a group of people set up a government in exile in Ghana. Houphouët-Boigny, who was then prime minister, reacted vigorously by arresting the king and other members of the elite. The leader was sentenced to ten years in prison. Houphouët-Boigny proclaimed that any treaties the French may have signed with the Sanwi state were henceforth invalid. The movement seemed to have been suppressed.[32]

Another attempted secession based largely on elite interests was that of the Lozi people in Barotseland, an area in the southwestern part of Zambia. In 1880, King Lewanika agreed to a protectorate under the British South African Company, and the state then became part of British-controlled Northern Rhodesia, later to become Zambia.

The king, called the Litunga, and his court survived under the British system but became alarmed when the British announced plans to amalgamate Northern Rhodesia with Southern Rhodesia, whose white-settler population would surely dominate. At that point, in the early 1950's, the Lozi threatened to secede. To calm them the British granted the king more power and made Barotseland Province into a separate protectorate within Northern Rhodesia. In return the Lozi agreed with the project of federation with Nyasaland and Southern Rhodesia.

In 1959 demands for secession were revived, but the British and the African nationalists resisted the demands. With the collapse of the federation and the approach of independence the king, increasingly fearful of his personal status within an independent Zambia, appealed to the British and, even more foolishly, to the South Africans for support. In 1964, as Zambia became independent, the most important party, the United Naitonal Independence Party (UNIP) of Kenneth Kaunda, agreed on a slightly different administrative status for Barotseland. It also allowed the king to control local government institutions. In 1965 the king refused to carry out some central government reforms; in reaction, the central government decreased his powers. The Litunga threatened secession but was unable to give much credibility to the threat because of his people's poverty.[33] The Lozi king now more or less supports any opposition party movements, even though such movements do not necessarily support Lozi separatism as such. Accordingly, Lozi irredentism seems quite weak at the moment.

A third example of elite-led separatism is that of Katanga, the richest province in Zaïre. During the disorder following independence on June 30, 1960, Katanga declared itself an independent state under the leadership of a businessman, Moïse Tshombe, son-in-law of a precolonial

[32] See Aristide R. Zolberg, *One-Party Government in the Ivory Coast*, rev. ed. (Princeton, N.J.: Princeton University Press, 1969), pp. 13, 288–94.

[33] Gerald Caplan, "Barotseland: The Secessionist Challenge to Zambia," in *The Journal of Modern African Studies*, VI: no. 3 (1968): 343–60. Our account comes largely from this article.

Lunda leader. Belgian businessmen with important investment in the copper of the province and European mercenaries supported Tshombe. The conflict between the Baluba and other ethnic groups also helped Tshombe, who was able to capitalize on the fact that here, as elsewhere, the Baluba from a neighboring province of Kasai occupied better jobs than the local Lunda: "Regional differences in the distribution of economic resources operated to aggravate latent tensions among ethnic groups, so that economic stratification tended to coincide with tribal divisions."[34] He was able to keep the state separate from the rest of the Congo until January, 1963, when, after United Nations intervention, the unity of the country was restored, after thousands of deaths in the conflict between the Central Army and Katanga's European-led army.

In a fourth example of secession, elite and mass interests seemed to coalesce, leading to extended and very destructive conflict. This was the secession of the eastern region of Nigeria, which called itself Biafra. War between the region and the rest of Nigeria lasted from 1967 to 1970.

Biafra was an attempt on the part of mainly Igbo-speaking people to set up an independent state, or, in other words, to transform an ethnic group into a nation. There had never been such an Igbo state before in history, although the Aro branch was beginning to unite them before the colonial period. Most groups of Igbo had no centralized government before the colonial period, and loyalties were to much smaller groupings.

The Igbo were one of three major ethnic groups in the country. Each group dominated one region: Hausa-Fulani in the north, Igbo in the east, and Yoruba in the west. (After independence in 1960, another region, the mid-west, was created, without any group being able to dominate it.) Ethnic groups also corresponded with political parties. The Igbo had the National Council of Nigeria and Cameroons (NCNC). The Yoruba had the AG, or Action Group, and the Hausa the NPC, or Northern Peoples Congress. Each group dominated the several minority groups in each region, in an effort to increase their weight in elections and distribution of benefits.

Although an Igbo man, Dr. Nnamdi Azikiwe, became the first President of Nigeria, a Hausa, Al Hadj Sir Abubakar Tafawa Balewa, became Prime Minister, a much more important post. Each region also had its prime minister and legislature. Sir Ahmadu Bello, Sardauna of Sokoto, held the very important position of prime minister of the north, the largest region and the one with the most representatives in parliament.

Because of conservative northern control of the government, widespread corruption, and increasing violence in elections in the western region, many members of Nigeria's elite concluded that significant change would be impossible with the government then in power. Conservative Hausa dominance—28 per cent of the total population, compared with about 18 per cent for the Igbo and 17 per cent for the

[34] René Lemarchand, "The Limits of Self-Determination: The Case of the Katanga Secession," in *The American Political Science Review*, LVI, no. 2 (June, 1962): 415.

Yoruba—seemed impossible to overcome, particularly after attempts to manipulate census data in an effort to decrease northern control failed.

Elections held in 1964 were violent and exacerbated tension, already high because of a general strike the same year. Added to this were unrest among minorities, particularly the Tiv in the north—who felt discriminated against by the three principle ethnic groups—the jailing of Chief Obafemi Awolowo, leader of the Action Group, a Yoruba party, and demands by northern Nigerian politicians to fire Igbo and other southern civil servants working in their region. Many said they preferred foreigners, British and Pakistanis, to southerners, who were more advanced in education and likely to control most positions for many years. Ethnic conflict grew during 1965, after the northern region again won a majority of seats in parliament, and the Igbo vice-chancellor of Ibadan University and the Igbo vice-chancellor of the University of Lagos were replaced by Yorubas.

On January 15-16, 1966, middle-grade army officers, mainly but not exclusively Igbo, revolted against the government and assassinated northern Hausa and western Yoruba politicians then in power, including Sir Ahmadu Bello, Prime Minister Tafawa Balewa, and Prime Minister Akintola, head of the western region's government. Few Igbos were killed: President Azikiwe was conveniently out of the country, and Dr. Okpara, Prime Minister of the East, survived, perhaps because he had foreign visitors. General Aguiyi-Ironsi, an Igbo, took over a new military government; he was the highest-ranking military man but had not been involved in the coup. He named military governments for the four regions, including Colonel Ojukwu as head of the eastern region.

The military government then began reforms by removing older politicians from office and decreeing that knowledge of the Hausa language was not necessary for civil servants working in the northern area. In May, 1966, the government abolished the four regions, thus destroying northern dominance.

Shortly thereafter riots broke out in the north, during which many Igbos were killed. Leaders encouraged the people to remain where they were, apparently believing it was a temporary outburst. General Aguiyi-Ironsi began a tour of the country in July, 1966, in hopes of uniting it, but on July 29 he was killed in Ibadan by northern soldiers who had organized a second coup. Immediately more riots against Igbos took place. On August 1, a northern (but not a Hausa or Fulani) officer, Yakubu Gowon, took over leadership of the military government, and he re-created the federal system. Further riots then took place in August, and Igbos fled the north and other regions back to the east, a region some of them had never known because they had been born in the north. Many died. It has been estimated that about 2 million Igbo moved to eastern Nigeria in a few months.

Beginning in September, a series of conferences brought together Colonel Ojukwu, emerging as the most important Igbo leader, and other members of the military government to discuss the crisis facing the country. Northerners talked of seceding from Nigeria, but then easterners began saying they might do so. Easterners asked for a greater share of oil revenue because, they said, they needed it to resettle refugees, and because oil was being produced in greater quantities in their region than elsewhere. At the same time, elites and masses were horrified at what had been done elsewhere in Nigeria to Igbo-speaking people. A meeting took place in Aburi, Ghana; in spite of hopes for a settlement, mutual accusations of bad faith followed the meeting, and there was a steady collapse in communication.

On May 30, 1967, Colonel Ojukwu declared eastern Nigeria independent, with the name of Biafra, and the federal government, in response to the wishes of minority groups all over Nigeria, angered by Igbo, Yoruba, and Hausa domination over the years, declared the whole country would henceforth be divided into twelve states based on ethnic identity. East Nigeria was divided into three states: East Central for Igbos; Rivers for Ejaw; and Southeast for Efik and Ibibio peoples.

War began shortly thereafter and lasted until January, 1970. Nigeria mobilized a huge army of at least 250,000, up from its 1966 level of a mere 8,000, and Biafra mobilized men, women, and children to fight. Weapons came from the Soviet Union and Great Britain to the Federal Military Government, and some weapons came from France and Israel to the Biafrans. South Africa and Portugal, congratulating themselves that war might prove Africans were incapable of governing themselves, helped the Biafrans and may also have indirectly helped the central Nigerian government too. Four African countries recognized Biafra— Tanzania, Zambia, the Ivory Coast, and Gabon. With the exception of Haiti, no other country in the world recognized it.

Estimates of the deaths during the war varied greatly, up to more than a million, but predicted massacres once the war ended did not occur. In spite of some discrimination against Igbos, the Federal Military Government, under the leadership of General Gowon, has taken many steps to reintegrate Igbos back into jobs and to restore to them property they owned outside the East Central State. A policy of generosity will go far in increasing the solidarity and unity of Nigeria.

The conflict in Sudan between north and south may also have come to an end after seventeen years of conflict. In 1955 southerners, who number about 3,000,000, or a quarter of the population, mutinied in the army, and a rebellion against Muslim northern dominance began. The Nuer, Shilluk, and Zandé peoples of the south organized themselves into a movement called the Anyanya and demanded autonomy or independence, because they believed they were being discriminated against "By the end of the 1960's the Anyanya had set up its own administration, and was attempting to provide basic services for at least the 600,000 to 700,000 people it claimed to control completely." [35] However, a peace

[35] David Roden, "Peace Brings Sudan New Hope and Massive Problems," in *Africa Report*, June, 1972, p. 15.

agreement was signed on March 27, 1972, providing for a measure of self-government in the south with a regional assembly and other protection against northern dominance. It has been estimated that during the decade 1963-72, when fighting was most intense, 500,000 died from disease and famine, 500,000 died in the fighting, and 1,000,000 Sudanese fled to neighboring Uganda, the Central African Republic, and other states.[36] Secessionist war continues in Ethiopia, where a group of Eritreans wants independence. About half of Eritrea's 1.8 million people are Muslim. More highly educated than elsewhere in Ethiopia, many were nonetheless unemployed, and they resented other forms of discrimination. Thus, they created the Eritrean Liberation Front in 1962 and began fighting the central government. Because the first head of the military government, General Andom, was Eritrean, many thought an agreement could be reached in 1974. His assassination and replacement at the end of the year opened a new, more intense conflict fueled by money from several Arab states.

Ethnic Manipulation for Policy Changes. Ethnic group identification may be manipulated for much less dramatic goals than unification or secession. A group may want to change a policy or change a government within frontiers that they accept. For example, the non-Arabic-speaking Mauritanians revolted in 1963 against an announced government policy to require that government employees speak Arabic. As a result of these ethnic groups' activities, government policy changed.

In 1963 the Berbers of Algeria, who live in a mountainous area not easily accessible to the outsider, rebelled against the government of Ahmed Ben Bella. Many of them had rallied around the newly formed Front des Forces Socialistes headed by the Berber leader Hocine Ait Ahmed. It seems to have been a bid for power on the part of Hocine Ait Ahmed rather than an ethnic uprising for purely ethnic goals. Although guerrilla action continued until the end of 1964, it was quickly suppressed.[37] Berbers in Morocco and Touaregs in Mali have refused to pay taxes, and military action has been undertaken against them.

Europeans and refugees have also acted, sometimes as a group, to attempt to influence government policy. We have already mentioned that Europeans had a role to play in the Katanga secession; they are a powerful force in Kenya, Zambia, and French-speaking countries, where they are allowed to vote, for example. They generally support vigorously the governments that protect foreign investments and rights of small European merchants. In East Africa, Indians have played an important role as a group, formerly controlling commerce in Tanzania, Kenya, and Uganda. Their expulsion from Uganda by General Amin and new governmental restrictions on them in Tanzania and Kenya have weakened their role.

[36] *Ibid.*, p. 16.
[37] See David and Marina Ottaway, *Algeria: The Politics of a Socialist Revolution* (Berkeley and Los Angeles: University of California Press, 1970), p. 42.

Southern African refugees have moved into Tanzania, Zambia, Swaziland, Lesotho, and Botswana. Angolans have moved to Zaïre, and Tutsi from Rwanda live in Zaïre and Burundi. They are sometimes a force within the country of refuge. For example, an attempt was apparently made to obtain help from refugees from the Republic of South Africa in an attempt to overthrow the government of Tanzania. Zambia and Senegal have found it necessary to limit the activities of refugees in order to protect their own interests. During the Guinea-Bissau war of liberation Senegalese territory was bombed by the Portuguese because of refugee operations from the country, and the government then restricted their operations to prevent further attacks. In the future these refugees may continue to play a role within their host states, particularly if they are unable to bring about change in South Africa and Rhodesia. Other countries where there might be conflict because of ethnic assertion are Libya, which is still divided into three major regions; Guinea, where the Fulani are systematically discriminated against; Zaïre, where General Mobutu appears to be discriminating against the once powerful Bakongo; Nigeria, where the tensions among ethnic groups have only slightly abated since the war; Tanzania, where there may be an underground conflict between Muslims who feel left out of the mainstream and the Christians who generally control the government; Kenya, where the tension between Luo and Kikuyu is high; Uganda, where northern-southern hostility is very close to the surface; Rwanda and Burundi, where Hutu and Tutsi antagonisms are very sharp; and Angola where the Bakongo may resist MPLA rule.

Countries where there should be little or no ethnic conflict in the next few years are Swaziland, Botswana, and Lesotho in the south; and Ivory Coast, Upper Volta, Mali, Egypt, Algeria, and the Central African Republic, where there is considerable ethnic homogeneity or where large groups are unorganized. As each country develops, of course, the chances of ethnic conflict over limited benefits may decrease.

Development: Concepts

Political and economic development facilitate nation-building, and nation-building facilitates development; the two processes are not separable. For example, most definitions of political modernization include three elements: greater centralization of power, increased participation, and "differentiation and specialization of political institutions.' [38] Both centralization and participation contribute to integration, which is basic to the development of a national community. Most definitions of economic modernization include an increase in per capita income, greater equalization of income, and decreasing unemployment, which is another way of saying greater integration into the national economic system. In

[38] Claude Welch, "Modernization and Political Institutions," in Claude E. Welch, Jr. (ed.), *Political Modernization: A Reader in Comparative Political Change* (Belmont, Calif.: Wadsworth, 1967), p. 203.

both types of development, the role of the institutions of the state are of key importance. Their "capabilities" may be measured in order to determine the degree of development.[39]

African governmental capabilities with regard to the above six characteristics of development are generally low and, in spite of some leaders' promises, are likely to remain low for some countries for a very long time. The absence of resources in countries like Tchad, Upper Volta, and Niger (in spite of the uranium) will seriously affect development, although it is true there are no rigid rules about how to achieve higher per capita income and greater participation.

Attempts by the Europeans, Americans, and Africans to analyze African economies in terms of the rules of European or American history are not always useful. Countries that do not have the so-called Protestant ethic may still develop; China, for example, certainly does not have the spirit of individualism that was so important in the development of Western countries. Although the extended family in Africa is often criticized as a barrier to development, it may in fact contribute to it by providing the cooperation and labor necessary to build a business or a dam. No one institution is absolutely necessary for development, and no one institution is an absolute barrier to development: "The requirements of development turn out to be more tolerant of cultural and institutional variety than we thought on the basis of our limited prior experience," Hirschman has written.[40]

Following American or European patterns may also be disadvantageous in other ways. José Ortega y Gasset complained that, with the triumph of technology and the ideal of liberal democratic forms of government in the West, old values have disintegrated. The process began in the United States, but all countries seem to be following the same path. People are increasingly optimistic that "tomorrow . . . will be still richer, ampler, more perfect,"[41] and as a result mass man has no respect for past standards. He expects the state to intervene in all aspects of human life, because he thinks it can modernize quickly and make him rich, Ortega y Gasset wrote.

By such intervention, the state homogenizes a population, thus creating a nation with a centralized government, high per capita income, high rate of participation, and so forth. Meanwhile, in Ortega y Gasset's view, "all spontaneous social effort" will be absorbed and "Society will have to live *for* the State, man *for* the governmental machine."[42] In such a situation, man may or may not be "happy," and even with a high

[39] See Gabriel A. Almond and G. Bingham Powell, Jr., *Comparative Politics: A Developmental Approach* (Boston and Toronto: Little, Brown, 1966).

[40] Albert O. Hirschman, "Obstacles to Development: A Classification and a Quasi Vanishing Act," in Harvey G. Kebschul (ed.), *Politics in Transitional Societies: The Challenge of Change in Asia, Africa and Latin America* (New York: Appleton-Century-Crofts, 1968), p. 373.

[41] José Ortega y Gasset, *The Revolt of the Masses* (London: George Allen and Unwin, 1951), p. 41.

[42] *Ibid.*, p. 88.

per capita income, can it be true that the slum-dweller in America's decaying cities is happier or better off than the Ghanaian peasant who has a lower income? On the other hand, it is not useful to romanticize or idealize precolonial African society. Development may be a little ambiguous, but African elites have decided, like elites elsewhere, that they want it. They are leading their countries toward what they call development and growth.

Development and Growth

Development is not the same thing as growth. Growth means more money and a larger civil service, for example. In economic and political terms, development means basic changes in structure inherited from the precolonial and colonial periods. It means "establishing new sources and uses of inputs, new kinds of outputs, new techniques for production, and new marketing systems for distribution."[43] In political terms, it means "change in political structures, in the pattern of resource flows and in the use of resources. New sources of inputs could come from mobilizing new sectors or from reorienting activity from local to national political markets."[44] Education and communication facilities can play a very important role in this kind of development by involving new groups of people and new regions in the development and nation-building processes.

One sign of development may be the increasing role of women in political and economic activities. At present, women may vote and be elected to public office in almost all African states, except for northern Nigeria and Libya. Women voted in most French-controlled and British-controlled areas before independence. In Ethiopia, women have voted since 1955; in Morocco, since 1959; in Tunisia, since 1957; and in Egypt, since 1956.[45] In Guinea, in Gabon, and in Algeria, leaders promised change to the women and got their support against rivals and the Europeans. In Guinea laws now make civil marriage mandatory, and since 1962 women legally have the right to refuse to marry men not of their choice. According to the same 1962 law, the dowry is limited and must be given to the wife instead of her family. Wives may oppose husbands' plans to take second wives, and divorce must take place in court. Schooling for girls has increased all over Africa, and there are usually more women in factories. Political parties have women's sections, and in many cabinets there is a woman minister. On the other hand, African repre-

---

[43] Norman Thomas Uphoff, "Ghana and Economic Assistance: Impetus and Ingredients for a Theory of Political Development" (paper delivered at the Annual Meeting of the American Political Science Association, Los Angeles, September, 1970), p. 6.

[44] *Ibid.*, p. 12.

[45] "Political Rights of Women in Member Nations of the United Nations," United States Department of Labor, Women's Bureau, from United Nations Report A/5153, August 1, 1962.

sentatives at a 1975, U.N.-sponsored meeting in Mexico City on the role of women followed the lead of Arab representatives by deflecting discussions of the main issues with irrelevant condemnations of Israel, where women and men are more equal than in any African state.

Another sign of structural change in some countries is the attempt to bring the rural areas into the mainstream of change. In Tanzania the Ujamaa village scheme sets up settlements in areas previously uncultivated. It has been reported that by 1976 about seven million people have been affected by this regroupment. Resistance and resentment contributed—along with a paucity of rain—to a decline in agricultural production, too. In Tunisia, a cooperative movement led by Ahmed Ben Salah was spreading throughout the country from 1962 to 1969: "The large programme to create viable rural organisations is now extended to roughly 10 per cent of the rural population and the *Perspective décennale* (1962–71) made the cooperative sector a distinct part of Tunisia's economic structure."[46] In September, 1969, the program was halted, however, as the government seemed to have second thoughts about the idea of complete cooperativization and perhaps about the ambitions of the dynamic leader, Ben Salah. In spite of this change, the country has maintained many cooperatives and has kept the idea of economic planning. The problems of self-management have been great for Algeria, but the country has made changes in its economic structure.

Most countries emphasize growth rather than the more fundamental change of development. Those leaders who fear their own positions might be undermined by basic change are content to announce figures of higher production of a particular industrial crop, pretending that this alone will change the country. Increasingly numbers of students in poor schools should not be considered a sign of development either. The confusion between development and growth is only one barrier to development.

Barriers to Development

Another possible barrier to development is a conflict of goals, particularly between participation on the one hand and institutionalization and centralization of power on the other. According to Huntington, institutionalization, "the process by which organizations and procedures acquire value and stability,"[47] is weakened by mobilization and participation. Agreeing with Ortega y Gasset, Huntington says that once people are awakened, so to speak, and participate in the political and economic system, they will make increasingly impossible demands on it. If the system is unable to satisfy their demands, disorder and decay result, and

[46] Douglas E. Ashford, "The Politics of Rural Mobilization in North Africa," in *The Journal of Modern African Studies*, VII, no. 2 (1969): 201.
[47] Samuel P. Huntington, "Political Development and Political Decay," reprinted in Welch (ed.), *Political Modernization*, p. 215.

the people follow any dynamic leader who promises them what they think they want.[48]

Demands for immediate material rewards will also threaten government plans for long-range slow development. The problem is that many countries' elites have made this claim as a justification for the absence of civil liberties and reasonable democratic institutions. The need for order is a convenient justification for dictatorship and oppression.

A second barrier to development is a possible attempt by some groups to prevent other groups from participation or the possibility that structural change may weaken the role played by one group. In Algeria, for example, men have resisted the participation of women, in spite of promises made and in spite of the important role played by women during the war of liberation. A deeply felt prejudice against participation by women exists in Islamic society and contributes to the problems in Algeria: "Women in Islamic culture suffer from a deeply rooted suspicion that they are morally unreliable, that there is something demonic, even unclean about them."[49]

Despite promises made to women in the Tripoli Program of July, 1962, they are still expected to wear veils; men are favored for jobs; their organization, the Union Nationale des Femmes Algériennes (UNFA) collapsed because of intense opposition from men; and the number of women deputies in the National Assembly has actually decreased since independence. Algerian women who fought as soldiers and engaged in the urban bombings that contributed to French withdrawal have fought back through books and novels in which men are accused of trying to keep women out of the mainstream of development for selfish reasons.

Gabon's first President, Léon Mba, created a woman's section of the army, but he made the mistake of paying women soldiers more than men, thus creating a deep antagonism among men that may have had something to do with the attempted coup d'état in 1964. The woman's section was abolished shortly after the coup attempt. Women increasingly work elsewhere in the police force and in civil services like the post office.

Economic change surprisingly has also been in some cases a barrier to liberation of women, at least in the view of some women. One complained that, among the Gusii of Kenya, the men now go off to work in the cities, leaving women to do their work. They have more duties in cultivation of the soil, but the men still maintain control over production and distribution by coming home at harvest time or by sending orders from the cities where they live.[50]

In Liberia, the coastal people still prevent the inland people from full participation in development. Although workers are recruited for

[48] *Ibid.*, pp. 224–29.
[49] David C. Gordon, *Women of Algeria*, Center for Middle Eastern Studies, Monograph XIX (Cambridge, Mass.: Harvard University Press, 1968), p. 12.
[50] Marjorie J. Mbilinyi, "The 'New Woman' and Traditional Norms in Tanzania," *The Journal of Modern African Studies*, X: no. 1 (1972): 61.

the foreign-owned enterprises, and although there has been a great increase in government revenue since the opening of a large iron mine, the money goes for wages for civil servants, most of whom come from the coast, and for the development of Monrovia.[51] The new President, Mr. William Tolbert, has said he is working to bring about the full participation of all Liberians, and perhaps he will be successful.

A third barrier to development is the continuing legitimacy of precolonial institutions. The existence of these institutions is not in itself a barrier. They may become a barrier if people feel threatened by the central government or if their leaders perceive they will lose their positions. For example, one of the problems in the conflict between north and south in Tchad is the rather heavy-handed way in which the central government has tried to impose civil servants on northern Muslim leaders.

In 1963 the government of Tchad took away the tax-collecting duties of canton chiefs, and in 1967 it took away their official judicial powers. Small uprisings began against the civil servants sent by the central government, and these agents were killed. People refused to pay taxes, and civil servants fled the rural areas for safer cities. President Tombalbaye also ordered that a leader of the nomads in the northernmost region of the country give up his rights as a judge of customary law. The leader then revolted against the central government. Everywhere, except in the south where President Tombalbaye came from, civil servants and military men were attacked. The President lost control of the country, regaining it only with the help of French troops.[52] In April, 1975, the Tchad military killed Tombalbaye and took over the government, but the new head of state, General Felix Malloum, was unable to bring peace. The kidnapping of Madame Claustre, a Frenchwoman, by the northerners brought the spotlight of the world press to Tchad and complicated relations with France.

African political systems without centralized institutions may resist all attempts to centralize authority. Suspicion of such authority is part of their culture. During the colonial period they developed techniques to escape from central authority, and they still use them against independent governments. Attempts to substitute judicial institutions for precolonial institutions have met with strong resistance all over Africa.

A fourth barrier to development is outside interference. European, Lebanese, and Asian control of industry and commerce in many countries permits a great outflow of money unless safeguards are taken. Some heavy industry is highly mechanized to save the companies money but does not contribute to an alleviation of unemployment. The countries may also resist economic planning.

A fifth barrier is lack of resources and technical skills, accompanied

[51] George Dalton, "History, Politics and Economic Development in Liberia," *The Journal of Economic History*, XXV, no. 4 (December, 1965): 573.
[52] See Gilbert Comte, "La Guerrilla du Tchad," in *Le Monde*, May 5, 6, 7, 1970.

by a fear of innovating. In spite of attempts to Africanize the educational system, some experts have complained that the introduction of a few courses on African history in place of courses on European history does not represent significant change or development in education. African children are still taught to disdain manual labor in schools,[53] and teaching in European languages in the beginning grades of school puts the African child at a disadvantage, according to educational experts.[54]

Corruption in government is a sixth barrier. Studies of corruption in Nigeria indicate that when political parties were legal "there was a general failure . . . to distinguish between public, party, and private financial interests, and . . . this gave the parties the opportunity to increase their own strength in a number of ways."[55] Public corporations' funds were used by political parties, and kickbacks on contracts let by the state for construction went to the party in Nigeria and in Ghana. In the latter country, "A kickback of from 5 to 10 per cent was expected in return for government contracts."[56] Whatever the reasons for corruption, it is a sign of lack of respect for regulations and squandering of the resources of the country. People who are asked to pay their taxes and obey governmental directives for purposes of development will find more ways to resist if they are convinced they will never see any benefits.

A last barrier is the small size of some developing nations. Countries with a million or even a few million people may not be able to use efficiently the dams and factories they wish to build. Industry needs a large market—the "economic space" of many countries is too small. The economist Samir Amin has said that a region the ideal size for development purposes would include Tchad, the Central African Republic, Congo-Brazzaville, Gabon, Cameroun, Zaïre, and Angola. Planning should be for the whole region: "Real industrial and agro-industrial specialization would be possible, and this would permit a linkage among these poles a system of axes of development while using particularly the basin of the Congo River."[57] Division, outward oriented

[53] See René Dumont, L'Afrique noire est mal partie (Paris: Seuil, 1962), pp. 72–74.

[54] Le Thanh Khoi, L'Enseignement en Afrique tropicale (Paris: Presses Universitaires de France, 1971), pp. 379–81.

[55] K. W. J. Post, The Nigerian Federal Election of 1959 (Dandon, 1961), reprinted in Wilfred Cartey and Martin Kilson (eds.), The Africa Reader: Colonial Africa (New York: Random House, 1970), p. 235.

[56] Herbert H. Werlin, "The Roots of Corruption—the Ghanaian Enquiry," in The Journal of Modern African Studies, X, no. 2 (1972): 252.

[57] Samir Amin and Catherine Coquery-Vidrovitch, Histoire économique du Congo: 1880–1968 (Dakar: IFAN, and Paris: Editions Anthropos, 1969), p. 151: "Des spécialisations directement industrielles et agro-industrielles véritables seraient alors possibles, qui permettraient de tisser entre ces pôles un réseau d'axes de développement, en utilisant notamment le bassin du fleuve Congo."

economies, and the political and economic pressures from outside the continent "block" development.[58]

African leaders are aware of these problems. They have sought solutions. Many think they have found an over-all solution to problems of nation-building and development in the one-party state and the idea of socialism.

---

[58] Samir Amin, *L'Afrique de l'ouest bloquée: L'Economie politique de la colonisation 1880–1970* (Paris: Les Editions de Minuit, 1971).

8 Attempted Solutions

> *In an attempt to solve the problems of material development and nation-building independent Africa has experimented with the one-party state and socialist ideology. Failures have facilitated the rise of military governments.*

Faced with the problems of development and nation-building, leaders of many independent African countries have resorted to one-party systems and have said that socialism is their guide. They have vigorously defended these choices in their writings. Acceptance of the single party and of socialism by the masses has been far from complete.

The One-Party State

The phenomenon of a state in which there is only one political party is not, of course, limited to Africa. At various times in the history of France, the United States, Mexico, Germany, the Soviet Union, and China, there has been only one organization for providing candidates for election to public office, developing programs, and winning elections. In some cases, second or third parties existed, but all power was in the hands of one organization. Until recently the Republican Party in the southern United States had no influence or power, even though it existed. Mississippi, Alabama, and Georgia were single-party states in microcosm.

In Communist countries, the Communist Party is usually the only legal party. The same was, of course, true for the Fascists in prewar Italy and Germany. In a nontotalitarian country like France, the Union pour la Nouvelle République (UNR) had such dominance under General de Gaulle, and other parties were so weak and divided, that one can say that the country was almost a single-party state, at least as far as national posts went. In Africa the following countries are among the many that have been dominated over several years by one party: Algeria, Tunisia, Egypt, Mauritania, Mali, Senegal, Liberia, Ivory Coast, Ghana, Tchad, Central African Republic, Gabon, Congo-Brazzaville, Zaïre, Malawi, Tanzania, Guinea-Bissau, Mozambique, and Angola.

Countries that have had more than one party for at least part of the period since independence have been Sierra Leone, Morocco, Malagasy, Gambia, Rwanda, Nigeria, Dahomey, Zambia, Lesotho, and Upper Volta, but the pressure to abolish opposition parties has been strong because ruling elites fear the loss of power. Ethiopia has had no parties at all. On the other hand, a Senegalese law passed in early 1976 made it possible for three parties to exist. The Senegalese Democratic Party (PDS) had already been functioning since July, 1974, and challenging the ruling Progressive Senegalese Union (UPS).

The party is identified with the nation in a single-party situation, but in varying degrees. In Algeria, Congo, and Ghana, the single-party system was put into the constitution. In Ghana the colors of the party's flag were adopted by the state to replace the previous colors. In Congo the president was chosen in the course of party meetings; in chapter 1, article 2 of the constitution, one reads: "Sovereignty resides in the people and from the people emanate all public powers through one Popular Party: The Congolese Labor Party whose organization is defined in its Statutes." And in chapter IV, article 36: "The President of the Central Committee of the Congolese Labor Party is President of the Republic and Head of State." Article 37: "The President of the Republic is elected for 5 years by the Congress of the Party in conformity with the statutes of the Party."

In most single-party states the chief executive is also head of the party, symbolizing the identification of party with state and nation. Although it is true that the Prime Minister of Britain and the President of the United States are the heads of their parties, too, they are the titular heads and do not hold administrative party positions. In Guinea, President Touré has been the chief executive as well as Secretary General of the PDG. Elsewhere, in the Ivory Coast, Houphouët-Boigny is president, but Philippe Yacé has been secretary general of the PDCI. And, in Guinea-Bissau Aristides Pereira is general-secretary of the PAIGC while Luis Cabral is Head of State.

Cabinet members in a one-party state are high-ranking officials in the party. The highest organ in Guinea's PDG, the *bureau politique*, generally has seven or eight of its twelve members in the cabinet. The national executive of Tanzania's TANU has at least half of its members in cabinet posts. It has been practically impossible in most states for a man or woman to gain a high position in the civil service without being a member of the party.

It is difficult to separate the party from the government, from the legislature and the administration, in a one-party state. Party officials become administrators or para-administrators. A high-ranking TANU official was named chief academic officer of the University of Dar es Salaam, replacing a scholar, for example. The party is also supposed to decide which secondary school students will have the privilege of continuing their education in university. There is a tendency to create a monolith in which everything is absorbed: youth movements, women's movements, trade unions, cooperatives. In the process of absorbing every local organization, the party, in a sense, disappears. If the party is everything, it may lose its reason for being. Without any competition, parties such as Ivory Coast's PDCI, Kenya's KANU, and Algeria's FLN have become moribund themselves.

What happens is that a few men and women at the top of the party use its organization and ideology to control everyone else. This small group is also united by bonds of personal friendship and the shared struggle against colonialism. Below the very top echelons of the single party are men who fear that in party competition they might lose their jobs. Thus, an advantage of the one-party monolith to those already in power is that criticism and challenge are reduced. This muting of opposition voices serves to protect jobs.

However, the original reasons for the development of the one-party state have nothing to do with keeping jobs. Parties evolved out of nationalist movements that struggled for the creation of a necessary common front against colonialism in order to bring about independence as quickly as possible. Colonial forces—the administration, business, the church—were fairly well united, so that unity of opposition was necessary. Besides, one organization was and is necessary to bring different ethnic groups together. At the end of a meeting of 30 parties and liberation movements in Tunis in July, 1975, participants affirmed that the party is the only organization capable of building national unity.

Single parties that took power at independence had also recognized the need to mobilize the masses as much as possible. In most cases, they were not in fact able to mobilize the majority of the population, but they did recruit more people and more diverse groups than had ever been recruited before.

For example, prior to the advent of the FLN in Algeria (which was never as unified as its leaders wished), Algerians who worked to bring about change were divided into many different groups: The Association of Ulama, the Democratic Union of the Algerian Manifesto (UDMA), Parti du Peuple Algérien, or Mouvement pour le Triomphe des Libertés Démocratiques (MTLD). In Guinea after the openly ethnic parties came alliances between groups to form the Parti Socialiste de Guinée, the Union Franco-Guinéenne, the Comité d'Entente Guinéenne, and the Parti Progressiste de Guinée. In 1947 the PDG, or Parti Démocratique de Guinée, was founded, and soon Sékou Touré became its most important leader. In 1954 the other parties formed the Bloc Africain de Guinée (BAG) and the Démocratie Socialiste de Guinée (DSG). Although the DSG, BAG, and PDG were not tied to ethnic groups or regions, only PDG leaders like Sékou Touré campaigned hard for the unity of all groups under its banner and for a unified country.

Touré used his descent from Samory Touré to advantage, for Samory had united many peoples under him and he had fought the French. In addition, Sékou Touré was able to surmount some divisions within the Malinké group, and he muted his party's socialist leanings in order not to antagonize the Muslims. In fact, he attracted to the PDG some

Muslim reform leaders. He also preached against ethnic conflict and jealousies and used various symbols to create new loyalties. He attracted Diallo Sayfoulaye, a leading Fulani, into the party, and got control of most elective offices. The other two parties united in 1958 to form a Guinean branch of the PRA, or Parti de Regroupement Africain, and they called for independence from France. In September, Sékou Touré called for a "no" vote on the French constitution, thus meaning Guinea would become independent. The others then joined with the PDG, so that by the end of 1958 Guinea had only one political party and was independent. Since 1958 the country has had only one political party.[1]

The PDG, unlike other parties, had campaigned in rural areas to get mass backing, and it had effectively led the country to independence. On these two bases, the party claimed to be Guinea. Without the PDG, the party claimed, Guinea would be neither independent nor one, and therefore it was a true emanation of the nation and could not be separated from it. Both FRELIMO in Mozambique and PAIGC in Guinea-Bissau succeeded in grouping together the various ethnic groups and thus avoided the fratricide of Angola.

In Tanzania the ethnic situation was particularly complex. There were small regional or ethnic organizations after World War II, such as the Sukuma Union and the Lake Province Growers Association in the northwest. As early as 1947 or 1948, the Sukuma Union tried "to form a new association to coordinate representation of the interests of all the tribes of the province."[2] This organization did not last, and the Sukuma Union developed into an increasingly political organization along with the TAA, the Tanganyikan African Association, founded in 1929. In 1954, leaders of TAA reorganized and changed the name of the association to Tanganyika Africa National Union, after it had begun to recruit in the countryside and had more or less absorbed the Sukuma Union and other ethnic associations.

TANU became the main articulator of anticolonial feeling. Quite late, other organizations were formed. In 1958 the African National Congress, "those skeptical of TANU's assertive thrust toward monolithic control at the local level, and others excluded by chance or circumstance from the inner councils of provincial, district and branch TANU organizations, struck independent postures."[3]

In 1962 TANU acted against the African National Congress by banning its public meetings. Then members were threatened with loss of jobs. The same year, the People's Democratic Party was founded, but leaders were removed from districts where they lived. In January, 1963, the National Executive Committee decided to make the country into

---

[1] Ruth Schachter Morgenthau, *Political Parties in French-Speaking West Africa* (Oxford: The Clarendon Press, 1964), pp. 231-53.

[2] G. Andrew Maguire, *Toward 'Uhuru' in Tanzania: The Politics of Participation* (Cambridge, England: Cambridge University Press, 1969), p. 78.

[3] *Ibid.*, p. 270.

Attempted Solutions 189

a one-party state. TANU thus absorbed the other parties, and Asian and European members were then permitted to join.

TANU acted to end the Sukumaland Federal Council, an institution set up by the British in 1946 to unite Sukuma chiefdoms, and in other ethnic groupings chiefs were replaced by civil servants, although in some cases these civil servants were chiefs or of chiefly families. "Predominantly elected divisional and village development committees would take over the functions of the former chiefdom and subordinate councils."[4]

TANU started to control the union movement by gaining control of the Central Tanganyika Federation of labor and then tried to increase the power of the Federation within the labor movement.[5]

Berg and Butler have pointed out that in some countries, like Guinea and Kenya, both of which became one-party states, the trade union was close to the party because the high officials of the union were also the high officials of the party. Sékou Touré was Secretary General of the PDG and head of the CGT union. Tom Mboya was the leader of the Kenya Federation of Labor and a leader of KANU.

In Ghana and Algeria trade unions supported the parties' nationalist activities before independence. Labor demonstrations supported party demonstrations. Labor was more or less independent from the CPP in Ghana, but the party wished to use the union and centralize authority in the central federation of the Trade Union Congress (TUC). However, the individual unions kept their autonomy. In 1958 the government legislated to centralize power in the party-controlled TUC. Laws were passed to prevent any union from remaining or becoming autonomous.

In Algeria, the Union Générale des Travailleurs Algériens was founded by the party in 1956 but was more active outside Algeria, where workers —in France, for example—had long participated in trade union activities. Leaders tried to reorganize after 1962. To gain control, the party sent men to vote at the meeting of the union. They succeeded in voting out the somewhat independent leadership, but angry union officials and workers struck.[6] In 1965 the party realized it had hurt its goals by its crude effort to crush the union. At another congress in 1965, President Ben Bella changed his tactics and allowed free choice of leaders, and the new leaders appeared both independent and committed to the FLN's program.[7]

After the military coup in 1965, some unionists were arrested, and the unions were intimidated. In 1968 the FLN began putting party men at the heads of the locals and accused the Union Générale des

---

[4] *Ibid.*, pp. 332, 330-31.

[5] Elliott S. Berg and Jeffrey Butler, "Trade Unions," in James S. Coleman and Carl G. Rosberg, Jr., *Political Parties and National Integration in Tropical Africa* (Berkeley and Los Angeles: University of California Press, 1964).

[6] Clement Henry Moore, *Politics in North Africa: Algeria, Morocco, Tunisia*, The Little, Brown Series in Comparative Politics (Boston: Little, Brown, 1970), p. 192.

[7] *Ibid.*, pp. 193–94.

Travailleurs Algériens of economic sabotage. The leadership of the union became divided, and membership decreased. This is in fact the situation in all countries with a single party. Attempts to control the unions are also made in other countries. Trade union activity, like that of the press, was freer during the latter days of colonialism than after independence. Party leaders attempt through the organization of the party and centralized leadership to control everything in the country.

Party Organization

It has often been said that the party in the single-party state has tried to organize like the Communist Party and has used Communist techniques. This is quite different from saying it is a Communist invention or that members are Communists. The point is that the Communist Party is a well-organized institution that has successfully ruled the Soviet Union and China.

In regard to some countries, however, it is not really worthwhile to talk at length about party structure, because it is moribund at the local level. Power is at the top only. Organization is at the top only, and the underpinnings are weak and unsure. KANU of Kenya, for example, seems to have disintegrated. Surprisingly, even the FLN, which had fought a war of liberation against the French, could not maintain its cohesion. After independence, the party's highest organ was the Political Bureau; next a hundred federations corresponding to the *arrondissements*, administrative units, and they in turn were "divided into 1,112 *kasmas* (districts) at the level of the communes." Within the communes were cells, whose functions were mainly educational, of no more than fifty members. These were the units at the bottom of the FLN pyramid, but they became inactive.[8] Although the FLN had a representative in a local area, he was not often respected. "The typical small town party official was a young man in a French-cut suit and Italian pointed shoes, hiding behind dark glasses and posing as an intellectual. Such officials were more interested in playing politics than in stimulating local initiative or mobilizing the people."[9] The leadership tried to reorganize the party in 1968–69, and the central party and the woman's and youth wings became much weaker at the grass-roots level. Control by the leaders is important to the leaders, but either they do not care to organize or they have not been successful when they have tried to organize. Problems of effective and long-lasting organization are typical of all African countries. One of the reasons given for allowing two new parties to form in Senegal in 1975 and 1976 was a desire to revive the ruling party through challenge and competition.

The Guinean PDG has claimed to have at least one-quarter of the

[8] David and Marina Ottaway, *Algeria: The Politics of a Socialist Revolution* (Berkeley and Los Angeles: University of California Press, 1970), p. 115.
[9] *Ibid.*, p. 116.

ATTEMPTED SOLUTIONS   191

population in its ranks. There have been 7,164 local committees at the base. These are located in villages and neighborhoods of cities like Conakry. Each committee has a ten-member executive that calls together the membership for the scheduled weekly meetings, at which party directives are discussed and party principles learned.

The executive represents the local committee at the district level. There are 169 district committees. The district elects an executive and sends representatives to the party organization at the level of the region. There are twenty-nine administrative regions in the country; thus, there are twenty-nine federations of the party plus an extra federation in Conakry, making a total of thirty. Each federation is directed by a seven-man board. At the top of the party and at the national level is the BPN, or National Political Bureau. The BPN has seventeen members. It is the organism that runs the party day to day and is, in effect, the most important part of the PDG. The BPN is elected once every three years by a National Congress of the party, which is supposed to give it general direction. The National Congress is composed of ten party delegates for each district. Therefore, there are approximately 1,690 delegates to these meetings. At each level of the party is a corresponding woman's and youth section. Places on the executive committees are reserved for women. There is always at least one woman on the BPN.

Although in theory higher officials in the party are elected by lower officials, the flow of direction is from top to bottom, with the BPN controlling who is elected to what post within the party. Normally no one is elected to the BPN or removed from it without the approval of the most important member, Secretary General Sékou Touré.

The structure of the single party of Cameroun, the Union Camerounaise (UC), is parallel to the country's administrative structure. Committees exist in villages and neighborhoods of cities. Above these committees are the *sous-sections* at the district level, and they make up a section at the level of a department. Each section sends representatives to a party congress, which supposedly sets the party line and elects the executive committee, as does Guinea's BPN.

The leaders of the Union Camerounaise claim that their party is not a "single party" but, rather, a "unified party." Other parties absorbed themselves into the UC, and party leadership claimed the UC was the only national party with control over many jobs. In the early 1960's, meetings of parties not absorbed in the UC were broken up by UC members, and their adherents were jailed on various pretexts. Many people then joined the dominant party: "Some were promised houses; others were given government positions; some were simply frightened into their new party affiliations."[10]

In elections in 1962 and 1963, the UC effectively discouraged opposi-

---

[10] Willard R. Johnson, *The Cameroon Federation: Political Integration in a Fragmentary Society* (Princeton, N.J.: Princeton University Press, 1970), p. 254.

tion parties by unfair practices, harassment, and threats. Like other single parties, the UC could henceforth claim massive majorities of all ethnic groups voting for it.

Elections

During much of the late colonial period, European administrators attempted to influence votes; some clearly falsified them when they had the chance. They did so to help candidates friendly to the colonial administration. But near the end of the colonial period these elections were more or less fair and democratic. One proof of this is that anti-colonialist forces in Tunisia, Guinea, Tanzania, and Ghana took office after elections held while the colonial administration was still intact—although the administration had earlier imprisoned these same anti-colonialists.

Worldwide, elections are seldom completely free and open. Attempts are made to intimidate the voter, ballot boxes are filled before the election begins, ballots are counted to suit the ruling group, choices are narrow. The use of sophisticated advertising techniques "pioneered" in the United States but now being used elsewhere to some extent opens the way toward a form of hypnosis of the electorate unknown as yet in Africa. Many Americans need go no further than a city like Chicago for reports of manipulation of the vote.

In most single-party states, efforts are made to get out the vote; to prevent opposition parties from forming, by law if necessary; and to ensure control over the choice of candidates, so that elected officials will know their future election depends on pleasing party officials and not the people who elected them. Those who do the nominating count. Further, to prevent the rise of popular individuals with close links to one constituency, the single-party state usually sets up a single constituency for the whole country. Voters are therefore not able to associate with a given candidate, even if he is the only candidate; they are presented with a list for the whole country and are to vote "yes" or "no" on the whole list. The freedom of the voter is even less than what it might be in a single-party situation.

A well-known exception to this general rule is Tanzania, where TANU says it permits any party member to run for the national assembly, and in most constituencies there is more than one candidate, assuring some choice. However, the president may appoint a losing candidate to the assembly. This is what happened, for example, in 1965, after the defeat of Dr. Nyerere's close associate, Paul Bomani, in the Mwanza area.

More than 3.25 milion registered voters could choose among 208 candidates for 107 seats in the national assembly. Anyone could present his name if he were a member of TANU and if twenty-five people supported him. He then appeared before a meeting of TANU members in his district, to submit to questions about his record. The conference then ranked the candidates in order of their own preference and forwarded them to the national committee. The committee approved of two candidates for almost every constituency, who then ran under the control of and at the expense of TANU and the government.

During the campaign government or party vehicles took candidates (together) to meetings, where they spoke from the same platform. The two candidates chosen to run per constituency chose between a house or a hoe as their symbol. They were required to speak Swahili, and they were forbidden to talk about any ethnic group. More than 2.25 million people voted, and ministers in addition to Bomani were defeated. Five non-Africans won, and only "10% of the members of the Assembly [were] carryovers from the old."[11] Five years later, in 1970, another election was held for the national assembly, and the results were similar. The elections provide a good outlet for people's feelings about government policy, even if they are unable to vote for a non-TANU candidate. Party elections in 1975 reportedly brought many new faces into the most important organs of TANU.

In all political systems the people's choice is limited. In most one-party states the people really have no choice at all, but in Tanzania there is an exception, probably one of the several reasons President Nyerere has been one of the most popular leaders in any country, whereas many elsewhere have been overthrown.

Coups

Many single-party governments have been overthrown, mainly by the military in unconstitutional coups d'etat. Multiparty states have experienced the same phenomenon. Greece, for example, and France, to say nothing of the Latin American republics, have seen coups. The military takes over when it feels its own professional interests are threatened; because it may be encouraged by outside forces; because it feels the regime is "evil" and it is the only other force that can act, for constitutional remedies are inadequate; and because military leaders have personal ambitions that can be satisfied only by taking over the government.

One institution or method of the one-party system that some people may find bad is "democratic centralism." The terminology, borrowed from the Communist Party, means in Guinea, for example:

1. Party leaders are directly and democratically chosen by the supporters who all enjoy full liberty of conscience and of expression within the Party;
2. The affairs of the State of Guinea are the affairs of all the citizens of Guinea. The programme of the Party is democratically discussed. As

[11] Ruth Schachter Morgenthau, "African Elections: Tanzania's Contribution," *Africa Report*, December, 1965, pp. 12–16.

long as no decision has been made, each is free to say what he thinks or what he wishes. But when, after extensive discussions in congress or in assembly, a decision has been arrived at by a unanimous vote or by a majority, the supporters and leaders are bound to apply it correctly;
3. The responsibility for leadership is not shared. Only the responsibility for a decision is shared. Thus, no breach of discipline can be permitted.[12]

What this seems to mean is that there is free discussion in the party, but once a decision is taken everyone must obey and follow the leaders. No outsider knows what goes on in party discussions. Perhaps there is completely free discussion, even when the president of the country is taking part in policy discussions, as well as choice of candidates, but what little information one gets from those who, at least at one time, participated in such discussion is that the president of the country almost completely dominates discussions and expects rigid compliance to what turn out to be his decisions.

Some African leaders claim the single party with one leader is in keeping with traditional African political systems when there was no formal opposition. Perhaps so, but there is an Ibibio story that says one chief sent a message summoning others: "Come to discuss this matter with me." No one came. He realized his mistake and sent another message: "Let us assemble so that we can discuss together." They all came. The emphasis on egalitarianism among those who have the right to discuss matters is probably not adhered to today in states headed by the strong leaders who have emerged in most African states. It is just this centralization of authority and decision-making in one person, what Professor Aristide Zolberg has called the "Presidential Monarch," that some military men may object to. But military men in power may also become presidential monarchs.

The first military coup in independent Africa took place in Egypt. In a sense, the coup of young Egyptian officers in 1952 can be considered the beginning of the country's period of independence. The officers, disgusted by the obvious corruption of the British-protected monarchy—supposedly independent since 1922 but heavily influenced by London—and angered by the loss of the Arab-Israeli war of 1948–49, took power and maintained themselves up to and beyond President Nasser's sudden death in 1970. They have changed ownership of land, nationalizing many holdings, and have taken control of locally owned industry. The government nationalized the Suez Canal and generally dislodged the old ruling class, giving poor people more opportunity to move up. Opening of the Aswan Dam should increase productivity to help feed Egypt's large population, but purchases of military equipment and continuing corruption compromise other gains.

In 1958 the military seized control of the Sudanese government;

[12] Sékou Touré, "Les principes du centralisme démocratique," cited in Victor D. Du Bois, "Guinea," in Coleman and Rosberg, *Political Parties and National Integration*, p. 207.

Attempted Solutions 195

civilians replaced them but in turn were replaced by other military leaders.

In 1960 a group of military men attempted a coup in the no-party state of Ethiopia during the emperor's absence on a visit in South America. The coup collapsed when the leader suddenly returned by airplane, but others succeeded in September, 1974, replacing the emperor with a Provisional Military Administrative Council first headed by General Aman Andom of Eritrean origins. After Aman Andom was killed by his own colleagues, Brigadier Teferi Benti, an Amhara, replaced him.

The next coup, or series of coups, took place in Congo-Kinshasa. In 1960, after the turmoil caused by an army mutiny, Belgian intervention, Katanga's secession, and the sending of United Nations troops, the military intervened to install a so-called Collège des Commissaires to run the government. Civilian government returned under Joseph Ileo at the end of 1960, and under Cyrille Adoula in 1961. The head of the military, Joseph Mobutu, who consolidated his own position in the face of rivals, continued to exert great influence on successive governments. The only force the government had in attempting to put down the various revolts and secessions in the country was Mobutu's Armée Nationale Congolaise (ANC). He took over the government again in 1965, keeping power after making himself president of the republic.

A series of coups began in Togo in January, 1963, with the overthrow and assassination of President Sylvanus Olympio, who had recently reduced the size and salaries of the army. The same year, the military, responding to labor union demonstrations, took over the Congo-Brazzaville government, then withdrew, as in Congo-Kinshasa, to permit civilian rule until 1968, when it seized power.

President Mba of Gabon was overthrown early in 1964 but returned after the intervention of French troops. In 1965, the army under Houari Boumediene overthrew President Ben Bella in Algeria, claiming it did so because of Ben Bella's dictatorial rule. The same thing happened several times in Dahomey (or Benin). In January, 1966, it was the turn of the Central African Republic, then Upper Volta, Nigeria, and Ghana. Coups took place in Mali, Uganda, Burundi, Somalia, Sierra Leone, and Libya. In 1971 an attempted coup took place in Morocco. In addition to the Ethiopian military takeover, Niger's government was toppled in April, 1974, and so were Tchad's and Nigeria's in 1975. General Murtala Muhammad replaced Yakuba Gowon, but was himself assassinated in another but unsuccessful coup attempt in Lagos in early 1976. Lt. General Olusegun Obasanjo then became the first Yonuba to head Niberia.

Another easily disenchanted group has been the students, who have vainly tried to keep their separate organizations, impossible within their homelands but usually possible in the foreign countries in which they study. The Algerian student organization opposed the 1965 coup d'état, and in the Ivory Coast Houphouët-Boigny spent years trying to either suppress or win over dissident students. Both Dr. Nkrumah and Dr. Nyerere found themselves at odds with local universities, and severe repression has taken place in Congo-Kinshasa and Ethiopia. Students do not, of course, have the power or the organization of the military.

African leaders feel too insecure to permit opposition or possible opposition. They say the single party will ensure that different ethnic and regional groups will work together, but the party is perforce organized at its basic level on ethnic and regional lines. The people of Mwanza are Sukuma and belong to one section of TANU; the people of Labé are Fulani and belong to one section of the PDG; the people of Tizi Ouzou are Kabyles and belong to one section of the FLN. What is to prevent these sections from struggling against the Chagga section in Moshi, the Malinké section in Kankan, the Arab section in Algiers? In the one-party system of the American south, the predominance of Democrats in Alabama never prevented competition between counties or between the industrial north and the rural midsection of the state.

Further, the single party is not an automatic solution for material development. It is too centralized, and leaders fear that local planning and decision-making will permit groups and individuals to compete for power with the central government. Leaders are afraid of losing control; they feel insecure about their positions.

The insecurity of leadership and the weak organization of both party and the administration are great problems that are likely to be with most African countries for a long time to come. The single party that has brought a country to independence, even after a long war, is not necessarily regarded by the people as a legitimate ruling organization, particularly if they sense corruption or internal conflict. The army is not a solution either because colonial rule alienated the military from its society and culture. Without the bonds African armies act like mercenaries or like social janissaries.[13] It took many years for the Communist Party to establish its legitimacy in the Soviet Union and China. In Africa there are still many people who do not feel they are getting any benefits, although the socialist program of the parties is appealing.

African Socialism

Socialism is popular in most states of Africa for civilians and the military and has great appeal to African youth. Although those who call themselves socialists came to an anticolonial position rather late in the imperial period, many of their doctrines are attractive as a justification for policies that will be taken in spite of ideology, as a rough guideline, and because they provide definite goals to give direction and legitimacy.

Unity is one of the most important aspirations of Africans—unity within the developing nation-state and unity across contemporary political frontiers. Socialism, defined as the "doctrine that the ownership

[13] Claude L. Welch, "Continuity and Discontinuity in African Military Organization" *Journal of Modern African Studies*, XIII, no. 2 (1975): 229–48.

Attempted Solutions

and control of the means of production—capital, land, or property—should be held by the community as a whole and administered in the interests of all,"[14] is unifying because it is anti-individualistic and it recognizes no ethnic divisions. The only divisions it recognizes are those based on class, and class divisions are purely materialistic—there is nothing racial, inborn, or mystical about them. The divisions can be conquered, suppressed, or prevented. The Tanzanian government restrictions on the private ownership of houses—under the Arusha declaration, a man may own only the house he is actually living in—are not designed to prevent the gathering of wealth by individuals as such but to prevent the exercise of power and influence through the possession of wealth. By preventing concentrations of wealth in private hands, the government and party will prevent, they hope, the concentration in private hands of power and influence that can be used to exploit people and influence public policy for narrow interests.

Second, Marxist doctrine presents a historical-progressive movement toward a specific goal: History is moving inexorably toward the rule of the proletariat, and independence for Africa can be seen as a step in that direction. As Fanon says, it may be that all of Africa is a proletariat.

Third, socialism provides a justification for the nationalization of both foreign-owned and locally owned businesses and factories of various kinds. It helps explain the need for planning, state ownership, and the single party.

In most African countries, with the exception of Nigeria, Morocco, Tunisia, Egypt, the Ivory Coast, and a few others, there are no businessmen or entrepreneurs with the capital necessary to develop large industries. The capital must come from the government or from outside the country. Some countries, including the Ivory Coast, Gabon, Malawi, Kenya, Liberia, and Senegal, have accepted foreign investments with a minimum of control in order to create jobs and encourage further investment. Ghana under Nkruma, Madagascar, Tanzania under Nyerere, Algeria and Egypt, and Mali under Modibo Keita, Guinea-Bissau under Luis Cabral, and Mozambique under Samora Machel began to exert considerable control over outside investments and nationalized them so they became the property of the state. They said they feared that foreign investors would not respect priorities of development and would be able to manipulate the economy. Centralized economic and social planning fit these leaders' plans for centralized political control.

Planning began in socialist and Communist countries but has been used by many other countries, such as France and India. Some planning goes on in the United States too, but because of the word's socialist connotations it is generally not called planning.

---

[14] Daniel Bell, "Socialism," in *International Encyclopedia of Social Sciences*, XIV (New York: Crowell Collier and Macmillan, 1968): 506, 527.

What development there was in Africa during the colonial period was in a way planned, although not very well. French and British economic development programs were set up for the colonies, with European interests uppermost in the planners' minds. Tunisia had its first development plan from 1948 to 1952, four years before independence.

Planning in independent countries is seen as a way to bring about effective "developmental socialism." This means "(1) social justice and higher living standards, (2) achieved through more or less democratic processes, (3) without colonialism, and (4) through the presumably rational processes of national planning."[15]

A fourth point about socialism that appeals to African leaders is its optimism about the future. Development can come, there is nothing innately preventing it. It is thus a nonracist, almost an antiracist, set of beliefs. Race, religion, and geography are irrelevant to socialism; all men are equal. This is of course a refreshing antidote to colonial doctrines, which implicitly or explicitly asserted a supposed African inferiority.

Socialism is appealing because of the successes of two countries once considered underdeveloped, the Soviet Union and China. Imperial Russia, not as underdeveloped materially as China, has become a great world power under a socialist-Communist government. China is probably the most spectacular example for Africans—it was under the influence of foreign powers, in a quasi-colonial status—but, after a long struggle that some people say ended only in 1949 with the victory of the Communists, socialism won and then proceeded to develop the country. China, though not a European Caucasian country, has equaled European countries in some technical achievements. Many Africans used to think that technical knowledge—the building of airplanes, radios, automobiles—might be the preserve of the European because of some inborn capacity. China proved this incorrect, particularly with its explosion of nuclear devices. Socialism is seen as a possible way to achieve sufficient power to forge unity, promote economic development, and free the nation from manipulative, exploitive forces.

The socialist terminology of Friedrich Engels can easily be flung at European powers. His "exploiting bourgeoisie" can be equated with the colonialists or, if need be, the African or Asian businessman. It was the African masses who "produced" and were kept down like the European workers in Engels's formulation. Surplus value explained the meaning of exploitation of colonial peoples.

Colonial peoples produced at low wages, but European owners made the profits. African countries produced agricultural products, and minerals were taken from their soil; they purchased from the Europeans needed manufactured goods at much higher prices. Engels wrote that

---

[15] Bertram Gross, in preface to Douglas Elliott Ashford, *Morocco-Tunisia: Politics and Planning*, National Planning Series (Syracuse, N.Y.: Syracuse University Press, 1965), pp. xiii, xiv.

ATTEMPTED SOLUTIONS   199

the proletariat would take over the government (independence in the African context) and transform industry and business so that they would belong to the people: "Socialized production upon a predetermined plan becomes henceforth possible." Classes disappear; the state vanishes; man is unified and free. It is the proletariat that can bring freedom and peace to the world.[16]

African leaders have done more than identify with socialism by name changes such as Congo People's Republic, and People's Republic of Mozambique and by proclamations in Benin, Congo, and Somalia that Marxism-Leninism is the official state ideology. Africans have insisted they are building African socialism. This is a reaction to the attempts of all Europeans, socialist or not, to be paternalistic toward non-Europeans. When the great West Indian poet Aimé Césaire broke with the Communist Party in 1956, he accused it of not understanding the aspirations of black peoples. The very refusal to recognize racial or religious differences on the part of the Communists became offensive to Africans and West Indians, who wished to free themselves *and* assert the richness of their civilizations and history.

African leaders have also objected to the idea of class warfare and the notion of materialism as the basis of scientific socialism. They say there are no classes to speak of in Africa, and they assert a humanism that insists on man's belief in forces beyond purely material ones. This assertion of *African* socialism frees Africa from becoming too closely associated with the socialist countries and thus helps maintain a certain level of neutrality.

President Léopold Sédar Senghor wrote specifically on the point that Africans were suppressed as a race, not a class. Europeans of all ideologies believe they have a monopoly on civilization and thought, in Senghor's view. The European proletariat—in spite of Marx's and Engels's appeals for unity—did not feel solidarity with colonial peoples, the Third World proletariat. Senghor wrote that times had also changed since Marx and Engels. New discoveries have been made in science, and new methods of thought developed. The Africans, he insisted, "have inherited, from our ancestors, our own method of knowledge."[17] It is on the basis of African values that, in President Senghor's view, socialism and the one-party state will revolutionize Africa.

Single Parties, Socialism, and Revolution

The word "revolution" is used with such frequency today that it has more or less lost whatever meaning it once had. A right-wing coup in Brazil replaces a government undertaking basic reforms, and the press calls it a revolution. The military in another country seizes power to

[16] Friedrich Engels, *Socialism—Utopian and Scientific*, trans. Edward Aveling (New York: International Publishers, 1935), pp. 74–75.
[17] Léopold Sédar Senghor, *Nation et voie africaine du socialisme* (Paris: Présence Africaine, 1961), pp. 99, 94–98.

protect the interests of the army, and the generals call it a "revolution" by the people and for the people. Shouting the word does not mean that a revolution is going on. As Robert Dahl has said, if Denmark were to proclaim itself a republic tomorrow and replace the king with an elected president, this single action would bring about far less change than the various social and economic and political transformations quietly taking place in that country over the past several years under a monarchical form of government.[18]

The replacement of Europeans by the African colonial elite and the creation of socialist one-party states did not mean a transformation of the political system. The real revolution has been the increasing acceptance of a new framework for political, economic, and social activities by a significant group of people. During the colonial period, the precolonial system began to lose its status as the highest loyalty group for an increasing number of people. Change in identity has therefore meant the beginnings of the transformation of precolonial political systems—those with states and those without states—into ethnic groups or distinct cultural communities within a larger cultural community that has political independence.

The willingness of some Malinke peoples of Guinea to extend their loyalty to the new state of Guinea, whose first president was a Malinke, and to consider other residents of that state to be Guineans just like themselves is a revolutionary change. This is true even if the Malinke do not completely lose their identity and loyalty to what are now ethnic values. Continuation of the process after independence in Ghana, for example, "helped to legitimize notions of a national society in which diverse peoples in Ghana played a role, to attach subelites to a national regime and give them national and participant orientations."[19] With the establishment of the new framework and the increasing ability of government to allocate goods and services, people orient themselves "to government output and to the need to affect government decision-making."[20] This change is significant.

Similarly, the concentration of power in civil service and a political party, operating at the level of the new state, and the use of police and an army to ensure compliance were revolutionary. The process began during the colonial period. The claim to legitimate authority by the head of a territory whose boundaries were delimited during the colonial period, or an independent state called Angola or Algeria, is revolutionary. Even where, as in Morocco, Swaziland, and Burundi, some state authority existed before the colonial period, the French, British, and Belgians, respectively, helped consolidate it.

[18] Robert A. Dahl, *After the Revolution? Authority in a Good Society* (New Haven, Conn.: Yale University Press, 1970), pp. 3–4.
[19] Jon Kraus, "Political Change, Conflict, and Development in Ghana," in Philip Foster and Aristide R. Zolberg (eds.), *Ghana and the Ivory Coast: Perspectives on Modernization* (Chicago: Chicago University Press, 1971), p. 70.
[20] *Ibid.*, p. 71.

ATTEMPTED SOLUTIONS 201

Centralization of power has been the single most important problem in the history of African politics. The creators of the colonial state introduced structures and methods to serve their own purposes, and in some cases these methods have become more rather than less like the European model, partly because they have been successful in solving problems of centralization. The replacement of white faces by black faces in African structures merely continues methods of centralization rather than introducing new revolutionary changes.

Centralization

After independence, the new rulers tried to consolidate institutional legitimacy and introduce their own personal legitimacy. They had already mobilized the masses against the Europeans by an articulation of their immediate grievances, but few proposed any basic change in institutions established in the late colonial period—such as an increase in elective offices, for example.

The continued development of this European type of administration is the most striking example of the unwillingness of the African elite to bring about basic change after independence. Efforts to monopolize power have even reversed what seemed to be a trend established by the colonialists themselves after World War II to allow some local initiative through elected regional councils and through the development of municipal government. The result is an increased concentration of power in the hands of European-trained African civil servants who operate at the center of the political system. The gap between these officials' salaries and the earnings of workers and farmers continues to grow; their control over industry as governments nationalize it increases apace. And, they are increasingly entrenched in power as new governments come and go after coup and counter-coup.

Partly as a result of the training these younger civil servants received, "administration procedures and bureaucratic controls have too often remained untouched" since independence.[21] This is true in areas formerly controlled by Britain, France, Belgium, and Spain, but is probably less likely in the former Portuguese areas. Statutes governing the civil services have rarely been altered significantly; the same salary scales and codes of behavior continue; administrative law books have not changed. The same elitist attitudes are absorbed, including a generalized disdain for elected officials and technicians, in spite of egalitarian socialist ideology.

After entry into the civil services of their respective countries, these men and women become more important than elected councilors or even members of national legislative assemblies. For example, in the three states of East Africa, leaders planned to permit free elections to

[21] A. H. M. Kirk-Greene, "The New African Administrator," in *Journal of Modern African Studies*, X, no. 1 (1972): 97.

town councils, but in Kenya after independence members have been appointed by the party, and in Uganda under President Obote the various ministers appointed them. Even if voters have a little choice in Tanzania, the ruling party nominates candidates, and high-ranking civil servants attend council meetings. These officials have the power to approve the agenda for the council meetings; they provide technical advice, which is an important influence, and they help obtain grants for the operation of the councils. The latter have little power to raise their own revenue or to hire and fire their own personnel. "The Kenya government has recently resumed direct control of primary education, road maintenance, and health services in the rural areas."[22]

The powers of local councils have also decreased in the Ivory Coast. Following strictly the colonial tradition, the administrative head of a region is also mayor of the principal town. As such, he tries to dominate the elected municipal councilors. Although Nigeria's central government spent only 42.4 percent of total government expenditures in 1963–64, its share increased to 70.5 percent in 1971–72, while state expenditures declined from 43.6 percent to 26.1 percent. During these years, town and city government shares declined from 14 to 3.4 percent. On the other hand, in 1976 the Nigerian military announced a revival of local authorities, and Guinea-Bissau's elected Regional Councils seem very much alive.

In Algeria, attempts were made just after independence at decentralization and increased participation in projects called "self-management" by workers on abandoned French farms and industrial enterprises. On farms, for example, Algerians elected management committees, which with an elected farm manager ran the large estates. Any profits would be divided among the workers. More than 16,000 farms were affected by decrees of March, 1963, officially establishing self-management. They amounted to "about eight hundred thousand hectares of the most fertile land and employing perhaps seventy thousand workers." In addition, "450 industrial enterprises . . . hundreds of hotels, restaurants, cafés, shops, and other commercial enterprises" were affected.[23]

The new government of Ben Bella announced these self-management projects as an experiment in socialism, but centralizing tendencies soon began to prevail. Centralized marketing organizations for the farm products and centralized institutions to control finances of the farms began after declines in productivity. Factories soon came under the control of government administrators in Algiers. After the overthrow of Ben Bella by Houari Boumediene, state corporations replaced some self-managed enterprises, and the number of self-managed farms decreased further.

In Algeria, a very dynamic trade union movement was crushed, just

---

[22] K. J. Davey, "Local Bureaucrats and Politicians in East Africa," in *Journal of Administration Overseas*, X, no. 4 (October, 1971): 270–71.

[23] Ottaway and Ottaway, *Algeria*, p. 61.

ATTEMPTED SOLUTIONS

as others had been in Tanzania, Ghana, Guinea, and elsewhere. In April, 1973, trade unions met in Addis Ababa to establish a unified all-African organization, but such efforts have little influence. Particularly in countries with a single party, these independent organizations, as well as churches, private professional societies, youth clubs, and women's groups, have been absorbed into the party to ensure centralized control.

In Ghana, some cocoa cooperatives marketed Ashanti-produced cocoa for years. Apparently fearful of local control over this product, the party created a centrally controlled United Ghana Farmers Council Cooperative (UGFCC), thus destroying local initiative and participation. Similarly, the party-controlled Trades Union Congress (TUC) absorbed all trade unions in Ghana, ensuring central control from Accra.[24] The formation of the UGFCC and the TUC coincidentally solved the problem of supplying good jobs to the party faithful. It created new offices in Accra to control workers and farmers, with salaries to be paid by farmers and workers, who did not want such offices in the first place. It could also put the party cadres in high positions in the civil service, which, of course, came under party control.[25]

In spite of many differences between Ghana and the Ivory Coast, Houphouët-Boigny's party, the PDCI, or Democratic Party of the Ivory Coast, has also monopolized power. Instead of opposing the bureaucracy, as it did during the colonial period, the PDCI has absorbed it, extending "the principles governing the colonial bureaucratic structure ... to the party and representative structures which previously embodied values of popular expression."[26] Administrators paid by the state collect party dues for the party, just as colonial administrators collected the head tax to pay the expenses of the colonial administration. It is difficult to understand how the masses could perceive any difference. Although locally elected party committees exist, rural people in particular have no choice in voting. Everyone must belong to the party and pay. There is no real participation of the masses in party decision-making. The people have no choice in local government or administration, although they must participate and show appropriate zeal in demonstrations organized on occasions like the visit of a foreign dignitary or their own head of state.

Apparently convinced of their own infallibility, presidents of most countries have a difficult time accepting criticism, and they have generated considerable fear on the part of subordinates within the party and administration. The subordinates fear to make decisions, because they know a mistake could mean prison, or worse, in many states. They

[24] See Martin Kilson, "The Grassroots in Ghanaian Politics," in Foster and Zolberg (eds.), *Ghana and the Ivory Coast*, pp. 114–21.
[25] Jon Kraus, "Political Change," pp. 33–72.
[26] Martin Staniland, "Single-Party Regimes and Political Change: The P.D.C.I. and Ivory Coast Politics," in Colin Leys (ed.), *Politics and Change in Developing Countries* (Cambridge, England: Cambridge University Press, 1969), p. 135.

prefer to depend on the president for decisions, even the smallest ones.

The attempt to concentrate power and authority in the capital can easily end with all power in the hands of one person, therefore. The inevitable result is a growing inability of the political system to respond intelligently, if at all, to messages coming from the periphery of the system, except in the case of an emergency. Needs and grievances remain, and the masses of people have in some cases become alienated from the new state. When this happens, people in the rural, nonindustrial, nonmining areas quickly perceive they have been cheated by independence, or what passes for it.

Disappointments: "Not Yet Mabadiliko"

The refusal of new African elites to permit the masses greater participation in the political process may not be seen as harmful by the masses themselves. During the colonial period elites wanted independence, or *Uhuru*, in order to participate and control the state. The masses were more interested in the satisfaction of very basic economic needs and the protection of core values that had been attacked by the colonial state; they therefore wanted change, or *Mabadiliko* in Swahili. Because political public opinion polling is not used in Africa, we cannot learn very much about attitudes by putting direct questions to large samples. Through more indirect methods, however, observers can know if the grievances of the ordinary man and woman have been solved, and whether they perceived that helpful change came about through single or multiple parties, through socialism or capitalism.

In Ghana the leaders of the independence movement told cocoa producers that they would stop the British expedient of destroying plants attacked by swollen shoot disease. Once they took power, they naturally continued the British program; they knew that to do otherwise would eventually mean the disappearance of all cocoa in the country. In Tanzania TANU had told irate cattle owners that they would stop the cattle-dipping begun by the British to rid cattle of parasites if the owners would support them. Naturally, the program was good for the cattle, protecting them from disease, and TANU knew it. The party continued it after independence, much to the surprise of the people.

Houphouët-Boigny and other leaders from French-controlled areas of West and Equatorial Africa promised an end to forced labor and succeeded in getting the French parliament to pass such a law before independence. Once these men took over the state apparatus, however, they announced that citizens would give up some of their time to build roads and bridges without payment. The program in one country was called *investissement humain* instead of forced labor. Tanzanian farmers were told they had to cultivate a specified number of acres just as the British had ordered. One might argue that a contribution of one's labor to community projects is praiseworthy. This may be true, but the people

ATTEMPTED SOLUTIONS

might still see no difference between building a road under a white civil servant and building a road under a black civil servant, if they perceive no benefit to themselves. These issues are relatively unimportant, however, compared with the grievances over land in Kenya still unsolved after independence.

For example, after 1960 the British colonial administration in Kenya permitted 5,000 African farmers, who already had some land, to purchase parts of European farms. Two years later, just before independence, they offered a plan for a larger group of African farmers and laborers to purchase land. President Kenyatta agreed that Africans would have to pay for land, even though, in their view, the Europeans had stolen the land from them in the first place. Some African ministers and civil servants also purchased European estates.

To prevent a flight of Europeans from Kenya, which might have disrupted the economy as a similar flight had done in Algeria, guarantees to the Europeans were written into the constitution, and if their land was forcibly purchased they were allowed to obtain land elsewhere. Africans were granted loans to purchase land, but the government would not permit them to have title to the land until they paid back the loans. The Kenya government therefore put itself in the position of demanding money for land that Kenyan peasants believed had belonged to them all along, and the Kenyan government can now evict people from their new land unless and until repayment of the loans is completed. It is likely that the Kenyans have the same sense of insecurity they had under European rule. The African government "since independence has shown little recognition of the historical objectives of African nationalism with respect to land," according to Harbeson.[27]

In his book *Not Yet Uhuru*, Oginga Odinga, the former vice-president of Kenya, asserted that President Kenyatta and others, by strictly regulating land sales, had refused to recognize the role of the Mau Mau freedom fighters in bringing about political change in Kenya. He implied they should get land free and that Europeans should not be paid for it by anyone, in spite of the fact that Kenya's Bill of Rights "contains the key clause on property rights which obligates us to pay compensation for settler farms . . . in cash."[28] As a result of his criticisms, Odinga was held under house arrest by the government, which accused him of falling under Communist influence, a canard once used frequently by colonial officials in similar attempts to discredit African leaders who first demanded changes and finally independence. Another popular critic of the government, J. M. Kariuki, was murdered in March, 1975, setting off a wave of dissatisfaction because people believed high officials in the government bore the responsibility.

---

[27] John W. Harbeson, "Land Reforms and Politics in Kenya 1954–1970," in *The Journal of Modern African Studies*, IX no. 2 (1971): 251.
[28] Oginga Odinga, *Not Yet Uhuru: An Autobiography* (New York: Hill and Wang, 1967), p. 259.

Elsewhere, certain ethnic groups saw their fears realized after independence. In Guinea the Fulani have been underrepresented in posts in the government, party, and civil service, the major sources of income. The reason may be revenge for their not having supported Sékou Touré, a Malinke, before independence. Many Fulani, as well as members of other groups, fled the country as the economic situation deteriorated and the government became more autocratic. Some 500,000 Guineans are reportedly in exile.

In Nigeria and Cameroun southerners felt the beginnings of discrimination against them for jobs because of northern control of the central government. In Ethiopia the Eritreans claimed discrimination, and non-Kikuyu of Kenya said they could not get the best jobs. In Gabon the Protestants complained that their regions received less benefits than Catholic areas because the president and the majority of ministers were Catholics. The Baganda of Uganda saw their king replaced as president by Milton Obote, and the Dahomeans of the three major ethnic groups felt their interests were not being served by a president from one of the other groups. The result in Dahomey was the creation of a tripresidential system, with one man serving as president for a period of time, to be replaced by president number two, and so on. Minority Tutsi control of Burundi continued, and the Hutu tried to revolt several times, with great loss of life in 1972. Northern Muslim Sudanese in control of the government tried to impose their culture and religion on southerners; the Moors of Mauritania did the same. Against these threats to their core values, Christians and non-Christians of the south revolted.

In all countries, access to schools has become easier, and the numbers of schools have increased greatly. Jobs for school graduates in the modern sector of the economy have not, however, increased at the same rate. As a result, independent states have growing problems of unemployment. In 1957, in colonial Guinea, there were 109,400 men and women salaried employees, but by 1966 the number had dropped to 90,000.[29] Supposedly socialist, one-party Guinea has not been able to provide new jobs and has not even been able to keep up the same rate of employment as before independence. Banks, insurance companies, and businesses were nationalized by the government, but the result has been a decrease in business activity. Mining operations, under the control of international consortia, tend to be highly mechanized and are thus unable to absorb many workers. As a result, "Kenya was estimated to have at least 200,000 hard-core unemployed in 1966. . . . Lagos was said to have 34 per cent of its laboring population out of work in 1965."[30] The effects of the increase in petroleum prices has been disastrous, although Africa produces 10 per cent of world production.

[29] Claude Rivière, *Mutations sociales en Guinée* (Paris: Marcel Rivière, 1971), p. 397.
[30] William A. Hance, "The Race Between Population and Resources," in *Africa Report*, January, 1968, p. 8.

ATTEMPTED SOLUTIONS

The flow of Algerian workers to France continued after independence because of the lack of job opportunities at home. As Algerians move up the hierarchy of jobs in France, they are replaced by the newly arrived Senegalese as street-cleaners and trash-collectors. Malawians still must travel to South Africa, Rhodesia, and Zambia to find employment in European-run mines. Dahomeans and Togolese, expelled from Congo-Brazzaville and the Ivory Coast in order to leave jobs for Congolese and Ivorians, now swell the ranks of the unemployed in their respective countries. A continued rise in the prices Africans pay for manufactured and imported goods without a concurrent rise in wages or in prices paid for African products creates further hardship. The 1973–74 drought, cutting across the continent from Mauritania to Ethiopia, made matters worse.

Salaries of high-ranking civil servants and politicians have not, however, remained so static. Oginga Odinga complained that in Kenya, three years after independence, the salaries of members of parliament rose from 620 pounds per year to 1,200 pounds.[31] Politicians, as in other countries of the world, use high salaries and perquisites to keep the loyalty and silence of other politicians; they use salaries for civil servants for similar reasons and to keep them from going into private corporations owned by expatriates. When they try to reduce salaries in the face of popular pressure, they risk a serious alienation of the civil servants or the military and may thus encourage opposition leaders to make a bid for power. Few civil servants and soldiers wish to give up the salary structure inherited from the colonial period.

Europeans are also still present. Many of the European district commissioners and *commandants de cercle* remained for years as advisers or as teachers, and new groups of European and American teachers, agricultural specialists, and businessmen arrived. In those countries where the actual physical presence of Europeans decreased, trade patterns did not and could not easily change, and investments continued, thus providing European leverage in policy that the people could feel. European troops even intervened in a few countries and were stationed in some.

Even though French civil servants in the states of West Africa, Equatorial Africa, and Madagascar decreased from 10,278 in 1960 to 8,423 in 1966, 1,500 more military men arrived to work as technicians, and 3,800 agricultural specialists were sent. Those Frenchmen still in administrative posts rose in rank, to have control over a greater number of African civil servants than in the past. For example, a European who may have been the head of a small region during the colonial period could be put in charge of several regions administered by Africans after independence.[32] Technical services are still very much under French control. In 1969 about 1,900 whites worked in power, transportation, and com-

---

[31] Odinga, *Not Yet Uhuru*, p. 302.
[32] See Brian Weinstein, "Africanization in French Africa," in *Transition*, no. 31 (June–July, 1967) p. 33.

munication facilities in fourteen African states. The same year there was one French technical assistant for every 1,331 people in Gabon; one for every 4,945 in Senegal, and one for every 5,337 in the Ivory Coast, not counting teachers and military advisers.[33] As late as 1976 Senegal's powerful Minister of the Interior was white.

In one Francophone city alone, Dakar, there were 29,000 Frenchmen in 1970.[34] Many of these men and women are in business for themselves; others are advisers in ministries, clerks in shops, and even secretaries. Their pattern of behavior toward Africans has not changed much since independence; they feel superior to blacks and show it, except to the black elite in power, with whom some have very close personal ties.

French troops were stationed in Madagascar, Senegal, and Tchad, under treaty arrangements made at independence. Smaller contingents are located in Ivory Coast and Gabon. They were sent to Gabon in 1964 to restore a government that had been overthrown by the Gabonese military; they went to Tchad in greater numbers to help put down an insurrection against the government, and to the Central African Republic to help the President maintain his position. They have refused to intervene elsewhere, but the French government has implied it would intervene to assist elites in the Ivory Coast and Senegal if they should be threatened by external or even internal forces.

There is a British presence in Kenya, and British advisers are used in Nigeria, Gambia, Sierra Leone, and Malawi. British troops have intervened in Kenya and Tanzania to protect African civilian authorities against their own armies. The British had a base in Nigeria just after independence and helped Americans and Belgians intervene in Zaïre in 1964 to rescue Europeans. The Belgians have been unable to maintain their hold on the Zaïre Republic, although they have tried; others, such as Americans and the French have begun to play an important role in that huge, rich country. South African civil servants work in Lesotho and Malawi. There are fewer Europeans in Morocco, Algeria, and Tunisia than in pre-independence days, although many French technical assistants remain. Algeria and Libya have received advisers and teachers from Egypt, as has Sudan. Numbers of Soviet, Vietnamese, Chinese, American, and Canadian technicians have gone to certain countries, but because they had no colonial past in Africa the Africans probably do not view them the same way they view the Belgians, French, British, Spanish, and Portuguese—or at least not at first.

If independence may be measured by balancing external influence on policy-making against internal influences on policy-making, many states of Africa are less rather than more independent, and their elites have been unable to fulfill earlier promises. The African masses have some-

---

[33] Edward M. Corbett, *The French Presence in Black Africa* (Washington: Black Orpheus Press, 1972), pp. 138, 140.
[34] Rita Cruise O'Brien, *White Society in Black Africa: The French of Senegal* (London: Faber and Faber, 1972), p. 17.

Attempted Solutions 209

times reacted to this situation by fleeing their home countries, by supporting counter-elites who want to take power in coups d'état, by indifference, and by retreating into their precolonial systems in the vain hope of escaping the new state. Malaise and alienation are widespread. Free elections are nonexistent. Some African novelists have made the new "black colonialists" the villains in their works. One of the most bitter examples is Ayi K. Armah's *The Beautyful Ones Are Not Yet Born*, dealing with Ghana in the 1950's and 1960's.

Some military men have written books to justify their coups. Colonel A. A. Afrifa, who participated in the coup that replaced President Nkrumah, wrote that he had become "convinced that Kwame Nkrumah had failed the country as a leader."[85] His reasons were a mixture of criticism about the lack of participation, the failure to redeem promises made, and the generation of new grievances among the masses and elites. He complained about the absence of civil liberties of particular concern to elites. No one was allowed to criticize the government or President Nkrumah, raised to the level of a god by official ideology: "Our glorious revolution which was to free us from the colonial yoke and to usher in freedom and justice was to be replaced by the black domination of one man. Nkrumah used every political trickery to wrest power from the hands of the people."[86] He claimed the country was thus moving toward Communism.

Colonel Afrifa, a former student at the British military school Sandhurst, also claimed to be speaking for the masses when he wrote that the family in Ghana had been weakened by the idea that the state and Nkrumah were supreme, that corrupt, dishonest sycophants were draining the country's resources, that the United Ghana Farmers Cooperatives Council—"imposed upon the farmers of this country against their will"—was also corrupt, that state farms were in contradiction with the tradition of small private holdings in Ghana. He said the Nkrumah regime had brought inflation and high taxes, and that Nkrumah had refused to follow good advice to reverse this trend. Instead, he had preferred incompetent and corrupt advisers. "There was therefore no other choice open to the people to restore their rights, except perhaps to turn to the Army."[37]

After four years, the military rulers voluntarily turned over the government to a popularly elected civilian government headed by Dr. Kofi Busia, but in 1972 the army seized power once again, claiming that the newly elected civilians were incompetent.

At each change of the government, photographs show enthusiastic demonstrators in Accra supporting their new regime. Because of the constant frustration of expectations of change, the enthusiasm might be

---

[85] Colonel A. A. Afrifa, *The Ghana Coup 24th February 1966* (London: Cass, 1967), p. 75.
[36] *Ibid.*, p. 76.
[37] *Ibid.*, p. 92.

less sincere than the photos indicate or the enthusiasm more constrained as government follows government. The masses may well have begun to see independence and politics within the new state as a device for the circulation of elites who have personal and narrow group interests to pursue, at the expense of the ordinary man.

The masses in many states may perceive that African rulers, like their white predecessors, monopolize power and enjoy the advantages of it. The ruled, subject to varying degrees of violence to ensure compliance, supply the rulers "with material means of subsistence and with the instrumentalities that are essential to the vitality of the political organism."[38] They may then conclude that a return to their precolonial political systems would serve them better than does the new state. If they do so believe, they will resist processes of nation-building and economic development for the new state, thus creating a deep crisis for African politics and, of course, for themselves.

Neither this crisis nor the tension in independent African politics justifies, however, a contention that the continent was not "ready" for independence. If peace and tranquility, confidence and majority rule were required for independence, few countries in the world would be independent today.

[38] Gaetano Mosca, *The Ruling Class*, trans. Hannah D. Kahn (New York: McGraw-Hill, 1939), p. 50; and Vilfredo Pareto, *The Mind and Society: A Treatise on General Sociology* (New York: Dover, 1935).

9 Adaptation of Institutions, Concepts, and Methods

Independent Africa has attempted to adapt institutions, concepts, and methods to its own needs.

Traditional Values in a Modern State

Many African leaders saw in independence not only the gateway to social and economic advancement but also an opportunity, at last, to express an African attitude in the affairs of their countries, subject for so long to imposed Western values. They foresaw eradication of the assumption that what was white and European was advanced and superior; what was black and African, backward and inferior. But they were well aware that they had a difficult task. A new generation of educated Africans tended to accept the paternalistic colonial judgment of Africa and, in doing so, permitted much that was worthwhile in African tradition to be pushed aside.

But the material benefits of the modernization that independence promised could not be ignored. For most of the people in the new states, independence meant such things as better roads, sewage, electricity, the cinema, radio, and television. And no political leader wishing to retain popular support could avoid trying to satisfy the people's craving for participation in the "good life" offered by the technological achievements of the twentieth century. Not that these leaders were themselves altogether free from the influence of European or American ideas. For Nkrumah, Nyerere, and Kenyatta, Britain; for Nkrumah, Azikiwe, and Banda, the United States; and for Senghor, Bourguiba, and Houphouët-Boigny, France had been the major sources of inspiration or instruction while they were developing as future national leaders. The Francophone leaders, in particular, came to independence—most of them have changed little since then—with a strong attachment to French ideas, attitudes, and style.

In spite of the weight of European and colonial tradition, African leaders are trying to maintain, within the framework of a modern state, a way of life that has an essentially African quality instead of being an imitation—to a greater or a lesser degree—of the way of life bequeathed by the departed colonial power. Traditional concepts and institutions were the product of societies based on a subsistence economy. They could hardly be expected to survive in African states that were clamoring to take their place in the modern world. But some of them—chieftaincy, the extended family, traditional land-holding—resisted the pressures of colonial rule and continue to be part of present-day African social structure. This is also true of many African ideas and values; they continue to flourish. Throughout independent Africa, essentially African ideas are asserted in a variety of ways; through schools of art and design, experimental theaters, dance groups, publications like *Black Orpheus* and *Transition*, and the constant interpretation of the real Africa by such writers as Camara Laye, Chinua Achebe, Ezekiel Mphahlele, and Ayi Armah.[1]

Since independence, the African states have been trying to adapt traditional concepts and institutions to the needs and aspirations of a modern state forming part of the new Africa. We turn now to consider four significant areas in which this process of adaptation is taking place: education, language, chieftaincy, and customary law.

Education

Both major colonial powers, Britain and France—although they differed in their conceptions of the function of education[2]—had established primary and secondary schools, and the young African attached great importance to possession of the appropriate diploma or certificate as the passport to a better job or a promising career. This attitude continued after independence, notwithstanding much talk among the leaders about the need to Africanize education. What the new independent states were urged to provide by their people—and have continued to do—were more schools. The demand was—and has largely continued to be—for a "good education," which meant for most young men seeking to improve themselves, simply increased access to the kind of education that had been provided by the colonial power.[3]

There has been a tendency, therefore, to look at education quantitatively rather than qualitatively; the emphasis has been on providing manpower needs as soon as possible. A review of educational development in Africa for the period 1961–67 showed that, while there has been substantial progress in increasing school enrollment, much re-

---

[1] For an excellent discussion of the place of African values in modern Africa, see the chapter entitled, "Rediscovery and Integration: The Search for Values," in Melville J. Herskovitz, *The Human Factor in Changing Africa* (New York: Knopf, 1962), pp. 451–78.

[2] See David Scanlon, "Education," in Robert A. Lystad (ed.), *The African World* (New York: Praeger, 1965), pp. 202–9.

[3] Philip Foster, *Education and Social Change in Ghana* (Berkeley: University of California Press, 1965), pp. 298–99.

mained to be done in improving the content and quality of education.[4]

But in recent years a few African countries have displayed growing opposition to the continuance of a system of education closely tied—by means of the school syllabus and the use of teachers from the metropolitan countries—to British or French ideas, standards, and practices. In these countries a new approach to education has developed.

Julius Nyerere has been outstanding among African leaders in seeking to make education truly responsive to needs and goals of the independent African states. He set out his views in the pamphlet *Education for Self-Reliance*.[5]

Traditional African society had a system of education that ensured the transmission of the society's values from one generation to the next. Children were educated in a variety of ways: There were stories by the elders about the history and traditions of their own tribe and its encounter with other tribes; day-to-day instruction, to which parents and grandparents devoted great care; and participation in the agricultural and pastoral activities of the community. The common belief that the African knew no education until the European came was due to the arrogant assumption by the colonial rulers that there could be no education without schooling as it was known in Europe.

The systems of education inherited by the African states inculcated alien values—the values of the colonial power. The basic motivation of colonial education was to provide for the training of a small minority of the indigenous population that was needed to serve the colonial power's interests. What was taught was essentially British or French, not African.

Nyerere's views, as stated in his pamphlet, have a general applicability. At independence, the Tanzanian system had not yet produced a sufficient number of educated people to satisfy the requirements of the administration, and the number of children then enrolled in the schools was not large enough to assure an early improvement in the situation.

Nyerere describes how Tanzania set about trying to correct the three "most glaring faults" in the inherited system. First, all racial and religious barriers to school enrollment were abolished, and all schools—whether governmental or government-aided—were made available to all Tanzanian children without distinction. Second, the number of children in school, at both the primary and the secondary levels, was greatly increased. Third, the content of education was transformed. African history has assumed increasing importance, national songs and dances are taught, and Kiswahili occupies a prominent place in the curriculum.

---

[4] Address by Robert K. A. Gardiner, Executive Secretary of the Economic Commission for Africa, at the 47th session of the Economic and Social Council, Geneva, July 24, 1969. See also Adam Curle, *Educational Problems of Developing Countries: With Case Studies of Ghana, Pakistan and Nigeria* (New York: Praeger, 1973).

[5] Included in Julius K. Nyerere, *Ujamaa: Essays in Socialism* (Dar es Salaam: Oxford University Press, 1968), pp. 44–75. Most of the material in this section is based on Nyerere's ideas as expounded in "Education for Self-Reliance."

Nyerere proceeds to demonstrate that, notwithstanding the improvements that have taken place, the existing system is not preparing the young people for full integration into the society that is being built, a socialist society "based on three principles: equality and respect for human dignity; sharing of the resources which are produced by our efforts; work by everyone and exploitation by none." He lists four aspects of the system that are unfavorable to such full integration: (1) the creation of a small intellectual elite with an attitude of superiority toward the rest of the people, which encourages the development of a class structure; (2) the fact that the schools and the universities are producing young men separated from the people of Tanzania as a whole; (3) the encouragement of an unbalanced respect for formal education with a consequent tendency to have insufficient regard for real wisdom and experience; (4) the fact that "our young and poor nation is taking out of productive work some of its healthiest and strongest young men and women." He suggests ways of correcting these faults, among them the idea of attaching a farm to every school in order to create a new kind of school community that would include people who are both teachers and farmers or both pupils and farmers. The welfare of the community would depend on the farm's output, and pupils would combine study with work on the farm, participating in decisions on the conduct of farming operations. The rationale for this and similar suggestions is that the "primary school graduates should be able to fit into and to serve the communities from which they come."

A syllabus has been drawn up in accordance with these new ideas. In 1970 the minister of national education announced the inauguration of a plan sponsored jointly by the government of Tanzania, UNESCO, and UNICEF to provide special training for teachers to qualify them to teach the new syllabus. It was anticipated that all teachers would have received the necessary training by 1975.

Among the other countries applying themselves to the adaptation of education is Algeria, which in 1969 established a National Council for Educational Reform; the council aims to create a system of education in keeping with Algeria's existing needs and future goals. In the Congo Democratic Republic, existing educational facilities are very good. Education between the ages of six and sixteen is compulsory and free, and about 77 per cent of the children go to school. Educational reform is being considered. There is a proposal to establish "people's schools" freed from "neo-colonialist" influence and adapted to the needs of the country, its socialist ideology, and the interests of Africa as a whole. In Guinea, which provides free compulsory education for a period of nine years, there has been substantial growth in the number of schools and in enrollment since independence. Education aims to satisfy the social and economic needs of the country and is related to the ideology of the one-party state. Cameroun has established a Rural Vocational Teachers Training School, with aid from the United Nations and UNESCO. Its function is to train teachers who will provide instruction designed to encourage their pupils to build careers in their own rural environment. Malagasy seems likely to move toward Malgachization of its educational system.

Language

Language is essential for human communication. The colonial rulers were therefore obliged to ensure that their subjects could use the metropolitan language; but, as a minority seeking to control the majority, they also found it necessary to make sure that extensive use of a common language did not unify the subject peoples. Confining the majority of the inhabitants to the use of different local languages, and excluding all but a select few from the means of mastering a universal language like English or French, could serve the dual purpose of keeping the people divided and limiting their exposure to the ideas disseminated by the press, literature, radio, and television of the outside world.

Colonial regimes often communicated with the people by using a body of trained African interpreters, particularly in a colony with several local languages. Where there was one dominant African language, colonial officials usually learned that language. The use of the metropolitan language between governors and governed was necessarily limited, because the colonial schools turned out few Africans who had an adequate command of it. This was so, however, much less in the French colonies, where all school instruction and all official communications were in French in West and Equatorial Africa and in Algeria.

To have one language in a country is an effective way of encouraging national unity. It is not surprising, therefore, that the new African states, except for Arab states, chose to make English or French the sole official language. This had the added advantage of providing a recognized means of communication with other African countries and the countries of Europe. But the European language is spoken regularly by only a very small proportion of the Africans. Thus, the divisive differentiation between a small educated elite and the mass of the people created under colonial rule was carried forward into the independent states.[6]

European countries have faced problems in recognizing different languages spoken by different ethnic groups. Belgian governments have fallen over language issues. Imposing a national language in a country with many languages spoken by different ethnic groups can lead to serious disruption. The decision by India in 1967 to recognize both English and Hindi officially led to serious riots—anti-English and anti-Hindu—in different parts of the country. In Africa, the Sudan provides an example of the explosive potential of language differences. The imposition on the southern region of Arabic as an official language was an important factor in starting a disastrous conflict that lasted seventeen years before it was settled in 1972.

[6] This material is based loosely on Leonard Thompson, "Historical Perspectives of Pluralism in Africa," in Leo Kuper and M. G. Smith (eds.), *Pluralism in Africa* (Berkeley: University of California Press, 1971), pp. 354–62.

In a few African countries the acknowledged dominance of an indigenous language operates as a unifying factor. In 1969 President Kenyatta pledged that Swahili would become the national language of Kenya, and in 1970 KANU announced a two-phase program that would provide for gradually increased use of Kiswahili, leading up to its adoption by law as the national language. In July, 1974, the President declared Swahili to be the official language of Kenya. It was ordered that Parliamentary debates and all other government business would thenceforth be conducted in Swahili and that passing an English test would no longer be a requisite for candidacy in elections.

At its second assembly in Cairo in 1975 the All Africa Teachers Organization resolved to ask the Organization of African Unity to adopt one of the three major African languages—Hausa, Arabic, Swahili—as the lingua franca for Africa. Such adoption would require that instruction in the language chosen be compulsory in all schools in Africa.[7]

Ghana and Sierra Leone indicated an interest in furthering the recognition of local languages. In Ghana a motion introduced in the national assembly during 1971 asked the government to establish a committee to promote and coordinate efforts to select a common Ghanaian language as a lingua franca. In support of the motion, it was stated that there were fifty-six languages and dialects in Ghana but that approximately 70 per cent of the people spoke one of the Kwa languages, while more than half the population spoke and understood the Akan languages. There was considerable support for the recognition of one or the other as a common language, to be known as "Ghanaian." But there was just as much support for the continued use of English as a lingua franca, for two reasons: because of the practical advantages offered by English, and because the choice of one Ghanaian language would lead to resentment among the users of other languages. The Minister of Education stated that the policy of his ministry was to treat all the main languages of the country equally in the schools, in the hope that one language would emerge as a dominant language acceptable to the country as a whole. The debate terminated with the adoption of an amended motion, which merely agreed to "take note" of the need for a common Ghanaian language as an important factor in creating national unity.

In Sierra Leone there has been criticism of the use of English. According to the annual report for 1969–70 of the Provincial Literature Bureau, 90 per cent of the population had no knowledge of English and very seldom heard it spoken. The report was opposed to the idea of adopting English as the second language. All Sierra Leoneans, it said, should be made to realize that to be regarded as educated in the true sense of the word, they should be able to carry on a conversation in at least Mende

[7] *West Africa* 3054, January 12, 1976, p. 17. For a well-reasoned case in favor of Swahili as the lingua franca, see Adewole John, "An International Language for Africa?" *West Africa*, 3053, pp. 7–8.

and Temne; this would also help to curb the growth of tribalism. In any event, Sierra Leone had neither the money nor the expertise to teach everyone English; furthermore, few Sierra Leoneans were likely to go abroad, where knowledge of English was most useful. The report went on to make it clear that "literacy" was understood to mean not the ability to read and write a foreign language—and English is a foreign language—but the ability to read and write one's own language. Literacy in a mother tongue could speedily be made available to the majority of the people if they were only willing to learn. The same could not be done with the English language.[8]

Chieftaincy

Immediately before independence came to Africa, two extreme views had crystallized on chieftaincy: the militant nationalist view, and the orthodox, traditionalist view. The former saw chieftaincy as incompatible with the interests of a modern state and insisted on its abolition. This was the attitude adopted by the first All-African People's Conference, held in Accra in 1958, which condemned chieftaincy as a traditional institution to be "annihilated" because it had supported colonialism and obstructed the African's advance toward freedom.[9] The orthodox view looked forward to the restoration of the traditional power and prestige of the chiefs once the restraints of colonial rule had gone. In fact, neither view prevailed in most of independent Africa once the leaders of the new states came face to face with the realities of independence. In the over-all pattern, militant nationalism conceded some role for chieftaincy in the modern African states, and the chiefs accepted the curtailment of their traditional power, influence, and prestige.

The power and influence of the chiefs varied from one country to another, according to the distribution of traditional authority within a particular country. As a rule, when the new nation comprised a number of tribes more or less equal to one another in influence and authority, the chiefs were not a significant political factor. But where there were few tribes within a country, among them one or more that were dominant and commanded extensive support in part of the country—for instance, the Ashanti of Ghana—the chiefs could constitute a political force and could emerge as the focus of competition with the new national leadership in the country.

In some countries the new national leader of the newly independent state came, in a sense, to usurp the role the chief had filled in traditional times. In Ghana, for example, there were times when the new nationalists seemed to display the same kind of emotional loyalty toward their leader, Kwame Nkrumah, that the peasant had displayed toward his chief.

[8] *West Africa*, no. 2817 (June 11, 1971), p. 655.
[9] Colin Legum, *Pan-Africanism*, rev. ed. (London: Pall Mall Press, 1968), pp. 253–54.

Before we consider independent Africa's attempts to adapt chieftaincy to its own needs, it is necessary to understand the extent to which the traditional status, authority, and power of the chiefs had already been diminished by the impact of colonial rule.[10]

Before the coming of the European, a number of African societies, such as the Zulu of South Africa and the Ashanti of Ghana, had sophisticated political systems with the chief at their center. The chief combined in his office supreme legislative, executive, judicial, and religious power. But his power was not absolute; it was subject to well-defined limitations. First, any action taken by him in the exercise of his functions had to conform to the traditional law and customs of his people. Second, every important decision taken by him had to reflect not his own whim but the wishes of his people—wishes to be ascertained by constant consultation with a council of elders and periodic consultation with the whole tribe. He ignored these limitations at his peril. Failure to observe them could result in his removal from office or in transference by disaffected members of his tribe of allegiance to a rival chief. Because he was looked up to as the father of his people, his responsibilities toward them were extensive. Within the framework of an essentially egalitarian society he exercised great power; as long as he conformed to the traditions of his office he enjoyed immense prestige.

Colonial rule severely undermined the chief's power, authority, and prestige. He became part of an alien administration imposed upon his people. He continued to perform his functions as a chief at the pleasure of the colonial rulers; his right to do so depended upon their recognition of his status. Once he had been recognized it was the colonial regime, not the traditions of his people, that determined the nature and extent of his powers. Part of the price he paid for accepting recognition was being required to carry out duties beneath his traditional dignity. More important, they were duties that often required him to carry out measures of the colonial administration that were bitterly resented by his people, for example, collect taxes imposed by the colonial government or interfere with traditional occupations by applying controls to cattle-grazing or land cultivation. Above all, all his actions were subject to the supervision or control of a colonial official.

The chief under colonial rule had to reconcile being the instrument of an alien administration with remaining the spokesman of his people. He could try to relieve his people of some of their disabilities by interceding with a colonial official on their behalf. But the two conflicting loyalties were not easily reconcilable. The people soon ceased to look

---

[10] In what follows, we have drawn heavily on Leslie Rubin, "Chieftaincy and the Adaptation of Customary Law in Ghana," in Jeffrey Butler and A. A. Castagno (eds.), *Boston University Papers on Africa: Transition in African Politics*, Praeger Special Studies in International Politics and Public Affairs (New York: Praeger, 1967), pp. 116–21. See also Michael Crowder and Obaro Ikime, *West African Chiefs: Their Changing Status Under Colonial Rule and Independence* (New York: African Publishing Corporation, 1970), pp. vii–xxviii.

upon the chief as the father of his people; more and more, he came to be thought of as no more than a servant of the colonial government. After all, he was paid by the government, and the government could, whenever it pleased, remove him from office.

The concomitants of colonial rule—economic development, education, and the introduction of Christianity—also contributed to a weakening of the people's allegiance to their chief. Improved communications and the rise of towns, with opportunities of paid employment by the white man, took men away from the tribe for longer or shorter periods; in some cases, they never returned. The Christian faith offered growing competition with the ancestral spirits, and the teachings of the missionaries weaned many tribesmen from adherence to traditional practices. Education—limited and inadequate though it might have been—encouraged individualism and independent inquiry, and planted the seeds of a new outlook that persuaded many that the chief was an obstacle to progress and advancement. Before long, all these influences produced a new class, young men fired by the cause of national independence and freedom from colonial oppression. For them, as we have seen, the chief was simply part of the machinery of colonial oppression. With the disappearance of colonial rule, they believed, the chief too had to go.

But the ardent young nationalists overlooked chieftaincy's deep roots in the fabric of African society. When the Coussey Committee, reporting in 1949 on the Gold Coast,[11] emphasized the close bonds between chieftaincy and "the life of our communities," it was describing a state of affairs that also existed in most of the rest of Africa.

Independence has brought little change in the position of the chief as compared with his position under colonial rule. In most of the African states the chiefs continue to be used by the government to carry out its policies, in much the same way the French or British administrations used them to carry out colonial policies. They continue to provide a link between the government and the people at the level of local government, to perform religious and ceremonial functions, and to have a role—in relation to customary law—in the legal system. There are variations in the political importance of chieftaincy, according to whether the chiefs are a focus of power in one part of the country or another. Nkrumah felt obliged to treat the Asantehene with some respect. He had every reason to fear that a hostile Asantehene might lead the Ashanti people into becoming a source of opposition to the Nkrumah regime.

A survey of chieftaincy in the independent Africa of today discloses an over-all pattern relegating the chiefs to a subordinate role, but the response to the persistence of chieftaincy within the framework of modernization has not been uniform. In three states, chieftaincy has

---

[11] Report to H. E. the Governor by the Commission on Constitutional Reform, 1949 (London: 1949). Colonial No. 248.9.

been abolished; at the other end of the scale, there is one state where a traditional chief exercises complete political control over his people. In between, there are different approaches to the task of fitting chieftaincy into the structure of a modern state.

Guinea, Tanzania, and Rwanda abolished chieftaincy. In Guinea doctrine had its way, and chieftaincy was treated as a reactionary institution. Besides, the Guinean chiefs had not, apparently, enjoyed much public support. There were no disturbances when the abolition was put into effect. In Tanzania, with eleven months of independence, the law providing for chieftaincy was repealed. But if the institution was legally dead, its incumbents remained very much alive:

> Chiefs were legally dethroned, but their influence did not end. As the Government moved to fill the administrative void with civil servants the chiefs and headmen moved to consolidate their remaining influence. Throughout the nation, examples of chiefs retaining power in a local area and gaining some governmental recognition were common. In these cases the government reaction was to appoint the chief a local government official; and where the situation demanded more administrative expertise, to appoint a deputy with the chief.[12]

In Rwanda, where chieftaincy also has been abolished,

> there is an obvious parallel between the previous division of authority between land chiefs and that which at present exists between various categories of bureaucrats and politicians.
>
> Just as in the past the presence of several chiefs, each exercising specific authority within the same administrative unit, resulted in a system of checks and balances, today in Rwanda the existence of "parallel hierarchies" seems ideally suited to provide certain institutional safeguards against possible abuses of authority.[13]

At the other end of the scale is Swaziland, the smallest independent state in Africa, where King Sobhuza II, Ngwenyama (the Lion) a paramount chief of colonial times, rules his 400,000 people, combining unquestioned traditional prestige with effective political power. But there are few countries like Swaziland in Africa. Unlike most other African leaders, Sobhuza is not troubled by the evils of tribalism; Swaziland is a country where the unusual equation "tribe = nation" applies. All the people over whom Sobhuza rules are Swazi.

Between these two extremes, the independent states have produced two approaches to the role of the chief. The first recognizes the right of chiefs, by virtue of their office, to participate (although admittedly to a limited extent) in the exercise of political power. The other denies

---

[12] Norman N. Miller, "The Political Survival of Traditional Leadership in East Africa," in Marion E. Doro and Newell M. Stultz, *Governing in Black Africa* (Englewood Cliffs, N.J.: Prentice-Hall, 1970), p. 272. See also David Brokensha, "Handeni Revisited," in *African Affairs*, vol. 70, no. 279 (April, 1970), pp. 166-67.

[13] René Lamarchand, *Rwanda and Burundi* (New York: Praeger, 1970), p. 273.

them any place in the political organs of the state by virtue of their office and confines their influence to the exercise of certain prescribed functions, of an advisory nature, in relation to customary law and the regulation of traditional matters.

Examples of the first approach were to be found in the Federation of Nigeria and in Sierra Leone before the military coups. Under the Nigerian constitution, each region had a House of Chiefs, which was one part of the bicameral legislature; in addition, the chiefs participated in the exercise of executive power at the regional level. At the federal level, they participated in the exercise of legislative power by being directly represented in the federal legislature; they also had a say in the choice of twelve federal senators who represented the regions. In Sierra Leone, the twelve paramount chiefs of the state were members of the unicameral legislature, and their power was reinforced by a constitutional entrenchment of "the office of Paramount Chief as existing by customary law."[14]

In Ghana under Nkrumah, each of the eight regions had a House of Chiefs, but these bodies (unlike the Houses of Chiefs in Nigeria) had no legislative power at all; they existed to advise the government on questions of customary law and to deal with disputes concerning the election or destoolment of a chief and allied matters.[15]

The overthrow of Nkrumah and the introduction of a constitution marked by a strong reaction against all he had stood for resulted in a considerable increase in the influence and prestige of the chiefs in Ghana. Dr. Busia, himself a descendant of the royal house of Wenchi (a distinguished chiefly family of Ghana), was elected as prime minister when the country returned to civilian rule in 1969; this promised enhanced respect for the institution of chieftaincy by the new government.

The report of a 1968 constitutional commission, which had been appointed by the National Liberation Council, includes a chapter devoted to chieftaincy. It embodies recommendations based on written and oral evidence received in the course of hearings throughout the country. The commission concluded that chieftaincy could be most useful by playing an essential part in the system of local government; it also recommended that chiefs have a say in the election of the president and be represented in the council of state, a body composed of distinguised members of the Ghanaian community whose function is to assist the president in the discharge of his duties.[16]

There were also proposals designed to prevent chieftaincy from being used for political purposes. One recommended termination of the practice of requiring government recognition of the enstoolment or destool-

---

[14] For further details of the chief's rights and powers in both countries, see Rubin, "Chieftaincy," pp. 118–19.

[15] Ibid., pp. 119–24.

[16] *The Proposals of the Constitutional Commission for a Constitution for Ghana.* SPC/A10613/5000/1/67-68. (Republic of Ghana, 1968), chap. 22, paras. 635–95.

ment of a chief; instead, it was proposed that there should merely be an announcement by the president in the *Gazette* that there had been an enstoolment or a destoolment, in accordance with "the procedure and usages established by customary law." Thus, the government would merely give effect to the decision already taken by the chiefs instead of itself deciding whether a chief should hold or retain office. It was also proposed that the president be empowered to deal with matters concerning the election and removal of chiefs and that the supreme court have jurisdiction to hear appeals concerning the status of paramount chiefs.[17]

The Ghana constitution, which came into force in 1969, gives the chiefs increased importance in the government and administration of Ghana and enhances the influence and prestige of chieftaincy as an institution.

First, chieftaincy finds a place in the preamble to the constitution, which declares that "we *the Chiefs* and people of Ghana" (instead of "we the people," as in the Nkrumah constitution) "adopt . . . this constitution." (Emphasis added.) Then there is the provision: "The institution of chieftaincy, together with its traditional Councils as established by customary law and usage, is hereby guaranteed." This guarantee is declared to be permanent and irrevocable. It is contained in Article 153, which parliament is prohibited from amending in any way whatsoever, at any time.[18] The president is elected by an electoral college comprising all the members of the national assembly (not less than 140 and not more than 150), representatives of the district councils (not exceeding a total of 120), and twenty-four chiefs (three for each region) elected by the Houses of Chiefs of the regions.[19] The council of state consists of three groups: (1) the prime minister, the speaker of the national assembly, the leader of the opposition, and the *president of the national House of Chiefs*; (2) not more than four persons, appointed by the president, each of whom must have held office in the past as president, chief justice, speaker, or prime minister; and (3) not more than eight persons, appointed by the president, of whom at least two must be women, and *not more than four must be chiefs*. Thus, out of a maximum membership of sixteen, the council of state may have up to five members who are chiefs.[20] The first council of state established under the constitution included only three, including the president of the national House of Chiefs. Only two of the four possible appointments were made by the President of Ghana; he appointed the paramount chief of the Dagomba traditional area and the Omanhene of the Sekondi traditional area.[21]

The constitution provides for a national House of Chiefs consisting of

[17] *Ibid.*, pp. 645–47.
[18] See Article 169(3), Constitution of Ghana.
[19] Article 41(3).
[20] Article 53(1).
[21] Keesing's Contemporary Archives (September 27–October 4, 1969), 23582.

representatives elected by each regional House of Chiefs (five chiefs from each region). The national House of Chiefs is empowered to: (1) receive appeals from decisions by a regional House of Chiefs; (2) advise authorities or other people who have duties in matters relating to chieftaincy; and (3) "undertake the progressive study, interpretation and codification of customary law with a view to evolving, in appropriate cases, a unified system of rules of customary law."[22] Each regional House of Chiefs, in addition to its jurisdiction in matters affecting the claims of a paramount chief, is empowered to receive appeals from traditional councils relating to the appointment or removal of chiefs.[23]

The system of local government provides for local councils, district councils, and regional councils. A local council consists of elected and traditional members, but the number of traditional members may not be more than half the number of elected members. In the case of a district council, two-thirds of the members are elected, and one-third are chosen by the traditional authorities in the district "in accordance with traditional and customary usage." The membership of a regional council includes "not more than two Chiefs from the House of Chiefs of the Region."[24]

The ouster of the Busia regime by a military coup has produced no significant change in the authority and influence of the chiefs. Six months after he came to power Colonel Acheampong, the new head of state, discussed chieftaincy more than once during a tour of Ghana's nine regions. While frequently emphasizing his government's recognition of the value of chieftaincy and declaring that there would be no interference "in chieftaincy matters," he also (as the Busia regime had done) criticized the chiefs for failing to provide leadership and for "using their position to indulge in wasteful and partisan politics."

Customary Law

The African state inherited dual systems of law. The colonial powers had introduced their own laws enforced by general courts, alongside the customary law enforced by African courts. In the British colonies there was the general law consisting of the English common law, the rules of equity, a number of English statutes, and enactments of the colonial government. Although the courts were to be "guided" by customary law in disputes between Africans, and English law was to be applied "subject to local circumstances," these requirements "were largely ignored and the British judges were solely guided by the law with which they were

---
[22] Article 154, Constitution of Ghana.
[23] Article 155.
[24] Articles 156–59. For a valuable discussion of the changes in chieftaincy in Ghana, see David Brokensha, "The Resilient Chieftaincy at Larteh, Ghana," in Michael Crowder and Obaro Ikime, *West African Chiefs: Their Changing Status Under Colonial Rule and Independence*, pp. 393–400.

familiar, i.e., English Law."[25] Customary law was applied in the African courts, but in the other courts it had to be proved by evidence in the same way as a question of fact, and in any event it applied only "so far as it was not repugnant to natural justice or morality."[26] In the French colonies too, the French Civil Code and other metropolitan laws applied; customary law was applicable to Africans considering themselves subject to it. As in the British colonies, a "repugnancy" principle operated; customary law applied only insofar as it was not contrary to *ordre public et bonne moeurs*.[27]

The colonial powers took no steps to resolve the problems arising from this dualism. Perhaps this is not surprising. It has been pointed out that the existence of different systems of law within a colony was a means of supporting colonial rule, because it helped to keep the population divided.[28] Neville Rubin and Eugene Cotran have described the colonial rulers' neglect:

> ... there appears to have been a general lack of interest in the problems arising from the content and application of customary law, and generally speaking there were no serious attempts at studying the subject, no attempts at recording customary law, developing it, reforming it, or unifying it with the other laws. Customary law remained to a large extent unwritten and was treated as a matter of fact rather than law in the courts. Lawyers were not in touch with customary law problems, and its study remained the domain of the social anthropologist or the administrative officer.[29]

Colonial rule maintained separate and parallel court systems. The English colonies had their "native courts," the French colonies their *tribunaux de droit coutumier*. This separation has largely disappeared since independence. Some states, such as Niger, Mali, and the Ivory Coast, have abolished customary courts; a single court system exists for all cases, with provision for a lay expert to sit with the judges when customary law is dealt with. Others, such as Ghana, Tanzania, and Senegal, while conferring on a lower court (a "court of justice of the peace," a "primary court," or a "local court," as the case may be) special jurisdiction in matters of customary law, empower all courts at all levels to deal with both customary law and the general law; thus, cases involving customary law can come before the highest court of appeal. Today, in most of independent Africa, there is, to a greater or lesser degree, a unified court system.

---

[25] Neville Rubin and Eugene Cotran, *Readings in African Law*, I (London: Frank Cass & Co., Ltd., 1970), xxi.

[26] In this section, we have drawn heavily on Rubin, "Chieftaincy," pp. 121–28.

[27] Thierry Verhelst, *Safeguarding African Customary Law; Judicial and Legislative Processes for Its Adaptation and Integration*, African Studies Center (Los Angeles: University of California, 1968).

[28] Hilda Kuper and Leo Kuper, "Introduction," in Hilda Kuper and Leo Kuper (eds.), *African Law: Adaptation and Development* (Berkeley: University of California Press, 1965), p. 21.

[29] Rubin and Cotran, *Readings in African Law*, p. xxi.

Some African states have applied themselves to the task of trying to create an integrated legal system. They have faced three distinct problems. First, there was the need to determine what the customary law is, to have an accurate written record of the content of the law. Second, there was the problem of creating a common customary law applicable to all the people in the state; for when we speak of the customary law of an African state, we are referring to what are, in fact, a number of systems of customary law, each observed and practiced by a separate tribe or community within the same state.[30] Third, there was the question whether customary law could, by adaptation, become acceptable to all the people in the state; for instance, was it possible to formulate one law of marriage applicable to all citizens of a state, irrespective of their tribal status, ethnic origin, or religious faith?

Some states have made considerable progress in projects for the detailed restatement of customary law. Kenya, Tanzania, Malawi, Zambia, Botswana, and Swaziland have already produced valuable material on different branches of personal law, such as the Swazi law of succession.[31] Tanzania has gone far toward completing a project that aims at unifying the different systems of customary law applicable to the numerous tribes in the country.[32] The North African countries, particularly Morocco, have dynamic courts operating on the basis of Islamic law.

In 1960 Ghana sought to create an integrated customary law within the country by introducing the new concept of "assimilated customary law." The customary law of Ghana was defined as consisting of "rules of law which by custom are applicable to particular communities of Ghana." Under the new procedure, if a rule applicable to a particular community was deemed suitable for general application, it could be assimilated as part of the common law, thus becoming part of the law of the land. This was done by executive action taken on the advice of the chiefs.

The minister responsible for local government could convene a joint committee of all the Houses of Chiefs to consider whether a rule of customary law should be assimilated. He could take this step in response to representations from any one House of Chiefs or on his own initiative. The joint committee would consider the representations and any evidence placed before it; it was also empowered to carry out such additional investigations as might be necessary. If the committee decided that the rule should be assimilated, it was required to draw up a declaration describing the rule, with such modifications, if any, as it might consider necessary, and to submit the declaration to the minister. The final de-

---

[30] See Antony A. Allott, "The Future of African Law," in Kuper and Kuper, *African Law*, p. 225.

[31] N. N. Rubin, "The Swazi Law of Succession: A Restatement," in *Journal of African Law*, IX, no. 2: 108–9.

[32] For a detailed description of this project, see E. Cotran, "Integration of Courts and Application of Customary Law in Tanganyika," *East African Law Journal* (1965), pp. 1–15.

cision was taken by the minister after consultation with the chief justice. If the minister was satisfied that the declaration should be put into effect, he could declare the rule—with or without modifications, at his discretion—to be assimilated. The rule would thereupon become part of the common law of Ghana, officially designated a "common law rule of customary origin."

The same action could be taken on the inititative of a traditional council. A traditional council, having considered the rule of customary law in its area and decided that it should be assimilated, was empowered to make representations to the House of Chiefs having jurisdiction, which would make the necessary representations to the minister.

There is no record of this procedure's being used by the Nkrumah regime; nor does there appear to be any plan to do so by the present government of Ghana. It deserves to be tried out by some of the African states. It seems to be a way of getting government and traditional authority to cooperate in trying to develop an integrated legal system that can preserve much that is worthwhile in the traditional African heritage.

Ghana under Nkrumah was responsible for the first attempt to unify the law of marriage, divorce, and inheritance. In 1961 a white paper announced the government's intention to consider appropriate legislation, but only after there had been full and free discussion; it called for "as many people as possible" to send in their views, so that they could be taken into account in drafting the proposed law. After a year the Marriage, Divorce and Inheritance Bill was published, but it was not enacted. In 1963 a new bill was substituted; it was accompanied by a memorandum stating that the bill incorporated principles based on the views of the public and the recommendations of a parliamentary committee. The bill aimed to combine traditional and modern ideas and procedures in a single legislative enactment.

The bill substituted for the existing Ghanaian marriage law—the recognition of parallel systems of marriage, one under the marriage ordinance, the other according to customary law—a uniform law applicable to all citizens, providing that no person could register more than one marriage. A man could have more than one wife, but only the registered wife could inherit his property if he died without leaving a will. In this way the proposed new law, while permitting polygyny, would expose it to pressures from women anxious to assure for themselves and their children support from the estate of a deceased husband and father.

The divorce provisions in the new law are innovative in adapting traditional ideas to modern conditions. Under customary law, divorce, like marriage, takes place according to a procedure that is based on the fundamental idea that divorce concerns the two families as much as it concerns the spouses. There are discussions between the heads of the two families, the spouses, and invited relatives and strangers, aimed at a reconciliation. Only after it is clear that reconciliation is not possible does a divorce take place; arrangements are made, by agreement, in regard to the property rights of the spouses, maintenance of the wife, and the custody and maintenance of the children. Under the proposed new law, in the first step in divorce proceedings the judge appoints a committee, over which he presides, to try to effect a reconciliation. The committee consists of four local inhabitants, believed to be persons "whose wisdom and experience are respected in the locality and who would be expected to bring to marriage problems sympathy and understanding." The proceedings take place not in open court but in the judge's chambers, and lawyers are not admitted except by special permission of the judge. The committee has the usual power to call and examine witnesses. If a reconciliation is held to be impossible, the committee grants a divorce, which is announced by the judge in open court.

These provisions reflect a constructive and sensitive approach to the problems of divorce, which might be profitably emulated beyond the borders of Africa; in some respects, they would appear to be an improvement on the usual divorce procedures of the Western world. Surely a hearing in the privacy of a judge's chambers—particularly when there are children—is more appropriate than subjecting the parties to the strains of a hearing in open court.

In dealing with inheritance, the proposed law had to cope with the existence of two systems of inheritance under customary law, in addition to the system under statute law: the patrilineal system, under which children may inherit from their father and the matrilineal system, under which they may not. The effect of the proposed law would be to wipe out this distinction. Applying to all the inhabitants of Ghana, it gives two-thirds of the deceased's property to the children, one-sixth each to the surviving spouse and the surviving parents. While only a registered wife may inherit, all children, whether born of a registered or an unregistered marriage, may do so.

Unfortunately, none of these provisions became law in Ghana. Presumably because there was insufficient public support, the government decided, after the bill had been before parliament on three separate occasions, not to proceed with its enactment. But the abortive bill undoubtedly embodies ideas that merit the consideration of other African states.

A commission appointed by the government of Uganda in 1965 recommended the adoption of virtually all the Ghanaian provisions, but no action has taken place. Two commissions appointed by the government of Kenya, reporting in 1968, have recommended unified laws in which essentially African legal ideas are embodied in a modern legal enactment.[33]

In 1970 Tanzania announced its intention to enact a uniform law of marriage. A lengthy draft bill, the Law of Marriage Act, 1971, appeared as a supplement to the *Gazette* of December 18, 1970. It contains 167 sections, with two schedules—"Written Laws Repealed," and "Written Laws Amended." Here are some of its more important provisions: A

[33] Rubin and Cotran, *Readings in African Law*, pp. xxv–xxvi.

marriage may be contracted in Islamic form, according to customary law in a church where both parties are Christians, in civil form, or in accordance with the rites of a specified religion; all marriages must be registered. A simple procedure is provided for a civil marriage, which is available to all persons whether or not the parties belong to the same religion. A marriage may be monogamous or polygamous. Every marriage according to customary law or in Islamic form is presumed to be polygamous; every other marriage is presumed to be monogamous. Parties to a marriage may convert it to a polygamous or a monogamous marriage by a declaration made before a judicial officer. The minimum ages for marriage are eighteen for males and fifteen for females, but persons below the minimum age may marry with the leave of the court. Both parties must freely and voluntarily consent. A female below the age of eighteen also requires the consent of the parent or guardian. The court may grant a decree of separation, when it is satisfied that a marriage has broken down; a decree of divorce, when it is satisfied that the breakdown is irreparable. Where the marriage was contracted under customary law or Islamic form, proceedings may be brought in the high court, a district court, or a primary court; otherwise in the high court or the court of a resident magistrate. No person may bring proceedings for divorce unless he has first appeared before a marriage conciliatory board, which has conducted the necessary inquiry and certified that it has been unable to effect a reconciliation. The government is empowered to establish a conciliatory board for every ward. In granting a divorce, the court may also order the division of the assets jointly owned by the parties and award maintenance to either party and the children. The court may make orders for the custody of children, the paramount consideration being the welfare of the child. A married woman has the same right as her husband to hold or dispose of property, to enter into a contract, and to sue and be sued in a court of law. Marriage does not affect the right of a spouse to his or her own property, except that his or her interest in a matrimonial home may not be disposed of without the consent of the other spouse. When one spouse receives a gift from the other, there is a presumption that the property given belongs to the spouse who has received it. The husband has a duty to maintain his wife and children, but if he is unable to earn by reason of physical or mental incapacity, and the wife has the means to maintain the family, then it is her duty to do so. When a man and a woman have lived together for two years or more in such circumstances that they have acquired the reputation of being husband and wife, there is a presumption that they were married, but the presumption may be rebutted by either party producing evidence that they were not. If the presumption is rebutted, the woman is entitled to maintenance for herself and the children of the union. It is an offense for a married woman to contract another marriage.

Many states have altered specific provisions of customary law by legislation. There have been far-reaching changes in the marriage law. Gabon and the Central African Republic have abolished the dowry; the Ivory Coast and the Central African Republic have abolished polygamy. Mali, in a new marriage law, declares customary law to be repealed but incorporates a number of traditional provisions—for example, the dowry, while recognized, may not exceed a specified amount. In Senegal traditional practice relating to the rights and duties of the *navetanes* (foreign agricultural workers) have been incorporated in an otherwise modern code of civil and commercial obligations. In 1960 Ethiopia enacted a comprehensive code of civil law providing for essentially Western laws and institutions and expressly repealing customary law. But in certain branches of family law, for example, betrothal, the code makes traditional rules of law applicable.

From the examples we have given it would appear that customary law —the law of traditional African society that had successfully resisted the inroads of colonial rule—has some place in the modern legal systems of Africa. Precisely what that place will turn out to be is not yet clear, because customary law is itself undergoing change. The continuing though gradual process of recording it, converting it into written codes (the restatement projects), its interpretation by the courts of law in the course of litigation—these are making it lose much of its original character. In some fields customary law may be doomed to defeat in trying to compete with institutions and ideas inherited from a European power. This is probably true of the traditional judicial process, which has been largely replaced by such Western systems as the British law of procedure and evidence, with its well-organized structure of detailed rules.

But in such fields as marriage, divorce, and other branches of family law, as we have seen, there is clearly room for much of the substance of African customary law. It is encouraging that some of the African states have taken steps to ensure that modernization does not mean that customary law must be jettisoned. Other African states should follow the example that such countries as Ghana, Kenya, Tanzania, Senegal, and Mali have set by seeking to fit into the structure of their modern systems of government such traditional African legal ideas as are worthy of preservation.

10 Cooperation Among the Independent African States

The African states recognize African unity as an ultimate goal but continue to base their programs and policies on national needs rather than the interests of independent Africa as a whole.

Roots of Pan-Africanism

When the independent states of Africa, meeting at Addis Ababa in May, 1963, established the Organization of African Unity, they were completing a process going back more than half a century. In 1900 a conference devoted to the idea of Pan-Africanism took place in London. Sponsored by a West Indian lawyer, H. Sylvester Williams, the conference aroused the interest of William Edward Burghardt Du Bois, who proceeded to devote a brilliant mind to the development of Pan-African ideas and activities. Du Bois was largely responsible for five other Pan-African conferences held between 1919 and 1945 and aimed at building unity among black people throughout the world, enlisting the aid of world powers in removing racial discrimination, and, finally, securing independence for the peoples of Africa. At the last of these conferences, held in Manchester, England, in 1945, the delegates included many young Africans later to make their mark in the struggle of their own countries for independence: Kwame Nkrumah, Jomo Kenyatta, and Hastings Banda, to name but three.

During the same period another black spokesman was making his contribution to Pan-Africanism. In 1920 Marcus Aurelius Garvey, a Jamaican by birth, founded his universal Negro Improvement Association and attracted millions of followers with the slogans "Africa for the Africans" and "Renaissance of the Black Race." Within five years the powerful mass movement founded by Garvey had disintegrated; but he had, within that short period, stimulated among millions of people in the United States an awareness of a community of interests and goals, and his message had spread to other parts of the world.

Garvey and Du Bois—each making his own special kind of contribution—combined to fashion the twentieth-century ideology of Pan-Africanism. The ideas, attitudes, and values that went to make up this ideology represented a community of interest among all black people arising from a shared history of suffering.

Embodied in the ideology of Pan-Africanism are the two related but distinct concepts of *négritude* and the African personality. The essence of the concept of *négritude* is the awareness of a distinctiveness shared by all black people, accompanied by the positive reaction of being proud of one's blackness and the negative reaction of rejecting the values of the white world. The poet Aimé Césaire, who was born in Martinique but studied in Paris, introduced the term *négritude* and discussed the concept in the famous poem *Cahiers d'un Retour au Pays Natal*, which dealt with his rediscovery of himself as a black man after he had returned to his birth place. Other black poets in the United States and Africa—Langston Hughes, David Diop, Léon Damas, Léopold Sédar Senghor—writing in a similar vein, helped to make the concept of *négritude* significant for many of the young men who were later to play an important part in the political emancipation of colonial Africa.[1]

Recently, *négritude* has come under attack in Africa on the ground that it is beginning to have a restrictive effect on black creative activity. At the first Pan-African Cultural Festival, held in Algiers in 1969, there was support for the view that *négritude* was inhibiting "cultural vitality" by encouraging "conformity of style and content" among black writers.[2]

The second concept—the African personality—while also embodying the sense of pride in being black, incorporates the additional idea that Africa has its own unique contribution to make to the world. This concept, first enunciated by the West Indian Dr. Edward Blyden in the nineteenth century, was expounded by Kwame Nkrumah in the broadcast address that preceded the opening of the Conference of Independent African States at Accra in 1958:

For the first time, I think, in the history of this great continent, leaders of all the purely African states which can play an independent role in international affairs will meet to discuss the problems of our countries and take the first steps towards working out an African contribution to international peace and goodwill. For too long in our history, Africa has spoken through the voices of others. Now, what I have called an African Personality in international affairs will have a chance of making its proper impact and will let the world know it through the voices of Africa's sons.[3]

Many years before the Accra Conference, the ideology of Pan-Africanism had begun to assume the form of an instrument designed to change the whole future of the people of Africa. The last of the six Pan-African conferences responded to the climate of world freedom after the defeat of Nazi Germany by demanding independence for Africa and calling on

[1] For further information on the work of these poets and on *négritude* generally, see Colin Legum, *Pan-Africanism*, rev. ed. (London: Pall Mall Press, 1965), pp. 15–19, 93–111.
[2] Colin Legum and John Drysdale (eds.), *Africa Contemporary Record: 1969–1970* (Exeter, England: Africa Research Ltd., 1970), C 271–272.
[3] Kwame Nkrumah, *I Speak of Freedom* (New York: Praeger, 1962), pp. 124–30.

the people in the colonies "to fight ... by all the means at their disposal" for the right "to govern themselves and control their own destiny." In the new world that started to take shape at the end of World War II, the Pan-African movement developed as a response to the challenge presented by the struggle between the two great world powers. In the introduction to *Pan-Africanism: The Coming Sruggle for Africa*, George Padmore, writing a year before the Gold Coast was to achieve independence, offered this interpretation of Pan-Africanism:

> For if there is one thing which events in Africa, no less than in Asia, have demonstrated in the post-war years, it is that colonial peoples are resentful of the attitude of Europeans, of both Communist and anti-Communist persuasion, that they alone possess the knowledge and experience necessary to guide the advancement of dependent peoples. Africans feel that they are quite capable of leading themselves, and of developing a philosophy and ideology suited to their own special circumstances and needs, and have come to regard the arrogance of white "loftiness" in this respect as unwarranted interference and unpardonable assumption of superiority. Africans are quite willing to accept advice and support which is offered in a spirit of true equality, and would prefer to remain on terms of friendship with the West. But they want to make their way under their own steam. If, however, they are obstructed they may in their frustration turn to Communism as the only alternative means of achieving their aims. The future pattern of Africa, therefore, will in this context, be in large measure determined by the attitudes of the Western nations.[4]

This chapter looks at the way in which Pan-Africanism stimulated the search among the individual African countries (beginning when they were still under colonial rule and continuing after they had attained independence), for ways of cooperating with each other in order to advance the interests of Africa as a whole; a search that finally led, after a variety of regional grouping and shifting alliances, to the association of all the independent states of Africa as members of the Organization of African Unity.

We turn first to developments during the colonial period.

West Africa

France administered its colonial empire in Africa in a manner calculated to provide a basis for cooperation between the individual territories. Unlike the British colonies, the French colonies were administered as two federations: *Afrique Occidentale Française* (AOF, or French West Africa), comprising eight territories, each with its own governor and all subject to the general direction of a governor general with headquarters at Dakar; and *Afrique Equatoriale Française* (AEF, or French Equatorial Africa), comprising four territories, each with its

---

[4] George Padmore, *Pan-Africanism: The Coming Struggle for Africa* (London: Dennis Dobson, 1956), pp. 17–18.

own governor, and all subject to the general direction of a governor general with headquarters at Brazzaville. As they moved in the direction of increased autonomy and, ultimately, independence, these colonies tended to seek the achievement of their objectives by combining in small groups. One example of this tendency was the formation of the *Rassemblement Démocratique Africain* (RDA), an interterritorial political party led by Félix Houphouët-Boigny of the Ivory Coast. RDA had been formed following a meeting of deputies in the French parliament representing territories in AOF and AEF to protest against disabilities suffered by them as members of the French Union created by the new constitution of 1946.

In 1959, the Mali Federation was planned, to comprise Senegal, the former French Sudan (the present-day Republic of Mali), Dahomey, and Upper Volta, but antagonistic pressures from France and from the Ivory Coast led to the ultimate rejection of the proposals by Dahomey and Upper Volta. A smaller Federation of Mali (comprising the Sudan and Senegal) attained independence within the French *Communauté* in June, 1960, but two months later the marked ideological differences between the two nations led to their separation as the independent states of Senegal and Mali. Meanwhile, to counter the Mali Federation as originally planned the *Conseil de l'Entente* came into existence. It originated in an agreement between the Ivory Coast and Upper Volta, but Niger and Dahomey joined later, and the four countries established close economic ties. With President Houphouët-Boigny dominating its activities, the *Entente* has continued to meet from time to time, concerning itself with the coordination of its members' policies within the framework of their loyalty to what is now called the *Organisation Commune Africaine Malgache et Mauricienne* (OCAM), the body comprising many of the states of Francophone Africa. In March, 1966, following the military coup that ousted Nkrumah, when President Sékou Touré was reported to have made threats against the military regime in Ghana, Houphouët-Boigny warned Sékou Touré that the Ivory Coast and its fellow members of the *Entente*, aided by France, would come to the defense of Ghana. When the fifth conference of the heads of state of OCAM took place in January, 1970, it was reported that representatives of the five member-states of the *Entente* (Togo had joined in 1966) had met a few days prior to the conference to coordinate their views. With the withdrawal of several members since 1970, OCAM has been much weakened.

The principle of self-determination propounded by President Woodrow Wilson at the end of World War I evoked a response in the British colonies in West Africa. In 1920 J. E. Casely Hayford, a lawyer in the Gold Coast, called a conference of leaders from Gambia, Sierra Leone, Nigeria, and the Gold Coast. While the conference naturally concerned itself with such questions as more representative African participation in the legislative councils of the individual colonies and the removal of disabilities suffered by Africans in the civil service, there was also reference to the ultimate establishment of a permanent National Congress of British West Africa. The congress met three times during the next ten years, but with Hayford's death in 1930 it went out of existence. The foundation of the congress was premature. On the one hand, the colonial administrations saw it as a threat to their authority. On the other hand, there was a widespread feeling that it represented a small group of educated men who did not speak for the people as a whole. There was opposition in particular from influential chiefs. But, during its brief existence, it did make a contribution to the development of Pan-African consciousness, at least in West Africa.[5]

There were activities outside Africa that kept Pan-African thinking alive. In 1925 the West African Students Union was formed in England, and in the years that followed men like Nkrumah, Azikiwe, Banda, and Kenyatta were being prepared for their subsequent careers as leaders in Africa by their exposure to Pan-African ideas then being discussed in England and the United States. In 1945 Nkrumah founded the West African National Secretariat in London. It supported the idea of a West African Federation—an idea that had the support of Azikiwe—as a step intended to lead in due course to a United States of Africa.

North Africa

The movement toward unity in North Africa, which culminated in recognition of the Maghreb as an entity based on significant ties between its constituent members, was born during the colonial period. Today the Maghreb, comprising Tunisia, Morocco, Algeria, and Libya, is a grouping of independent states that share political and economic interests within the framework of their membership in the Arab bloc. Many years before these states achieved independence, Arab nationalist leaders in Tunisia and Morocco preached the importance of Maghreb unity, which came to be accepted as a goal by the independent states. The constitution of Tunisia, for example, declares the Tunisian Republic to be "part of the Great Maghreb," and the people to be determined to remain true to their "membership of the Arab family" while cooperating "with the African peoples in building a better future."

In 1958 representatives of the political parties of Tunisia, Morocco, and Algeria met to discuss the Algerian war and methods of achieving North African unity. The following resolution was passed:

The Conference resolves to work for the realization of the unity of the Arab Maghreb, and considers that the federal form corresponds to the circumstances of the participating countries. For this purpose, the conference proposes the establishment during the transitional phase of a Conservative Assembly of the Arab Maghreb, formed from the National Assemblies of Tunisia and

[5] For a detailed description of the foundation and development of the congress, see David Kimble, *A Political History of Ghana* (Oxford: The Clarendon Press, 1963), pp. 389–403.

Morocco and the National Council of the Algerian Revolution. The Assembly will be empowered to study questions of common interest and to make recommendations to the local executive bodies.

The Conference recommends that the Governments of countries of the Arab Maghreb should not enter into engagements in the field of foreign relations or defense until federal institutions have been established.

It was also decided to create a 6-member secretariat.

A permanent secretariat was established, but the other provisions of the resolution were not put into effect. The proposal that there be a federal relationship between the member-countries was not discussed at subsequent meetings. Since then the Maghreb states have been content to cooperate in various ways in the light of their common interests, without creating close formal bonds.

Ideological differences between Algeria and the others led at one time to serious conflict. There was an interruption of diplomatic relations between Morocco and Tunisia, and Tunisia refused to adopt the policy of militant hostility toward Israel shared by the other three, but since 1964 meetings have taken place at the ministerial level, and close economic coordination has been worked out among the four countries in many spheres. In January, 1969, President Boumediene paid his first official visit to King Hassan II of Morocco, and following talks between the two heads of state a "Treaty of Solidarity and Cooperation" was concluded between the two countries.[6] Since the Yom Kippur war of 1973, Tunisia's stance has tended to conform to that of the Arab world.

East, Central, and Southern Africa

In East Africa, the British colonial government had laid a foundation for possible cooperation between Tanganyika, Kenya, and Uganda by setting up the East African High Commission, which provided for a measure of useful economic and administrative coordination among the three countries. In 1961 a British commission, set up to review economic relations between the three countries, advised that the East African common market area be continued but recommended a redistribution of revenues to compensate for the fact that Kenya was reaping the greatest benefit from the common market. The commission concluded also that the name of the East African High Commission gave rise to misunderstanding about its functions and recommended that it be changed.

Later in the same year, at a conference held under the chairmanship of the British colonial secretary, it was agreed that Tanganyika would continue to share in common services with Uganda and Kenya after it attained independence, and that the East African High Commission

[6] For more recent developments in the Maghreb, see Legum and Drysdale, *Africa Contemporary Record, 1969–1970,* C 433. See also Abderrahman Robana, *The Prospects for an Economic Community in North Africa: Managing Economic Integration in the Maghreb States* (New York: Praeger, 1973). See also later discussion in this chapter.

would be known as the East African Common Services Organization.

The establishment of the East African Common Services Organization provided a basis for the growth of economic and political ties, which, it was hoped, would lead in due course to the creation of an East African Federation. The federation has not yet materialized, nor are present indications of its ultimate creation at all promising. But the functioning of the organization is one of the examples of fruitful cooperation between three African states that deserves attention. However, the subsequent development of this cooperation is part of the record of events after all three countries had become independent and will therefore be discussed later.

Meanwhile, there had been attempts to establish machinery for cooperation among the respective political parties in the countries of East and Southern Africa. In 1954 Kenneth Kaunda of Northern Rhodesia (now Zambia) had tried to arrange for the African leaders of Central, Southern and East African countries to meet. A meeting took place, but of local leaders only. The British colonial immigration authorities refused to allow the delegates from Kenya, South Africa, and the other countries to enter Northern Rhodesia. In 1958 representatives of a number of political parties met at Mwanza, Tanganyika, in large measure through the initiative of Julius Nyerere. It was at this meeting that the Pan-African Freedom Movement of East and Central Africa (PAFMECA) was formed, representing political parties in Tanganyika, Kenya, Northern and Southern Rhodesia, Nyasaland, and Zanzibar. When the outlawed African National Congress (ANC) and Pan-African Congress (PAC) of South Africa joined in 1962, it became the Pan-African Freedom Movement of East, Central, and Southern Africa (PAFMECSA).

PAFMECSA continued to be an important focus for cooperation among the new nations south of the Sahara and for the idea of Pan-African unity until it went out of existence in 1963 following the creation of the Organization of African Unity. The African nationalist movements that brought PAFMECSA into existence committed themselves to the goal of a federal relationship among the states to be created once independence had been achieved. For them, the framework of a future federal state comprising Tanganyika, Kenya, and Uganda was much more than a romantic dream; so much that in 1960 Julius Nyerere, speaking for Tanganyika, which was due to attain independence in 1961, declared his readiness to delay his own country's independence until Kenya and Uganda had also become independent, in the belief that this would make achievement of the federal goal easier. The fact that the Central African Federation, which had combined Northern Rhodesia, Southern Rhodesia, and Nyasaland in a federal relationship, was by then in a state of incipient dissolution—it ceased to exist three years later—did not undermine the faith of the PAFMECSA leaders in federalism as a means of building unity. They understood the difference between, on the one hand, a federal structure imposed on countries by the colonial power without taking due account (until it was too late) of the wishes of the people and, on the other, a federal structure resulting from the genuine belief of recognized nationalist leaders that federalism would advance the cause of African unity.

PAFMECSA came into existence at a time when the outlook for independence in East Africa was not encouraging: The emergency declared by Britain to cope with the surge of nationalism in Kenya was still in force. But there was a new climate of enthusiasm for Pan-African planning following on the grant of independence to Ghana. It was in 1958 that Nkrumah called the first meeting of the All-African People's Organization in Accra. Many of the young men associated with the foundation of PAFMECSA attended the Accra meeting and were inspired by contact with other future nationalist leaders who had accepted Nkrumah's invitation.

From the developments we have described, it is clear that the final stages of the decolonization process saw the emergence of what might be called concrete Pan-Africanism. Thus, despite the differences between their respective situations toward the close of the colonial period, North Africa, West Africa (both Anglophone and Francophone), East Africa, and Southern Africa had all provided evidence that there was a basis for planned and organized Pan-African cooperation in the future. The process of building a structure of Pan-African unity would commence in earnest when colonial rule had come to an end, and the new independent states had the power to relate their individual development to the future of Africa as a whole.

Toward African Unity, 1958–63

The attainment of independence by the Gold Coast in 1957 (the first British colony in Africa to do so) ushered in a period of intensive Pan-African thinking and activity. Under Nkrumah, Ghana became the center of the enthusiastic continuation in Africa of the Pan-African planning outside Africa that had culminated in the conference at Manchester in 1945. In April, 1958, Nkrumah arranged the first Conference of Independent African States in Accra. In December of the same year the All-African People's Conference took place, also in Accra, and in the succeeding years, until the Organization of African Unity was founded in 1963, Nkrumah's drive, energy, and persistence were an inescapable part of the process that was to make cooperation among the independent African states possible.

Let us look more closely now at events and developments during the period 1958–63, perhaps one of the most important periods in recent African history.

The Accra Conference of April, 1958, was a meeting of all the independent states of Africa except South Africa, namely Ghana, Liberia, Ethiopia, Egypt, Tunisia, Libya, Sudan, and Morocco. The fact that five of them were Arab and Muslim proved to be less important than the recognition that they all shared a concern for each other as part of

Africa. The declaration issued at the conclusion of the conference included the following passages:

We, the African States assembled here in Accra, in this our first Conference, conscious of our responsibilities to humanity and especially to the peoples of Africa, and desiring to assert our African personality on the side of peace, hereby proclaim and solemnly reaffirm our unswerving loyalty to the Charter of the United Nations, the Universal Declaration of Human Rights, and the Declaration of the Asian-African Conference held at Bandung.

We further assert and proclaim the unity among ourselves and the solidarity with the dependent peoples of Africa as well as our friendship with all nations. We resolve to preserve the unity of purpose and action in international affairs which we have forged among ourselves in this historic Conference; to safeguard our hard-won independence, sovereignty and territorial integrity; and to preserve among ourselves the fundamental unity of outlook on foreign policy so that a distinctive African personality will play its part in co-operation wth other peace-loving nations to further the cause of peace.

An important step in the direction of bringing about Pan-African cooperation was the conference decision that the representatives of the eight independent African states at the United Nations should act as a group for purposes of ensuring coordinated action on matters of common concern.

It was at the All-African People's Conference, held in December, 1958, also in Accra, that Nkrumah's ideas on Pan-African unity were presented. Just as the Conference of Independent African States was intended to provide for cooperation at the governmental level, the All-African People's Conference was intended to do the same at the non-governmental level. It was a gathering of representatives of political parties and trade unions from twenty-eight countries, most of them not yet independent. Many of the young men who attended, then unknown beyond the borders of their own countries, were later to become important figures on the African scene. The chairman was Tom Mboya from Kenya. Among the delegates were Patrice Lumumba, who was to return to the Belgian Congo (Zaïre) fired with a nationalist fervor that contributed very soon thereafter to an unexpectedly early grant of independence, and a quiet-spoken man called Joseph Gilmore, later, as Holden Roberto, to become known as the founder of the *Uniao das Populaçoes de Angola* (UPA) (The Union of Angolan Peoples), which launched the rebellion against Portuguese rule. There were white delegates representing the Liberal Party and the African National Congress of South Africa.

The resolutions—each of them lengthy and detailed—dealt with four topics, entitled: Imperialism and Colonialism; Frontiers, Boundaries, and Federations; Racialism and Discriminating Laws and Practices; and Tribalism, Religious Separatism, and Traditional Institutions.

In the resolution on Frontiers, Boundaries and Federations, the conference, *inter alia*, declared that the existence of separate states in Africa is fraught with the dangers of exposure to imperialist intrigues and of resurgence of colonialism even after their attainment of independence, unless there is unity among them. . . . The ultimate objective of African nations is a Commonwealth of Free African States.

It went on to resolve that it

(a) endorses Pan-Africanism and the desire for unity among African peoples;
(b) declares that its ultimate objective is the evolution of a Commonwealth of Free African States;
(c) calls upon the independent States of Africa to lead the people of Africa towards the attainment of this objective; and
(d) expresses the hope that the day will dawn when the first loyalty of African States will be to an African Commonwealth.

The Resolution on Tribalism, Religious Separatism, and Traditional Institutions reflected the radical outlook of the delegates and their great concern at that time about the role of chieftaincy in delaying the advance toward independence. It reads:

Whereas we strongly oppose the imperialist tactics of utilizing tribalism and religious separatism to perpetuate their colonial policies in Africa;

Whereas we are also convinced that tribalism and religious separatism are evil practices which constitute serious obstacles to (i) the realization of the unity of Africa: (ii) the political evolution of Africa; (iii) the rapid liberation of Africa;

Be it resolved that steps be taken by political, trade union, cultural and other organizations to educate the masses about the dangers of these evil practices and thereby mobilize the masses to fight these evils.

That in addition to any action taken by independent countries, the independent countries shall (a) allow their governments to pass laws and through propaganda and education, discourage tribalism and religious separatism; (b) encourage their governments to give the dependent countries and their leaders effective aid in the fight to realize their common objectives rapidly.

Whereas the Conference realizes that some of the African traditional institutions, especially chieftancy, do not conform to the demands of democracy;

And whereas some of these institutions actually support colonialism and constitute the organs of corruption, exploitation and repression which strangle the dignity, personality and will of the African to emancipate himself;

Be it resolved that those African traditional institutions whether political, social or economic which have clearly shown their reactionary character and their sordid support for colonialism be condemned.

That all conscientious peoples of Africa and all African political leaders be invited to intensify and reinforce their educational and propaganda activities with the aim of annihilating those institutions which are incompatible with our objectives of national liberation.

And that governments of independent countries be called upon to suppress or modify these institutions.

The All-African Peoples' Organization (AAPO) was established with headquarters and a "permanent secretariat" in Accra. The first secretary-general was George Padmore; after his death in 1959 the post was occupied by Abdoulaye Diallo, the resident minister representing Guinea in Ghana. Two further conferences took place, one in Tunis in 1960 and the other in Cairo in 1961. At both, resolutions were passed dealing with detailed measures relating to specific problems in Africa, for instance, at the Tunis conference the resolution on South-West Africa proposed that South Africa's performance of its obligations under the mandate granted by the League of Nations be made the subject of proceedings before the International Court of Justice; at the Cairo conference there was a resolution calling on the independent states of Africa "to press for and impose sanctions on South Africa, economic, diplomatic, and otherwise."

Meanwhile, the second Conference of Independent African States had taken place in 1960 at Addis Ababa. There were now fifteen member-states, and it was at this conference that two divergent approaches to the question of African unity emerged. The divergence was to lead to rival groupings that seemed at one stage to threaten Pan-African cooperation. One approach was that of Nkrumah. Ghana's Foreign Minister Ako Adeji expressed it in addressing the conference:

To us in Ghana the concept of African Unity is an article of faith. It is a cardinal objective in our policy. We sincerely believe that the Independent African States can, and may some day, form a real political Union—the Union of African States. . . . It does not matter whether you start with an Association of African States or whether with economic or cultural co-operation . . . we must start from somewhere, but certainly the Union can be achieved in the end.

Nkrumah had already furnished added proof of his conviction on this question by entering into the Ghana-Guinea Union in 1959.

The other view, directly opposed to that of Nkrumah, was put by Yusuf Maitima Sule, leader of the Nigerian delegation. He said:

No one in Africa doubts the need to promote pan-Africanism. . . . But we must not be sentimental; we must be realistic. It is for this reason that we would like to point out that at this moment the idea of forming a Union of African States is premature . . . we feel such a move is too radical—perhaps too ambitious—to be of lasting benefit. Gradual development of ideas and thoughts is more lasting . . . we must first prepare the minds of the different African countries—we must start from the known to the unknown. At the moment we in Nigeria cannot afford to form a union by government with any African States by surrendering our sovereignty.

In June, 1960, Ghana had become a republic under a constitution that reaffirmed Nkrumah's dedicated commitment to political unity as the answer to Africa's problems. The preamble affirmed the hope that the people of Ghana would, by adopting the new constitution, "help to further the development of a Union of African States."

In November, 1960, Nkrumah extended the scope of the Ghana-Guinea declaration with the announcement that Ghana and Mali had agreed to have a common parliament, but there was no information as to how this agreement was to be implemented. In December, 1960, after talks in Conakry, the capital of Guinea, among the three presidents—Nkrumah, Sékou Touré of Guinea, and Modibo Keita of Mali—a joint communiqué was issued announcing that they had decided to establish a union of the three states, with common diplomatic representation and a common economic and monetary policy. In 1961, after several days of secret talks in Accra, a joint communiqué stated that the three presidents had signed a charter to be submitted to their parliaments for ratification, which provided for the establishment of a Union of African States, to be "regarded as the nucleus of the United States of Africa."

The Ghana-Guinea-Mali Union never functioned as a supranational structure, but it was significant in establishing at least a temporary closer relationship among three West African states to demonstrate that a commitment to Pan-African cooperation could prove stronger than the French-English language barrier.

Meanwhile, two events—the Algerian civil war and the conflict in the Congo—were to play a major role in overshadowing such limited cooperative efforts as the Ghana-Guinea-Mali Union, clearly demarcating two camps among the independent African states in their movement toward unity, namely, the Brazzaville group and the Casablanca group. Following a meeting called by the Ivory Coast in 1960 to deal with the Algerian situation, the Union Africaine et Malgache (UAM) was created out of the Brazzaville group. It comprised the Ivory Coast, Senegal, Mauritania, Upper Volta, Niger, Dahomey, Tchad, Gabon, the Central African Republic, Cameroun, and Madagascar. Its aims were "organizing cooperation between its members in all fields of external policy in order to reinforce their solidarity, ensure their collective security and their development, and maintain peace in Africa, Madagascar, and the world." Membership was not restricted; any state accepted unanimously by the existing members could join, and general policy would be formulated by the heads of state and government meeting in ordinary session twice a year and in special sessions when necessary. The UAM members would constitute a group at the United Nations, meeting beforehand on all important issues in order to work out a coordinated policy.

The open breach that developed between Kasavubu and Lumumba in the Congo (today's Zaïre) was one of the main reasons for the emergence of the Casablanca group. The leading sub-Saharan countries in this group were Ghana, Guinea, and Mali, all unequivocally aligned with Lumumba. The alliance was born at a 1961 conference at Casablanca, called by Morocco because of its dispute with Mauritania, which had joined the Brazzaville group. The other African delegations were from the United Arab Republic, Libya, and the Algerian Provisional

Government. One of the resolutions passed at the Casablanca conference denounced Israel "as an instrument in the service of imperialism and neo-colonialism not only in the Middle East but also in Africa and Asia." This was the first time that the United Arab Republic had been able to persuade a group of African countries to identify themselves with the Arabs in their conflict with Israel. Nkrumah's decision to join in this resolution did not, however, disturb the close relations that then existed between Ghana and Israel. Israel was cooperating with Ghana in a number of economic and medical projects, and relations between the two countries at the diplomatic level remained cordial.

In May, 1961, twenty African states met at Monrovia. This was the largest gathering of African states to that time, and it included, in addition to the members of the Brazzaville group, Liberia, Nigeria, Somalia, Sierra Leone, Togo, Ethiopia, Libya, and Tunisia. Perhaps its most significant feature was the cooperation within the same grouping of African states of all the Francophone states and a number of Anglophone states. The initiative in bringing about the Monrovia conference was taken by President Senghor of Senegal, but he chose to remain in the background, and the conference was finally called under the co-sponsorship of President Sylvanus Olympio of Togo, President Tubman of Liberia, and Prime Minister Sir Abubakar Tafawa Balewa of Nigeria. Ghana and the other Casablanca states did not attend, and the months that followed saw a spate of newspaper attacks from Ghana on the Monrovia conference, which drew in return an equally vigorous barrage of press attacks on Ghana from Nigeria.

Efforts to heal the breach between the Monrovia and the Casablanca groups and to create a framework for cooperation by all the independent African states continued. Nigeria provided the major impetus behind these efforts, and the prime minister, Sir Abubakar, aided by the president, Dr. Azikiwe, played a leading role in negotiations and discussions, which resulted in another conference in January, 1962, held in Lagos. The representatives of twenty countries attended, and although the Casablanca powers once more stayed away the discussions indicated there was a strong belief that it was important to build unity among the newly independent states. Prime Minister Julius Nyerere of Tanganyika, who attended the Lagos conference, had anticipated its mood when he said, in an address to the World Assembly of Youth in the previous year, that "the African national state is an instrument for the unification of Africa, and not for dividing Africa; African nationalism is meaningless, is dangerous, is anachronistic if it is not at the same time Pan-Africanism."

On the one hand, African thinking appeared to be polarized, with the Casablanca group (led by Ghana) standing for a radical, militant, and left-oriented approach, and the Monrovia group (with Liberia and Nigeria in the forefront) standing for a conservative, moderate, and Western-oriented approach. On the other hand, this ideological conflict was not strong enough to prevent a steady movement toward Pan-

African unity. It was decided that there would be another conference, this time at Addis Ababa. Now Haile Selassie, Emperor of Ethiopia, presenting a new image as an African elder statesman, assumed a leading role in the planning of further steps. Soon he and Sir Abubakar were either themselves visiting various African countries or sending delegations to them to smooth over differences and widen possible areas of agreement. They discovered an unexpected ally in President Sékou Touré of Guinea—the union with Ghana and Mali agreed upon in December, 1960, still existed on paper only—whose unfortunate experience at this time of Soviet Russia's attempted interference in his country's affairs had induced him to seek closer ties with the West. Their joint efforts during 1962 and 1963 were responsible for the first summit meeting of African heads of state in May, 1963, and the establishment at that meeting of the Organization of African Unity.

African Trade Unionism

Before we discuss the OAU, we must refer briefly to the attempt to build unity among Africa's workers. At the first All-African People's Conference in Accra in 1958 there was a unanimous resolution calling for the establishment of an All-African Trade Union Federation (AATUF). This was reaffirmed at the second conference, held at Tunis in 1960, which declared its support for the convocation of an African Trade Union Congress. The AATUF was established at a conference at Casablanca in 1961, but it represented only a small percentage of the workers of Africa and, far from contributing to unity in the sphere of African trade unionism, became the center of bitter conflict.

Three international bodies competed for the support of African trade unions. They were the International Confederation of Free Trade Unions (ICFTU), a non-Communist organization; the World Federation of Trade Unions (WFTU), which was Communist-dominated; and the International Federation of Christian Trade Unions (IFCTU). Before independence, Sékou Touré established his own trade union in Guinea and persuaded the Senegalese trade union to break its ties with the WFTU. By 1957 his emphasis on an autonomous African trade union movement had resulted in the *Union Générale des Travailleurs de l'Afrique Noire* (UGTAN), which represented the workers of Francophone Africa and had no ties either with international bodies or with trade union organizations of metropolitan France. The establishment of UGTAN had inspired the decision taken at the Accra meeting that resulted in the creation of the AATUF.

When the AATUF came into existence in 1961, the ICFTU had succeeded in securing the affiliation of the majority of African trade unions. The Ghana Trade Union Congress had disaffiliated, but a number of trade unions, particularly those of Kenya (with the influential Tom Mboya as their spokesman) and Tunisia, continued to argue that the African trade union movement should retain its ties with ICFTU.

Ghana replied that AATUF would wage "total war" on African unions refusing to disaffiliate, and bitter recriminations between Ghana and Tunisia followed.

When the Organization of African Unity came into existence in 1963, there was a fairly clearly defined division in the ranks of the workers of Africa. The majority of the trade unions continued their affiliation, but a significant group (those of Ghana, Guinea, Mali, and the United Arab Republic) had an undivided commitment to AATUF. They had absented themselves from a conference held at Dakar in January, 1962, at which it was decided to establish a new body, the African Trade Union Confederation (ATUC). In the ATUC, forty-one union organizations were represented, twenty-one affiliated with ICFTU, twelve affiliated with IFCTU, and the remaining eight without ties to any international bodies. The countries represented comprised most of the Francophone states, as well as Tunisia, Libya, Kenya, Sierra Leone, and Nyasaland. It was decided that, while the confederation would not join any trade union international, the individual national organizations were free to maintain affiliation with international bodies. Among the principal aims of the confederation were (1) total "liberation" of Africa, (2) African unity, (3) creation of a "distinctive African socialist society," and (4) establishment of an African common market.

Even before the conference had opened, the Ghanaian trade unionist John Tettegah, secretary general of the AATUF, had denounced it as a "hoax" organized by "a clique of reactionary African trade union stooges supported and financed by the ICFTU." Nevertheless, at the conclusion of the conference the hope was expressed that members of the AATUF would in due course join the confederation.

Since the establishment of the OAU—which set up an economic and social commission with functions including the coordination of activities concerning the interests of African workers—the earlier divisions referred to have virtually disappeared, and the conflicting allegiances to the different international trade union bodies have ceased to play any significant part in relations between African states.

The Organization of African Unity

Meeting at Addis Ababa from May 22 to May 25, 1963, the independent states of Africa established the Organization of African Unity (OAU). A meeting of foreign ministers a week earlier had completed the detailed arrangements for the gathering of heads of state that on May 25 adopted a charter stating common aims, formulating common principles, and setting up a number of organs designed to achieve the purposes of the organization. The successful outcome of the summit meeting at Addis Ababa was a decisive reply to the chorus of political Cassandras throughout the world, who, pointing to the divisions that had developed in Africa since 1958, were convinced that Pan-African unity was an ideal bound to disintegrate once it confronted the realities of the African situation.

The creation of the OAU may fairly be described as a landmark in the recent history of international relations. Thirty states,[7] presenting a wide diversity at many levels—historical background, culture, political structure, language, ideology—were able to reach unanimous agreement on aims and objectives providing a basis for cooperative action in the interests of Africa as a whole. While the ultimate significance of the organization remained to be tested by subsequent developments, the fact that divisive factors were submerged in favor of dedication to a common purpose was generally recognized as a tribute to the statesmanship displayed by the leaders of the new African nations.

The two different approaches to African unity that had been part of the conflict between the Casablanca and the Monrovia groups were clearly defined during the discussions at the summit meeting. Nkrumah tried to obtain support for proposals designed to create a union of African states "along the lines of the U.S.A. or the U.S.S.R." The first step would be to set up an all-African committee of foreign ministers, charged with the task of establishing a permanent body of officials and experts to "work out machinery for the Union Government of Africa." The conclusions reached by this body would be submitted to a presidium consisting of the heads of government of the independent African states, which would meet in order to adopt a constitution and take other steps necessary to bring the "Union Government of Africa" into existence. Separate commissions would be set up to formulate plans for a common foreign policy, a common system of defense, a common industrial and economic program, and common African citizenship. The essence of Nkrumah's approach was that it called for a partial surrender of national sovereignty to the "Union Government of Africa."

Almost unanimously, the conference rejected Nkrumah's proposal in favor of the idea of a functional combination of sovereign states cooperating in the achievement of common goals. Sir Abubakar Tafawa Balewa, prime minister of Nigeria, said:

Some of us have suggested that African Unity should be achieved by political fusion of the different states in Africa; some of us feel that African unity could be achieved by taking practical steps in economic, educational, scientific, and cultural co-operation and by trying first to get Africans to understand themselves before embarking on the more complicated and more difficult arangement of political union. My country stands for the practical approach to the unity of the African continent.

It was the concept, inherent in this statement, of a gradual approach

[7] Morocco withdrew from the conference after a formal appearance, owing to its dispute with Mauritania. Togo was not represented, because the new government under Nicholas Grunitzky had not been recognized by all the African states. Both have since adopted the charter. Kenya and Zanzibar adopted it later in the year, when they achieved independence. By 1976 membership of the OAU had grown to 48 states.

to African unity that was unequivocally rejected by Nkrumah. "This view," he told the conference,

takes no account of the impact of external pressures. Nor does it take cognizance of the danger that delay can deepen our isolation and exclusiveness; that it can enlarge our differences and set us drifting further apart into the net of neo-colonialism, so that union will become nothing but a fading hope and the great design of Africa's full redemption will be lost, perhaps forever.

The decision of the conference to establish a functional union, it should be noted, did not mean the rejection of political union as a long-term goal. It reflected, rather, a wise refusal on the part of the overwhelming majority of the heads of state at Addis Ababa to assume that under existing circumstances in Africa a political union involving the partial surrender of sovereignty was desirable, or even possible.

Nkrumah did not see the Addis Ababa decision as a defeat for his point of view. When he returned to Ghana, his address to the national assembly hailed the establishment of the organization as a significant landmark on the road to a union of African states.

The OAU Charter

The Charter of the Organization of African Unity, adopted on May 25, 1963, comprises a preamble and thirty-three articles that state the purposes of the organization and the principles to which the member-states adhere and provide for a number of institutions through which the organization will accomplish its aims. Membership is open to any independent African state, and all member-states "enjoy equal rights and have equal duties." A state may renounce its membership by written notification, and after the expiration of one year from the date of the notification, such a state ceases to belong to the organization and to be subject to the provisions of the charter.[8]

The charter rests firmly on the basis of cooperation with the United Nations. In the preamble, the signatories declare themselves to be persuaded that "the Charter of the United Nations and the Universal Declaration of Human Rights . . . provide a solid foundation for peaceful and positive cooperation among states," and Article 26 provides for the submission of questions by member-states of the organization to the United Nations. In one of six resolutions adopted, the conference reiterated "its desire to strengthen and support the United Nations," and reaffirmed "its dedication to the purposes and principles of the United Nations Charter, including financial obligations."

The organization is declared to have five purposes: the promotion of African unity; the achievement of a "better life for the peoples of Africa"; the defense of the sovereignty of the African states; the eradica-

---

[8] Since 1963, each African state has joined the OAU on attaining independence, and, despite serious interstate conflict from time to time, no state has renounced membership. Today, all the independent states of Africa are members, and all, to a greater or lesser degree, participate in the OAU's activities.

tion "of all forms of colonialism from Africa"; and the promotion of "international co-operation having due regard to the Charter of the United Nations and the Universal Declaration of Human Rights." The member-states undertake to achieve the five stated purposes through cooperation in the fields of political activity, economic development, cultural advance, scientific and technical progress, public health, defense, and security. (The formal description of the purposes of the organization was elaborated in six lengthy resolutions passed by the conference. They dealt with decolonization; *apartheid* and racial discrimination; Africa, non-alignment, and the United Nations; general disarmament; economic problems; and the future of the Commission for Technical Co-operation in Africa.

In pursuing these purposes, the member-states:

solemnly affirm and declare their adherence to the following principles:
(1) the sovereign equality of all member-states
(2) non-interference in the internal affairs of states
(3) respect for the sovereignty and territorial integrity of each member state and its inalienable right to independent existence
(4) peaceful settlement of disputes by negotiation, mediation, conciliation, or arbitration
(5) unreserved condemnation, in all its forms, of political assassinaton as well as subversive activities on the part of neighboring states or any other states
(6) absolute dedication to the total emancipation of the African territories which are still dependent
(7) affirmation of a policy of non-alignment with regard to all blocs

The fifth principle (which is logically unnecessary, since the activities it deals with are examples of the "interference" covered by the second principle) reflects the strong feelings displayed at the conference about the suspected complicity of Ghana in the assassination in January, 1963, of President Olympio of Togo.[9] As to the third principle, it is difficult to envision any meaningful Pan-African cooperation without respect for territorial sovereignty. Pragmatically, therefore, the inclusion of this principle was unavoidable. It is necessary, however, to recognize that, in adopting this principle, the independent states of Africa were declaring their refusal to become involved in the difficult and emotionally charged question of redrawing the admittedly arbitrary and often unjust boundaries drawn by the colonial powers. Only five years earlier, in 1958, the first All-African People's Conference, which met in Accra, had passed a resolution stating that the conference

denounces artificial frontiers drawn by imperialist powers to divide the peoples of Africa, particularly those which cut across ethnic groups and divide people of the same stock; calls for the abolition or adjustment of such fron-

[9] President Houphouët-Boigny of the Ivory Coast who had, himself, recently escaped assassination, had told the conference, "We must have a clear and unequivocal attitude about assassinations, murders organized from outside or with the complicity of other countries, to overthrow a regime in the interests of a few adventurers."

tiers at an early date; calls upon the independent states of Africa to support a permanent solution to this problem founded upon the wishes of the people.

But the independent states of Africa took the wise decision, when creating a structure for the future development of Africa as a whole, of using to the best advantage what each of them had inherited from the colonial power, rather than running the risk of involvement in the multifarious conflicts bound to arise if a restructuring of the map of independent black Africa were undertaken. President Sylvanus Olympio had articulated the reasoning behind this decision as follows:

> In their struggle against the colonial powers the new African states, arbitrary and unrealistic as their original boundaries may have been, managed at last to mobilize the will of their citizens towards the attainment of national independence. Achieved at great sacrifice, such a reward is not to be cast away lightly; nor should the national will, once unified, be diluted by the formation of nebulous political units.[10]

The sixth principle is elaborated, reinforced, and given practical effect in the resolutions on decolonization and *apartheid* and racial discrimination. The first, calling for an immediate end to what still remained of colonial rule in Africa, "informs the allies of the colonial powers that they must choose between their friendship for the African peoples and their support of powers that oppress African peoples." It promises support for national liberation movements in the dependent territories and calls for a trade boycott of Portugal and South Africa. It establishes a special fund to assist the national liberation movement and a nine-nation committee to manage the fund and plan the assistance. The second resolution stresses the urgency of putting an end to the policy of *apartheid*; it provides for the creation of a fund to assist anti-*apartheid* movements in South Africa and the grant of aid to refugees from South Africa. All governments having diplomatic and economic relations with South Africa are called upon to break off relations and to "cease any other form of encouragement for the policy of *apartheid*." The resolution concludes by expressing "the deep concern aroused in all African peoples and governments by measures of racial discrimination taken against communities of African origin living outside the continent and particularly in the United States of America" but adds "appreciation of the efforts of the United States of America to put an end to these intolerable malpractices."

The charter states that its aims are to be achieved through four main institutions and a number of specialized commissions. The main institutions are the Assembly of Heads of State and Government; the Council of Ministers; the General Secretariat; and the Commission of Mediation, Conciliation, and Arbitration.

[10] "African Problems and the Cold War," in *Foreign Affairs*, XL, no. 1 (October, 1961): 51.

The assembly, which is described as the supreme organ of the organization, has an essentially deliberative function. It is required to "discuss matters of common concern to Africa" and has the right to review the activities of other organs and agencies of the organization. It comprises the heads of state or government (or their representatives) and meets at least once a year. An extraordinary session of the assembly must take place if requested by any member-state. Two-thirds of the total membership of the OAU constitutes a quorum at any meeting of the assembly, and all resolutions must be supported by two-thirds majority before they can take effect.[11]

The council of ministers has an essentially executive function. It is charged with the obligation to implement decisions taken by the assembly. It acts on the instructions of the assembly in coordinating inter-African activities and must deal with any matter referred to it by the assembly. The council meets regularly twice a year, but extraordinary sessions take place when requested by a member-state, provided that such a request has received the approval of two-thirds of all member-states, whose representatives are either the foreign ministers or such other ministers as the states may designate. As in the case of the assembly, two-thirds of the total membership of the council constitutes a quorum, but all decisions are taken by a simple majority of the members.[12]

The general secretariat comprises an administrative Secretary-General, together with one or more assistant Secretaries-General. The charter provides for the appointment of the Secretary-General by the assembly on the recommendation of the council of ministers, the functions of the secretariat being governed by the provisions of the charter and by regulations approved by the assembly. The Secretary-General and his staff are responsible only to the organization. To ensure the strict impartiality of the secretariat, the charter provides that (1) it may not, in performing its duties, act on the instructions of any government or other external organization, and (2) no member of the organization will seek to influence the secretariat in the discharge of its responsibilities.[13]

The charter embodies a decision to establish a commission of mediation, conciliation, and arbitration, whose function is to give effect to the pledge of member-states "to settle all disputes among themselves by peaceful means," but its composition and "condition of service" are left to be determined at a later date by the assembly.[14]

[11] Articles 8–10. The United Nations General Assembly requires a two-thirds majority only for "important questions." For all other questions, a simple majority is sufficient. (United Nations Charter, Article 18.)

[12] Articles 12–41. The Council lacks the inherent powers and rights of independent action, which are conferred upon the Security Council by the United Nations Charter. (United Nations Charter, Article 24.)

[13] Articles 16–18. These provisions follow the corresponding provisions of the United Nations Charter. (United Nations Charter, Articles 97 and 100.)

[14] Article 19. In this provision, the OAU envisages a special organ to perform the function that, under the United Nations Charter, is the responsibility of the Security Council. (United Nations Charter, Articles 33–38.)

There is no limit to the number of specialized commissions that may be established, but the charter makes specific provision for the following: Economic and Social Commission; Educational and Cultural Commission; Health, Sanitation, and Nutrition Commission; Defense Commission; and Scientific, Technical, and Research Commission. Additional commissions may be established by the assembly as it sees fit. Commissions are composed of ministers designated by the memberstates. The functions of the commission are governed by the provisions of the charter and by regulations approved by the council of ministers.

The OAU is financed by contributions of the member-states. The budget, prepared by the Secretary-General and approved by the council of ministers, provides for contributions based on the scale of assessment prepared by the United Nations, subject to the stipulation that no member-state may be required to contribute an amount exceeding 20 per cent of the annual budget of the organization.

Addis Ababa was chosen as the seat of the organization's permanent headquarters, and Diallo Telli of Guinea, who had been Chairman of the United Nations Special Committee on *Apartheid*, became the first Secretary-General, with four assistant secretaries from Algeria, Dahomey, Kenya, and Nigeria. He continued in the office until 1972, when he was replaced by Nzo Ekangaki, who was replaced in 1974 by Eteki Mboumduawas; both are Camerounian. The Committee of National Liberation (often referred to as the Committee of Nine) was established, comprising Tanganyika, Uganda, Guinea, the United Arab Republic, Algeria, Nigeria, Ethiopia, Zaïre, and Senegal, with headquarters in Dar es Salaam. The fund to assist the national liberation movements came into existence. It was planned originally that memberstates should contribute 1 per cent of their national income to the fund, but this idea was abandoned. In 1963 about $17 million was contributed, Ghana alone refusing, following vigorous criticism of the activities of the committee by Nkrumah. The various organs of the Organization of African Unity have continued to meet regularly since 1963. New permanent commissions have been established, and decisions have been taken from time to time designed to facilitate the working of the machinery of the organization. But the structure set up a Addis Ababa in 1963 remains unchanged; it has continued to provide what appears to be an adequate framework for cooperative action among the independent African states.[15]

The 13th Assembly of the OAU, held in 1975 in Uganda, was preceded by unsuccessful attempts by several African states to prevent General Amin from being elected to the presidency. The Assembly, while calling for increased aid for the Southern African liberation movements, approved the negotiations by Zambia and Tanzania with South Africa aimed at accelerating majority rule in Rhodesia. The 14th

[15] This section is based on Leslie Rubin, "The Organization of African Unity: Machinery, Problems, and Prospects," in S. Okechekwu Mezu (ed.), *The Philosophy of Pan-Africanism* (Washington, D.C.: Georgetown University Press, 1965).

Assembly, held in 1976 in Mauritania, was addressed by Dr. Kurt Waldheim, United Nations Secretary-General, who condemned the Soweto "massacre" as "the inevitable consequence of the brutal policy of *apartheid*."

The Organization of African Unity: Achievements and Failures

The record of the Organization of African Unity, which we shall now examine, covers a decade. Developments during that period, as we shall see, while encouraging in a number of respects, when taken together reveal the fluidity of political patterns in Africa. It will probably be many years before these patterns crystallize and one can speak with some assurance of clearly defined trends in the processes of African unity. Those who are quick to express dogmatic opinions on the state of African unity after a single decade must be reminded of the European experience. The history of attempts to achieve unity in Europe during the past half-century (with its record of two disastrous wars, and the city of Berlin still divided between two hostile regimes) should be a warning against the dangers of expecting too much too soon from the efforts of the new Africa to build its unity.

The problems that face the OAU are perhaps more insistent and more complex than any that faced the League of Nations after World War I or that face the United Nations today. Already the organization represents forty-eight independent states (when the liberation of Africa is complete the number could rise to over fifty) and speaks in the name of more than 350 million people, who present a wide diversity in terms of historical background, political structure, language, ideology, and economic strength. In addition, many of the African states are destined to seek the achievement of their national goals, severely handicapped by the colonial legacy of borders that have left one tribe or nation (for instance the Ewe of Ghana and Togo; the Somali of the Somali Republic, Kenya, and Ethiopia) arbitrarily split up among two or more independent states. The organization also faces problems that relate to the size, geographical situation, and viability of some of its member-states. Most of them have small populations; some of them, populations of less than 1 million (such as Equatorial Guinea, 300,000; Swaziland, 400,000; Gabon, 500,000). Five states—Nigeria, the United Arab Republic, Ethiopia, Zaïre, and Algeria—together account for approximately half the population of the continent. Two examples of problems arising from geographical factors are Lesotho and Gambia; each is an enclave within another state, the former within the Republic of South Africa, the latter within Senegal.

Commitment of Member-States. The OAU's potential in many fields has been limited by the failure of most of the member-states to fulfill their obligations. It has been hampered by shortages of funds, because many of them, at different periods, have not paid the contributions levied under the charter.

The OAU has also been hampered in its work because of the unwillingness of member-states to participate in the activities of various organs. For instance, the secretariat was unable for some years to convene a session of the Commission of Jurists for lack of a quorum.[16]

In marked contrast was the action of President Nyerere in calling for an extraordinary meeting of the council of ministers in 1964, *after* the mutiny of the army of Tanganyika had been quelled. His purpose in doing so was to affirm his commitment to the organization by reporting on what had occurred and thus giving his fellow members an opportunity to express their views on the action he had taken, as well as to discuss with him the wider implications of the mutiny.

For most member-states, however, the organization continues to be the symbol of a Pan-African unity that they wish to preserve, rather than a political force that they can look to for the practical solution of their problems. Absorption in their own—and usually pressing—national problems has tended to militate against the growth of a spirit of full commitment to the organization. But this, as we shall see, has not prevented the organization from being able to claim a number of significant achievements in the short period of its existence.

Interstate Conflict. The two major sources of conflict among member-states have been border disputes and the existence in one state of refugees from another.[17]

The Organization of African Unity was born in an atmosphere of interstate conflict. One of the absentees from the Addis Ababa conference in 1963 was Morocco. It refused to participate because of its persistent claim to the territory of Mauritania (which was represented at the conference) ever since that country attained independence in 1960. Tension beween the two countries had grown, and Mauritania had threatened military steps to deal with alleged subversive action by Morocco, but discussions were opened between them and the conflict was resolved. Both have participated in subsequent OAU meetings.

Later in the same year, the organization was presented with a more severe test of its capacity to ensure adherence to its principles and goals when fighting broke out between Algeria and Morocco over disputed claims to territory. A ceasefire was arranged, and in November, 1963, the council of ministers appointed a seven-nation arbitration commission, which met several times and was instrumental in bringing about a settlement. In May, 1964, diplomatic relations between Algeria and Morocco were fully restored, and by the beginning of 1965, complete agreement had been reached on all outstanding differences between them. But by 1975, Morocco's takeover of most of Spanish Sahara had led to further friction that culminated in the rupture of diplomatic relations between the two countries and the possibility of armed conflict.

[16] Paul Saenz, "The Organization of African Unity in the Subordinate African Regional System," in *African Studies Review*, XIII, no. 2 (September, 1970): 204
[17] *Ibid.*, p. 215.

A third dispute, involving the Somali Republic, Kenya, and Ethiopia, proved to be less easily resolved. A ceasefire in the border warfare between Ethiopia and the Somali Democratic Republic, called for by the council of ministers, was short-lived. Attempts at mediation were made by President Abboud of the Sudan and Presidents Nkrumah and Nyerere, but they were of no avail, and Somalia threatened to place its complaint before the U.N. Security Council if its demands were not satisfied. In 1964 the council of ministers set up a special committee to deal with the dispute, to ensure that an approach to the United Nations was averted and that settlement was negotiated within the OAU framework. It took three years before the dispute was settled, but the challenge to the organization had been met. The settlement had been achieved by the use of OAU machinery. At the fifth summit meeting of the OAU, held in Kinshasa in September, 1967, Kenya and Somalia reached agreement, and in October the president of Kenya and the prime minister of Somalia met under the auspices of the OAU, with President Kaunda of Zambia acting as mediator, to sign the necessary documents. Meanwhile, in September a communiqué issued simultaneously in Ethiopia and Somalia had recorded the agreement of the two states to "eliminate all forms of tensions" and to take various specified steps to establish cooperation between them.

The suppression of opposition in some of the African states, and internal conflict resulting in violence, has created a refugee problem in Africa. The difficulty has been to distinguish between the simple grant of asylum to refugees from another country and the support of efforts by the refugees to undermine or overthrow their own governments. The OAU is attempting to deal with this problem by laying down a set of principles designed to govern the behavior of each African state in relation to the internal affairs of all other African states. These principles are to be found in three sources: (1) the Protocol on the Status of African Refugees, (2) the Declaration on the Problem of Subversion, and (3) decisions of the Commission on African Refugees. Examples are undertakings by all the states not to permit their own territories to be used for subversion directed against any fellow member-state of OAU and not to engage in propaganda directed against any fellow member-state.

The conflict between Tanzania and the Amin regime in Uganda, following the overthrow of President Obote, is dealt with below.

Internal Conflict. Civil war in three African states presented the OAU with special problems. The situations in Zaïre, Nigeria, and Angola resulted in a division of loyalties among the other African states that gave rise to interstate friction and led to intervention by non-African states. The complex ramifications of both situations placed a great strain on the OAU's desire to see internal peace restored while respecting the principle enshrined in the charter of respect for the sovereignty and independence of each state.

The situation in Zaïre (1964-65, then called Congo) produced strong feelings among many African states against the Tshombe regime because of its use of foreign mercenaries against the rebels and its acceptance of foreign intervention in the form of military aid provided by the United States. The OAU set up a nine-nation Congo Conciliation Commission under President Jomo Kenyatta of Kenya, which held meetings with the regime and with representatives of the rebels. Its activities served to antagonize both the United States and the government of the Congo. The OAU proved powerless to prevent support for the rebels by Algeria, the United Arab Republic, and Ghana, and both the conciliation commission and the council of ministers spent a great deal of time in inconclusive debates. The assumption of power by Mobutu in November, 1965, marked the beginning of the process that was to bring order and stability to the Congo during the next two years, but the OAU was not entitled to claim credit for this. On the contrary, what had been demonstrated was the weakness of the OAU when faced with a combination of strong feelings within Africa and powerful external pressures.

The Nigerian civil war is an example. The federal government was aided by Britain, the Soviet Union, and the United Arab Republic, while Biafra received limited military aid from France. During the first year of the war, the Igbos gave every indication of being determined to carry on their resistance for many years. In September, 1967, the OAU condemned the secession of Biafra and set up an advisory commission composed of the heads of state of Ethiopia, Ghana, Cameroun, Niger, Zaïre, and Liberia. There were visits by members of the commission to Lagos, and in 1968 discussions took place between representatives of the federal government and Biafra under OAU supervision, but they ended in a deadlock. Meanwhile, Tanzania had accorded official recognition to Biafra, Nyerere having argued persuasively that, however desirable the maintenance of Nigerian unity in theory, the conclusion of the Igbo nation that only independence could ensure its future security was fully borne out by the facts of the situation. Zambia, the Ivory Coast, and Gabon followed Tanzania's example but the OAU reaffirmed its earlier decision to insist on the maintenance of Nigerian unity and therefore to side with the federal government. Biafran resistance continued for almost three years but the superior federal forces, together with the effects of famine and disease, proved too much for the Igbo people. Ojukwu's forces surrendered on January 12, 1970.

In the case of Nigeria, too, the OAU had been proved incapable of rallying the forces of independent black Africa to bring about a peaceful settlement of conflict with a member-state.

The OAU found itself deadlocked when after Portugal's withdrawal armed conflict erupted among the three Angolan liberation movements, which led to intervention by the Soviet Union, Cuba, South Africa, and the United States. Attempts to bring about a government of national unity failed. A destructive civil war ended in 1976 with victory for the

MPLA, which the OAU recognized as the legitimate government of the new state. The OAU did not prevent the partitioning of Spanish Sahara between Morocco and Mauritania after Spain's withdrawal, notwithstanding vigorous opposition by Algeria.

The Liberation of Africa. As we have seen, the National Liberation Committee started its existence with financial problems stemming from failure of member-states to pay their contributions. Most member-states continued to be in arrears with their contributions. In most cases this reflects widespread dissatisfaction with the committee's activities.[18]

The major source of dissatisfaction is the fact that the liberation forces are divided between rival organizations, with the result that much of the money provided by the committee has been dissipated in the unnecessary duplication of activity. At the summit meting in 1966 the OAU set up a committee to consider ways and means of making the National Liberation Committee more effective. Much of the criticism expressed is based on the impatience of many member-states because the guerrilla movements have not yet been able to achieve their goals, but at the 1970 summit meetings of the OAU (which was preceded by a meeting of the committee) there was a full discussion of various aspects of the committee's activities, followed by a decision to provide increased aid for the committee.

While the national liberation movements have found it necessary to seek independent supplementary aid (both financial and in terms of equipment and training) for their guerrilla activity, from individual African countries, such as Algeria and the United Arab Republic, as well as from the Soviet Union, China, and such countries as Sweden and Israel among the Western powers, the National Liberation Committee continues to perform the valuable function, through its administrative and consultative machinery in Dar es Salaam, of coordinating the activities of the various movements. In some cases it has helped to terminate rivalry within a national liberation movement, for example, by increasing aid to the African National Congress (ANC) of South Africa while suspending aid to the rival Panafricanist Congress (PAC). In addition, the consistent dedication of President Nyerere (with the support of President Kaunda of Zambia) to the cause of eradicating white supremacy from South Africa has been an important factor in sustaining the morale of the various national liberation movements that have offices in Dar es Salaam.[19]

Dissidence of Member-States. As we have noted in a previous chapter,[20] one of the member-states of OAU, Malawi, has openly defied the organization by establishing diplomatic relations and building close

[18] *Ibid.*
[19] For details of the various liberation movements, see Chapter 6.
[20] See Chapter 6.

economic ties with South Africa. There are no indications that other member-states might follow Malawi's example. (For a discussion of the unsuccessful attempt of President Houphouët-Boigny of the Ivory Coast to persuade the OAU to enter into a dialogue with South Africa, see Chapter 6.)

African Influence in the International Community. There is evidence that, since the establishment of the OAU, the independent African states have become a significant pressure group in the field of international affairs. The African Caucusing Group at the United Nations has been influential in getting a number of treaties concluded that control nuclear activity. African representation on the Security Council, and a number of other United Nations agencies, has been increased. In exercising its influence, the OAU has kept faith with its commitments to nonalignment, that is, the African states have avoided involvement in conflicts that have developed between the world powers.[21]

Economic Cooperation. The record in the sphere of long-range planning of economic cooperation among the independent African states is most encouraging. The activities of the Economic and Social Commission of the OAU in this sphere have recently been described as follows:

The commission has made initial preparatory arrangements for (1) the coordination of national economic development plans so as to avoid competition which would be harmful to the effective development of the entire continent, (2) the establishment of regional institutions for more judicious exploitation of Africa's natural resources and markets, (3) the development of a "common united front" in all international organizations dealing with economic and social problems. In addition, it has formulated plans to (1) coordinate and harmonize the activities of African Ministers of Labor and Social Affairs on common problems; (2) safeguard the interests of African workers; (3) achieve labor cooperation in the development of the continent; (4) incorporate the Pan-African Youth Movement into the framework of the OAU; (5) coordinate vocational training throughout Africa by means of an OAU Center for Higher Technical and Vocational Training; and (6) sponsor a full exchange program of festivals, work camps, jamborees, sports games and so forth. . . .

In attempting to promote the establishment of an African common market the Commission has been following a policy of encouraging the adoption of various programs. . . . For example, the Commission has promoted (1) the creation of regional institutions for economic integration and (2) the strengthening of existing groups in order to make them more effective. In accordance with this policy, the Commission has enthusiastically supported (1) the complete reorganization of the Equatorial Customs Union, (2) the establishment of the Central African Customs and Economic Union, (3) the continuation of the East African Common Services Organization,

---

[21] Saenz, "Organization of African Unity," pp. 212–13. For relations with Arab world, see Chapter 11.

(4) the creation of a West African common sugar market, (5) the development of a West African integrated iron and steel industry centered in Liberia, (6) the joint exploitation of the Lake Chad Basin, and (7) the development of the Senegal River by the riverine states.[22]

Another OAU commission, the Transportation and Communications Commission, is concerned with programs that will facilitate economic cooperation. There are plans to coordinate transportation services, for instance, by airline companies, which can respond to the needs of two or more countries, and to take similar steps in regard to postal and telecommunication services, such as having a uniform postage rate adopted on certain kinds of mail transmitted from one state to another.

Scientific and Technical Research. The OAU Scientific, Technical and Research Commission took over the functions of the Commission for Technical Cooperation in Africa in 1964. Since then it has been responsible for a number of programs concerned with such matters as the training and exchange of personnel and joint research undertakings, which are likely to promote significant advances in the cooperative exploitation of Africa's great potential in hydroelectric power and mineral resources.[23]

Education and Cultural Development. The OAU Educational and Cultural Commission has formulated several ambitious plans relating *inter alia* to teacher-training, adult literacy, and instruction in English and French, which could play an important part in speeding the process of modernization throughout Africa.[24]

Military and Defense Planning. The OAU Defense Commission is working with a department of defense within the secretariat and a committee of defense composed of members of the general staffs of the member-states on plans aimed at the ultimate establishment of an integrated system of defense covering Africa as a whole. It is generally recognized that achieving this goal belongs to a very distant future, but there is evidence that useful preliminary measures have been taken that could form part of a foundation for a military Pan-African structure one day. An example is the success of the OAU in arranging for a number of African states from time to time to share training facilities and small quantities of equipment.[25]

---

[22] *Ibid.*, p. 213.
[23] *Ibid.*, pp. 215–16.
[24] *Ibid.*, p. 216.
[25] *Ibid.*, and Legum and Drysdale, *Africa Contemporary Record: 1970–1971*, A37–38.

Regional Pan-African Groupings

Following the establishment of the OAU, the grouping of Francophone states which had come into existence in 1961 (the UAM)[26] decided to cease operating as a political body but to continue in existence for purposes of cooperation in economic, cultural, and technical spheres under a new name, *Union africaine et malgache de coopération économique* (UAMCE). In 1965, however, UAMCE was replaced by the *Organization commune africaine et malgache* (OCAM), with headquarters at Yaoundé. OCAM announced its aim and objects as follows:

> The new Organization . . . is an African grouping which has the aim, within the framework of the OAU, of reinforcing cooperation and solidarity among the African states and Madagascar in order to accelerate their development in the *political*, economic, social, technical, and cultural spheres.

Functioning on an administrative apparatus that parallels the OAU, since 1965 OCAM has continued to hold regular annual conferences of heads of state, usually preceded by meetings of its Council of Ministers. At the 1970 conference, Mauritius became the fifteenth member of the organization, whose name was then changed to *Organization commune africaine, malgache et mauricienne* (OCAM).

At first there was a tendency among most member-states of the OAU to regard the existence of OCAM as a divisive factor on the Pan-African scene. It was felt that OCAM expressed an unhealthy belief among the Francophone states that their interests should take precedence over the interests of Africa as a whole, and its continued existence was thought to present a threat to African unity. But it seems the pursuit by the member-states of OCAM of the economic and cultural interests they share has not prevented them from participating in the activities of the OAU. Furthermore, the common interests that bind them to each other have not prevented a divergence of outlook on many important questions. For example, the militant opposition of Cameroun to *apartheid* and white minority rule in Southern Africa is in marked contrast to the moderate attitude of the Ivory Coast, which has urged that even economic pressures by the OAU be abandoned in favor of direct talks with the South African government. These and other differences have considerably weakened the OCAM in recent years. But at its ninth conference, held in 1974, despite the resignation of Cameroon, Tchad, and the Malagasy Republic and the threats of resignation by Gabon and Togo, they decided to remodel the organization, making it a "purely economic" body designed to ensure effective cooperation among its member-states.

We have already referred to the regional grouping of Tanganyika,

---

[26] See page 241 of this chapter.

Uganda, and Kenya.[27] There had been encouraging steps in the direction of a federal union of these countries before they attained independence. At a meeting in June, 1963, it was agreed that, after Kenya had become independent, the three states would combine to form a federation. Before long, however, it became apparent that differences in the patterns of development of the three countries created obstacles to a federal union. In 1965 the three heads of state concluded the "Kampala Agreement," which provided for the distribution of certain major industries among the three countries and introduced a system of quota restrictions on the importation of commodities by one state from either of the others. The East African common currency was discontinued, and separate currencies were established.

Today Kenya, Uganda, and Tanzania form the East African Economic Community, participate in a common market, and combine in the operation of a number of common services. There is an East African Legislative Assembly empowered to make laws on all matters concerning the community—including the collection of customs and excises, civil aviation, income tax, and transfer taxes—which meets regularly. In 1976 the inclusion of Mozambique and a form of associate membership for Zambia were under consideration.[28] The unexpected overthrow of the Obote government in Uganda in January, 1971, threatened to have unfavorable effects on the immediate future of the community. President Nyerere of Tanzania refused to recognize the new military regime under General Amin, announced officially that the deposed President Obote (who was granted asylum in Tanzania) would be regarded as the lawful head of state, and launched a vigorous public attack on General Amin. Later in 1971, there were clashes between units of the Ugandan and Tanzanian armed forces, and tension between the two countries increased greatly. By the end of the year, through the conciliatory efforts of President Kenyatta, Uganda and Tanzania were moving toward the resumption of former joint activities within the community. The OAU's recognition of the Amin regime as Uganda's lawful government seemed to ensure normal relations within the community, but the brutality of the Uganda regime coupled with Amin's outbursts of aggressive behavior led to a serious breach with Tanzania. In 1975, when Amin's candidacy as President of OAU was under consideration, the Tanzanian government described him as "a murderer, an oppressor, a black fascist, and a self-confessed admirer of fascism." Relations between the two countries have continued to deteriorate. With friction between Kenya and Uganda in 1976, and growing policy differences between Kenya and Tanzania, the East African Economic Community showed signs of disintegrating.

A number of other groupings have come into existence, most of them concerned mainly with the advancement of shared economic interests. In 1968 Senegal, Guinea, Mali, and Mauritania combined to form the

[27] See pages 235-36 of this chapter.
[28] *Africa Diary*, XVI, no. 16 (April 15-21, 1976).

Organization of Senegal River States (OERS), with the primary object of developing the resources of the Senegal River basin. Following serious tension between Senegal and Guinea after the invasion of Guinea in 1971, Guinea ceased to participate, Senegal resigned, and OERS ceased to exist. It was replaced by a new organization comprising Senegal, Mali, and Mauritania called the *Organisation pour la Mise en Valeur du Fleuve Sénégal* (OMVS, Organization for the Development of the Senegal River). Meeting in 1974, OMVS adopted a forty-year plan involving an expenditure of $2000 million on a number of hydro-electric, agricultural, mineral, and industrial projects. About the same time, the United States of Central Africa (UEAC) was established, comprising Tchad, Zaïre, and the Central African Republic, as a means of advancing their mutual economic interests, but it was short-lived. The same year saw the creation of the West African Regional Group comprising Guinea, Ghana, Liberia, Gambia, Mali, Mauritania, Nigeria, Senegal, Sierra Leone, and Upper Volta. In 1975 the Economic Community of West African States (ECOWAS), comprising most of the states of the area, came into existence; its main goals, to be achieved in stages, were, *inter alia*, the termination of customs duties and other trade restrictions and the establishment of a common commercial policy.

A grouping of East and Central African States continues to hold annual summit conferences devoted to political as well as economic questions. It comprises fourteen states: Zambia, Ethiopia, Burundi, Tanzania, Uganda, the Central African Republic, Tchad, Congo-Brazzaville, Kenya, Zaïre, Malawi, Rwanda, Somalia, and Sudan. This grouping was responsible for the Lusaka Manifesto dealing with Southern Africa, referred to in Chapter 6. The ninth summit conference of these East and Central African States, held in 1974, was attended by representatives of several African liberation movements and decided, among other plans, to grant aid to the newly independent African states.

We have selected some of the more important groupings. The circumstances in which they came into existence, their aims and objectives, and the record of their activities suggest that they are supplementary rather than competitive in relation to the OAU. They appear to reflect a natural desire for cooperation on a limited basis in response to mainly economic needs, within the framework of recognition of the OAU as the effective instrument for achieving broader objectives and maintaining an over-all unity among all the independent African states. An encouraging feature of many of the groupings is the extent to which they have been able to break through the barriers—linguistic, cultural, and economic—that tend to keep the Anglophone and the Francophone states of Africa apart.

Federalism

As we have seen, a number of attempts at federation failed: the Mali Federation, because of ideological differences between Senegal and the

Sudan; the Ghana-Guinea-Mali Union (which never developed beyond a loose and imprecisely defined association), because movement toward closer political association was frustrated by the bad relations between Ghana and Guinea; and the hoped-for East African Federation, because Kenya and Uganda did not share Tanganyika's dedication and were deterred by the possible sacrifices federation would require of them. But it is important to remember that, however faint the present prospects of an East African federation may be, the close economic ties that have been forged and institutionalized provide a basis on which a political unification of the three states could be built at some future date.[29]

The most important federation that exists in Africa today is Nigeria. Nigeria inherited a federal structure when it achieved independence in 1960. Britain had dealt with the heterogeneity of the population of this large colony by dividing it into three regions corresponding to the three major ethnic groups—the Hausa, Yoruba, and Igbo—which were joined under a federal constitution. But the way the country was divided transgressed a basic principle of successful federation, namely, that the component units of the federation should be approximately equal in power, so that no one unit can dominate another unit or subject the federal government to its own control. The northern region, which was dominated by the Hausa, was much larger than the other two regions combined. The creation of a fourth region—the mid-western region— after Nigeria became a republic in 1963 did not sufficiently alter the existing imbalance of the component parts of the federation. The successive military coups of 1966 and the civil war that followed had much to do with the defective constitutional structure. For, while there were much deeper causes of the bloody strife that plagued Nigeria, there is no doubt that the constitutional legitimization of Hausa dominance served to stimulate ethnic fears and to encourage regional rather than national loyalty.

An obvious way of removing the imbalance would have been to divide the country into a number of small states, and perhaps if such a redivision had been achieved in 1963 strife would have been avoided.[30] As it was, when General Gowon announced early in 1967 that twelve states would replace the old regions, Igbo fears of concealed attempts to ensure the continuance of northern dominance had by then taken too strong a hold, and the secession of Biafra followed soon after. The Biafran failure naturally strengthened the determination of the Gowon regime to make the new federal structure work. Prospects for success are reasonably good. Only a year after the end of the civil war, there were indications that the Nigerian economy had made a significant re-

---

[29] For an interesting discussion of federation in Africa, see Ayo Ogunsheye, "Problems of Federation in Africa," in H. Passin and K. B. Jones-Quartey (eds.), *Africa: The Dynamics of Change* (Ibadan, Nigeria: Ibadan University Press, 1963), pp. 86–107.

[30] For a useful discussion of Nigerian federal problems, see Kalu Ezera, "The Failure of Nigerian Federalism and Proposed Constitutional Changes," in *African Forum*, II, no. 1 (Summer, 1966): 17–30.

covery, with oil production at a level of a million barrels a day and exports rising steadily. The encouraging economic development already achieved by 1976 gave every reason to anticipate that the new states would be viable long before 1979, the date set for the return to civilian rule. Two changes of government since 1974 appear to have left unaltered Nigeria's determination to produce an effective constitution based on division of power among the federal government and nineteen states. The impressive Constitutional Commission chaired by Chief Rotimi Williams has selected some of the country's best brains to serve on a number of committees assigned the task of building the political structure of the new civilian-governed Nigeria. In 1976 a draft constitution was published embodying a Bill of Rights and providing for a structure closely resembling that of the United States. It would come before a Constituent Assembly for ratification in 1977. Independent black Africa may yet prove to have learned from the admittedly costly Nigerian experience a useful lesson about the potential of federalism as a means of curbing ethnic divisiveness and creating regional unity.

Cameroun is an example of unification of Anglophone and Francophone states. The Republic of Cameroun came into existence in 1961, when the former Cameroun Republic (French) and the former Southern Cameroons (British) combined as the states of East Cameroun and West Cameroun, respectively, under a federal constitution, which recognized French and English as official languages and sought to bring about the political integration of the two populations by providing for a substantial degree of centralization. Language differences and the introduction of the CFA currency gave rise to a number of political, social, and economic problems at the outset of the republic's existence, but it succeeded in satisfying most of the more important needs of the two states. By the time the tenth anniversary of independence was celebrated, in January, 1970, the militant insurgency led by the outlawed *Union des Populations du Cameroun* (UPC), which had continued for many years, was almost at an end, and the central government was feeling sufficiently certain of its control over the whole country to provide a right of amnesty for political prisoners in certain circumstances and to lift partially a curfew that had been imposed. In addition, there had been substantial economic progress, aided by considerable improvement in communications between the two states. Later in 1970, President Ahmadou Ahidjo and Vice-President John Ngu Foncha (who had been prime minister of West Cameroun) were re-elected for a further five-year term. The single legal political party, the *Union nationale camerounaise* (UNC) is led by Ahidjo. It came into existence in 1966 by amalgamating six existing parties, one of them, the Kamerun National Democratic Party, having been founded and led by Foncha.

Neville Rubin writes of the wider implications of the Cameroun experience as follows:

Cameroun's potential as an important living example of the functioning of African unity has long been recognized, both inside the country and abroad; ... Cameroun has successfully withstood many of the strains imposed by the problems of national integration, and it has done a good deal better than most other attempts at unity between states on the African continent. . . . Cameroun has . . . solved a number of her own internal problems, and may well be able to provide the solution to those which remain.[31]

The Future of African Unity

In seeking to evaluate the prospects of African unity in the light of developments considered in this chapter, we must bear in mind that the OAU is not and was not intended to be a supranational institution based on the surrender of sovereignty by its member-states. It therefore lacks the power to compel any of them to carry out its decisions. It follows that its capacity to act for independent black Africa as a whole rests on persuasion and therefore depends on the member-states' voluntary compliance with its wishes. It is to be expected, therefore, that such compliance is usually forthcoming only when it does not entail any sacrifice of a member-state's interests.

In addition to this serious handicap, the OAU lacks the military power or economic strength to challenge any important European power, and it is surprising that it has to its credit, after a decade, even the limited achievements already discussed. There are others worthy of mention. As part of the pressures through the United Nations, often initiated and strongly backed by the OAU, South Africa has been excluded from a number of international bodies. Among these are the Economic Commission for Africa, the Commission for Technical Assistance in Africa, UNESCO, the International Labor Office, the Food and Agricultural Organization, the World Health Organization, and the Olympic Games. At its summit meeting in 1970 the OAU appointed a deputation, led by President Kaunda, that presented Africa's protest to Britain and a number of European countries against the proposed British supply of arms to South Africa.

The activities of the OAU until now fall into three distinct broad categories. First, it has been a forum for the exchange of views on matters concerning Africa. Second, it has been a means of curbing disagreement and building further cooperation among the African states. Third, it has provided a platform from which independent black Africa is able to present its view as a continental entity to the rest of the world.[32] Its success in the first category can hardly be questioned. Despite the periodic tensions and strains caused by such occurrences as

[31] Neville Rubin, *Cameroun: An African Federation* (New York: Praeger, 1971), pp. 193, 195. In May, 1972, following a referendum, Cameroun converted to a unitary state. President Ahidjo announced that the reasons for the change were to reduce the costs of governing the country and to conduct public affairs more efficiently. The conversion appeared to meet with widespread approval in both states. The new constitution guaranteed language rights, and eight of the twenty-four ministers in the new cabinet were from the former West Cameroun, now divided into two provinces. The former East Cameroun was divided into five provinces.
[32] Yashpal Tandon, "The Organization of African Unity as an Instrument and Forum of Protest," in Robert I. Rotberg and Ali A. Mazrui (eds.), *Protest and Power in Black Africa* (New York: Oxford University Press, 1970), pp. 334–46.

the Congo-Kinshasa situation, the Nigerian civil war, the unexpected overthrow of Nkrumah and the Angolan civil war, membership of the organization has remained intact, and disagreements and grievances have continued to be freely aired. Although it has had to contend with divisive and dissident factors, the OAU has also been able to heal breaches and promote cooperation. Here, the strong, emotionally charged commitment of the overwhelming majority of the African states to the eradication of *apartheid* has been a dominant unifying factor.

Looking back over the past decade, one is aware of issues that spurred independent black Africa into bursts of unified activism. Among these were the Rhodesian UDI (1965), the Nigerian civil war (1967–70), the invasion of Guinea (1971), and the Angolan situation (1975). It is true that the weakness of the African states, combined with the behavior of the world powers (either refusal to act or pressures contrary to independent black Africa's interests), prevented effective concerted action at all times. Nevertheless, the record since 1963 suggests that the goal of African unity has a real meaning for the African states and that bonds are slowly forming that can one day provide the foundation for a closer political association. It is true that African states still act in response to national needs rather than in response to Pan-African considerations, but what Nyerere has called "the sentiment of Africanness" goes deep.

11 Africa in the World Context

Despite Africa's increasing role in world affairs, politics in Africa continues to be dominated by world politics and world economics.

Africa and the International Community

The interaction between Africa and the rest of the world is one of the major developments of the twentieth century. It has two distinct aspects: the impact of the new independent black Africa on the international community and the impact of the international community on the new independent black Africa. The first aspect has been touched on in previous chapters: in Chapter 6 we discussed the influence of the African states on the United Nations in regard to Southern Africa. It is the second aspect—the way in which Africa has been and is being influenced by developments in the rest of the world—that we are concerned with here.

To see this influence in its proper perspective, it is helpful to distinguish three phases in the relationship between Africa and the outside world. First, there was the period before World War II when Africa, parceled out as colonies among the European powers, was the object of, rather than a participant in, world politics. The second phase covers the period from 1945 to the emergence of the former colonies as independent states. This phase saw the growth of African nationalism and the decision of the colonial powers to liquidate their African empires. Pressure on the colonial powers to hasten decolonization mounted with the universal postwar emphasis on the importance of national freedom, as expressed in particular by the Charter of the United Nations. The third phase corresponds to the period beginning with the independence of Ghana in 1957 and reaching up to the present time. During this period, forty-two independent African nations have come into existence, bringing the total number to forty-eight. They are a significant element in the United Nations and have become a force in world politics. Most of them became independent only in 1960 and even later, and in discussing the impact of world politics on them, we are attempting judgments and conclusions based on a very short period in any nation's history.

But the end of colonial rule did not mean the immediate termination of European influence in Africa; nor did it result in the severance of all ties between the European powers and their former colonies. Both Britain and France—the two major empire builders in Africa—continue to influence their former colonies, though they now enjoy full constitutional independence. The nature of this influence and the way in which the Anglophone and Francophone states have responded to it are part of the subject matter of this chapter.

Another aspect of the influence of world politics on Africa is the role of the United Nations in providing the new states with a forum for the discussion of their demands and their goals and with a base for the coordination of their activities.

A third aspect is the interaction between the African states and the leading world powers. Having come into existence as independent states in the postwar world, they could not avoid becoming involved, to a greater or a lesser degree, in the conflict between the Western world and the Communist powers. Their future development was bound to be affected, directly or indirectly, by the competition for world power between the United States, Soviet Russia, and Communist China.

Finally, there is the impact of the outside world on Africa, which flows logically from the fact that the African states are regarded as "underdeveloped." This term has been defined as applicable "loosely to countries or regions with levels of real income and capital per head of the population which are low by the standards of North America, Western Europe, and Australia."[1] As underdeveloped countries, the African states are generally considered to be entitled to aid (whether in the form of loans or grants of money, or technical advice and assistance) from the developed countries of the world. Such foreign aid, whether provided by individual European or Asian nations or by such international agencies as the World Bank, affects political developments in the recipient countries. Sometimes aid is given to an African country as the expression of a continuing interest in the progress of a former colony. Trade between Europe and Africa is often associated with the recognition of an obligation to assist in reducing "underdevelopment." Whatever the circumstances, such aid is part of an economic network that influences African politics.

In this chapter we shall discuss the four questions mentioned: (1) the impact of the United Nations, (2) the persistance of the influence of the former colonial powers, (3) the relations between Africa and the world powers, and (4) the effect of world economics on African politics.

The United Nations

When the United Nations was established at the conclusion of World War II, the victorious allied powers were determined to prevent a recurrence of the horrors of racial oppression and brute force practiced by

[1] P.T. Bauer and B. S. Yamey, *The Economics of Underdeveloped Countries* (London: James Nisbet, 1957), p. 3.

Nazi Germany. The United Nations Charter condemned racial discrimination, placed great emphasis on the preservation of human rights, and recognized the right of dependent territories to achieve self-government. But the fundamental human rights and freedoms that the Charter described in general terms remained to be formulated more specifically. This task was performed by the United Nations Commission on Human Rights. The commission drew up the Universal Declaration of Human Rights, which was adopted on December 10, 1948.[2] The overriding principles, which apply to all the specific rights and freedoms formulated in the Declaration, are contained in Article 2:

Everyone is entitled to all the rights and freedoms set forth in this Declaration, without distinction of any kind, such as race, color, sex, language, religion, political or other opinion, national or social origin, property, birth or other status.

Furthermore, no distinction shall be made on the basis of the political, jurisdictional or international status of the country or territory to which a person belongs, whether it be independent, trust, non-self-governing or under any other limitation or sovereignty.

The Declaration, although it has no legal force, has come to be accepted as an authoritative statement of principles of sound and stable government. In the United Nations it is constantly used as the test to determine whether charges made against member-states are justified. Examples are the General Assembly resolutions that certain laws of the government of South Africa were "contrary to the Charter and the Universal Declaration of Human Rights" and that South African racial policies were "a flagrant violation" of the Charter and the Declaration."[3] In some African states, provisions of the Declaration are embodied in the constitution as a bill of rights.[4] In others, the constitution declares adherence to the Declaration in general terms.[5]

Committed as it was to the principles and goals we have described, the United Nations soon became a forum for discussing African grievances and asserting African demands. For many years before independence was achieved, African aspirations were expressed at the United Nations by representatives of India and Pakistan. Sometimes the interests of these two countries and those of the still dependent African countries coincided. One example was the discussion by the General Assembly in 1946 of the racial discrimination practiced by the South African government against its Indian population. India's complaint about

[2] The adoption was unanimous, with the Soviet bloc, Saudi Arabia, and South Africa abstaining.
[3] Resolutions 719(vii) of 1953, and 285(iii) of 1961.
[4] For example, Zambia (1964) and Ghana (1969).
[5] For example "[le peuple camerounais] affirme son attachement aux libertés fondamentales inscrites dans la Delaration universelle des droits de l'homme et la Charte des Nations Unies." (Constitution de la Republique du Cameroun, 4 mars 1960, preambule.)

the treatment of Indians in South Africa was the first use of the United Nations to direct the attention of the international community to discrimination on the grounds of race or color in contravention of the principles of the Charter.

The formation of an African-Asian group in the United Nations in 1950 saw the beginning of a period of Afro-Asian relations that continued for fifteen years; it finally came to grief because of a bitter conflict between the Soviet Union and the People's Republic of China. United by bonds of shared opposition to colonialism and a common experience of victimization on grounds of color, the African and Asian states acted as a bloc with some influence at the United Nations. The Bandung Conference in 1955, comprising representatives of twenty-nine states, six of them African, showed that Asia and Africa could combine in trying to influence world affairs. The first Afro-Asian Peoples Solidarity Conference met in 1957. Subsequent meetings took place until 1965, but by then friction between Russia and China had become serious. Following a decision taken in the previous year, a second Afro-Asian Conference modeled on the Bandung Conference of 1955 was planned for 1965 in Algiers. It was never held. The Chinese government had declared its opposition to the participation of Russia, and despite several postponements of the date of the conference aimed at reconciliation, the breach within the Communist ranks remained. The bitterness of Soviet-Chinese mutual hostility had made institutionalized Afro-Asian cooperation impossible. There have been no attempts since then to call another conference; nor are there any indications that an improvement in Soviet-Chinese relations would make another Bandung-type conference likely in the near future.[6]

During the period 1945 to 1960 the United Nations had a significant impact on Africa through its various organs, particularly the Trusteeship Council, and its numerous specialized agencies, such as the U.N. Educational, Scientific and Cultural Organization (UNESCO) and the World Health Organization (WHO). Through the visits of Trusteeship Council missions to Trust territories and the practice of permitting petitioners to present their case in person to the Trusteeship Council and sometimes before the General Assembly, the political awareness of the African people grew, and the desire to press for independence was stimulated.[7]

From 1960 onward, independent black Africa took shape as a bloc with growing importance in the United Nations. By December, 1975, 48 of the 144 United Nations members were Africans. Suddenly the voice

[6] For Afro-Asian relations up to 1961 see Vernon McKay, *Africa in World Politics* (New York: Harper and Row, 1963), pp. 102–6; for subsequent developments, see *Keesing's Contemporary Archives*, 1964, 20364–65; 1965, 20983–84; 1969, 23377, 23438.
[7] For an excellent description of these developments see McKay, *Africa in World Politics*, pp. 21–49.

and the vote of Africa had assumed a new significance; the United Nations had provided the new Africa with a means of influencing world affairs. Admittedly, its capacity for dictating to the international community was severely limited; ultimate control of the United Nations, through their veto power in the Security Council, was vested in the five world powers (U.S.A., U.S.S.R., Britain, France, and China). But Africa has been able by negotiation and diplomacy to wield some influence on the world powers on such issues as the elimination of racial discrimination, the termination of what remains of colonial rule, and the obligation of the developed nations to respond to the problems of underdevelopment. In 1975, support by most African states—in response to Arab pressure—for the United Nations resolution declaring Zionism "a form of racism and racial discrimination" was met with a barrage of severe criticism throughout the western world. There were indications that the African vote had been ill-conceived; sympathy with African goals was undermined, and international support for the eradication of *apartheid* was weakened.

The story of Africa's response to the opportunity afforded by the United Nations begins even before 1960. Already in 1958 Kwame Nkrumah had recognized the potential of the United Nations as an instrument for achieving African goals. At the first Conference of Independent African States in 1958,[8] a foundation was laid for planned coordinated action as a group in the United Nations by the eight African countries then independent. The declaration issued in the name of those eight states included the following statement: "We have charged our Permanent Representatives at the United Nations to be the permanent machinery for coordinating all matters of common concern to our States; for examining and making recommendations on concrete practical steps for implementing our decisions." The record of these African states in the United Nations during that early period was impressive, but in 1960 the unity that had been forged was damaged, largely as a result of the conflicting allegiances created by the situation in the Congo. Colin Legum has described both their achievements within the United Nations framework and their failure to remain united when faced by the Congo disaster:

Until the fissure opened in the Central Government between Lumumba and Kasavubu, the African states in the United Nations enjoyed their finest hour. They worked in unison, compelling the Security Council to operate effectively; they stayed off the incipient "cold war" threat in the Congo. The presence of Africa as a force in the councils of the world had been made real for the first time in history. There is a great deal still to be written about that period: about Ghana's role as mediator and moderator; about Guinea's role as irritant and militant, outflanking Ghana on the left; about the French African leaders' negotiations with Mr. Tshombe and President Kavasubu; and

[8] See Chapter 10, pp. 231, 237–38.

about Nigeria's incursion through Mr. Jaja Wachuku's chairmanship of the UN Conciliation Commission. But for our purposes it is enough to record that, faced with its first major test in an African crisis, the African states were disunited.[9]

The growth of that disunity—as reflected in the conflict between the Monrovia and the Casablanca groups—and the developments that finally led to the establishment of the Organization of African Unity have been described in Chapter 10.[10]

The Organization of African Unity stressed the importance of the United Nations in its own charter; at the first summit conference in 1963, one of the six resolutions was entitled "Africa and the United Nations." This resolution, after reaffirming the belief of the independent states of Africa that the United Nations is "an important instrument" for ensuring the advancement of the interests of "all peoples" and their desire to "strengthen and support the United Nations," went on to specify three measures calculated to ensure a more influential African participation in the affairs of the international community. First, the resolution called for a "more equitable representation" of Africa in the organs of the United Nations and in its specialized agencies. Second, African governments were asked to instruct their United Nations representatives to take "all possible steps" to achieve such representation. Third, African governments were invited to instruct their United Nations representatives "to constitute a more effective African group, with a permanent secretariat to bring about closer cooperation and better coordination in matters of common concern."

Only seven months later, the African states saw the first fruits of their faith in the United Nations. On December 17, 1963, the General Assembly adopted resolutions providing for an increase in the membership of the Security Council, the Economic and Social Council, and the General Committee of the Assembly (the steering committee that organizes the work of the session and decides on the agenda). Membership of the Security Council was to be increased from eleven to fifteen, five representing the African and Asian countries; membership of the Economic and Social Council, from eighteen to twenty-seven, seven representing the African and Asian states. The resolution dealing with the General Committee of the Assembly provided for an increase in the number of vice-presidents of the General Assembly on the basis of "equitable geographical representation" and for the "equitable geographical representation" of the office of president. This resolution became effective immediately. The other two resolutions, which called for amendment of the Charter, required ratification within two years by two-thirds of the member-states, including the five permanent members of the Security Council; they came into effect after the requisite number of ratifications on August 31, 1965.

[9] Colin Legum, *Pan-Africanism*, rev. ed. (London: Pall Mall Press, 1965), p. 49.
[10] See Chapter 10, pp. 242–46.

Some of the detailed steps taken by the United Nations in regard to *apartheid* and the situation in Southern Africa have been described in the previous chapters.[11] The record of this activity at the United Nations shows that pressure on the Western powers by the African states (with the support of the Asian states) has had a marked effect on the attitude of the international community. The majority of members of the United Nations have moved from being content with verbal condemnation to calling for diplomatic, economic, and even military steps against South Africa. While it is true that neither the United States nor Britain is yet prepared to support action by the Security Council treating the situation as a threat to international peace and security, when one looks back over the last two decades a significant toughening in the attitude toward Southern Africa by the two leading Western powers is discernible. As *The Oxford History of South Africa* puts it, the United Nations:

in institutionalizing the hostility against South Africa, contributed in great degree to giving apartheid a universal connotation in the minds of politicians and their publics. *The African and Asian states played the crucial role, forcing the Western powers into taking a position which, but for this pressure, might have remained one of relative indifference to the domestic affairs of a small power, traditionally prepared to offer support at times of crisis and one having ties of kinship, trade and historical connections.* [Emphasis added.][12]

Neo-Colonialism

It would be naïve to expect the grant of independence to produce the immediate termination of all ties between the former colonial power and the newly independent state. While African political leaders recognized that some colonial influence could be expected to persist after independence, they were well aware of the risk that a colonial power could deliberately use its superior power—whether economic, technical or military—to retain, in large degree, the actual control it had formerly exercised long after constitutional power had been transferred to the new state. "Neo-colonialism" is the term used to describe this threat of continued subjection to colonial power after political independence.

Almost immediately after Ghana had become independent, Nkrumah emerged as the leading African spokesman on this question. In the years that followed he continued—in his public addresses, his writings, and through the medium of the conferences that he was instrumental in convening—to stress its importance. He undoubtedly indulged in much

---

[11] See Chapter 6, pp. 111–34 and 145–47, and Chapter 10, p. 242. For a useful discussion of United Nations action against South Africa, see Monica Wilson and Leonard Thompson, eds., *The Oxford History of South Africa*, II (Oxford: The Clarendon Press, 1971): 512–24. A valuable source on Southern Africa as a whole is the publications of the United Nations Special Committee on *Apartheid*, which have appeared frequently since 1963.

[12] Wilson and Thompson, *Oxford History of South Africa*, II: 523.

rhetorical condemnation of colonialism, but he also paid attention to the need for appropriate practical steps to resist neo-colonialism where it was found to exist. His practical approach is illustrated by the activities of the All-African People's Organization, which came into existence at a conference called on his initiative and held in Ghana in 1958. At this first conference, no mention was made of neo-colonialism. This was not surprising. At that stage, the representatives of African nationalist movements seeking their countries' freedom from colonial rule were not concerned with the possible influence of the colonial power *after* independence had been granted. At the second conference of the organization, held in Tunisia in January, 1960, at a time when Belgium had promised independence to the Congo and France was engaged in a bitter struggle with the people of Algeria, there was only a passing reference to neo-colonialism in a general resolution covering several topics. By the time the third conference was held—in March, 1961, in Egypt—neo-colonialism had become an important issue, calling for thorough study designed to produce appropriate action. A lengthy resolution was adopted dealing exclusively with neo-colonialism; there was an introductory section and three further sections entitled "Manifestations of Neo-Colonialism," "Agents of Neo-Colonialism," and "Means of Fighting Neo-Colonialism." The introductory section, describing neo-colonialism as "the greatest threat" to African countries, whether already independent or only approaching independence, and referring to the situation in the Congo, concluded by naming the United States, West Germany, Israel, Britain, Belgium, Holland, South Africa, and France as "the main perpetrators of Neo-colonialism." Among the "Manifestations of Neo-Colonialism" that the conference formulated were: the colonial power's "economic entrenchment" while it was still in control of the colony, followed by the continued "economic dependence" of the former colony after independence; the use by a "foreign power" of financial aid and technical assistance to infiltrate the economy of a former colony after independence; and the establishment of military bases "sometimes introduced as scientific research stations or training schools" either before independence or as a condition of granting independence. Examples of the "Agents of Neo-Colonialism" listed by the conference were: embassies and missions of the former colonial powers "serving as nerve centers of espionage and pressure points on the local African governments"; "so-called foreign and United Nations technical assistants who ill-advise and sabotage national political, economical, educational and social development"; and "the representatives from imperialist and colonial countries under the cover of religion, Moral Re-armament, cultural, Trade Union and Youth or Philanthropic Organizations." Under the heading "Means of Fighting Neo-Colonialism," the proposals included: an invitation to the independent African states to come to the assistance of the African countries still under colonial rule; a request that those independent states still having "military or para-military bases" in their territories liquidate them as soon as possible; and the urging of independent states to "intensify their efforts" to create machinery enabling them to cooperate economically, socially, and culturally "in order to frustrate Neo-Colonialism."[13] The especial concern of the third conference with neo-colonialism, as well as much of the content and the strong language of the resolution, was due to the fact that the Congo crisis was then at its height.

But Nkrumah's passionate support of the struggle against neo-colonialism continued long after the shock of the Congo situation had begun to wear off. In his book *Africa Must Unite*, published in 1963—the year that saw the number of independent African states grow to thirty-four—he launched a vigorous attack against neo-colonialism in the introduction and also devoted a lengthy chapter to it. The introduction sums up the dangers of neo-colonialism, actual and potential, as follows:

> Imperialism is still a most powerful force to be reckoned with in Africa. It controls our economies. It operates on a worldwide scale in combinations of many different kinds: economic, political, cultural, educational, military; and through intelligence and information services. In the context of the new independence mounting in Africa, it has begun and will continue to assume new forms and subtler disguises. It is already making use, and will continue to make use, of the different cultural and economic associations which colonialism has forced between erstwhile European masters and African subjects. It is creating client states, which it manipulates from the distance. It will distort and play upon, as it is already doing, the latent fears of burgeoning nationalism and independence. It will, as it is already doing, fan the fires of sectional interests, of personal greed and ambition among leaders and contesting aspirants to power. *These and many others will be the devious ways of the neo-colonialism by which the imperialists hope to keep their stranglehold on Africa's resources for their own continued enrichment.* [Emphasis added.][14]

In the chapter, Nkrumah moves away from generalization about the colonial powers and examines in detail the methods used by France to ensure that its former colonies remained within the French orbit after they had been granted independence. He contrasts the pressure—direct and indirect—applied to maintain the ties between the Francophone states and France with the completely voluntary nature of the association between the Anglophone states and Britain, as fellow members of the Commonwealth.

Since 1963, when *Africa Must Unite* was published, thirteen more independent African states have come into existence. The peoples of the continent (except for those of the white supremacist states of Southern Africa) have achieved their goal of freedom from colonial rule. The situation in independent black Africa, in terms of both internal develop-

---

[13] For the complete text of the Resolution on Neo-Colonialism, see Legum, *Pan-Africanism*, pp. 272–75.

[14] Kwame Nkrumah, *Africa Must Unite* (London: Heinemann, 1963).

ments and external pressures, has changed greatly during the last decade. As a result, the earlier neo-colonialist thesis is, in many respects, no longer applicable. But in its broader aspects it continues to have validity as a means of throwing light on the process by which undesirable ties can continue to exist between a colony and the colonial power after independence has been achieved. It should be borne in mind, too, that whether neo-colonialism is an actual threat may be less important for an understanding of African politics than the prevalent belief among African leaders that it *is* inimical to the true interests of their countries.

Anglophone and Francophone Africa

Let us turn now to a discussion of the present ties between the two leading colonial powers in Africa—Britain and France—and their former colonies. There is a marked contrast between the British and the French relationship. The cultural ties between France and the Francophone states are very close, and the dependence of the states upon France for financial aid and military support is extensive. The political leaders of Francophone Africa have seen no contradiction between their political independence and the continued reliance on Frenchmen to man their administrative services and their armies. In countries like the Ivory Coast and Gabon, the number of expatriates from France has more than doubled since independence was achieved. As the African tours of Presidents Pompidou during 1971 and 1972 and Giscard d'Estaing during 1975 demonstrated, the over-all relations between France and its former African colonies are marked by considerable warmth and goodwill (see Brian Weinstein, "Francophonie: a Language-based Movement in World Politics," *International Organizations*, Vol. 30, no. 3, Summer 1976, pp. 485–508). This does not mean that there is complete uniformity among them. On the one hand, loyalty to France has enabled them to overlook the fact that France is a major source of the supply of arms to South Africa. On the other hand, when President Houphouët-Boigny of the Ivory Coast proposed a dialogue with South Africa (an idea believed to owe much to the influence of the discreetly powerful Jacques Foccart, Secretary General for African Affairs under both de Gaulle and Pompidou), only five of the sixteen Francophone states supported him; among the remainder were such consistently vigorous and outspoken opponents of *apartheid* as Cameroun, Guinea, and Algeria. There are variations, also, in the influence of French economic and military factors on the former colonies. In almost every Francophone state, France remains the dominant trading partner. Guinea was an exception, but it has recently moved tentatively toward closer relations with France. Algeria, following a crisis caused by the nationalization of French oil companies, has extended its trade relations with other countries of the Western world. Throughout Francophone Africa there are signs of a steady growth of American, Japanese, and West German participation in trade, within the framework of a commitment to France, although it is true that French commercial relations with Algeria have decreased considerably since American companies have begun to purchase Algerian petroleum products and gas. But it is in the area of military involvement that one finds the most striking difference between Francophone and Anglophone Africa. French troops have been stationed in several of the former colonies. In 1964, a French military force put down an attempted coup in Gabon and ensured the continuance of a regime known to be acceptable to France. In 1971, President Tombalbaye was using 3,000 French troops to deal with a rebellion in the north of Tchad; but the situation in Tchad could spark off a process leading to ultimate military disengagement. In October, 1970, the death of a number of young French soldiers in Tchad led to a heated debate in the French National Assembly culminating in a promise by the French government that all the troops in Tchad would be back home by the end of 1971.

The mutually satisfying pattern of relationship constructed with great skill by General de Gaulle has not changed noticeably since de Gaulle's death; the signing of new cooperation agreements between France and a number of states since 1973 has reinforced it.

Britain's association with its former colonies has been somewhat different. Ever since independence, the countries of Anglophone Africa have emphasized the importance of avoiding continued dependence on Britain.[15] In these countries, the cry has been for "Africanization," that is, replacing expatriate British personnel (in the civil service, the judiciary, the universities, and all other spheres) as soon as possible with officials drawn from the local population or from some other African country. Africanization seems to have proceeded more quickly than in Francophone states. The government and administration of Ghana, Sierra Leone, Tanzania, and the Sudan are more in the hands of nationals than the government and administration of Ivory Coast and Gabon. On the other hand, there has probably been more Africanization in Algeria and Tunisia, and Mauritania and Togo, formerly under French control, than in Kenya, northern Nigeria, and Botswana, formerly under British control. Francophone states of West and Equatorial Africa have turned more readily to French military power than Anglophones and North Africans have turned to the Europeans.

Anglophone states have turned to Britain but their attitude has been different. The behavior of President Nyerere when Tanganyika was faced by army mutiny in 1964 is a striking example. Rioting with loss of life and destruction of property followed a revolt by the soldiers of the First Battalion Tanganyikan Rifles against their British and

---

[15] Malawi (because of President Banda's refusal to conform to the policies adopted by the majority of African states), Lesotho, Botswana, and Swaziland (because of their special position geographically, economically, and politically in relation to South Africa), in varying degrees, display departures from the practices and attitudes of the Anglophone states as described.

Tanganyikan officers and NCOs. The rioting spread, but it was first reported that the government of Tanganyika had rejected that British troops be called. However, following army mutinies in the adjoining countries of Kenya and Uganda, President Nyerere asked Britain for assistance in bringing the Tanganyikan army under control. A British marine commando was promptly landed at Dar es Salaam, and the mutiny was put down within two days with very little loss of life. In a public broadcast, President Nyerere apologized to the people of Tanganyika for having called in British troops. Later he requested an emergency meeting of the foreign and defense ministers of the Organization of African Unity to enable him to explain the action he had taken. Addressing the meeting in Dar es Salaam on February 12, 1964, Nyerere said that he wished to enable the independent African states to discuss, within the context of African unity, the situation that had arisen as a result of his action. He continued: "Our national humiliation arises from the necessity of having non-Tanganyikan troops do our work for us.... Already it is clear that there are some people who will seize this opportunity to play upon the natural fears of neo-colonialism in the hope of sowing seeds of suspicion between African states." He explained that it would take time to reconstruct the Tanganyikan army and that he could ask the British troops to remain until that had been done, but he suggested that the African states might come to Tanganyika's assistance. The OAU ministers agreed in principle that the British troops then in Tanganyika should be replaced by African troops and established a committee to consider ways and means of doing this. On March 20, 1964, it was announced that, following discussions in Lagos between the British Foreign Secretary and the Tanganyikan Minister of External Affairs, the Nigerian government had agreed to provide troops. On April 1, the third battalion of the Nigerian army was flown to Dar es Salaam in RAF aircraft, which took the members of the 41st Royal Marine Commando back home. The third battalion served in Tanganyika until September, 1964, when it returned to Nigeria.

The Commonwealth

The Commonwealth is an association of sovereign independent states. It is the result of the evolutionary process by which Britain gradually moved its colonies to complete independence while seeking a framework within which mutually fruitful ties with the new states could be continued after independence. Neither the status of the Commonwealth nor the mutual relationship of the member nations is capable of precise definition. The first attempt to define the Commonwealth is to be found in the statement at the Imperial Conference of 1926, which described the member nations as "autonomous communities within the British Empire, equal in status, in no way subordinate one to another in any aspect of their domestic or external affairs, though united by a common allegiance to the Crown, and freely associated as the British Commonwealth of Nations."

India had achieved independence in 1947 under a constitution affirming its allegiance to the Crown and had become a member of the British Commonwealth. In 1949 India decided to become a republic but wished to continue its membership in the British Commonwealth. As a republic, it could not owe allegiance to the Crown, and, if it were to remain a member, it would have to be on some other basis. An appropriate formula was devised. The new basis for India's membership, formulated at a conference of Commonwealth Prime Ministers, was that it accepted "the King as the symbol of the free association of its independent member nations and as such Head of the Commonwealth." In addition, Britain quietly permitted the "British Commonwealth of Nations" to become simply the "Commonwealth of Nations."

Ghana was the first African state to follow India's example. From the date of its independence ("attainment of fully responsible status within the British Commonwealth of Nations") in 1957 until it became a republic in 1960, Ghana owed allegiance to: "Elizabeth the Second, Queen of Ghana and Her other Realms and Territories, Head of the Commonwealth." Like India, Ghana remained in the Commonwealth after it became a republic, but the Queen had ceased to be Queen of Ghana. Instead, Ghana now accepted the Queen as the symbol of Ghana's free association with her fellow members and, as such, the Head of the Commonwealth. Constitutional autochthony became the mark of true independence for the independent states of Africa; most of them, in due course, following Ghana's example by changing from monarchical to republican status under constitutions that declared that "We the People of . . . , Do Hereby Enact and give to ourselves this Constitution." Today Africa's voice in the Commonwealth is significant. Of the thirty-two members, thirteen are African, ten of them republics.

The Commonwealth enjoys the distinction of having been approved by some of the foremost critics—and victims—of British colonialism. Jawaharlal Nehru and Kwame Nkrumah, both of whom spent some time in British colonial jails because of their opposition to British colonial rule, have been generous in their praise of the achievements of the Commonwealth in creating a mutually enriching voluntary association of all the former colonies with one another and with Britain. Writing in 1963 on the dangers of neo-colonialism, Nkrumah had this to say:

States emerging from the tutelage of other colonial powers have not always understood Ghana's attachment to the Commonwealth and the sterling area. That is because the loose *ad hoc* nature of the structure is not correctly comprehended by those who have been or are members of a more formal association. It is difficult for those not accustomed to a *free* connection with Europe to appreciate that the Commonwealth is an association of sovereign states, each of which is free from interference from the others, including the

United Kingdom. Each decides for itself its own foreign and domestic policies and the pattern of its government.... Members have the right to criticize each other and do.[16]

The machinery through which the Commonwealth performs its functions is designed to ensure constant voluntary consultation among the member-nations. There is an emphasis on informality in its activities. Without being bound to do so by rules or regulations, the member-countries recognize that they have an obligation to consult with each other beforehand on a proposed course of action likely to affect another member-country's interests. Until recently, the Commonwealth even operated without the usual bureaucratic apparatus. It was only in 1964 that the decision was taken to set up—for the first time in its history—a secretariat; in 1965 a Canadian diplomat, Arnold Smith, became its first Secretary-General.

Consultation takes place mainly through the medium of a wide range of conferences. The most important of these is the Conference of Commonwealth Heads of Government (formerly known as the Commonwealth Prime Ministers' Conference). In keeping with the traditional practice of avoiding formality, these conferences, held at regular intervals, usually have no fixed agenda and issue no official report of the proceedings. Instead, a final communiqué, purporting to express the shared views of all member-countries, is issued at the conclusion of the conference. In addition to these regular highest-level meetings, there are, from time to time, meetings of finance ministers, foreign ministers, and defense ministers; there are also economic conferences. An important part in the process of Commonwealth consultation is played by high commissioners, who represent commonwealth countries in the capitals of their partner countries. They have a status equal to that of ambassadors, and it is through them that governments of Commonwealth countries usually communicate with each other. There is regular consultation among all the high commissioners in London and between them and the British Secretary of State for Commonwealth Relations. In addition a number of Commonwealth organizations provide machinery for the exchange of information, and for collaboration and cooperation in many spheres.

On several occasions the African members of the Commonwealth have sought to assert an African point of view. The fact that South Africa ceased to be a member of the Commonwealth is because of the pressure brought to bear by the African members. At the Prime Ministers' Conference in March, 1961, the Prime Minister of South Africa, having applied in advance for continued membership after South Africa had become a republic (a change planned to take place later in the year), withdrew his application before the conclusion of the conference. Although no official statements were issued, it was known that

[16] Nkrumah, *Africa Must Unite*, pp. 185–86.

the African and Asian members, joined by Canada, had voiced very strong criticism of *apartheid*. In addition, the day before South Africa's application to remain in the Commonwealth was considered, *The Observer* carried an article by Julius Nyerere (then Chief Minister of Tanganyika, whose independence was imminent), which declared that, if South Africa were permitted to remain in the Commonwealth, Tanganyika would not apply for admission. In the course of his article, Nyerere described South Africa as "a State deliberately and ruthlessly pursuing a racialist policy" and went on to explain Tanganyika's decision as follows:

We believe that the principles of the Commonwealth would be betrayed by an affirmative answer to South Africa's application for re-admission as a republic . . . we are forced to say that to vote South Africa in is to vote us out. . . . The world would take the readmission of South Africa as a condonation of her policies, or at least as a cynical dismissal of all principles of human political activity. No one realizes better than we, who have been looking forward to our admission, that this question could wreck the very structure of the Commonwealth. But if this happens it will be the result of South Africa's attitude not of ours. Her policies are a daily challenge to the basic concepts of the Commonwealth.[17]

The South African Prime Minister contended, when he reported to the South African parliament on his return from Britain, that South Africa had withdrawn its application because it was unwilling to be a member of the changed Commonwealth, now a multiracial grouping of nations, most of which were hostile to South Africa, instead of the old Commonwealth consisting of Britain and the white dominions.[18] The contention does not hold water. Dr. Verwoerd knew at the time he applied that the Commonwealth had changed and what the views of the majority of its members were regarding his country, and he was still quite prepared to have South Africa be a member. The real reason for the withdrawal of the application was that there was no doubt in his mind that, if the application were not withdrawn, it would be refused. Understandably, from South Africa's point of view, he decided that withdrawal was preferable to expulsion.

The unilateral declaration of independence by the Smith regime in Rhodesia (UDI) was another occasion for asserting a specifically African point of view within the Commonwealth. Feeling ran high in the African member-countries; there were vigorous protests by Kenya and Nigeria and demonstrations against the British High Commission in Tanzania. In the negotiations that followed between Britain and the Smith regime in the search for a settlement, Britain was subjected to steady pressure (from Zambia and Tanzania, in particular) to refuse

[17] *The Observer*, London, March 12, 1961. *The Times*, London, described the article as "a piece of powerful advocacy in the battle over South Africa."
[18] Wilson and Thompson, *Oxford History of South Africa*, II: 487–88. This work fails to state that Verwoerd's contention is not borne out by the facts.

recognition of the rebel regime unless it declared unequivocal commitment to the establishment of majority rule.

A major confrontation between Anglophone Africa and the Commonwealth followed the announcement by the new Conservative government in Britain during 1970 that it intended to supply arms to South Africa. A hostile reaction from a number of member-countries (particularly Zambia and Tanzania) persuaded Britain to postpone a final decision until the Commonwealth Heads of Government Conference in 1971. The conference, held in Singapore, January 14–22, opened in a mood of pessimism, with predictions in some quarters that the Commonwealth would not survive the wide gulf that had emerged. There was much bitterness on both sides. Prime Minister Edward Heath insisted on Britain's right to supply the arms "for maritime defense purposes only" because of the buildup by Soviet Russia of its naval power in the Indian Ocean. The African leaders contended that Britain's action in supplying arms to South Africa necessarily implied support of *apartheid* and was therefore incompatible with the principles upon which Commonwealth association was based.

On the opening day of the conference, President Kaunda of Zambia urged the adoption of a Declaration of Commonwealth Principles intended to "define what we stand for" and "declare what we believe in and what we are determined to work for or to work against." The declaration included the following paragraph: "We recognize racial discrimination as an unmitigated evil of society and racial prejudice as a dangerous sickness threatening the healthy development of the human race: we therefore seek every means of combating these evils; we shall deny all regimes which practice them any assistance which could consolidate or strengthen them."

Objections were raised to this paragraph by the British and Australian delegations, and agreement was reached on a compromise version: "No country will afford to regimes which practice racial discrimination assistance which *in its own judgment* directly contributes to the pursuit of this evil policy." (Emphasis added.)

In its original form, the declaration would have imposed an obligation on the Commonwealth countries to refrain from providing assistance likely to "consolidate or strengthen" a regime that practiced racial discrimination. The inclusion of the words "in its own judgment" in the revised version made it clear that it was left to each country, exercising a sovereign right of independent action, to take the final decision. Thus, it would be for Britain *alone* to decide whether the supply of arms to South Africa would "directly contribute to the pursuit or consolidation" of the policy of *apartheid*.

Nevertheless, the paragraph in its revised form was included in a Declaration of Commonwealth Principles adopted unanimously by the thirty-one delegations at the conclusion of the conference, which otherwise followed, in the main, the draft that had been presented by President Kaunda. Among its other provisions were the following:

Membership of the Commonwealth is compatible with the freedom of member-governments to be non-aligned or to belong to any other grouping, association or alliance. Within this diversity all members of the Commonwealth hold certain principles in common. It is by pursuing these principles that the Commonwealth can continue to influence the international society for the benefit of mankind.

We recognize racial prejudice as a dangerous sickness threatening the healthy development of the human race, and racial discrimination as an unmitigated evil of society. Each of us will vigorously combat this evil within our own nation.

We believe that the wide disparities in wealth now existing between different sections of mankind are too great to be tolerated. They also create world tensions. Our aim is their progressive removal. We therefore seek to use our efforts to overcome poverty, ignorance, and disease, in raising standards of life and achieving a more equitable international society.

To this end our aim is to achieve the freest possible flow of international trade on terms fair and equitable to all, taking into account the special requirements of the developing countries, and to encourage the flow of adequate resources, including governmental and private resources, to the developing countries, bearing in mind the importance of doing this in a true spirit of partnership and of establishing for this purpose in the developing countries conditions which are conducive to sustained investment and growth.

The dominant question at the conference was the proposed supply of arms to South Africa. At the conclusion of a closed session, it was announced that an eight-nation study group would be set up to consider the arms issue in the context of the agreements relating to the naval base at Simonstown, and the question of security in the Indian Ocean. British Prime Minister Heath read a statement affirming Britain's right to proceed with the supply of arms to South Africa, if so advised, even *before* the study group had presented its report. In the discussion at the plenary session that followed, Heath denied that the arms sales would confer a "certificate of respectability" on South Africa, reiterated that South Africa had given an assurance that the arms would not be used for aggressive purposes and concluded with a statement that, while Britain was ready "to narrow down to the minimum" the equipment to be supplied, she was obliged to make some delivery of arms in the interests of maritime security. Strong opposition was expressed to the supply of any arms at all by a number of African leaders; and President Nyerere, stating that Tanzania was unable to accept the South African assurances, said: "*Apartheid* is aggression; weapons will be used in its defense against the freedom fighters, and may be used in what is usually called a 'pre-emptive strike' against countries bordering the white states which give moral support to these freedom fighters."

Speculating on the future of the Commonwealth in the light of a somewhat arrogant statement made by the British Prime Minister, Nyerere added:

If any of us compromise with racialism under any circumstances, except the direct and most urgent necessity of national survival, then either we have to leave the Commonwealth, or we destroy the Commonwealth by denying its very meaning. It has been said by the British Prime Minister that the Commonwealth could survive if a few of its members left. Of that there is no doubt at all. Whether the Commonwealth has 31 members or 30, or 20 or less, does not particularly matter. But if the Commonwealth has no meaning at all it will not survive. It will either collapse or gradually die a natural death.

By the time the conference ended, the numerous prophets of doom had been proved false prophets. Although the discussions had generated dangerous tensions, attacks on Britain by some African delegations had shocked observers by their emotional bitterness, and the differences had seemed, at times, to be quite irreconcilable, the Commonwealth proved capable of withstanding the severe strains to which it was subjected this time.

The British Prime Minister returned from Singapore claiming a diplomatic victory.[19] Within a month of his return, it was announced from London that Britain was prepared to sell arms to South Africa, although it was stipulated that only Wasp antisubmarine helicopters would be sold. South Africa replied immediately by ordering seven helicopters, the total order being valued at about $2.4 million. It was also reported that Britain would supply any other maritime equipment considered essential for the defense of the Cape sea route. Thus, Britain started its trade in arms with South Africa even before the eight-nation study group set up at Singapore met. And, while it was clear that Heath gave no undertaking that Britain would wait for the study group's report before it acted, it was reasonably certain that six of the eight member-countries[20] regarded Britain's precipitate action as a breach of the spirit of the agreement entered into at Singapore.[21]

When the heads of government met again—at Ottawa in 1973—the helicopters had not been delivered, and the supply of arms to South Africa was no longer an issue. The 1973 meeting was marked by considerable emphasis (readily endorsed by Great Britain) on the Commonwealth's obligation to assist the Africans of Southern Africa in achieving their goals. In the final communiqué the heads of government recognized the "legitimacy of the struggle to win full human rights and self determination," agreed "on the need to give every humanitarian assistance" to the people's efforts to achieve self-determination, and

---

[19] At least one recognized authority on Africa disagreed. Reporting from Singapore at the conclusion of the conference, in *The Observer*, London, Colin Legum wrote, "The British Commonwealth Conference concluded here yesterday with strong evidence that British Prime Minister Edward Heath had taken a beating, although he prefers to see it differently."
[20] The eight member-countries were Britain, Australia, Canada, India, Jamaica, Kenya, Malaysia, and Nigeria.
[21] For a variety of instructive comments on the Singapore Conference and the future of the Commonwealth, see *Commonwealth*, The Journal of the Royal Commonwealth Society, XV: 2, (London: April, 1971).

called on those Commonwealth members in a position to do so to endeavor to "persuade Portugal to grant a negotiated independence to its African colonies." Decisions at the Commonwealth meeting in 1975 reflected the most positive British posture on Southern Africa since the return of the Labor Party to power. Southern Africa received special attention because of the end of Portuguese colonial rule, and the Commonwealth committed itself to support for the liberation forces in Zimbabwe.

Nonalignment

The rivalry that developed between the United States and Soviet Russia after the end of World War II was gathering force at the time that the countries of Africa were moving toward independence. It was thus natural that, during the growth of African nationalism, and from the beginning of their existence as independent states, African countries should be concerned about the effect on their future of the conflict between the great world powers. Out of this concern was born the doctrine of nonalignment, resting essentially on the determination of the African states to avoid involvement in the conflict between the two blocs into which the postwar world had divided—the Communist and the non-Communist (or Western) blocs. Nonalignment has both a positive and negative motivation: on the one hand, the belief of an independent state that policies should be based on domestic interests rather than on those of a foreign power; on the other hand, the determination of a weak nation to avoid the destructive consequences of war between the great powers. At African conferences, peaceful coexistence among all the nations of the world has always been emphasized. In the Charter of the Organization of African Unity, one of the seven principles is stated simply as: "Affirmation of a policy of nonalignment with regard to all blocs."

The African states tend to interpret and apply nonalignment pragmatically. It is not to be equated with neutrality; on the contrary, it calls for participation in world affairs. But the participation does not rest on an obligation to side with one power or another; nor does it call for loyalty to one bloc or another. It leaves a state free to make the choice in its own interests; it may side with one power on one issue, with a different power on another. In practice, however, the states of Africa have tended to lean toward one bloc or another, and one can distinguish with resonable accuracy between states that are (1) nonaligned but tend toward the West and (2) nonaligned but tend toward the Communist bloc.[22] However, all states claiming to be nonaligned would be expected

[22] The African states do not fit easily into the conventional East-West/Communist-capitalist categories. Guinea, ideologically very close to the Communist world, does not hesitate to look to the West in planning economic development. The exploitation of very valuable new bauxite deposits has been undertaken by Guinea, in partnership with American, Canadian, French, and West German corporations.

not to take part in such organizations as the North Atlantic Treaty Organization (NATO) or such alliances as the Warsaw Pact, nor to allow their territory to be used for a foreign military base. In the economic sphere, nonalignment boils down to avoiding exclusive dependence on one country for aid, and achieving a balance between Communist and non-Communist powers in the over-all source of aid. The emphasis is on "aid without strings," that is, accepting aid from a foreign power while not necessarily being identified with its ideology or policies. Nonalignment implies a preference for aid from bodies like the United Nations International Bank for Reconstruction and Development (IBRD), and the International Monetary Fund (IMF), because they are not controlled by a single power. Increasingly, however, the African states tend to practice nonalignment by trading with, and receiving aid from, both Communist and non-Communist nations, often at the same time. They appear to assume that the best way to avoid commitment to either the West or the Communist bloc is to maintain economic ties with both. The indications are that the nations dealing with them, whether capitalist or Communist, are willing to permit relations to continue on this basis for the foreseeable future.[23]

The proceedings at the United Nations that culminated on October 25, 1971, in the expulsion of Nationist China and the admission of Communist China provided a revealing test of African nonalignment: the African states displayed an impressive resistance to American pressure. The United States had mounted a strong campaign for the retention of both Chinas, notwithstanding widespread support (which cut across East-West divisions) for the seating of Communist China alone, in which Britain and France joined with the Soviet Union.

There were two resolutions. The first, declaring the expulsion of Nationalist China an "important matter" and therefore requiring a two-thirds instead of a simple majority vote, was defeated by 59 votes to 55, with 15 abstentions; the African voting was 16 in favor, 16 opposed, 5 abstentions. The second resolution, to seat Communist China and expel Nationalist China, was carried by 76 votes to 35, with 17 abstentions. On this resolution—a humiliating setback for the United States—the African voting had the appearance of a concerted rejection of American pressures: 26 in favor, 14 against, 1 abstention. While four states had been absent in the first vote, every one of the forty-one states participated in this one.

In 1970 there was an attempt to give new meaning to the principles of nonalignment and to further cooperation among nonaligned nations. The third summit conference of nonaligned countries took place in

[23] For a discussion of various aspects of nonalignment, see Legum, *Pan-Africanism*, pp 59–63; 113–18. For an analysis of changing African attitudes to nonalignment, see Fred L. Halsted, "Africa and the World: Non-alignment Reconsidered," in Marion E. Doro and Newell M. Stultz (eds.), *Governing in Black Africa* (Englewood, N.J.: Prentice Hall, 1970), pp. 342–51. For a discussion of nonalignment in the context of conflicts between African states and the world powers, see Vernon McKay (ed.), *African Diplomacy* (New York: Praeger, 1966), pp. 15–19.

Lusaka, Zambia, under the chairmanship of President Kaunda, but the ceremonial opening of the conference was presided over by President Tito of Yugoslavia, chairman of the first conference of nonaligned nations, held in Belgrade in 1961. The Lusaka conference drew representatives of fifty-four countries (thirty-three of them African); nine others (eight of them African) having ignored invitations to attend.[24] Also present were observers from seven Latin American countries, the Barbados, Finland, leaders of the African Liberation movements, and Madame Nguyen Thi Binh, "Foreign Minister" in the "Provisional Revolutionary Government" of South Vietnam.

The conference adopted two declarations and passed a number of resolutions. The "Lusaka Declaration on Peace, Independence, Development, Cooperation and Democratization of International Resolutions" referred to the barriers within the international community that

... divide countries into the developed and the developing, oppressors and the oppressed, the aggressors and the victims of aggression, into those who act from positions of strength, either military or economic, and those who are forced to live in the shadow of permanent danger of covert and overt assaults on their independence and security.

The declaration argued that, while a movement toward negotiation between the superpowers had reduced the immediate risk of major conflicts, this did not contribute to the security of the smaller or the developing nations, nor did it remove the danger of local wars. The countries represented also promised to do all they could to have the "great military alliances" dissolved. The conference declared that the aims of nonalignment continued to be

the pursuit of world peace and peaceful co-existence by strengthening the role of non-aligned countries within the United Nations so that it will be a more effective instrument against all forms of aggressive action and the threat or use of force against freedom, independence, sovereignty, and territorial integrity of any country; the fight against colonialism and racialism which are a negation of human equality and dignity; the settlement of disputes by peaceful means; the ending of the arms race followed by universal disarmament; opposition to great power military alliances and pacts; opposition to the establishment of foreign military bases and foreign troops on the soil of other nations in the context of great power conflicts and colonial and racist suppression; the universality of, and the strengthening of the efficacy of the United Nations; and the struggle for economic independence and mutual cooperation on a basis of equality and mutual benefit.[25]

[24] One of these was Malawi. The day before the conference opened, President Banda was reported as saying he had "no time to go prancing around Africa passing resolutions condemning everybody."
[25] *Lusaka Declaration on Peace, Independence, Development, Co-operation and Democratization of International Relations and Resolutions of the Third Conference of Heads of State or Government of Non-Aligned Countries.* Lusaka, Zambia. September 8–10, 1970. (Published by the Ministry of Foreign Affairs. Printed by the Government Printer, Lusaka.)

The "Declaration on Nonalignment and Economic Progress" recorded the concern of the countries represented at the widening gap between the rich and the poor nations and their adoption of a "Programme of Action," set out in considerable detail under the headings, *inter alia*, of "Trade, Cooperation and Development"; "Industrial, Mineral, Agricultural and Marine Production"; and "Application of Science and Technology." The United Nations was urged to undertake specified measures designed to bring about an early improvement in the economic condition of the developing countries.[26]

Among the resolutions passed was one on "Apartheid and Racial Discrimination," condemning the United States, France, Great Britain, Western Germany, Italy, and Japan which "by their political, economic, and military cooperation encourage and incite the government of South Africa to persist in its racist policies." Another on Indochina demanded the "immediate, complete and unconditional withdrawal of all foreign forces from Vietnam" and expressed the hope that the Paris peace talks would result in an early settlement enabling the people of Vietnam to determine their own future.[27]

In order to increase future cooperation among the nonaligned nations, the conference decided that foreign ministers should meet annually, with a summit conference every four years, but more often if called for by the international situation. At the 1972 meeting of foreign ministers, held in Guyana, Prime Minister Forbes Burnham called for financial and military support for the liberation of Southern Africa, but no concrete measures were discussed.

In October, 1971, President Tito said that he expected the end of Communist China's isolation, following on the new American policy, to be to the advantage of the small countries of the world. He emphasized, however, that the new diplomacy of the superpowers would not be effective unless the interests of these countries were taken into account.

The fourth conference of nonaligned countries, which took place in Algiers in 1973, approved a political declaration (which reaffirmed solidarity with the African liberation movements), an economic declaration (which included the decision to create an economic and social development fund), and a number of resolutions on specific subjects. It was decided that the fifth conference would be held in 1976. It was announced during the 1973 conference that Jamaica had offered $160,000 to the "national liberation movements."

Africa and the United States

As compared with the European powers, the United States was a late arrival on the African scene. Until the 1950's American interest in Africa was limited; neither the government nor the people had displayed any significant interest in African developments, which were

[26] *Ibid.*, NAC/CONF. 3/Res. 14, pp. 22–28.
[27] *Ibid.*, NAC/CONF. 3/Res. 2, NAC/CONF. 3/Res. 5.

becoming increasingly important for colonial powers like Britain and France. America's serious involvement in Africa coincided with the beginning of the process of decolonization and the emergence of a large number of independent states. In the course of the two decades that have elapsed since then, the ties between the United States and Africa have become extensive. At the private level there have been, *inter alia*, considerable growth of trade and investment, the development of programs concerned with Africa in the 2,000 American universities and other institutions of higher education, and the provision of generous funds for various aspects of African development by such organizations as the Ford and Rockefeller foundations and the Carnegie Endowment.[28] At the governmental level, the United States has concerned itself with the protection and advancement of its military, economic, and diplomatic interests in Africa, motivated largely by resistance to the growth of Russian influence and the desire to secure the preservation of Western political ideas and institutions.[29]

Despite two major statements during 1970—a report by Secretary of State Rogers at the conclusion of his visit to Africa and discussion of Africa at some length in President Nixon's "State of the World" address —it is difficult to say with any precision what present United States policy on Africa is. When actions and official statements during the last few years are taken together, ambiguities and contradictions emerge. It is, however, possible to suggest four factors that have played an important part in the fashioning of United States African policy as it is at present: (1) The gravity of United States involvement in Southeast Asia, together with the dangers inherent in the Middle East situation, have relegated Africa to the bottom of the list of international priorities; (2) when a statement of policy or action of some kind is called for in regard to Africa, it is customary to do what Britain does rather than take an independent line; (3) cold war considerations tend to determine relations between the United States and a particular African country, rather than the realities of the situation (at times, the American attitude toward an influential African leader is based on a naïve belief that he is pro-Communist rather than on a sound evaluation of his influence and prestige); and (4) the United States tends to see its role in Africa as being largely limited to the provision of economic aid and technical assistance, and it is assumed that most of Africa's foreign aid will continue to come from the European nations, so there is a trend toward reducing American aid to Africa.

A factor influencing American policy, specifically toward Southern Africa[30] is the pressure of black American opinion on the administration. With a growing tendency of sections of the black community to

---

[28] See Vernon McKay, *Africa in World Politics* (New York: Harper and Row, 1963), pp. 245-70.

[29] *Ibid.*, pp. 271-87.

[30] See Chapter 6, pp. 133-34; see also John Marcum, "The Politics of Indifference: Portugal and Africa, a Case Study in American Foreign Policy," *Issue*, II, no. 3 (Fall, 1972) (African Studies Association).

identify with the African struggle against *apartheid*, the administration sometimes considers it wise to display (or at least to appear to display) a sensitivity to complaints about the situation in Southern Africa. American policy on Southern Africa as expressed through the Rogers report and the President's address consists of cautious general statements reaffirming adherence to recognized democratic principles and support for African goals, while avoiding any commitment to action designed to put an end to *apartheid*.

But the sympathetic stance of the Nixon Administration was contradicted by events during the period 1969–71. In 1970 a number of distinguished experts known to be strongly anti-*apartheid* were dropped from the State Department's panel of advisers on Africa; a much smaller body, including at least one well-known apologist for *apartheid* and many people representing conservative business interests, was substituted.[31] About the same time, President Nixon was unable to receive President Kaunda of Zambia (whom he had praised lavishly in the "State of the World" address), although arrangements had been made for this influential African leader to visit the White House as a spokesman for the Organization of African Unity. A year earlier President Nixon had acted against the advice of the State Department in declining to meet President Nyerere of Tanzania—another influential African leader in the vanguard of the fight against *apartheid*—while he was passing through the United States on a visit to Canada. In 1971 the United States withdrew from membership of the United Nations Colonialism Committee. This action—the first United States resignation from a United Nations body—could only feed African suspicions that United States condemnation of white minority rule was empty rhetoric not backed by a genuine intention to fight it.

On one important issue that arose in 1971 the United States departed from its practice of following Britain's lead. When Britain, ignoring intense opposition by the African states, announced its intention to supply arms to South Africa, the United States opposed Britain's decision, true to its own strict observance since 1963 of the United Nations resolution calling for a cessation of military supplies by all member-nations. There was influential American support for the African contention that the arms deal would undermine the influence of the West by making it easier for Russia to establish a sphere of influence in the Indian Ocean.[32]

United States policy appeared, at first, to be more forthright on

[31] No change has been made since President Nixon's resignation.

[32] For details of African opposition to the arms deal with South Africa, see pp. 279–83 of this chapter) In 1976 forty-one members of the United States House of Representatives called on President Ford to refuse an application by a South African government corporation, then being considered by the administration, for a loan from the Export-Import Bank. The refusal was urged pursuant to a ban imposed on loans to South Africa in 1964, and has been observed continuously since then.

Rhodesia than it was on South Africa. Economic sanctions against the Smith regime were maintained, and the consulate-general was closed in 1970. The closing was accompanied by a personal statement from the Secretary of State, an unusual step intended to emphasize American sympathy with the strong feelings of independent black Africa.

Then, in November, 1971, the United States acted to reverse existing policy. Congress voted to permit the importation of chrome from Southern Rhodesia in breach of the sanctions invoked by the Security Council and in violation of its own pledged support for the United Nations. The vote was on a motion introduced by Senator Harry Byrd of Virginia, based on the false argument that the ban on Southern Rhodesian chrome made the United States dependent on the Soviet Union for its supplies. (In fact, stockpiled supplies exceed American needs by more than 2 million tons, and there are plans to sell part of the surplus.) The decision came in the wake of American anger over the expulsion of Nationalist China and reflected a mixture of Southern racism (exploited by big business operating through the Southern Rhodesian lobby), traditional American anti-Communist sentiment, and current hostility toward the United Nations. An attempt to repeal the Byrd motion in June, 1972, was defeated by a 40 to 36 vote in the Senate. The failure of this attempt exposed the duplicity of the Nixon Administration. While the State Department openly supported the repeal, the White House refused a request before the vote was taken to convey its views to six senators who were doubtful. The result was that the United States stood condemned of a dishonorable repudiation of United Nations authority with its implication of support for white minority rule in southern Africa.

South Africa's continued defiance of the United Nations decision according international status to Namibia has led to action by the United States. All American diplomatic representation in Namibia has been withdrawn. Strong condemnation of South Africa's behavior was emphasized by the presence of a representative of the American embassy throughout the trial of a number of Namibians under the South African Terrorism Act. In 1970 the administration, announcing its decision to discourage American investment in Namibia, described South Africa's behavior as "a unique international wrong in the perpetuation of South African rule." It was also announced that the Export-Import Bank would be prohibited from granting credit guarantees in respect of trade with Namibia and that the government would not protect American investors whose rights were acquired after the United Nations decision of 1966 against claims made by a "future lawful government" of Namibia; other nations would be encouraged to take similar action. The written submission presented by the United States to the International Court of Justice in 1971 criticized South Africa much more severely than the submission of any other nation. South Africa was accused of practicing "a systematic policy to effect political, economic, social, and educational repression," and it was argued that South Africa's occupation of Namibia "by force against the will of the international authority entitled to administer it, was as much belligerent occupation as the hostile occupation of the territory of another state." The investment by American firms in Namibia, although negligible as compared with investment in South Africa, totals about $45 million, mostly in mining and exploration for metals.[33]

United States policy on Africa may be summed up as follows: The overriding consideration is to avoid any serious political commitment anywhere in Africa—at least for as long as the present involvement in Southeast Asia continues; subject to that consideration, diplomatic ties are maintained and economic and technical aid continued, preference being given to those African states believed to lean toward the West rather than toward the Communist world. As to Southern Africa, the official attitude may be described as a combination of condemnatory rhetoric and indirect economic support (through the medium of considerable trade and investment) in relation to white supremacy in South Africa, and limited but somewhat more concrete opposition to white supremacy in Namibia.

In 1976, however, the United States announced a more forthright policy on Africa as a whole and Southern Africa in particular. Secretary of State Kissinger visited six African countries, including Zaire, Zambia, and Tanzania. While in Zambia, Kissinger made a policy statement described as "a message of commitment and co-operation" that called for common United States–African action to achieve "the great goals of national independence, economic development, and racial justice" in Africa; submitted a ten-point proposal for majority rule in Rhodesia within two years; and described American policy on South Africa as "based on the premise that within a reasonable time we shall see a clear evolution toward equality of opportunity and basic human rights for all South Africans."

Africa and the Soviet Union

The Soviet Union's first attempts to export Communism to Africa met with little success. The frequent shifts during the 1950's in applying Communist ideology to African nationalism confused potential converts among the African leaders. Many of those leaders, among them Nasser and Nkrumah, were described in 1952 as "reactionary representatives of the bourgeoisie"; only three years later they were being recognized as leaders of a "great popular independence movement." But a less doc-

[33] For a perceptive analysis of American policy on Southern Africa, see Vernon McKay, "Southern Africa and its Implications for American Policy," in William A. Hance (ed.), *Southern Africa and the United States* (New York: Columbia University Press, 1968), pp. 1–32. For a useful criticism of American policy in relation to Namibia, see Elizabeth Landis, *Namibia: The Beginning of Disengagement*, Studies in Race Relations, Center on International Race Relations, Graduate School of International Studies, vol. II, no. 1 (Denver, Colo.: University of Denver, 1971).

trinaire approach toward the African situation developed as steps were taken to improve Soviet knowledge of Africa. The Soviet universities began to introduce African studies, the Oriental Institute of the U.S.S.R. Academy of Sciences trained personnel and sent scholars to Africa, and studies of various African questions were published. By 1959 a separate Africa Institute had been established under the direction of Professor I. I. Potekhin.

Despite these developments, the record of the first decade of Communist activity in Africa was hardly encouraging to the Soviet Union. Most African countries had no organized Communist parties, and very few of the nationalist leaders were Communist supporters or sympathizers. Communism had made little headway by using infiltration to subject African political movements to control by Moscow. Similar tactics in relation to the trade union movement by using the World Federation of Trade Unions (WFTU) and various front organizations, such as the World Federation of Democratic Youth and the World Peace Council, met with very little success; many young Africans had returned from their studies at Soviet universities critical of what they had learned and of the teaching methods used. In addition, the Communist diagnosis of the African colonial revolution had been proved false. The sudden abandonment of colonial power that had, in fact, occurred from 1960 onward was the opposite of the bloody struggle for continued imperialist control that the Leninist text books had so dogmatically predicted. Vernon McKay summarizes the result of Russian activity during this period as follows:

... after 40 years of world communism, (1) there were relatively few Communists in Africa, (2) Communists had failed in most of their efforts to gain control of African political movements, (3) the number of Communists in the trade unions had declined by the end of the 1950s, (4) Communist influence in front organizations had often been exposed, (5) Communist efforts with African students had not been altogether successful, and (6) the opportunist and cynical tactics of communism had been unintentionally revealed by ideological shifts and by such actions as the suppression of Hungarian nationalists in 1959, the Chinese invasion of Tibet in 1956, Khrushchev's callous attack on Secretary General Hammarskjöld at the U.N. General Assembly in 1960, and his deliberate resumption of nuclear testing during the conference of neutralists at Belgrade in September 1961.[84]

This assessment is largely applicable to the present situation. The large-scale invasion of Czechoslovakia in 1968, the occupation of Prague and other large cities, the ruthless suppression of every vestige of Czechoslovak resistance to Soviet power, the adamant refusal of the Soviet Union to make any concession to the search for a more flexible form of Communism, and the final humiliating removal from the scene of Alexander Dubcek and his supporters and sympathizers—all these com-

[84] McKay, *Africa in World Politics*, p. 221.

bined to constitute a reminder to African leaders of the Soviet Union's political methods. At the level of direct contact with the people of the African countries, designed to establish trust and confidence, the Soviets fared badly as compared with the Americans, British, and French, who according to Marxist-Leninist teachings should have trailed far behind the Soviets in being trusted by people with the injustices of colonial rule still fresh in their minds. Even while the Peace Corps program was being condemned by the African politicians in the country as an instrument of American "imperialism," most volunteers were establishing excellent relations with the people. The attitude of most Africans to the Soviets in their midst was in marked contrast; it was one of uneasy tolerance rather than complete acceptance, although there was a favorable response to Soviet ideology. The African reaction to Soviet ideas and methods was considered at a conference held in the United States in 1965, at which American authorities on Africa joined with a few visiting African politicians in discussing the determinants of African foreign policy. The published report of the conference,[35] suggesting proposals for further study, included the following:

The African attitude is expressed in the phrase, "We dislike this foreign country's policies, but we trust the people who expound and administer them." Analysis of the reasoning behind continued membership in the Commonwealth, and of popular feeling for British royalty and traditional British symbols and traditions could be instructive. Such an enquiry could also apply to the African image of Communism. Its application to Moscow and Peking might be: "We like your ideas but we don't like your methods, and we're not sure we trust your representatives."[36]

The proceedings at the OAU summit meeting on Angola in 1976 demonstrated Africa's cautious attitude toward the Soviet Union. The meeting divided equally—22 states on either side—in choosing between the Soviet-backed MPLA (clearly on the verge of victory) and a coalition between MPLA and the two western-supported rival movements. The meeting adjourned without deciding either way. This action underlined the determined attitude of the moderate African states, and was undoubtedly a rebuff to Moscow.

At the governmental level, the Soviet Union has taken various steps to advance its interests in Africa since the end of World War II. These may be considered conveniently under the following categories: (1) international, (2) diplomatic, (3) economic, and (4) cultural.

The United Nations provided the Soviet Union with a base for furthering its own influence and undermining the influence of the non-Communist world. It used the Trusteeship Council in particular, but also the General Assembly, to build an image of itself as the friend and ally of peoples under colonial rule, while at the same time presenting

[35] Vernon McKay (ed.), *African Diplomacy* (New York: Praeger, 1966).
[36] *Ibid.*, p. 207.

the United States to the rest of the world—often by using false propaganda—as the supporter of colonialism.

In 1958 a department devoted exclusively to African Affairs was established within the Soviet Foreign Ministry; since then diplomatic and consular relations with the independent states of Africa have expanded steadily, and trade has increased. Cultural relations have been established; there are radio programs to Africa in a number of African languages, and there is mutual communication in cinematography, science, drama, and the arts.[37]

By the end of the 1960's Africa appeared to have moved to the bottom of the list of Soviet priorities. Military aid to the Nigerian government during the Biafran war has led to closer economic and cultural relations with the Soviet Union, but Nigeria's traditional ties with the West have not significantly changed.[38] The Soviet Union has suffered disappointments in the last few years. The overthrow of Nkrumah in Ghana in 1966 and that of Keita in Mali in 1968 removed two influential socialist-oriented countries from the African scene. Guinea, though still maintaining close ties with the Soviet Union, appears to be seeking a restoration of good relations with France. After the United Arab Republic, Algeria is the African country receiving the largest share of Soviet economic aid, and Soviet involvement in the mining, oil, and steel industries is considerable, but there are indications of a more cautious Algerian attitude toward Russian influence in the Mediterranean and possible closer relations with the United States resulting from the sales of natural gas.

Since 1970 discussion of the British plan to sell arms to South Africa has focused attention on the Soviet Union naval presence in the Indian Ocean. Not yet regarded as a threat by Britain or the United States, Soviet influence in this area could lead to serious problems in the future. For example, if Britain delivers arms to South Africa as protection against the alleged threat of Russian dominance in the Indian Ocean, the African states may well retaliate by welcoming a Soviet presence and providing the Russians with the facilities they now lack.

The Soviet Union's consistent support of the national liberation movements (supplementing the meager aid available from the Organization of African Unity with money, arms, equipment, and training) has naturally given it useful channels of communication with these movements. It has also resulted in its recognition by the African states as a world power sharing their own commitment (unlike the Western powers) to the use of force in completing the decolonization of Africa. But these developments have not led to a Soviet sphere of influence in Southern Africa; the relations with the Soviet Union operate within the framework of the principles of nonalignment.

[37] For details, see McKay, *Africa in World Politics*, pp. 227–36.

[38] For details of recent economic cooperation between the Soviet Union and Nigeria, see Colin Legum, *Africa Contemporary Record 1970–1971* (London: Rex Collings, 1971), A60–61, B423–24.

Although the success of the MPLA in Angola has increased Soviet prestige and influence in Southern Africa, it would be unwise to assume that Angola will see alignment with Russia as the answer to her problems, once she settles down to the tasks of nation-building and economic development. Future Soviet influence in Southern Africa may be determined by the response of the United States and other Western powers to the developmental needs of Angola.

Africa and the People's Republic of China

Communist China's influence in Africa originated with the visits of Chinese delegations to African countries in 1958 following the contacts established at the Bandung Conference in 1955.

Claiming a special basis for close relations with the Africans, because they were also nonwhite (thus implicitly denying to the Soviets the same identification with African aspirations), and emphasizing that they (unlike the Soviets) supported the national liberation movements as a people themselves once subject to colonial rule, the Chinese had established close ties with several African states shortly after independence. By 1961 there were diplomatic relations with Ghana, Guinea, the Sudan, Mali, the Somali Republic, and the United Arab Republic. Chinese propaganda gave prominence to Peking's commitment to revolution as the instrument for world change, in contrast with Moscow's policy of coexistence. On a tour of Africa in 1964, Premier Chou En-lai made the famous pronouncement, "Revolutionary prospects are excellent throughout Africa." It was repeated during a second tour in 1965. Chinese tactics began to be feared as a threat to internal security. There was evidence that Chinese embassies in some African countries, for example, Niger and the Central African Republic, were active in supporting attempts to overthrow the existing governments. With the overthrow of Nkrumah in 1966, a stronghold of Chinese influence suddenly collapsed, and the African states were encouraged to take steps against the dangers of Chinese subversive activity. For many African leaders, concern for the security of their regimes outweighed a natural sympathy with the Chinese doctrine of revolution in Africa. A number of African states broke off relations with Communist China; some suspended relations; others, while leaving diplomatic relations unaltered, imposed limitations on Chinese activity within their countries. Among the third group was Kenya, which insisted on a substantial reduction in the embassy staff and prohibited the dissemination of Chinese propaganda. Peking's concern with Africa appeared to decline, but two years later it was clear that interest had revived, and by 1969 the Chinese were pursuing an increasingly important role. Since then there has been continued support of guerrilla activity in Southern Africa and an expanded program of economic aid. In addition, steps were taken to create a new image of China: no longer interested in subversion, but in Africa only to help. Most African states continued to be cautious, but over-all relations between them and Peking showed signs of steady improvement. The marked lessening in East-West tensions, culminating in China's admission to the United Nations in 1971 and the visit of President Nixon in 1972 (with its important consequences and implications, both political and economic), is likely to add considerably to China's future prestige and influence in Africa.

Communist China's outstanding achievement in Africa is the building of the Tanzam railway—the link between the copper mines of Zambia and the Indian Ocean ports of Tanzania—and its related projects. Taking advantage of the lack of foresight displayed by the Western world—China was approached only after applications had been turned down by the United States and the World Bank—Peking is responsible for a project that has been described as "comparable with, and perhaps even more spectacular than, the Soviet's Aswan Dam in Egypt."[39] The amount involved is approximately $400 million, the work on the 1100-mile railway, which got under way toward the end of 1969, is expected to be complete by 1975, and it was estimated that some 13,000 Chinese were employed on the project in 1971. Two hundred Tanzanians and Zambians will go to the Northern China Communications University for training in senior management and technical posts for the railways. Tanzania and Zambia meet the local costs, including the salaries of Chinese staff and purchases of goods and equipment in Africa, by buying Chinese goods. This has resulted in goods manufactured in China replacing some British goods. China has provided training for the army and the police force of Tanzania and has assisted in the planning of a naval base at Dar es Salaam. Since the inauguration of the Tanzam project, it has built up a reputation with several African countries for efficiency and rapid results in a variety of fields. Mauritania has learned to appreciate the results of China's expertise in the development of rice fields; in Zanzibar, a team of Chinese doctors has done excellent work in the fight against tropical diseases; in Congo-Brazzaville, Chinese engineering is responsible for the construction of a river dockyard; in countries as far apart as Zambia, the Somali Republic, and Mali, Chinese money, planning, and work have been behind new manufacturing and construction projects.

China, like other powers, aims at increasing trade and promoting cultural exchange, and these are bound to grow as time goes on. It is also likely that an engineer trained in China will want to buy Chinese machinery, just as a British-trained engineer will look to Britain for his needs. But there are no signs yet of any deliberate policy by Tanzania or Zambia to reduce purchases from Britain or other Western sources. The picture is rather one of China's engaging in normal competition for the trading opportunities available.

At the diplomatic level, Peking has made striking progress during the

[39] W. A. C. Adie, "China's Year in Africa," in Colin Legum and John Drysdale, *Africa Contemporary Record. Annual Survey and Documents 1969–1970* (Exeter, England: Africa Research, Ltd., 1970), A 50.

past few years. At the end of 1970 diplomatic relations were established with Ethiopia, and close ties were forged with Equatorial Guinea. Early in 1971 there was recognition by Nigeria, regarded in the Western world as one of the most important countries in Africa. The opening of the Communist Chinese embassy in Lagos in April, 1971, probably marked a turning point in Peking's relations with independent black Africa. Since then diplomatic relations have been established with Botswana, the Gambia, Niger, Mozambique, Senegal, and Gabon.

A comparison of Communist China (before it was admitted to the United Nations on October 25, 1971) with Nationalist China shows that, although many states recognized Taiwan, those recognizing Peking accounted for more than two-thirds of the total population of Africa and more than half its area. In September, 1971, the scoreboard was as follows: the twenty-three countries recognizing Peking were Algeria, Burundi, Congo-Brazzaville, Cameroun, Ethiopia, Ghana, Guinea, Equatorial Guinea, Kenya, Libya, Mali, Mauritius, Morocco, Mauritania, Nigeria, Uganda, United Arab Republic, Somali Democratic Republic, Sierra Leone, Sudan, Tanzania, Togo, and Zambia. Three of these—Burundi, Ghana, and Mauritius—had not agreed to exchange ambassadors. The eighteen countries still maintaining relations with Taiwan were Botswana, the Central African Republic, Tchad, Zaïre, Dahomey, Gabon, Gambia, the Ivory Coast, Lesotho, Liberia, Madagascar, Malawi, Niger, Rwanda, Senegal, Sierra Leone, Togo, and Upper Volta. By December, 1973, the Malagsy Republic, Rwanda, Dahomey, Tchad, Zaïre, and Senegal had recognized Peking.

Peking's aid to Africa is roughly estimated at four times the amount of Taiwan's, most of it going to the five countries with which it appears to have the closest ties: Algeria, Congo-Brazzaville, Guinea, Mauritania, and Tanzania. There have been loans to Senegal and Togo. Economic, trade, and technical agreements have been made with Nigeria, Gabon, Togo, Somalia, and the Malagasy Republic. Peking is believed to conduct substantial trade—through Hong Kong—with Rhodesia and South Africa, but this does not appear to have damaged its standing with independent black Africa; nor, it seems, does Peking itself see any conflict between providing economic support for white supremacy in Southern Africa and giving aid to the guerrillas who seek its overthrow. It was estimated in 1971 that Chinese aid to developing countries throughout the world exceeded $750 million; the figure for the Soviet Union and the countries of Eastern Europe together was $500 million.

The bitter conflict between Peking and Moscow has had its repercussions in Africa, where Chinese money and arms have been used to split some of the liberation movements. In 1968, for example, Peking was accused of supporting the Pan-Africanist Congress of South Africa (PAC) from which Zambia had withdrawn its support, to the detriment of the African National Congress (ANC). The ANC, recognized by the Organization of African Unity as the legitimate instrument of South African resistance, was receiving support from the Soviet Union.

The mutual hostility between the two Communist powers continues, although the Soviet Union has attempted conciliation. On the occasion of the fiftieth anniversary of the founding of the Chinese Communist Party (July 1, 1971), an official article in *Pravda*, referring to the long-term common interests the two powers shared, went on to state "the need for restoring and developing mutual cooperation and friendship." But there was no corresponding softening of Peking's past attitudes. On the contrary, an editorial in a Chinese publication attacked "Soviet revisionist social-imperialism," together with "United States imperialism" and "Japanese militarism."

Relations between Russia and China rest on a basis of deep-seated mutual fear. Each of them maintains a large armed force along the border between the two countries, and in both countries talk is common in official circles about the possibility of attack. The underground air-raid shelters that are a feature of Chinese cities indicate how seriously Peking treats the possibility of attack by Russia.

The outlines of Peking's foreign policy for the future began to take shape in 1971, with emphasis on a more pragmatic approach in international relations while remaining committed to the concept of world revolution and support for movements of national liberation. With its admission to the United Nations—and the simultaneous expulsion of Taiwan—Peking, rather than aiming to become a superpower itself, is likely to move toward leadership of the Third World, the bloc of smaller nations combining to resist domination—whether economic, political, or military—by the Soviet Union and the United States.

Included in the wide-ranging activities of Premier Chou En-lai intended to achieve this objective have been discussions with Rumania and Yugoslavia, public support for Britain's admission to the European Community, on the ground that a strengthened Europe would reduce the influence of the United States, and a planned visit to Peking of representatives of the parliamentary opposition in Australia about the possibility of Chinese purchases of Australian wheat.

There is, therefore, no doubt that Peking's wooing of Africa will continue, and most of the African states can be expected to maintain and strengthen relations with Peking as long as the fundamental principles of nonalignment are respected. But bitter conflict with Russia is implicit in China's Africa policy. An official Chinese publication, commenting in 1976 on the Angolan situation, said that the Russians by their successful support of MPLA had demonstrated their "wild ambitions to step up expansion, plunder and domination of Africa."

But there are puzzling—and perhaps frightening—contrasts for the African states between China as a revolutionary friend and protector of small weak nations and China as a pragmatic world power. It will not be easy for them to forget the paradox of China, in theory the champion of freedom for the people of Asia, in fact supporting Pakistan—a reactionary regime that brutally tried to suppress Bengali national liberation—and, in the process, finding itself in the company of the Nixon Administration.

The reference to Africa in the lengthy address to the United Nations

General Assembly by the Chinese Deputy Foreign Minister, Chiao Kuan-hua, in October, 1972, was noticeably brief. The Africans, while assured of China's sympathy with the liberation struggle, were told that it was "impossible to put an end to colonialist rule by relying on other people." And there was no promise of financial or military aid.

Africa and the Arab World

A concerted effort to increase Arab influence on the African states was made in 1974 with a meeting between representative of the Organization of Arab Petroleum Exporting Countries (OAPEC) and a special committee of the OAU. It was agreed that the oil requirements of the African states would be met and that the promised creation of an Arab bank for African development would be accelerated with an increased capital of $500 million. This was followed by creation of a $200 million "revolving fund" to compensate African states for the effects of the increase in the world price of oil.

Meeting in Cairo in 1975 representatives of 23 African and Arab countries discussed future cooperation in various areas following serious complaints by many African leaders that the Arab states had not carried out promises of compensation and aid that were to take effect after their countries had broken diplomatic relations with Israel. A declaration was issued that called for cooperation in trade, industry, and other areas, and was to be ratified at a joint meeting of the Arab League and the OAU. The OAU, at its thirteenth meeting, agreed to hold a summit conference of Arab and African heads of state and government on future Arab-African cooperation.

A few months later the United Nations General Assembly carried, by an overwhelming majority, an Arab-sponsored resolution against Israel that equated Zionism with *apartheid*. It was not surprising that two-thirds of the 47 African states supported it; twelve of them abstained, only four voted against.

The Impact of World Economics

We turn now to the fourth question raised in this chapter, the impact of world economics on the political development of the independent states of Africa.

That impact in its specific effect on African government may be described succinctly as follows: The capacity of the government of an independent African state to satisfy the demands of its people for significant economic advancement is determined largely by the nature and extent of the assistance it receives from external sources. Like all developing countries, the African states find themselves compelled to seek—directly from individual countries, or from international organizations—aid in the form of money or technical assistance. But very many of the African states, it seems, compare unfavorably even with other underdeveloped countries. Robert K. A. Gardiner, Executive Secretary of the Economic Commission for Africa, has said:

Various classifications of countries according to levels of development seem to agree on two things: that a very large number of the least developed countries among the developing countries are located in Africa; and that a large proportion of African countries fall within the rubric of the least developed countries.[40]

The term "underdevelopment" can obscure the stark reality of African poverty. Upper Volta has a population of 5,500,000, with only 29,000 persons in paid employment. About 95 per cent of the population depend on what their land produces for their livelihood. In a good year, a family of five can expect to earn $84. One out of every five children born dies in infancy; the average life-expectancy is thirty-five years. There is a grave shortage of water. It is a common occurrence for a woman to walk twelve miles (usually with a child on her back) to draw a bowl of water from a well.

Internal resources are not, in themselves, capable of ensuring the required economic growth, and the African states consequently depend on the developed world for the capital and the technical skills essential for their economic development.[41]

The development in Africa since the former colonies attained independence has been because of (1) aid provided by United Nations programs; (2) financial assistance in the form of loans or grants by the governments of the developed countries, such as the United States, Britain, France, the Soviet Union, Communist China, and some of the smaller European countries; and (3) aid in the form of trade and investment by private persons and corporations in the developed countries.

Since the end of World War II, the United Nations has been instrumental in providing the independent African states with considerable capital and a wide range of technical aid. These have come from the United Nations itself, its specialized agencies, and a number of other organizations participating in its activities. Capital requirements are dealt with by the International Bank for Reconstruction and Development (IBRD), usually known as the World Bank, which grants loans for projects in such fields as agriculture, transportation, and electric power. The International Development Association (IDA), an affiliate of the World Bank, makes capital available on easier terms for projects not acceptable to the World Bank. Technical assistance, embracing the provision of experts to be available in the countries to teach, conduct programs, and advise officials, as well as the training of suitable persons from the countries in overseas institutions, is provided in many fields by a variety of organizations. Among these are: The United Nations Food and Agriculture Organization (FAO), the International Labor Organization (ILO), the United Nations Educational, Scientific, and Cultural Organizaiton (UNESCO), the World Health Organization (WHO),

---

[40] In an address delivered at the forty-seventh session of the Economic and Social Council, Geneva, July 24, 1969.
[41] Andrew M. Kamarck, "Economic Determinants," in McKay, *African Diplomacy*, pp. 56–63.

and the International Civil Aviation Organization (ICAO). The United Nations Children's Fund (UNICEF), although not one of the specialized agencies, is another instrument with which the United Nations has provided invaluable assistance to a number of African countries by establishing and equipping health centers and providing essential medicinal supplies.[42] In 1971 the United Nations Development Program approved aid to ninety-six developing countries in amounts, totaling $140 million, which covered 129 new projects; of these, fifty projects were in Africa, as compared with thirty-two in Asia and the Far East and twenty-five in the Middle East. In the ten years that the program has been in operation, 1,363 projects have received aid, at a total estimated cost of $1.3 billion.

The decision by the government of a developed nation to grant aid to a developing country is not determined solely by the need of the country seeking aid. Governments usually dispose of the capital they can spare in order to serve their own interests. As we have seen in reviewing the activities of the world powers in Africa, whether aid is forthcoming, the form it takes, its value, and the time when it is offered are all questions influenced strongly by political considerations and often closely associated with the rivalry between world powers. As to trade, the African states cannot, under existing conditions, expect much; ordinary commercial association with Africa has little to offer the developed nations. Even the former demand for raw materials produced in Africa is diminishing as a result of the development of substitutes, such as various plastic materials instead of metal. In recent years, too, some nations have reduced aid to the developing countries in response to internal factors. Since 1966 there has been a downward trend in foreign aid, because two leading nations in the Western world have felt obliged to economize; Britain, because of its own deteriorating economic position, and the United States, because of the drain on its resources resulting from the enormous cost of the war in Indochina.

Since the end of World War II the United States has provided foreign aid on a large scale throughout the world and through a number of agencies; after 1961 the foreign aid program was expanded and reorganized through the activities of the U.S. Agency for International Development (AID). The countries of Africa figured prominently among the recipients of American aid and through the 1950's and the early 1960's there was a steady growth in economic assistance to Africa. But by the end of the 1960's there was growing public criticism of the policy of devoting to foreign aid money badly needed to alleviate unsatisfactory conditions at home.[43] Pressures created by the war in Vietnam and internal problems of poverty and racial discrimination have encouraged the view that the United States ought to think in terms of priorities;

[42] For a detailed description of United Nations aid to Africa up to 1961, see McKay, *Africa in World Politics*, pp. 50–67.

[43] For a description of American aid to Africa up to 1961, see McKay, *Africa in World Politics*, pp. 361–78.

that the war must end and pressing domestic problems be solved before the needs of foreign nations can receive attention. The inevitable result has been a substantial reduction in foreign aid.[44]

Growing concern at the failure of the developing nations to show significant improvement, accompanied by the widening gap between them and the developed nations—the problem of poor nations staying poor while the rich nations grow richer—led to attempts to develop a global approach to this question. The great extent of this gap appears from a comparison of the *gross annual sales* of some American corporations with the *gross national products* of some countries, for example, (the figures are in billions of dollars): General Motors 24.3, Standard Oil of New Jersey 16.5, Ford Motors 14.9, Nigeria 5.8, Algeria 4.2, Morocco 3.3, Libya 3.1. The members of the international community tackled the problem through a new organization, the United Nations Conference on Trade and Development (UNCTAD). Two meetings, in 1964 and 1968, formulated proposals for bringing about a more equitable distribution of wealth throughout the world. They were (1) a voluntary tax on the rich nations, corresponding approximately to 1 per cent of the gross national product: (2) increasing the prices of primary products and ensuring that they were maintained at an adequate level; and (3) granting preference in respect of goods produced in the factories of the developing countries. The general aim behind these proposals was approved, and the proposals themselves accepted in principle. A third meeting in 1972 failed to produce concrete measures and left the African states (together with the developing countries of Asia and Latin America) in a state of frustration. Negotiations intended to alleviate the economic weakness of the developing countries proved futile, the main reason being the abstention of the United States (often supported by other capital-exporting countries like Britain, France, and West Germany) on proposals that the International Monetary Fund should allocate a specified quota of "paper gold," or special drawing rights, to them. Except for minor concessions, the pleas of the poor nations were ignored. Implementation of UNCTAD's admirable goals—which could bring about a wide redistribution of the world's resources—seemed to be a long way off.

The problem relating to the future economic relations between the countries of Anglophone Africa and Britain and the effect on the other members of the Commonwealth of Britain's membership in the European Economic Community (EEC) was raised at the Commonwealth Conference in 1971.

Under the Yaoundé Convention, a number of African states (not members of the Commonwealth) after 1963 enjoyed preferential access to the markets of the EEC, in return for reciprocal preferences granted by them on exports from the community to their markets, and received

[44] Tom Soper, "Western Attitude to Aid," in Legum and Drysdale, eds., *Africa Contemporary Record, 1970–1971,* C. 407–9.

development aid from the community. Under the Arusha Convention, signed in 1968, Kenya, Tanzania, and Uganda participated in similar arrangements, except that the preferences covered a more limited range of goods, and there was no provision for development aid.

When Britain decided to join the EEC, a white paper was issued that set out three options available to Commonwealth African countries: (1) association with the community under a revised Yaoundé Convention, modified to provide development aid for the new as well as the existing associate states; (2) some other forms of association similar to that provided by the Arusha Convention; and (3) a commercial agreement to facilitate and expand trade with the community.[45]

After negotiations commenced in 1973, agreement was finally reached at the Lomé Convention between the EEC and forty-six African, Caribbean, and Pacific states covering, *inter alia*, the grant of duty-free access to imports of the latter and increased development aid to all of them. The Convention, having been ratified, as required, by the necessary number of African, Caribbean, and Pacific states, and by all the members of the Community went into effect in April, 1976.

Africa appears to be on the threshold of a period in its history that is likely to see far-reaching changes in its own economic condition and in its relations with and influence upon, the Commonwealth, Europe, and the international community as a whole.

The Dynamism of African Politics

The political scene in Africa early in the second decade of independence presents contrasting features. There has been progress and retrogression; disorder and reconstruction; civil war and national reintegration; military intervention and the restoration of civil rule; repression and liberalization. The period since 1957 must be characterized as one of political uncertainty. It was darkened by periodic outbreaks of internecine strife, bloodshed, and destruction, but it should be remembered that not a single African state has yet produced the institutionalized dehumanization created by *apartheid* nor the day-to-day brutality of South Africa's police-state apparatus.

There have been examples during this period of encouraging recovery from social and economic disruption and the reconciliation of conflicting goals and interests that had seemed irreconcilable. Nigeria seems to have come through a devastating civil war with a developing economy (boosted by immense oil resources), considerable reconstruction in the damaged areas, and, above all, the Igbo progressively returning to normal participation in the political, intellectual, and economic life of the country. The Sudan has seen the end of a long, bitter, and destructive conflict between north and south, with a negotiated agreement provid-

[45] *The United Kingdom and the European Communities*, Cmnd. 4715, July 7, 1971.

ing for autonomy for the southern region and the removal of language and religious barriers. Zaïre has moved into a phase of apparent economic and political stability.

The extent to which military coups have left their mark on Africa remains to be seen. They have varied in their motivation. Some, like Libya, have sought to remove reactionary regimes; others have represented a conservative reaction to militant regimes, as in the first Ghana coup; others again have represented the army's emergence as a means of correcting civilian inadequacy, as in the Dahomey coups. Little, if any, of the military intervention in Africa seems to correspond to the army takeovers in many Latin American countries, where a group of officers ousts an elected government in order to assume and retain power for themselves. Most African coups have been followed by the promise to restore civilian rule, sometimes by an announced date; in some cases the promise has been kept and the soldiers have returned to their barracks, as in Sierra Leone. The military rulers of Nigeria, having promised to restore civilian rule in 1979, have already set in motion machinery designed to provide an appropriate constitution. In some cases, when the military has remained in power it has taken steps to achieve legitimacy by becoming the core of a single party and holding elections, as in Zaïre.

The one-party state presents differences. In Ghana, with almost no prior public discussion, a proposed amendment to the constitution was submitted to a referendum, duly approved by an overwhelming majority, and enacted. In Tanzania President Nyerere appointed a commission to take evidence throughout the country, with the object of obtaining suggestions for ensuring maximal popular participation in government within the one-party framework. The results of the election that followed went a long way toward justifying his contention that the one-party system did not preclude the free exercise of political choice. Of the thirteeen former members of the national assembly who stood for re-election nine were defeated, among them two ministers and two junior ministers. Zambia has followed Tanzania's example. In 1972 President Kaunda, announcing his intention to introduce one-party rule, appointed his vice-president as chairman of a "Commission on One-Party Democracy," which received evidence throughout the country on proposals for making the one-party system as representative as possible of the people's wishes.

Political innovation was provided by Malawi. President Banda introduced a system for the 1971 national assembly elections aimed at reducing undue influence on the voters by candidates and encouraging voters to express their wishes freely in choosing candidates. Electoral committees were established for each district, each committee consisting of ten members each from the district committee of the single party, the youth league, and the women's league, as well as mayors, district councilors, chiefs, and subchiefs. Each committee met representatives of the party's national headquarters and was thereafter required to submit to the president's office not less than three nor more than five names, together with reasons for the choice in each case. The president made his selection from the lists presented by the electoral committees and declared those chosen by him to be duly elected to the national assembly.

Three quite unexpected developments in 1972 illustrate the dynamism of African politics. The first was the overwhelming rejection by the African voters in Rhodesia of proposals for a new constitution, which had been agreed to by Britain and the Smith regime subject to their acceptance by the people. The widely held view that government pressures, the conservatism of the chiefs, and police-state controls of the urban Africans would combine to make acceptance virtually certain proved to be wrong. The African National Council, a new organization, displayed considerable political skill and organizing ability in taking advantage of the Pearce Commission's presence to provide a voice for all shades of African opinion. An overwhelming African "no" compelled Britain to abandon the proposals and to reaffirm its policy of economic sanctions against the Smith regime.

The second surprising development was the strike by Ovambo workers in Namibia (action calling for considerable courage in a country subject to South Africa's police-state laws), which disrupted mining activities and offered a serious threat to overseas investors, as well as to the internal economy. Troops were flown in from South Africa, but the strike ended with the negotiation of minor improvements in the working conditions of the strikers. The personal intervention of Kurt Waldheim, the new Secretary-General of the United Nations, followed. He visited Namibia, then had discussions with the South African prime minister about the territory's future.

The third development came in Malagasy. Widespread strikes, demonstrations, and rioting compelled President Tsiranana to transfer power to the army. Soon afterward, the foreign minister of the new military regime announced that all official links with South Africa would cease immediately. South Africa had received no advance notice of the decision. A contract under which the South African government was to build a five-star hotel in Malagasy was summarily canceled. An important reason for this reversal of policy was the reaction of Malagasy students to the behavior of the South African authorities in relation to anti-*apartheid* demonstrations by South African students; the police had beaten up students engaged in peaceful protest, and the prime minister had publicly endorsed police action. The break with Malagasy was a major setback to South Africa's so-called outward policy of building good relations with independent black Africa, leaving the Ivory Coast as virtually the only African state openly committed to the much-discussed "dialogue" between the independent states and South Africa.

These recent developments prove that, notwithstanding the diversity of this huge continent, 350 million Africans recognize that agreement about the broad issues of development, nation-building, peace, and security is more important than their differences.

Appendix
African States, 1976

AFRICAN STATES 1976—ECONOMY

Country	Capital City	Area (Nearest '000 sq. miles)	Population (Thousands)	Dates of Independence	Per Capita Gross National Product (USA $s)
Algeria	Algiers	920	15,700	July 3, 1962	650
Angola	Luanda	481	6,500	November 11, 1975	580
Benin, People's Republic of (Dahomey)	Porto-Novo	43	3,100	August 1, 1960	120
Botswana	Gaborone	232	690	September 30, 1966	270
Burundi	Bujumbura	11	4,000	July 1, 1962	80
United Republic of Cameroon	Yaoundé	184	6,400	January 1, 1960	260
Cape Verde	Praia	1.5	.29	July 5, 1975	340
Central African Republic	Bangui	241	1,700	August 12, 1960	200
Chad (see Tchad)					
Comoro Islands, People's Republic of	Moroni	150	300	July 6, 1975	170
Congo, People's Republic of	Brazzaville	132	1,300	August 15, 1960	380
Egypt, Arab Republic of	Cairo	386	35,100	February 29, 1922	280
Ethiopia	Addis Ababa	471	29,500	In antiquity	90
Equatorial Guinea	Malabo	12	310	October 12, 1968	260
Gabon	Libreville	103	600	August 17, 1960	1,560
The Gambia	Banjul	4	500	February 18, 1965	170

Country	Capital	Area	Independence	Population
Ghana	Accra	92	March 6, 1957	9,900	350
Guinea	Conakry	95	October 2, 1958	4,400	120
Guinea-Bissau	Bissau	14	September 24, 1973	600	330
Ivory Coast	Abidjan	125	August 7, 1960	4,900	420
Kenya	Nairobi	225	December 12, 1963	13,400	200
Lesotho	Maseru	12	October 4, 1966	1,200	120
Liberia	Monrovia	42	July 27, 1847	1,600	330
Libya, Arab Republic of	Co-Capitals: Tripoli, Benghazi	667	December 24, 1951	2,400	3,360
Madagascar, Democratic Republic of	Tananarive	227	June 26, 1960	7,500	170
Malawi	Lilongwe	46	July 6, 1964	5,000	130
Mali	Bamako	479	September 22, 1960	5,600	70
Mauritania, Islamic Republic of	Nouakchott	398	November 28, 1960	1,230	230
Mauritius	Port Louis	1	March 12, 1968	900	480
Morocco, Kingdom of	Rabat	172	March 2, 1956	17,500	430
Mozambique	Maputo	303	June 25, 1975	9,100	420
Niger	Niamey	489	August 3, 1960	4,600	100
Nigeria	Lagos	357	October 1, 1960	80,000	240
Rwanda	Kigali	10	July 1, 1962	4,200	80
Sao Tome and Principe	Sao Tome	0.372	July 12, 1975	.08	470
Senegal	Dakar	76	August 20, 1960	4,400	320
Seychelles	Victoria	75	June 28, 1976	75	Not available
Sierra Leone	Freetown	28	April 27, 1961	3,000	180
Somali Democratic Republic	Mogadishu	246	July 1, 1960	3,200	80

AFRICAN STATES 1976—ECONOMY (cont.)

Country	Capital City	Area (Nearest '000 sq. miles)	Population (Thousands)	Dates of Independence	Per Capita Gross National Product (USA $s)
South Africa	Pretoria and Cape Town	471	25,100	May 31, 1910	1,200
Sudan	Khartoum	967	12,300	January 1, 1956	150
Swaziland	Mbabane	7	500	September 6, 1968	400
United Republic of Tanzania	Dar-es-Salaam	363	15,500	Tanganyika: Dec. 9, 1961 Islands of Pemba & Zanzibar: Dec. 6, 1963 Union Formed: April 23, 1964	140
Tchad	Ndjamena	496	4,000	August 11, 1960	90
Togo	Lomé	22	2,200	April 27, 1960	210
Tunisia	Tunis	63	5,800	March 20, 1956	550
Uganda	Kampala	91	11,500	October 9, 1962	160
Upper Volta	Ouagadougou	106	6,000	August 5, 1960	80
Zaire Republic	Kinshasa	906	24,000	June 30, 1960	150
Zambia	Lusaka	291	4,900	October 24, 1964	480

AFRICAN STATES 1976—POLITICS

Country	Major Ethnic Groups	Head of State & Head of Government	Official Language	Political Parties
Algeria	Arab, Berber	*President:* Houari Boumediene	Arabic	National Liberation Front
Angola	Ovimbundu, Kimbundu, Bakongo, Chokwe	*President:* Agostinho Neto *Prime Minister:* Lopo do Nascimento	Portuguese	Popular Movement for the Liberation of Angola (MPLA)
Benin	Fon, Adja, Bariba, Yoruba	*President:* Mathieu Kerekou	French	Benin People's Revolutionary Party
Botswana	Batswana	*President:* Seretse Khama	English	The Botswana Democratic Party Botswana People's Party Botswana Independence Party Botswana National Front
Burundi	Hutu, Tutsi, Twa	*President:* Jean-Phillipe Bagaza	French	Party for the National Unity and Progress of Burundi
Cameroon, United Republic of	Fulani, Bulu, Bamiléké, Bamoun	*President:* Ahmadou Ahidjo	French	The National Cameroonian Union
Cape Verde	Mainly Mulattoes (Creole), Mixture of Blacks	*President:* Aristides Pereira *Prime Minister:* Pedro Pires	Portuguese	African Party for the Independence of Guinea and Cape Verde (PAIGC)
Central African Republic	Baya, Mandjia, Banda	*President:* Jean Bedel Bokassa	French	Movement for Social Evolution in Black Africa
Chad (see Tchad)				
Comoro Islands, People's Republic of	Arab, Indian, Malgache, African-Shirazi	*Head of State:* Ali Soilih *Prime Minister:* Abdullah Mohamed	French	National United Front, National Council of the Institutions

African States 1976—Politics (cont.)

Country	Major Ethnic Groups	Head of State & Head of Government	Official Language	Political Parties
Congo, People's Republic of	Bakongo, Batéké, Mbochi, Sangha	*President:* Marien N'gouabi *Premier:* L. S. Goma	French	Congolese Workers Party
Egypt, Arab Republic of	Arab, Copt	*President:* Anwar al-Sadat *Prime Minister:* Abdul Aziz Hegazy	Arabic, English	The Arab Socialist Union
Ethiopia	Amhara, Tigreans, Galla	Chairman of the Provisional Military Govt. of Socialist Ethiopia: Teferi Banti	Amharic	None
Equatorial Guinea	Bubis, Fernandinos, Fang	*President:* Macias Nguema	Spanish	National Unity Party
Gabon	Fang, Eshira, Bakota, Omyènè	*President:* Omar Bongo	French	Gabonese Democratic Party (PDG)
The Gambia	Bapunu, Wolof, Fulani, Jola, Malinke	*President:* Dawda K. Jawara	English	Progressive People's Party, United Party, National Liberation Party
Ghana	Akan, Ga, Ewe, Moshi-Dagomba	Chairman of Supreme Military Council: I. K. Acheampong	English	None
Guinea	Fulani, Malinke, Soussou, Kissi	*President:* Sékou Touré	French	Democratic Party of Guinea (PDG)
Guinea-Bissau	Balante, Fulani, Mandyako, Malinke, Pepel	*President:* Luis Cabral *Prime Minister:* Francisco Mendes	Portuguese	African Party for the Independence of Guinea and Cape Verde Islands (PAIGC)

Country	Ethnic Groups	Leaders	Language	Political Parties
Ivory Coast	Agni-Ashanti, Kroumen, Malinke, Senoufo, Dan, Gourou,	*President:* Felix Houphouët-Boigny	French	Democratic Party of the Ivory Coast (PDCI)
Kenya	Kikuyu, Luo, Baluhya, Kamba	*President:* Jomo Kenyatta	English, Swahili	Kenya African National Union
Lesotho	Basotho, Colored, Asian	*Head of State:* King Moshoeshoe II *Prime Minister:* Leabua Jonathan	English	Basutoland National Congress Basutoland Congress Party
Liberia	Kru, Malinke, Gola, Americo-Liberian	*President:* William R. Tolbert, Jr.	English	True Whig Party
Libya, Arab Republic of	Of mixed Arab and Berber descent	*Revolutionary Command Council Leader:* Mummar al-Qadafi *Prime Minister:* Abdul Salam Jalloud	Arabic	None
Madagascar, Democratic Republic of	Merina, Betsileo, Betsimisaraka, Sakalava, Bara	*President:* Didier Ratsiraka *Prime Minister:* Justin Rakotoniaina	French, Malgache	Malagasy Socialist, National Front for the Defense of the Revolution
Malawi	Matari, Nyanja, Tumbulca, Yao	*President:* H. Kamuzu Banda	English	Malawi Congress Party
Mali	Bambara, Malinke, Sarakolle, Fulani	*Military Committee of National Liberation President:* Moussa Traore	French	None
Mauritania, Islamic Republic of	Maures, Toucouleur, Sarakole, Fulani, Wolof	*President:* Moktar Ould Daddah	Arabic	Mauritanian People's Party (PPM)

AFRICAN STATES 1976—POLITICS (cont.)

Country	Major Ethnic Groups	Head of State & Head of Government	Official Language	Political Parties
Mauritius	Creoles, Indians, Chinese, Europeans	Governor-General: Abdul Raman Mohammed Osman Prime Minister: Seewoosagur Rangoolam	English	Labor Party Parti Mauricien Social Démocrat L'Union Démocratique Mauricienne Comité D'Action Musulmane Independent Forward Bloc
Morocco, Kingdom of	Arab, Berber	Chief of State: King Hassan II Prime Minister: Ahmed Osman	Arabic	Front for the Defense of Constitutional Institutions Socialist Democratic Party National Union of Popular Forces Moroccan Labor Union
Mozambique	Tsonga, Changones, Sera, Manica, Nianja, Macuas, Nakondes	President: Samora Machel	Portuguese	Mozambique Liberation Front (FRELIMO)
Niger	Hausa, Djerma, Touaregs, Toubous, Fulani	President: Seyni Kountche	French	None
Nigeria	Hausa, Fulani, Ibo, Yoruba	Head of Federal Military Government: Olusegun Obasanjo	English	None
Rwanda	Hutu, Tutsi, Twa	President: Juvenal Habyalimana	French	The Party of the Hutu Emancipation Movement
Sao Tome and Principe	Mainly mixture of Blacks; some Mulattoes	President: Manuel Pinto da Costa Prime Minister: M. Trouvoada	Portuguese	Movement for the Liberation of Sao Tome and Principe

Country	Ethnic Groups	Leaders	Language	Political Parties
Senegal	Wolof, Serere, Toucouleur, Fulani	*President:* Léopold Sédar Senghor *Premier:* Abdou Diouf	French	Senegal Progressive Union (UPS), Senegal Democratic Party (PDS), Senegalese National Democratic Assembly (RND)
Sierra Leone	Temne, Mende, Creole	*President:* Siaka Stevens	English	All People's Congress Sierra Leone People's Party
Somali Democratic Republic	Somali	Supreme Revolutionary Council *President:* Mohamed Siyad Barre	Italian, Arabic, English	None
South Africa	Xhosa, Zulu, Sotho, Europeans, Colcreds, Asians	*Head of State:* Nicolaas Diederichs *Prime Minister:* Balthazar Johannes Vorster	Afrikaans, English	The National Party, The United Party, The Progressive Reform Party
Sudan	Beja, Nuba, Arab, Nuer	*President:* Jaafar M. al-Numeiri	Arabic	Sudan Socialist Union
Swaziland	Swazi, Europeans	*Head of State:* King Sobhuza II *Prime Minister:* Makhosini Dlamini	English	None
Tanzania, United Republic of	Sukuma, Meru, Chagga, Wanyakyusa, Masai	*President:* Julius K. Nyerere *Prime Minister:* Rashidi Kawawa	Swahili, English	Tanganyika African National Union (TANU)
Togo	Kabrai-Losso, Ewe, Aga-Quatehi	*President:* Gnassingbe Eyadema	French	None
Tunisia	Arab, Berber	*President:* Habib Bourguiba *Prime Minister:* Hedi Nouira	Arabic, French	Destourian Socialist Party
Uganda	Baganda, Iteso, Ankole, Busoga	*President:* Idi Amin	English, Swahili	None

African States 1976—Politics (cont.)

Country	Major Ethnic Groups	Head of State & Head of Government	Official Language	Political Parties
Upper Volta	Mossi, Bobo	*President:* Sangoule Lamizana	French	None
Zaire Republic	Bakongo, Baluba, Bayeke, Lunda	*President:* Mobutu Sese Seko	French	The Popular Movement of the Revolution (MPR)
Zambia	Barotse (Lozi), Bemba, Lunda, Ngoni, Bisa	*President:* Kenneth D. Kaunda	English	United National Independence Party

African Dependencies 1976—Economy

Country	Capital City	Area (thousands of sq. miles)	Population (thousands)	Gross Nat'l Product (millions of dollars)	Per Capita Income	Present Political Status
Ceuta and Melilla	None	—	20	52.0	315	Department of Spain
The French Territory of Afars and Issas	Djibouti	9	230	80	300	French Overseas Territory. Independence planned for 1977.
Namibia (South West Africa)	Windhoek	318	890	400	615	*De jure* under United Nations, *de facto* part of the Republic of South Africa
Rhodesia	Salisbury	150	6,600	2,493	406	British Colony in Rebellion
Western Sahara	El Aaiun	120	80	Not available	Not available	Divided between Moroccan and Mauritanian control. Polisario, backed by Algeria, attempting to gain independence.

AFRICAN DEPENDENCIES 1976—POLITICS

Country	Major Ethnic Groups	Official Language	Head of State & Government	Political Parties or Movements
Ceuta and Melilla	Mostly Spanish	Spanish	Controlled by Metropolitan Spain	
The French Territory of the Afars and Issas	Afar/Danakils Somalis, Issa, Ishaak	French	*Prime Minister:* Abdullah Mohammed Kamil	Afar Democratic Rally, Democratic Union of Issa, National Independence Union, African People's League for Independence
Namibia (South-West Africa)	Ovambo, Damara, Herero, Hottentot, Okavango, Whites	English, Afrikaans	*Administrator* (appointed by the government of the Republic of South Africa): J.G.H. Van der Wath	*White:* The Nationalist Party, Federal Party of South West Africa *Black:* South-West African People's Organization, National Convention of Freedom Parties
Rhodesia	Mashona, Matabele, Europeans	English	*President:* J. Wrathall *Prime Minister:* Ian Smith	*White:* Rhodesian Front, Rhodesia Party *Black:* African National Council Zimbabwe African National Union Zimbabwe African People's Union

African and World Totals

Area	Population Estimate (Millions)	Rate of Population Growth (Annual, Percent)	Urban Population (Percent)	Population Projection to 2000 (Millions)
Northern Africa	100	2.6	37	190
Western Africa	120	2.6	17	242
Central Africa	47	2.4	22	88
Eastern Africa	117	2.8	12	238
Southern Africa	29	2.7	44	56
Africa Total	413	2.6	23	815
World Total	4,019	1.8	38	6,214

Sources: Agency for International Development, *Africa: Economic Growth Trends* (Statistics and Reports Division, Office of Financial Management, Bureau for Program and Management Services, March 1976); AID, *Selected Economic Data for the Less Developed Countries*, July 1974; AID, *Gross National Product: Estimates for Non-Communist Countries for 1973*, July 1975; United Nations, *Monthly Bulletin of Statistics*, May 1976; *Africa Report*, 1975; *Area Handbooks* for various African countries published by U.S. Government Printing Office; African Embassies Washington, D.C.; *World Population Data Sheet of the Population Reference Bureau, Inc.*, 1976.

Readings

Chapter 2. Political Systems in Africa

ALEXANDRE, PIERRE, ed. *French Perspectives in African Studies.* London: Oxford University Press, for the International African Institute, 1973. Essays, some political, but most anthropological.

BALANDIER, GEORGES. *Daily Life in the Kingdom of the Kongo: From the Sixteenth to the Eighteenth Century.* Trans. HELEN WEAVER. New York: Pantheon, 1968. Precolonial kingdom under influence of Portuguese.

BLOCH, MAURICE. *Political Language and Oratory in Traditional Society.* New York: Academic Press, 1975.

CRUISE O'BRIEN, DONAL B. *The Mourides of Senegal: The Political and Economic Organization of an Islamic Brotherhood.* Oxford: Clarendon Press, 1971. Best study of origins of a religious-political-economic movement.

DAVIDSON, BASIL. *The Lost Cities of Africa.* Boston and Toronto: Little, Brown & Co., 1959. Early assertion of richness of African history.

DIAGNE, PATHÉ. *Pouvoir, politique traditionnel en Afrique occidentale.* Paris: Présence Africaine, 1967. On Senegal.

DIOP, MAJHEMOUT. *Histoire des classes sociales dans l'Afrique de l'ouest, I: Le Mali.* Paris: François Maspero, 1971. Important Marxist approach. Study of slavery.

EMERSON, RUPERT. *From Empire to Nation: The Rise to Self-Assertion of Asian and African Peoples.* Cambridge, Mass.: Harvard University Press, 1960. Basic introduction to African politics.

FORTES, M., and E. E. EVANS-PRITCHARD. *African Political Systems.* London: Oxford University Press, 1940. Basic, seminal study.

GAILEY, HARRY A. *The Road to Aba: A Study of British Administrative Policy in Eastern Nigeria.* New York: New York University Press, 1970. The Igbos and the reasons for the Aba riots of 1929.

JULY, ROBERT W. *A History of the African People.* New York: Charles Scribner's Sons, 1970. Excellent introduction; nothing on northwest Africa.

MAIR, LUCY P. *Primitive Government.* Harmondsworth, England: Penguin Books, 1962.

MAQUET, JACQUES. *Africanité traditionnelle et moderne.* Paris: Presence Africaine, 1967. Author believes black Africa quite distinct culturally from North Africa.

———. *The Premise of Inequality in Ruanda: A Study of Political Relations in a Central African Kingdom.* London: Oxford University Press, 1961. Brilliant Study of Tutsi and Hutu relations that led to revolution.

MIDDLETON, JOHN, and DAVID TAIT, eds. *Tribes Without Rulers: Studies in African Segmentary Systems.* London: Routledge & Kegan Paul, 1958. Companion volume to Fortes and Evans-Pritchard, but dealing with political systems without governments.

PADEN, JOHN, and EDWARD W. SOJA, eds. *The African Experience.* 2 vols. Evanston, Ill.: Northwestern University Press, 1970. Huge collection of short essays for teachers.

SANDERS, EDITH R. "The Hamitic Hypothesis: Its Origin and Functions in Time Perspective," *Journal of African History*, 10, no. 4 (1969): 521–32. Origins of racist attitudes toward Africa.

SENGHOR, LÉOPOLD SÉDAR. *Les fondements de l'Africanité ou Négritude et Arabité*. Paris: Présence Africaine, 1967. Diversity between North and Middle Africa, but basic unity.

SKINNER, ELLIOTT P. *The Mossi of the Upper Volta: The Political Development of a Sudanese People*. Stanford, Calif.: Stanford University Press, 1964.

THOMPSON, LEONARD. *Survival in Two Worlds: Moshoeshoe of Lesotho, 1786–1870*. New York: Oxford University Press.

VANSINA, JAN. *The Kingdoms of the Savanna*. Madison: University of Wisconsin Press, 1966. Area of Zaïre, Rwanda, Burundi.

WATERBURY, JOHN. *The Commander of the Faithful: The Moroccan Political Elite —A Study in Segmented Politics*. New York: Columbia University Press, 1970. Excellent analysis of Moroccan traditional politics.

Chapter 3. Colonialism and African Politics

ABBAS, FERHAT. *La nuit coloniale*. Paris: Julliard, 1962. Personal reflections about colonialism by early nationalist.

AJAYI, J. F. ADE, and IAN ESPIE, eds. *A Thousand Years of West African History: A Handbook for Teachers and Students*. Ibadan: Ibadan University Press & Nelson, 1965. Important selections dealing with colonial period.

AVINERI, SHLOMO. *Karl Marx on Colonialism and Modernization*. New York: Doubleday, 1968. Alleges Marx saw colonialism as a modernizing force.

BRUNSCHWIG, HENRI. *French Colonialism 1871–1914*. Trans. WILLIAM G. BROWN. New York: Praeger, 1966. Examination of French nationalism as a source of colonial expansion.

BUELL, RAYMOND LESLIE. *The Native Problem in Africa*. London: Frank Cass, 1965. Classic work. Much information about African society under colonialism.

COHEN, WILLIAM B. *Rulers of Empire: The French Colonial Service in Africa*. Stanford, Calif.: Hoover Institution, 1971. Analysis of administrators and history of colonial service.

CÉSAIRE, AIMÉ. *Discours sur le colonialisme*. Paris: Présence Africaine 1955. West Indian poet denounces colonialism.

COLE, PATRICK. *Modern and Traditional Elites in the Politics of Lagos*. New York: Cambridge University Press, 1975. Yoruba chiefs and professionals compete with each other and then against the British, 1890s–1920s.

DANQUAH, JOSEPH B. *Self-Help and Expansion: A Review of the Work and Aims of the Youth Conference*. Accra: n.p., 1943. Point of view of Ghanaian elite.

DELAVIGNETTE, ROBERT. *Freedom and Authority in French West Africa*. London: Frank Cass, 1968. Liberal French view.

GABRE-SELASSIE, ZEWDE. *Yohannes IV: A Political Biography*. Oxford: Clarendon Press, 1975. Tigrean leader began unification of Ethiopia before Menelik II.

GIFFORD, PROSSER, and WILLIAM ROGER LOUIS, eds. with assistance of ALISON SMITH. *Britain and Germany in Africa: Imperial Rivalry and Colonial Rule*. New Haven and London: Yale University Press, 1967. Rich collection of essays.

GIRARDET, RAOUL. *L'Idée coloniale en France, 1871–1962*. Paris: La Table Ronde, 1972. Origins of colonialism in France.

GUÈYE, LAMINE. *Itinéraire Africain*. Paris: Présence Africaine, 1966. Autobiography of member of Senegalese elite.

KHADDURI, MAJID. *Modern Libya: A Study in Political Development.* Baltimore: Johns Hopkins Press, 1963. Best study available.

MANGONGO-NZAMBI, ANDRÉ. "La délimitation des frontières du Gabon (1885–1911)," *Cahiers d'Etudes Africaines,* 9, no. 33, (1969): 5–53. Frontier between Cameroun, Guinea, and Gabon.

MASON, PHILIP. *Patterns of Dominance.* London: Oxford University Press, for the Institute of Race Relations, 1970. Colonialism seen as one of many forms of dominance.

MOORE, CLEMENT HENRY. *Politics in North Africa: Algeria, Morocco, and Tunisia.* Boston: Little, Brown & Co., 1970. Important section on effects of colonial rule.

MORTIMER, EDWARD. *France and the Africans 1944–1960: A Political History.* New York: Walker, 1970. African participation in French politics during Fourth Republic.

OBICHERE, BONIFACE I. *West African States and European Expansion: The Dahomey-Niger Hinterland, 1885–1898.* New Haven and London: Yale University Press, 1971.

OGOT, B. A., and J. A. KIERAN, eds. *Zamani.* Nairobi: EAPH and Longmans, 1968. East Africa.

SURET-CANALE, JEAN. *Afrique Noire: L'Ere coloniale 1900–1945.* Paris: Editions Sociales, 1964. Marxist approach; full of information.

THOM, DERRICK J. *The Niger-Nigeria Boundary, 1890–1906: A Study of Ethnic Frontiers and a Colonial Boundary,* Papers in International Studies, Africa Series, Number 23. Athens: Ohio University Center for International Studies, 1975.

TURNER, VICTOR, ed. *Colonialism in Africa 1870–1960.* Vol. III: *Profiles of Change: African Society and Colonial Rule.* Cambridge, England: Cambridge University Press, 1971.

WEINSTEIN, BRIAN. *Eboué.* New York: Oxford University Press, 1972. Biography of a black French governor in Equatorial Africa.

———. "Eboué and the Chiefs: Perceptions of Power in Early Oubangui-Chari," *Journal of African History,* 11, no. 1 (1970): 107–26. Points of view of Africans and French compared.

Chapter 4. The End of Colonialism

AZIKIWE, NNAMDI. *My Odyssey: An Autobiography.* New York and Washington: Praeger, 1971. Nigeria's first President's evolution into a nationalist.

BOITEAU PIERRE. *Madagascar: Contribution à l'histoire de la nation malgache.* Paris: Editions Sociales, 1958. 1946–47 movement against French.

BURKE, EDUMUND. "Pan-Islam and Moroccan Resistance to French Colonial Penetration 1900–1912," *Journal of African History,* 13, no. 1 (1972): 97–118. Help to the Moroccan resistance from Ottoman Empire and Egypt.

CROWDER, MICHAEL, ed. *West African Resistance.* London: Hutchinson, 1971. Rich collection.

GANN, L. H., and PETER DUIGNAN, eds. *Colonialism in Africa 1870–1960.* Vol. 1. Cambridge, England: Cambridge University Press, 1969. Rich collection of writings.

IGBAFE, PHILIP A. "Western Ibo Society and Its Resistance to British Rule: The Ekumeku Movement, 1898–1911," *Journal of African History,* 12, no. 3, (1971): 441–60. Igbo opposition to transformations of their society by British.

ITOTE, WARUHIU. "The Nature of the Mau Mau Movement," in WILFRED CARTEY and MARTIN KILSON, eds., *The Africa Reader: Independent Africa.* New York: Vintage, Random, 1970, pp. 111–17. Mau Mau seen as independence movement.

JANKOWSKI, JAMES P. *Egypt's Young Rebels: Young Egypt, 1933–1952.* Stanford: Hoover Institution Press, 1975.

JOHNSON, G. WESLEY, JR. *The Emergence of Black Politics in Senegal: The Struggle for Power in the Four Communes 1900–1920.* Stanford, Calif.: Stanford University Press, for the Hoover Institution, 1971.

KENYATTA, JOMO. *Facing Mount Kenya.* New York, Vintage, Random, 1962. Autobiography and Kikuyu reaction to British.

LEVINE, VICTOR T. *Leadership Transition in Black Africa: Elite Generations and Political Succession,* Munger Africana Library Notes, Number 30, May 1975. Pasadena: California Institute of Technology, 1975. Detailed analysis of elite characteristics.

MORGENTHAU, RUTH SCHACHTER. *Political Parties in French-Speaking West Africa.* Oxford: Clarendon Press, 1964. Rise of opposition and politics in Guinea, Mali, and Ivory Coast.

NGUBANE, JORDAN KHUSH. *An African Explains Apartheid.* New York: Praeger, 1963. Important history and analysis of South African problems.

NGUGI, JAMES. *Weep Not, Child.* London: Heinemann, 1964. Novel about effects of Mau Mau.

NKRUMAH, KWAME. *Ghana: The Autobiography of Kwame Nkrumah.* New York: International Publishers, 1957. Important book by first President of Ghana and pan-Africanist.

QUANDT, WILLIAM B. *Revolution and Political Leadership: Algeria 1954–1958.* Cambridge, Mass.: MIT Press, 1969. Discussion of rise of various opposition movements in Algeria.

RABEMANANJARA, JACQUES. *Nationalisme et problème malgaches.* Paris: Présence Africaine, 1958. Statement by Malgache poet and nationalist politician.

ROTBERG, ROBERT I., and ALI A. MAZRUI, eds. *Protest and Power in Black Africa.* New York: Oxford University Press, 1970. Essays about movements opposed to colonial rule.

SEMBÈNE, OUSMANE. *Les bouts de bois de Dieu.* Paris: Amio-Dumont, 1960. Railroad strike in Senegal described in novel.

TOURÉ, SÉKOU. "African Emancipation," in PAUL E. SIGMUND, JR., ed., *The Ideologies of the Developing Nations* (New York and London: Frederick A. Praeger, 1963), pp. 155–69. Articulation of urban dweller's opposition to colonial rule.

TURTON, E. R. "Somali Resistance to Colonial Rule and the Development of Somali Political Activity in Kenya 1893–1960," *Journal of African History,* 13, no. 1 (1972): 119–38. Somali Youth Club and other organizations.

Chapter 5. Independence

ABUN-NASR, JAMIL M. "The Independence Movements in the Maghrib," *Tarikh,* 4, no. 1 (1971): 54–67.

AFRIFA, COLONEL A. A. *The Ghana Coup, 24th February 1966.* London: Cass, 1967. Justification for Nkrumah's overthrow, by participant.

BOURGES, HERVÉ. *L'Algérie à l'épreuve du pouvoir (1962–1967).* Paris: Bernard Grasset, 1967. Internal conflict and competition.

CRUISE O'BRIEN, RITA. *White Society in Black Africa: The French of Senegal.* London: Faber & Faber, 1972. Attitudes of Frenchmen today.

FANON, FRANTZ. *Toward the African Revolution: Political Essays.* New York: Grove Press, 1967. Call for complete destruction of colonial structures (pp. 95–105) and importance of Algeria as a symbol of independence (pp. 144–49).

GREENFIELD, RICHARD. *Ethiopia: A New Political History.* London: Pall Mall, 1965. One of best histories of Africa's oldest independent state.

HARBESON, JOHN W. "Land Reforms and Politics in Kenya 1954–1970," *Journal of Modern African Studies*, 9, no. 2, (August, 1971): 231–52. Failure of Kenya's government to distribute land to peasants.

KILSON, MARTIN. "The Grassroots in Ghanaian Politics," in PHILIP FOSTER and ARISTIDE R. ZOLBERG, eds., *Ghana and the Ivory Coast: Perspectives on Modernization* (Chicago: Chicago University Press, 1971), pp. 103–24. Party attempts to control local organizations.

International Monetary Fund, Surveys of African Economies: Vol. 4: *Congo-K, Malagasy Republic, Malawi, Mauritius, and Zambia.* Washington: 1971. Basic information, helpful for judgments about development.

LOFCHIE, MICHAEL F. "The Zanzibari Revolution: African Protest in a Racially Plural Society," in ROTBERG and MAZRUI, eds. *Protest and Power in Black Africa*, pp. 924–67. Africans vs. Arabs.

LOWENKOPF, MARTIN. *Politics in Liberia: The Conservative Road to Development.* Stanford: Hoover Institution Press, 1975.

MARCUM, JOHN. *Angolan Revolution.* Cambridge, Mass.: MIT Press, 1966. Sympathetic and accurate.

MICAUD, CHARLES A., with LEON CARL BROWN and CLEMENT HENRY MOORE. *Tunisia: The Politics of Modernization.* New York: Praeger, 1964. Independence movement in Tunisia.

ODINGA, OGINGA. *Not Yet Uhuru: An Autobiography.* New York: Hill & Wang, 1967. Criticism of independent Kenya by former Vice President.

OTTAWAY, DAVID, and MARINA OTTAWAY. *Algeria: The Politics of a Socialist Revolution.* Berkeley and Los Angeles: University Press, 1970. Important discussion of self-management and other socialist measures.

POTHOLM, CHRISTIAN P. *Four African Political Systems.* Englewood Cliffs, N.J.: Prentice-Hall, 1970. See Chapter 6 on Somali independence.

UKPABI, S.C. "The Independence Movement in the Sudan," *Tarikh*, 4, no. 1 (1971): 41–53. How Sudan became independent of both Great Britain and Egypt.

VATIKIOTIS, P.J., "Some Political Consequences of the 1952 Revolution in Egypt," in P. M. HOLT, ed., *Political and Social Change in Modern Egypt* (London: Oxford University Press, 1968), pp. 362–87. Author sees military as a unique form of rule.

WEEKS, JOHN F. "Wage Policy and the Colonial Legacy: A Comparative Study," *Journal of Modern African Studies*, 9, no. 3 (October, 1971): 361–88. Civil servants and soldiers want to keep colonial salary structures.

YOUNG, CRAWFORD. *Politics in the Congo: Decolonization and Independence.* Princeton, N.J.: Princeton University Press, 1965. Chapters 3, 7, 8, and 13 particularly; complicated independence period examined.

Chapter 6. Southern Africa

ADAM, HERBERT. *Modernizing Racial Domination.* Berkeley and Los Angeles: University of California Press, 1971. Excellent in-depth analysis of South African politics.

BARBER, JAMES. *South Africa's Foreign Policy, 1945–1970*. New York and London: Oxford University Press, 1973. The determinants of South African foreign policy.

BOWMAN, LARRY W. *Politics in Rhodesia*. Cambridge, Mass.: Harvard University Press, 1973. An excellent analysis of Rhodesian society and politics.

BUNTING, BRIAN. *The Rise of the South African Reich*. Rev. ed. Baltimore: Penguin Books, 1969. Excellent description and analysis of *apartheid*.

DAVIS, JOHN A., and JAMES K. BAKER. eds. *Southern Africa in Transition*. New York: Praeger, 1966. Excellent on developments and problems up to 1963.

HALL, RICHARD. *The High Price of Principles: Kaunda and the White South*. London: Hodder & Stoughton, 1969. Zambia's role.

HANCE, WILLIAM A., ed. *Southern Africa and the United States*. New York: Columbia University Press, 1968.

HARVEY, CHARLES, et al. *Foreign Investment in South Africa: The Policy Debate*, Study Project on External Investment in South Africa and Namibia. Uppsala: Africa Publications Trust, 1975. An excellent comprehensive analysis.

HORRELL, MURIEL. A *Survey of Race Relations in South Africa*. South African Institute of Race Relations. Berkeley and Los Angeles: University of California Press, 1974.

KUPER, LEO. *An African Bourgeoisie: Race, Class and Politics in South Africa*. New Haven, Conn.: Yale University Press, 1965. Outstanding social and political and analysis.

LEGUM, COLIN, and MARGARET LEGUM. "South Africa in the Contemporary World," *Issue*, vol. 3, no. 3 (African Studies Association, 1973). An excellent analysis of twenty-five years of *apartheid*.

LUTHULI, ALBERT. *Let My People Go*. New York: McGraw-Hill, 1962. African nationalism and resistance in South Africa.

MANDELA, NELSON. *No Easy Walk to Freedom*. New York: Basic Books, 1965. An African on resistance to *apartheid*.

MARQUARD, LEO. *Peoples and Policies of South Africa*. 4th ed. London: Oxford University Press, 1969. Excellent combination of historical background and contemporary situation.

MATTHEWS, A. S. *Law, Order and Liberty in South Africa*. Berkeley and Los Angeles: University of California Press, 1973. *Apartheid* legislation.

MONDLANE, EDUARDO. *The Struggle for Mozambique*. Baltimore: Penguin Books, 1969. African resistance from within.

NIELSEN, WALDEMAR A. *African Battle Line: American Policy Choices in Southern Africa*. New York: Harper & Row, 1965. International implications of southern African situation.

SACHS, ALBIE. *Justice in South Africa*. Berkeley and Los Angeles: University of California Press, 1974. A cogent, well-written analysis of the role of the judicial system in maintaining white supremacy.

PATON, ALAN. *Hofmeyr*. Abridged ed. New York: Charles Scribner's sons, 1965. Life and ideas of a white South African liberal.

PIKE, JOHN G. *Malawi: A Political and Economic History*. New York: Praeger, 1968. Political developments in a historical context.

POTHOLM, CHRISTIAN, P. *Swaziland: The Dynamics of Political Modernization*. Berkeley and Los Angeles: University of California Press, 1972. Political developments since World War II.

POTHOLM, CHRISTIAN P., and RICHARD DALE, eds. *Southern Africa in Perspective*. New York: The Free Press, 1972.

ROTBERG, ROBERT I. "The Modern Emergence of Malawi and Zambia," in STANLEY DIAMOND and FRED G. BURKE, eds., *The Transformation of East Africa: Studies in Political Anthropology* (New York: Basic Books, 1966).

ROUX, EDWARD. *Time Longer Than Rope*. 2d. ed. Madison: University of Wisconsin Press, 1964. Excellent history of African resistance in South Africa.

RUBIN, LESLIE. *Apartheid and the International Community*. New York: United Nations, Unit on Apartheid, No. 11/73, 1973. International implications of internal opposition.

———. *Apartheid in Practice*. New York: United Nations, OPI/553, 1976. Description of *apartheid* laws.

RUBIN, NEVILLE. "Botswana's Last Exit to Freedom," *Venture*, vol. 22, no. 8 (September, 1970). Botswana's road link to Zambia.

———. *Law, Race and Color in South Africa*. New York: United Nations, Unit on Apartheid, no. 19/73, 1973. Discrimination and repression within a system of law.

NOLUTSHUNGU, SAM C. *South Africa in Africa: A Study in Ideology and Foreign Policy*. New York: Africana Publishing Company, 1975. A valuable analysis of South Africa's relations with the rest of Africa up to 1973.

STEVENS, RICHARD P. *Lesotho, Botswana and Swaziland*. New York: Praeger, 1967. A comprehensive historical and political study.

VAMBE, LAWRENCE. *An Ill-Fated People*. London: Heinemann, 1972. Historical background to contemporary Rhodesia.

VIGNE, RANDOLPH. *A Dwelling Place of Our Own: The Story of the Namibian Nation*. London: International Defense and Aid Fund for Southern Africa, 1973.

WALSHE, PETER. *The Rise of Nationalism in South Africa*. Berkeley and Los Angeles: University of California Press, 1971. An excellent history of the origin and development of the African National Congress through 1952.

WELSH, DAVID. "Capital Punishment in South Africa," in ALAN MILNER, ed., *African Penal Systems* (New York: Praeger, 1969). South Africa's world record in executions.

WILSON, MONICA, and LEONARD THOMPSON, eds. *The Oxford History of South Africa*. New York: Oxford University Press, vol. 1, 1969, vol. 2, 1971. Background and developments until 1966.

Chapter 7. "Modernization" in Independent Africa

AMIN, SAMIR. *Le Développement inégal: Essai sur les formations sociales du capitalisme périphérique*. Paris: Les Editions de Minuit, 1973. Important study of economic barriers to development.

ASHFORD, DOUGLAS E. "The Politics of Rural Mobilization in North Africa," *Journal of Modern African Studies*, 7, no. 2, (1969): 187–202. Cooperative movement in Tunisia.

CARTER, GWENDOLEN M., ed. *National Unity and Regionalism in Eight African States*. Ithaca, N.Y.: Cornell University Press, 1966. Good collection of chapters about little-discussed countries.

COHEN, ABNER. *Custom and Politics in Urban Africa: A Study of Hausa Migrants in Yoruba Towns*. Berkeley and Los Angeles: University of California Press, 1969. Economic foundations of ethnicity.

COLEMAN, JAMES S. ed. *Education and Political Development*. Princeton, N.J.: Princeton University Press, 1965. Excellent collection.

DALTON, GEORGE. "History, Politics, and Economic Development in Liberia," *Journal of Economic History*, 25, no. 4, (December, 1965): 569–91. Social organization keeps country underdeveloped.

DEUTSCH, KARL W. *Nationalism and Social Communication: An Inquiry into the Foundations of Nationality.* New York: The Technology Press, John Wiley, 1953; reprint Cambridge: MIT Press, 1962. Models for study of nation-building.

DEUTSCH, KARL W., and WILLIAM F. FOLTZ, eds. *Nation-Building.* New York: Atherton, 1963. Good collection of essays, theory and examples.

DUMONT, RENÉ. *False Start in Africa.* 2d ed. New York: Praeger, 1969. Criticism of most policies of independent governments.

GORDON, DAVID C. *Women of Algeria.* Cambridge, Mass.: Harvard University Press, 1968. Disappointments after revolution.

GOUELLAIN, RENÉ. *Douala: Ville et Histoire.* Paris: Institut d'Ethnologie, Museé de l'Homme, 1975.

HOROWITZ, DONALD L. "Multiracial Politics in the New States: Toward a Theory of Conflict," in ROBERT J. JACKSON and MICHAEL B. STEIN, eds., *Issues in Comparative Politics* (New York: St. Martins Press, 1971), pp. 164–80. Reasons for elite ethnicity.

———. "Three Dimensions of Ethnic Politics," *World Politics*, January, 1971, pp. 232–44. Analysis of dynamic group identity.

HUNTINGTON, SAMUEL P. "Political Development and Political Decay," *World Politics*, 17 (April, 1965): 386–430. Distinctions made between growth and development.

JOHNSON, WILLARD R. *The Cameroon Federation: Political Integration in a Fragmentary Society.* Princeton, N.J.: Princeton University Press, 1970. Discussion of theories of integration and detailed discussion of problems in Cameroun.

KOFF, DAVID, and GEORGE VAN DER MUHLL. "Political Socialization in Kenya and Tanzania: A Comparative Analysis," *Journal of Modern African Studies*, 5, no. 1, (1967): 13–52. Attitudes of students surveyed.

LEMARCHAND, RENÉ. "The Limits of Self-Determination: The Case of the Katanga Secession," *American Political Science Review*, 56, no. 2, (June, 1962): 404–16. Reasoned analysis of why some secessions are wrong.

———. *Rwanda and Burundi.* New York: Praeger, 1970. Brilliant discussion of change and revolution.

MAFEJE, ARCHIE. "The Ideology of 'Tribalism,'" *Journal of Modern African Studies*, 9, no. 2 (1971): 253–61. Developing classes will be more important than ethnic divisions.

MERCIER, PAUL. "Remarques sur la signification du 'Tribalisme' actuel en Afrique noire," *Cahiers Internationaux de Sociologie*, July–December, 1961, pp. 61-80. Ethnicity and other factors that divide and unite.

MITTELMAN, JAMES H. *Ideology and Politics in Uganda: From Obote to Amin.* Ithaca: Cornell University Press, 1975.

NASSER, GAMAL ABDEL. *Egypt's Liberation: The Philosophy of the Revolution.* Washington: Public Affairs Press, 1955.

ROTHCHILD, DONALD. "Ethnic Inequalities in Kenya," *Journal of Modern African Studies*, 7, no. 4 (1969): 689–711. Kikuyu dominance.

———. *Racial Bargaining in Independent Kenya: A Study of Minorities and Decolonization*, for the Institute of Race Relations. London, New York: Oxford University Press, 1973.

ROUCH, JEAN. "Migrations au Ghana: Enquête 1953–1955," *Journal de la Société des Africanistes*, vol. 31, nos. 1 and 2 (1956). Important study of "supertribalization" in cities.

SENGHOR, LÉOPOLD SÉDAR. *Nation et voie africaine du socialisme.* Paris: Presence Africaine, 1961. President Senghor's view of nation-building.
WELCH, CLAUDE, ed. *Political Modernization: A Reader in Comparative Political Change.* Belmont, Calif.: Wadsworth, 1967. Essays plus introductory synthesis.
WEINSTEIN, BRIAN. *Gabon: Nation-Building on the Ogooué.* Cambridge, Mass.: MIT Press, 1967. Details on Gabon and model proposed for study of nation-building.

Chapter 8. Attempted Solutions

ASHFORD, DOUGLAS ELLIOTT. *Morocco-Tunisia: Politics and Planning.* Syracuse, N.Y.: Syracuse University Press, 1965.
BERG, ELLIOTT J. "Socialism and Economic Development in Tropical Africa," *Quarterly Journal of Economics,* 78, no. 4 (November, 1964): 549–73. An economist's approach.
BERG, ELLIOTT J., and JEFFREY BUTLER. "Trade Unions," in COLEMAN and ROSBERG, eds., *Political Parties and National Integration* (see below), pp. 340–81. Absorption of trade unions by parties.
COLEMAN, JAMES S. *Nigeria: Background to Nationalism.* Berkeley and Los Angeles: University of California Press, 1958. Best background on Nigerian politics.
COLEMAN, JAMES S., and CARL G. ROSBERG JR. eds. *Political Parties and National Integration in Tropical Africa.* Berkeley and Los Angeles: University of California Press, 1964. Good collection on parties.
CRUISE O'BRIEN, DONAL B. *Saints and Politicians: Essays in the Organization of a Senegalese Peasant Society.* New York: Cambridge University Press, 1975. Views of masses and elites.
ENGELS, FRIEDRICH. *Socialism—Utopian and Scientific.* Trans. EDWARD AVELING. New York: International Publishers, 1935. Clear statement of meaning of Marxist analysis.
FOSTER, PHILIP, and ARISTIDE R. ZOLBERG, eds. *Ghana and the Ivory Coast: Perspectives on Modernization.* Chicago: Chicago University Press, 1971. Comparison of socialist and capitalist approaches.
FRIEDLAND, WILLIAM H., and CARL G. ROSEBERG, JR., eds. *African Socialism.* Stanford, Calif.: Stanford University Press, Hoover Institution, 1964. General essays.
HUNTINGTON, SAMUEL P., and CLEMENT H. MOORE, eds. *Authoritarian Politics in Modern Society: The Dynamics of Established One-Party Systems.* New York and London: Basic Books, 1970. Examples from all over the world. Africa set in a larger context.
KILSON, MARTIN L., JR. "Authoritarian and Single-Party Tendencies in African Politics," *World Politics,* 15, no. 2, (January, 1963): 262–94. General explanation for development of single parties.
———. *Political Change in a West African State.* Cambridge, Mass.: Harvard University Press, 1966. Politics in Sierra Leone.
MAGUIRE, G. ANDREW. *Toward 'Uhuru' in Tanzania: The Politics of Participation.* Cambridge, England: Cambridge University Press, 1969. History of evolution toward one-party state in Tanzania.
MORGENTHAU, RUTH SCHACHTER. "African Socialism: Declaration of Ideological Independence," *Africa Report,* 8, no. 5 (May, 1963): 3–6. Why Africans emphasize the "African" part of socialism.
NKRUMAH, KWAME. *Consciencism.* New York: Monthly Review Press, 1964. Ideology for Africa.

NYERERE, JULIUS K. *Ujamaa: Essays on Socialism.* Dar es Salaam: Oxford University Press, 1968. Explanations by President of Tanzania.
PADMORE, GEORGE. *Pan-Africanism or Communism.* New York: Roy, 1956. Important statement by West Indian who worked with Nkrumah.
POTEKHIN, I. I. "On 'African Socialism,'" *International Affairs* (Moscow), January, 1963, pp. 71–79. The Russian view.
ROSS, MARC HOWARD. *Grass Roots in an African City: Political Behavior in Nairobi.* Cambridge, Mass.: MIT Press, 1975. Cynicism grows as the masses are left out.
SKLAR, RICHARD L. *Nigerian Political Parties: Power in an Emergent African Nation.* Princeton, N.J.: Princeton University Press, 1963. Nigerian party development.
SPIRO, HERBERT J. *Politics in Africa: Prospects South of the Sahara.* Englewood Cliffs, N.J.: Prentice-Hall, 1962.
———. ed. *Africa: The Primacy of Politics.* New York, Random House, 1966.
STANILAND, MARTIN. *The Lions of Dagbon: Political Change in Northern Ghana.* New York: Cambridge University Press, 1975. Views of masses, on whom development ultimately depends.
SURET-CANALE, JEAN. *La République de Guinée.* Paris: Editions Sociales, 1970. Considerable information with a Marxist interpretation.
WELCH, CLAUDE E., JR., ed. Soldier and State in Africa. Evanston, Ill.: Northwestern University Press, 1970. Examines recent coups by military.
WELCH, CLAUDE L. "Continuity and Discontinuity in African Military Organization," *Journal of Modern African Studies,* 13, no. 2 (1975): 229–48. Precolonial, colonial, and postcolonial roles of the military.
ZARTMAN, I. WILLIAM. "Europe and Africa: Decolonization or Dependency?," *Foreign Affairs,* 54, no. 2 (January 1976): 325–43. Shows increasing real independence of Africa. Disputes neocolonial ideas.
ZOLBERG, ARISTIDE R. *Creating Political Order: The Party-States of West Africa.* Chicago: Rand-McNally, 1966. How single parties come into being and operate.
———. *One-Party Government in the Ivory Coast.* Rev. ed. Princeton, N.J.: Princeton University Press, 1969.

Chapter 9. Adaptation of Institutions, Concepts, and Methods

APTER, DAVID E. "The Role of Traditionalism in the Political Modernization of Ghana and Uganda," in JOHN WILLIAM HANNA, ed., *Indebendent Black Africa: The Politics of Freedom.* Chicago: Rand-McNally, 1964.
BASCOM, WILLIAM R., and MELVILLE J. HERSKOVITS, eds. *Continuity and Change in African Cultures.* Chicago: University of Chicago Press, 1962.
BROKENSHA, DAVID. *Social Change in Larteh, Ghana.* Oxford: Clarendon Press, 1966.
CLIGNET, REMI P., and PHILIP FOSTER. "Potential Elites in Ghana and the Ivory Coast," in MARION E. DORO and NEWELL M. STULTZ, eds., *Governing in Black Africa.* Englewood Cliffs, N.J.: Prentice-Hall, 1970. A comparison of student aspirations.
CROWDER, MICHAEL, and OBARO IKIME. *West African Chiefs: Their Changing Status Under Colonial Rule and Independence.* New York: Africana Publishing, 1970. Historical development and contemporary problems.
DILLON, WILTON S. "Universities and Nation-Building in Africa," *Journal of Modern African Studies,* vol. 1, no. 1 (1963).
DRAKE, ST. CLAIR. "Social Change and Social Problems in Contemporary Africa," in WALTER GOLDSCHMIDT, ed., *The United States and Africa,* rev. ed. New York: Praeger, 1965, pp. 222–69. Perceptive study of response to modernizing factors.

Education and Training and Alternatives in Education in African Countries. Dar es Salaam and Uppsala: Institute of Development Studies and The Dag Hammarskjold Foundation, 1974.
EISENSTADT, S. N. "Social Change and Modernization in African Societies," in DORO and STULTZ, eds., *Governing in Black Africa.* Excellent analysis of problems of modernization.
FOSTER, PHILIP. *Education and Social Change in Ghana.* Berkeley and Los Angeles: University of California Press, 1965. Perceptive analysis of educational problems.
HERSKOVITS, MELVILLE J. *The Human Factor in Changing Africa.* New York: Knopf, 1962. Chapter on "Rediscovery and Integration: The Search for Values" provides an excellent discussion of traditional concepts.
HUNTER, GUY. *The New Societies of Tropical Africa.* London: Oxford University Press, 1962. Chapter "From the Old Culture to the New" treats transition from traditionalism to modern ideas.
KUPER,, HILDA, and LEO KUPER, eds. *African Law: Adaptation and Development.* Berkeley and Los Angeles: University of California Press, 1965. Problems of changing customary law.
KURTZ, LAURA S. *An African Education.* New York: Pageant/Poseidon, 1972. Tanzanian education and social change.
MORRISON, DAVID. *Education and Politics in Africa: The Tanzanian Case.* C. Hurst, 1974.
NYERERE, JULIUS. "Education for Self-Reliance," in NYERERE, *Ujamaa: Essays in Socialism.* Statement of Tanzania's goals.
OWUSU, MAXWELL. *Uses and Abuses of Political Power.* Chicago: University of Chicago Press, 1970. Outstanding study of chieftaincy and political change in Ghana.
RUBIN, LESLIE. "Chieftaincy and the Adaptation of Customary Law in Ghana," in JEFFREY BUTLER and A. A. CASTAGNO, eds., *Boston University Papers on Africa: Transition in African Politics.* New York: Praeger, 1967, pp. 115–34.
RUBIN, NEVILLE. "Customary Law in Southern Africa: Its Place and Scope," in J. N. D. ANDERSON, ed., *Family Law in Asia and Africa.* New York: Praeger, 1968, pp. 255–72.
RUBIN, NEVILLE, and EUGENE COTRAN, eds. *Readings in African Law.* 2 vols. London: Cass, 1970. Invaluable text and source of reference material.
University of Ife, Law Faculty, ed. *Integration of Customary and Modern Legal Systems in Africa.* New York: Africana Publishing, 1971. Papers by several experts; most useful.

Chapter 10. Cooperation Among the Independent African States

AWOLOWO, OBAFEMI AWO. *The Autobiography of Chief Obafemi Awolowo.* Cambridge, England: Cambridge University Press, 1961. Nigerian attitudes toward African unity.
AZIKIWE, NNAMDI. "The Future of Pan-Africanism," *Presence Africaine,* vol. 12, no. 40 (1962). An African assessment.
CERVENKA, ZDENEK. *The Organisation of African Unity and Its Charter.* New York: Praeger, 1969. A valuable, detailed analysis.
JOHNSON, WILLARD R. *The Cameroon Federation: Political Integration in a Fragmentary Society.* Princeton, N.J.: Princeton University Press, 1970. An excellent political analysis.
LEGUM, COLIN. *Pan-Africanism: A Short Political Guide.* Rev. ed. New York: Praeger, 1965. Excellent history and contemporary analysis.

Mezu, S. Okechukwu, ed. *The Philosophy of Pan-Africanism*. Georgetown, Va.: Georgetown University Press, 1965. Papers on historical background and contemporary problems.

Mushkat, Marion. "Problems of Political and Organizational Unity in Africa," *African Studies Review*, vol. 13, no. 2 (1970). An excellent analytical review.

Nkrumah, Kwame. *Africa Must Unite*. New York: International Publishers, 1970. Vision of a "united Africa, great and powerful."

Nye, Joseph S. Jr. *Pan-Africanism and East African Integration*. Cambridge, Mass.: Harvard University Press, 1967. An excellent analysis.

Nyerere, Julius K. "A United States of Africa," *Journal of Modern African Studies*, vol. 1, no. 1 (1963). African evaluation of prospects for African unity.

Padmore, George. *The Coming Struggle for Africa*. London: Dennis Dobson, 1956. Excellent study of events up to 1955.

———, ed. *Fifth Pan-African Congress, Manchester, England, 1945: History of the Pan-African Congresses*. 2d ed. London: Hammersmith Bookshop, 1963. An invaluable record of source materials.

Rubin, Leslie. "The Organization of African Unity: Machinery, Problems, and Prospects," in Mezu, ed. *Philosophy of Pan-Africanism* (see above). Analysis of structure and significance.

Rubin, Neville. *Cameroun: An African Federation*. New York: Praeger, 1971. An excellent analysis of political and constitutional problems.

Saenz, Paul. "The Organization of African Unity in the Subordinate African Regional System," *African Studies Review*, vol. 13, no. 2 (1970).

Timothy, E. Bankole. "African Personality: A Cultural Evaluation," in *Africa in the Seventies* (London: The Royal Africa Society, 1970). A contemporary African assessment.

Wallerstein, Immanuel. *Africa: The Politics of Unity*. New York: Random House, 1967. An excellent survey and analysis.

Williams, Maurice J. "The Aid Programs of the OPEC Countries," *Foreign Affairs*, 54, no. 2 (January 1976): 308–24.

Woronoff, Jon. "African Unity: The First Ten Years," *Africa Report*, May–June, 1973. A review of achievements and failures.

Chapter 11. Africa in the World Context

Abelin, Pierre. *La Politique Française de Coopération*. Paris: La Documentation Française, 1975. Shows change in French orientation.

Bauer, P. T., and B. S. Yamey. *The Economics of Underdeveloped Countries*. London: James Nisbet, 1957; reprint, New York: Cambridge University Press, n.d. The problems of underdevelopment.

Bowles, Chester. *Africa's Challenge to America*. Berkeley and Los Angeles: University of California Press, 1956. The importance of Africa to the United States.

Brzezinski, Zbigniew, ed. *Africa and the Communist World*. Stanford, Calif.: Stanford University Press, 1963. The impact of Communism on the independent states of Africa.

Dumoga, John. *Africa Between East and West*. London: Bodley Head, 1969. Impact of international affairs on Africa.

Emerson, Rupert. *Africa and United States Policy*. Englewood Cliffs, N.J.: Prentice-Hall, 1967. An excellent analysis.

Hadsel, Fred L. "Africa and the World: Nonalignment Reconsidered," *The Annals*, vol. 371 (1967).

HEVI, EMMANUEL JOHN. *The Dragon's Embrace: The Chinese Communists and Africa.* New York: Praeger, 1967. An African student's experiences in Communist China.

JONES, J. D. F. "Post-Ottawa Thoughts," *Commonwealth* (Royal Commonwealth Society, London), December, 1973–January, 1974.

KILSON, MARTIN (ed.). *New States in the Modern World.* Cambridge, Mass.: Harvard University Press, 1975.

LARKIN, BRUCE D. *China and Africa.* Berkeley and Los Angeles: University of California Press, 1971. Africa-China relations since 1949.

MCKAY, VERNON. *Africa in World Politics.* New York: Harper & Row, 1963. An excellent survey.

———. *African Diplomacy: Studies in the Determinants of Foreign Policy.* New York: Praeger, 1966.

———. "Southern Africa and Its Implications for American Policy," in HANCE, ed., *Southern Africa and United States* (see under Chapter 6). Perceptive analysis of American policy toward southern Africa.

MAZRUI, ALI A., and HASU PATEL. *Africa in World Affairs: The Next Thirty Years.* New York: Third Press, 1973. Assessment of Africa's future international role.

NIELSEN, WALDEMAR A. *The Great Powers and Africa.* New York: Praeger, 1969. The international factor in the development of independent black Africa.

NKRUMAH, KWAME. *Neo-Colonialism: The Last Stage of Imperialism.* London: Nelson, 1965. Attributes Africa's poverty and weakness to neo-colonialism.

QUAISON-SACKEY, ALEX. "Africa and the United Nations," in PETER JUDD, ed., *African Independence* (New York: Dell, 1962). An African conception of the United Nations.

RUBINSTEIN, ALVIN Z. (ed.). *Soviet and Chinese Influence in the Third World.* New York: Praeger, 1975.

SCALAPINO, ROBERT A. "Sino-Soviet Competition in Africa," *Foreign Affairs*, vol. 42, no. 4 (1964). An excellent analysis.

SKLAR, RICHARD. *Corporate Power in an African State: The Political Impact of Multinational Mining Companies in Zambia.* Berkeley: University of California Press, 1975. Relates current general research to Africa.

Index

Abako party, 88
Abbas, Ferhat, 45, 81–82
Abboud, Ibrahim, 253
Acheampong, Colonel, 223
Achebe, Chinua, 212
Achimota College (Ghana), 45
Adams College, 80
Adjei, Ako, 240
Adoula, Cyrille, 195
Africa Must Unite (Nkrumah), 273
African National Congress: Rhodesia, 138–39; South Africa, 126–29, 236, 238, 255, 296; and TANU, 188; Zambia, 87
African Trade Union Confederation (ATUC), 244
Afrifa, Colonel A. A., 166, 209
Afrikaans, 111
Afrikaners, 89, 112, 116, 123
Afro-Shirazi party, 102
Aggrey, J., 82
Aguiyi-Ironsi, General, 174
Ahidjo, Ahmadou, 262
Ahomadegbe, Justin, 25
aid, foreign, 95, 266, 287
Akan, 52
Aku, 31, 48
Alawite dynasty, 14, 24, 37
Algeria, 27, 34, 38, 43, 46, 48–54, 56, 60–62, 64, 70, 77, 80–82, 87, 92–97, 99–101, 103, 104, 107, 140 149, 164, 166, 176, 177, 179, 181, 185–87, 189–90, 195, 197, 200, 205, 208, 214, 215, 234, 241–42, 246, 250, 254–55, 272, 274, 275, 296, 301
Algerian workers in France, 207
All-African People's Conference (AAPC), 94, 217, 237–39, 243, 247
All-African People's Organization (AAPO), 240, 272
All-African Trade Union Federation (AATUF), 243–44
Amba political system, 11, 19–21
Amin, General Idi, 25, 166, 176, 250, 259

Amin, Samir, 183–84
Andom, Aman, 195
Anglophones and Francophones, 5, 57, 97, 211, 237, 242, 258, 260, 262, 266, 273–76, 280, 301
Angola, 4, 27, 29, 31, 34, 44, 51, 52, 57, 61, 69, 80, 95, 99, 101, 104, 130, 136, 144, 145, 156, 169, 170, 177, 183, 185, 188, 200, 247, 248, 250, 253, 254, 264, 292, 294, 297, 302
apartheid, 97, 109–35, 141, 144–46, 264, 298; Commonwealth and, 280–81; future of, 144; international reaction to, 132–34; opposition to, 111, 117–18, 122–23, 126–29, 141, 274, 286, 303, 304; United Nations and, 133–34, 145–47, 288
Arabs, 4, 5, 13, 18, 29, 33, 34, 72, 102, 149, 153, 168, 176, 180, 194, 198, 215–16, 234–35, 237, 269, 298
Armah Ayi K., 209, 212
Arusha Declaration, 167, 197, 302
Ashanti, 4, 11, 15–17, 37, 42, 52, 70, 104, 166, 171, 203, 217–19
Assimilation: and "association," 42–44, 46; in nation building, 154, 160; in Senegal, 73–74
Atlantic Charter, 80
Awolowo, Chief Obafemi, 88, 174
Azikiwe, Nnamdi, 82, 93, 173, 174, 211, 234, 242

Baganda, 4, 25, 37, 42, 96, 153, 164, 206
Bakongo, 29, 51, 62, 88, 169, 177
Balandier, Georges, 33
Balewa, Al Hadj Sir Abubakar Tafawa, 23–24, 173, 174, 242, 243, 245
Balozi, 11, 37, 52, 168–69
Bamiléké, 73
Banda, 11, 47, 157
Banda, Dr. Hastings Kamuzu, 137, 211, 230, 234, 303
Bandung Conference, 79, 168, 268, 294
Bangassou, Sultan, 67

Bantu areas, 116–19, 165
Bantu Authorities System, 117–18, 120
Bantu Homelands Constitution Act, 120
Batéké, Kingdom of, 27
Béhanzin, 83
Bello, Al Hadj Sir Amadu, 23–24, 173, 174
Ben Bella, Ahmed, 180
Ben Salah, Ahmed, 180
Benti, Teferi, 195
Berbers, 13, 53, 149, 157, 166, 176
Berlin Conference, 31
Biafra, 42, 173, 175, 254, 261, 293
Biffot, Laurent, 163
Binger, Louis, 33
black Americans, 145–46, 287–88
Blyden, Dr. Edward, 231
Bomani, Paul, 192, 193
Botswana, 25, 31, 97, 109, 110, 129, 143, 149, 177, 225, 275, 296
Boumedienne, Houari, 195, 202, 235
Bourguiba, Habib, 24, 26, 88, 107, 211
Brazzaville Conference (1944), 64
Brazzaville Group, 241–42
Broederbond, 112
Buganda, 25, 37, 40, 42, 55, 97
Bunyoro, 21
bureaucracy: Africanization of, 275; influence of colonialism on, 57–59; in Morocco, 14
Burundi, 24, 25, 40, 149, 177, 195, 200, 206, 260, 296
Busia, Dr. Kofi, 209, 221, 223
Buthelezi, Chief Gatsha, 26, 121
Byrd, Harry F., 289

Cabral, Amilcar, 82, 88, 101, 186
Cabral, Luis, 186, 197
Caetano, Marcello, 130
Cameroun, 40, 42, 54–57, 61, 62, 73, 93, 94, 101, 104, 105, 107, 157, 165, 170, 171, 173, 183, 191, 206, 214, 241, 250, 254, 258, 262–63, 274, 296
Cape Verde, 5, 48, 88, 101
Casablanca Group, 5, 241–42, 245, 270
Casely Hayford, J. E., 233–34
Central African Republic, 4, 11, 22, 37, 47, 56, 60, 61, 67, 71, 149, 153, 157, 171, 176, 177, 183, 185, 195, 208, 229, 241, 260, 294, 296
centralization: colonialism and, 52–60; examples of, 13–19; and foreign rule, 35–41; problems of, 11, 21; process of, 201–4; as revolution, 200–201
Césaire, Aimé, 96, 199, 231
Chad, see Tchad
Chagga, 11, 26, 196
Chiao Kuan-hua, 298

chiefs and chieftaincy: abolition of, 26, 219; Bamiléké and, 73; and colonialism, 41, 49, 218; and contemporary politics, 25–27, 217–23; House of Chiefs, 220–21; Ghana constitution and, 221–23; Igbo and, 71; weakening of, 218–19
Chilembwe, John, 77–78, 84
China, 27, 30, 79, 80, 97, 145, 149, 178, 190, 196, 198, 208, 255, 266, 269, 284, 289, 291, 294–99
Chou En-lai, 294, 297
churches: separatist, 78, 87; and South Africa, 146
civil service: Africanization of, 102, 273; after independence, 95, 162, 164–66, 179, 201–2; and protest against colonialism, 73; salaries in, 207; in Sudan, 81
"colonial situation," defined, 33–34
colonialism: administrative traditions of, 58–59; and African authority, 43–47; African perceptions of, 67–75; Belgian, 28, 38, 40; British, 28, 29, 35, 55, 56, 73; by country, 31–32; defined, 28; and dual economy 59–63; effects of, 29, 34, 65; French, 29, 37–39, 56; German, 32, 40, 69–70, 72; and legal dualism, 223–29; opposition to, 66–89; and reaction to nationalism, 89; resistance to, 32; and Turks, 29
Coloureds, 110, 113–14, 121–23, 126, 141
Committee of National Liberation (OAU), 250
Commonwealth, 276–83, 301, 302
Communauté, 105–7, 233
communications: in colonial period, 61–63; in nation-building, 154–57, 166
Communists: accused, 199, 209; aid from, 276; and democratic centralism, 193–94; and single-party systems, 185, 190; and South Africa, 145; weakness of, 96, 291
Comoro islands, 5, 97
Conference of Independent African States (1958), 231, 238, 240, 269
Congo-Brazzaville, 29, 48, 51, 54, 61, 88, 140, 170, 171, 183, 185, 186, 195, 199, 207, 214, 260, 295, 296
Congo-Kinshasa, see Zaïre
Conseil d'Entente, 233
Contact Zones, 156–59, 161–62
Convention People's Party, 104
cooperatives: in Ghana, 203; in Tunisia, 180
Cotran, Eugene, 224

coups, 193–96, 209, 303; in Algeria, 195; in Ghana, 223; in Uganda, 25
courts, "native," 224
Coussey Committee, 219
Creoles, 31, 48, 73, 149
Curtin, Philip D., 30

Dahl, Robert, 200
Dahomey, 25, 31, 32, 71, 83, 105, 186, 195, 206, 207, 233, 241, 250, 296, 303
Damas, Léon, 231
De Gaulle, Charles, 94, 100, 105, 106, 185, 274, 275
Delavignette, Robert, 39
democratic centralism, 193–94
Deutsch, Karl W., 8–9, 154
development: Aswan Dam and, 194; barriers to, 180–84; concepts of, 177–79; growth and, 179–80; institutionalization of, 178; result of, 299
Diagne, Blaise, 74
Diallo, Abdoulaye, 240
Diallo, Sayfoulaye, 188
Diallo, Telli, 250
Diop, David, 231
Diop, Mahjemout, 23
Djibo, Bakary, 105
Du Cann, Edward, 145
DuBois, W. E. B., 4–5, 30, 230
Dutch trade, 29

East African Association, 79
East African Common Services Organization, 235
East African Economic Community, 259
East African High Commission, 235
Eboh, Okotie, 50
Eboué, Félix, 38–39, 64
Ecole Coloniale, 58
economic relations, 298–302
economies, dual, 59–63
education, 212–15; African opposition and, 80–81; in colonial period, 44–45; and modernization, 82–83
Education for Self-reliance (Nyerere), 213
Egbe Omo Oduduwa, 88
Egypt, 3, 11, 27, 30, 33, 37, 52–54, 73, 80, 87, 90–93, 96, 97, 99, 140, 149, 152, 153, 155, 166, 168, 177, 179, 185, 194, 197, 208, 237, 240–42, 244, 251, 254, 255, 272, 293–96
Ekangani, Nzo, 250
elites: accept colonial framework, 89, 90, 201; circulation of, 210; created by colonialism, 42–46, 72–73; interests of, 148, 179, 181; nation-building and, 47–48, 148, 153; "neo-traditional," 26; in Nigeria, 107, 175; oppose Europeans, 73, 97; separatism of, 173; slave trade and, 30; study European organization, 87–88, 208–9
Equatorial Guinea, 54, 103, 104, 157, 170, 171, 296
Ethiopia, 3, 4, 5, 24–25, 28, 52, 61, 69, 80, 83, 90–91, 93, 107, 135, 153, 154, 164, 171, 176, 179, 186, 195, 196, 206, 207, 237, 242, 243, 250, 251, 253, 254, 260, 296
Ethiopianism, *see* churches, separatist
ethnic groups: colonialism and, 46–50; conflict between, 103, 152, 155, 166, 173, 174, 176–77; defined, 148–50; fears of, 204; importance of, 22–23; manipulated, 169–76; and nation-building, 152, 154, 168; in Tanzania, 189; unity of, 161, 163, 170, 171, 196
European Economic Community (EEC), 297, 301, 302
Europeans, 11–12, 66, 95, 97; in post-independence Africa, 265–66; and secession movements, 176
Evans-Pritchard, E. E., 11
Ewe, 53, 80, 166, 170, 251

Fang, 11, 42, 47, 153, 157–63, 170, 171
Fanon, Frantz, 93, 98, 197
Farouk, King, 24, 37
Federation of Rhodesia and Nyasaland, 137
Fernando Po, 103, 171
Foccart, Jacques, 274
Foncha, John Ngu, 262
Fortes, M., 11
Fouta Djalon, 14–16, 23, 26, 53, 107
France, 4, 22, 24, 28, 37, 71, 89, 95, 96, 99–101, 104–6, 134, 150, 167, 171, 175, 185, 187, 193, 197, 198, 207, 208, 211, 212, 219, 224, 233, 266, 269, 272, 274, 275, 283, 284, 286, 287, 292, 293, 299, 301
FRELIMO, 101, 188
French territory of Afars and Issas, 61, 107
Front de Libération Nationale (FLN), 82, 99–100, 187, 189, 190
Front of the Liberation of Zimbabwe (FROLIZI), 139
Fulani, 3–4, 11, 14–15, 23–24, 26–27, 36–37, 42, 51–53, 56, 71–72, 98–99, 157, 167, 173, 174, 177, 187, 196, 205

Gabon, 11, 34, 42, 47, 49, 54, 61, 76, 97, 101, 130, 153, 156–64, 170, 175, 179, 181, 183, 185, 186, 195, 197,

Gabon (cont.)
  206, 208, 228–29, 241, 251, 254, 258, 274, 276, 296
Gailey, Harry A., 21
Gambia, 31–32, 48, 53, 149, 208, 233, 251, 260, 296
Garvey, Marcus A., 230
Germany, 4, 150, 185, 231, 267, 272, 274, 301
Ghana, 4, 5, 11, 16, 24, 26, 31, 37, 42, 44, 48, 52, 55, 61, 62, 70, 74, 76, 80, 87, 93–95, 104–5, 107, 137, 140, 155–56, 166, 170–72, 175, 179, 183, 185–87, 189–92, 195, 197, 200, 203, 204, 206, 209, 216–18, 221, 223–27, 229, 237, 240–44, 246, 247, 251, 254, 260, 264, 265, 269, 271–72, 293, 296, 303
Ghana-Guinea-Mali Union, 240–41, 243, 260
Gluckman, Max, 16
Gowon, Yakubu, 174, 175, 195, 261
Grunitzky, Nicholas, 105
Guinea, 4, 11, 14–15, 25, 26, 42, 51, 53, 57, 61, 62, 74–76, 88, 93–95, 97, 98, 104–7, 131, 140, 157, 166, 177, 179, 186–93, 200, 203, 214, 220, 232, 240, 241, 243, 244, 250, 259–61, 269, 274, 275, 277, 283, 294, 296
Guinea-Bissau, 27, 44, 48, 80, 99, 101, 104, 168, 177, 185–87, 197, 202
Gusii, 181

Hamites, 3–4
Hance, William, 61
Harbeson, John W., 205
Hassan II, 24, 235
Hausa, 37, 88, 98–99, 173–75, 216, 261
Heartland Zone, 156–57, 161–63, 170
Heath, Edward, 281
Hehe, 69
Hetman, Sultan, 37–38
Hirschman, Albert O., 178
Hocine Ait Ahmed, 176
Hodgkin, Thomas, 35
Houphouët-Boigny, Félix, 105, 130, 171, 172, 186, 195, 203, 204, 211, 233, 247, 256, 274
Huggins, Sir Godfrey, 138, 139
Hughes, Langston, 231
Huntington, Samuel P., 180
Hutu, 18–19, 103, 149, 177, 206

Ibo, see Igbo
identity card (South Africa), 113
Idris, King, 24
Igbo, 11, 21, 40, 71, 88, 173–75, 254, 261, 302
Ikime, Dr. Obaro, 48

Ileo, Joseph, 195
independence: disappointments of, 100, 204–10; promise of, 148, 208, 211
Indians: in East Africa, 31, 176; in South Africa, 113, 122, 267–68
indigénat, 41
indirect rule: Belgian, 40; British, 35–40; French, 38–39; German, 40; Portuguese opposition to, 40
integration: concept of, 150–52; and decision-making, 165–68; and development, 75; measurement of, 154
International Confederation of Free Trade Unions (ICFTU), 243, 244
Islam: brotherhoods, 21–22, 150; Fouta Djalon and, 14–15; in Morocco, 14, 16, 225; Samory and, 76; and Somalis, 84
Ivory Coast, 4, 25, 31, 34, 52, 56–58, 61, 76, 97, 106, 130, 153, 171–72, 175, 177, 185–87, 197, 202, 203, 207, 208, 224, 229, 233, 241, 247, 254, 256, 274, 275, 296, 304

Jeune Algérie, 45
Jihad, 98–99

Kader, Abd el, 70
Kamerun, 262
Karamoko Alfa, 15
Kariuki, J. M., 205
Kasavubu, Joseph, 103, 170, 241, 269
Katanga, 25, 40, 103, 169, 172–73, 176
Kaunda, Kenneth, 80, 86–88, 128, 137, 172, 236, 253, 255, 280, 285, 288, 303
Keita, Mobido, 25, 92, 241, 273
Kenya, 11, 34, 42, 54–56, 61, 63, 68, 72, 78–79, 84, 85, 94, 97, 101–2, 107, 149, 153, 164–66, 171, 176, 177, 181, 187, 189, 190, 197, 202, 205–8, 216, 225, 227, 229, 235–38, 243–45, 250–54, 259–61, 275, 279, 294, 296, 302
Kenya African National Union (KANU), 102, 186, 189, 190, 216
Kenyatta, Jomo, 85, 102, 205, 211, 216, 230, 234, 254, 259
Kikuyu, 11, 68–69, 72, 78–79, 84–85, 153, 165, 166, 177, 206
Kilson, Martin, 25, 26, 64
King, Martin Luther, Jr., 145
kinship, 19–22, 27, 41
Kissinger, Henry A., 99, 143, 290

Land Apportionment Act (Rhodesia), 137
language and nation-building, 149–50, 164, 182–83

INDEX

languages, African: ignored, 33; increased use of, 215–17
law, customary, 223–29
Leabua Jonathan, 108
Legum, Colin, 269
Lenin, V. I., 96
Lesotho, 24, 31, 62, 76, 97, 109, 110, 129, 149, 177, 186, 208, 251, 296
LeVine, Victor T., 80
Liberia, 28, 48, 61, 80, 90–93, 130, 135, 181–82, 185, 197, 242, 254, 256, 260, 296
Libya, 5, 22, 24, 32, 54, 56, 61, 80, 84, 91, 93, 149, 177, 179, 199, 195, 208, 234, 237, 241, 242, 244, 296, 303
Lomé Convention, 302
Lugard, Lord, 35, 55
Lumumba, Patrice, 95, 103, 238, 241, 269
Lusaka Manifesto, 133–34, 260, 285–86
Luthuli, Chief Albert, 80, 82, 126
Lyautey, Marshal, 37, 38

Macemba (Machemba), 69
Machel, Samora, 197
McKay, Vernon, 291
Madagascar, 5, 11, 17, 29, 32, 34, 51, 57, 62, 71, 85–86, 97, 104, 105, 149, 185–86, 197, 207, 208, 241, 258, 296, 304
Mahdi of Sudan, 22, 80
Maji-Maji revolt, 72, 84
Makerere University, 81
Malagasy, see Madagascar
Malawi, 34, 54–56, 74, 77–78, 109, 110, 129, 130, 137, 143, 172, 185, 191, 207, 208, 215, 225, 236, 244, 255–56, 260, 285, 296, 303
Mali, 23, 25, 38, 61, 62, 71, 76, 140, 153, 176, 177, 185, 195, 197, 224, 229, 233, 241, 243, 244, 259–60, 293–96
Margai, Sir Milton, 26, 64
Matanzima, Kaiser, 120, 121
Mau Mau, 84–85, 101–2, 205
Mauritania, 4, 21, 25, 52, 56, 61, 62, 97, 104, 140, 176, 185, 206, 207, 245, 251, 252, 255, 259–60, 275, 295, 296
Mauritius, 140, 258, 296
Mayolle island, 97
Mazrui, Ali, 79
Mba, Léon, 160, 170, 181, 195
Mboumduawas, Eteki, 250
Mboya, Tom, 94, 189, 238, 243
Menelik II, 25, 69, 83, 91
mining, 60–61
Mkwawa, 69
mobilization, 75, 155–57

Mobutu, Joseph, 177, 195, 254
modernization, 148, 179–83, 211
Mogho Naba, 17, 37
Monckton Commission, 137
Mondlane, Edouardo, 82, 88–89, 101
Monrovia Group, 5, 242, 245, 270
Moore, Clement, 13–14, 27
Moorosi, 76–77
Morand, Charles-Albert, 124
Morocco, 3, 5, 11, 13–14, 16, 17, 21, 24, 25, 30–31, 37, 42, 44, 45, 52–54, 56, 57, 62, 70, 77, 97, 99, 100, 104, 149, 153, 157, 164, 166, 176, 179, 185, 195, 197, 200, 225, 234–35, 237, 241, 245, 252, 255, 275, 296, 301
Mossi, 17–18, 37
Moulay er-Rachid, 14
Mourides of Senegal, 21–22
Mozambique, 27, 34, 44, 61, 65, 80, 95, 97, 99, 101, 104, 130, 131, 136 143–45, 168, 185, 188, 197, 199, 259, 296
Mphalele, Ezekiel, 212
MPLA (Angola), 101, 130, 131, 143, 177, 255, 292, 294
Muhammad, Ahmad, see Mahdi of Sudan
Mohammad, Murtala, 195
Muhammad V., 24
Muhammad Ali, 91, 99
Munongo, Godefroid, 25
Mutesa II, 25
Muzorewa, Bishop Abel, 142

Namibia, 6, 54, 66, 70, 109–10, 128–31, 134–36, 144, 147, 240, 289–90, 304
Nasser, Gamal Abdel, 92, 168, 194, 291
nation-building: barriers to, 168–70; and civic education, 166; concepts of, 148–52; in Gabon, 156–63; ideology of, 167; precolonial, 149; process of, 152–56
National Congress of British West Africa, 234
national cultures and belief systems, 163–64
National Liberation Committee (OAU), 128, 255
National Liberation Council (Ghana), 221
National Liberation Movement, 104
nationalism, 6, 34, 151–52
Nationalist Party (South Africa), 112
Nationalizing Zone, 156–63
négritude, 5, 231
neo-colonialism, 7, 207–8, 271–74
Néo-Destour Party, 88, 107–8
Neto, Dr. Agostinho, 82, 88, 101
Ngoni, 84

Niger, 61, 62, 105, 106, 178, 195, 224, 233, 241, 254, 294, 296
Nigeria, 4, 5, 11, 12, 21, 23–25, 31, 34–40, 42, 44, 48–51, 53–57, 61, 63, 71, 83, 93, 98, 107, 129, 152, 153, 164–66, 173–75, 177, 179, 183, 186, 195, 197, 202, 206, 208, 221, 233, 240, 242, 250, 251, 253, 254, 256, 261–62, 264, 270, 275, 276, 279, 293, 302, 303
Nixon, Richard M., 133, 134, 287, 288, 294, 296, 297, 301
Nkomo, Joshua, 138–39, 143
Nkrumah, Kwame, 24, 26, 82, 88, 94, 104, 166, 196, 197, 211, 233–34, 237, 238, 240–42, 245, 246, 250, 253, 264, 269, 271–73, 277, 291, 293, 294
North Atlantic Treaty Organization (NATO), 96, 284
Northern People's Congress, 37
Northern Rhodesian African Congress, 87
Nuer, 11, 155, 175
Nyerere, Julius, 24, 26, 81, 128, 147–48, 192, 193, 196, 197, 211, 213, 214, 236, 242, 252–55, 259, 264, 275–77, 281, 288, 303

Obasanjo, Olusegun, 195
Obote, Milton, 25, 202, 206, 253, 259
Odinga, Oginga, 205, 207
Ojukwu, Colonel Odumegwu, 174, 175, 254
Olympio, Sylvanus, 80, 105, 156, 195, 242, 247, 248
Organisation Commune Africaine, Malgache, et Mauricienne (OCAM), 233, 258
Organization of African Unity (OAU), 91, 110, 128–30, 216, 242–63, 288, 292, 293, 296, 298; and nonalignment, 283; and Pan-Africanism, 5, 230, 232, 236, 237; Portuguese territories and, 248; Tanzania and, 276; United Nations and, 270
Organization of Senegal River States (OERS), 259
Ortega y Gasset, José, 178, 180
Ould Daddah, Moktar, 25
Ourada, Muhammad, 39
Ovambo, 70, 136, 304
Owerri, 12

Padmore, George, 96, 232, 240
Palley, Claire, 142
Pan-African Freedom Movement of East Central and Southern Africa (PAFMECSA), 236–37

Pan-Africanism, 4–5, 230–43, 245–46, 258–60
Pan-Africanist Congress (PAC), 126–27, 255, 296
Pankhurst, Richard, 83
Paton, Alan, 125
PDG (Guinea), 191
Pearce Commission, 142, 304
Pemba islands, 102
Pompidou, Georges, 274
Portugal, 27–29, 33, 40–41, 69, 70, 97, 99, 110, 130, 175, 177, 208, 248, 254, 283
precolonial systems: centralized, 11, 13–19; contemporary governments and, 22–27, 193–94; decentralized or stateless, 11, 19–22, 27, 40–42; described, 11–22, 217–18; importance of, 8, 181–82; law of, adapted, 224–29; persistence of values of, 211–12
presidents, 166, 186, 194, 203–4
Principe, 5, 101
protégé system, 30–31
Providence Industrial Mission, 77–78, 84

Qadiriyya, 21

Rabemananjara, Jacques, 86
Rassemblement Démocratique Africain (RDA), 96, 233
Rekayi Tangwena, 26
revolution, meaning of, 199–200
Rhodesia, 4, 6, 26, 34, 56, 61, 62, 66, 85, 97, 99, 109–10, 128–30, 136–44, 147, 149, 165, 172, 177, 207, 236, 250, 264, 289, 290, 296, 304
Rhodesian Front, 138
Rio Muni, 103
Robben Island, 127
Roberto, Holden, 101, 238
Rodney, Walter, 60
Rogers, William, 133, 287
Rubin, Neville, 224, 262–63
Rwanda, 18–19, 24, 40, 97, 102–3, 149, 177, 186, 220, 296

Sadiki College, 44–45
Salah ben Youssef, 107
Sanwi, 171–72
secessions: Biafra, 171; Ethiopia, 176; Katanga, 172, 176, 195; Lozi, 170–71; Sanwi, 171–72
Selassie, Haile, 29, 91, 154, 243
Sembène, Ousmane, 71
Senegal, 4, 5, 21, 23, 26, 29, 34, 38, 40, 43–46, 51–53, 56, 61, 62, 71, 73, 75, 76, 98, 105, 107, 131, 144, 153, 167–68, 177, 185, 186, 190, 197, 199, 207,

INDEX

208, 224, 229, 233, 241, 242, 250, 251, 259, 296
Senghor, Léopold Dedar, 5, 26, 105, 136, 211, 231, 242
Senoussiya (Senusi), 22, 84
Seretse Khama, Sir, 25
servicemen: in Ghana, 77; in Kenya, 85; in Madagascar, 85–86; recruitment of, 78; in Zambia, 86–87
Sharpeville massacre, 95, 127, 132
Sidi Bou Outhman, battle of, 77
Sierra Leone, 25–27, 31, 61, 63–64, 71, 76, 185, 195, 208, 216–17, 221, 233, 242, 244, 260, 275, 296, 303
single-party state, 185–96; and coups, 193–96; elections in, 192–93; ethnicity and, 196; justifications for, 185–90; structure of, 186, 189–91
Sithole, Reverend Ndabaningi, 139
slave trade, 4, 24, 30, 31, 70, 155
Smith, Ian, 130, 138, 139, 141–44, 279, 304
Sobhuza II, 24, 220
socialism, African, 6, 168, 184, 189, 196–99
Somalia, 4, 5, 54, 55, 84, 104, 107, 149, 171, 195, 199, 242, 251, 253, 260, 294–96
South Africa, Republic of, 6, 26, 34, 56, 61, 62, 66, 72, 80, 89, 90, 92, 93, 97, 109, 137, 140, 141, 143–47, 165, 172, 175, 177, 207, 218, 236–38, 240, 248, 250, 251, 254–58, 272, 289, 290, 296, 302; arms sale to, 144, 253, 282, 295; Commonwealth and, 278, 279, 281; United Nations and, 263, 267, 271, 304
South-West Africa, *see* Namibia
South-West African People's Organization (SWAPO), 128, 129, 136
Southern Africa: defined, 109–11; future of, 144–47; population of, 4, 110
Sudan, 3, 11, 22, 23, 39, 43, 53–54, 62, 80, 91–92, 97, 140, 155, 156, 166, 175, 176, 194, 206, 208, 215, 237, 273, 260, 275, 294, 296, 302
Sule, Yusuf Maitima, 240
Swahili, 69, 102, 149, 164, 165, 192, 204, 216
Swaziland, 24, 52, 97, 109, 110, 126, 149, 177, 200, 220, 225, 251

Tan-Zam Railway, 165, 295
Tanganyika, *see* Tanzania
Tanganyika African National Union (TANU), 26, 27, 81, 186, 188–89, 192–93, 196, 204
Tanzania, 11, 24, 26, 32, 34, 40, 48, 54, 55, 69, 81, 84, 128, 139, 140, 143, 149, 153, 165, 167, 175–77, 180, 185, 186, 188–89, 192–93, 197, 202, 204, 212, 220, 224, 225, 227, 229, 235, 236, 242, 250, 252, 254, 258, 259–61, 275–77, 279–81, 288, 290, 295, 296, 299, 302, 303
Tchad, 22, 32, 38–40, 42, 47, 56, 62, 105, 155, 178, 182, 183, 195, 208, 246, 260, 275, 296
Tekrur, 11, 38
Terrorism Act (South Africa), 124, 129
Tettegah, John, 244
Thuku, Harry, 78–79
Tijaniyya, 21–22, 26
Todd, Garfield, 138
Togo, 31, 55, 56, 81, 93–95, 104–5, 107, 130, 156, 164, 170, 195, 207, 242, 245, 247, 251, 258, 275, 296
Tolbert, William R., 93, 182
Tombalbaye, François, 47, 182, 275
Tomlinson Commission, 116–17
Toucouleur, 11
Touré, Samory, 25, 75–76, 187
Touré, Sékou, 25, 26, 87, 94, 106, 107, 186–89, 191, 206, 233, 241, 243
Trade Union Congress (TUC), 189
trade unions, 64, 189, 203, 243–44
Transkei, 119–21
tribe, defined, 12; *see also* ethnic groups
Tshombe, Moïse, 25, 172–73, 254, 269
Tsiranana, 105, 304
Tubman, William V. S., 93, 242
Tunisia, 3, 24, 26, 31, 44, 45, 54, 56, 80, 88, 100, 107–8, 149, 179, 180, 185, 192, 197, 208, 234–35, 237, 242–44, 272, 275
Turkey, 3, 29, 77, 99
Tutsi, 4, 18–19, 40, 97, 103, 149, 177, 206

Uganda, 11, 19, 25, 31, 37, 40, 42, 55–56, 97, 149, 153, 164–66, 176, 177, 195, 202, 206, 227, 235, 236, 250, 253, 259–61, 276, 296, 301
ujamaa villages, 180
UNCTAD, 301
Unilateral Declaration of Independence (UDI), 139, 140, 264, 279
Union Africaine et Malgache (UAM), 244, 258
Union Camerounaise (UC), 191
Union des Populations du Cameroun (UPC), 101, 262
Union Générale des Travailleurs Algériens, 189
Union Générale des Travailleurs de l'Afrique Noire (UGTAN), 243

Union of Populations of Angola (UPA), 101, 238
Union of Soviet Socialist Republics, 10, 89, 96–97, 101, 130, 131, 143, 145, 149, 150, 152, 153, 175, 190, 196, 198, 208, 243, 245, 254, 255, 266, 268, 269, 280, 283, 284, 288, 290–97
UNIP (Zambia), 87, 137, 172
UNITA (Angola), 101, 131, 169
United Nations, 80, 91, 100, 103–5, 109, 110, 121, 125, 132–36, 140, 141, 143, 147, 173, 180, 214, 238, 241, 246–47, 250, 251, 253, 263–72, 284–86, 288, 289, 292, 295, 297–300, 304
United States of America, 29, 89, 92, 96, 111, 133–36, 145, 146, 149, 150, 154, 166, 167, 178, 185, 186, 192, 208, 211, 231, 245, 248, 254, 266, 268, 272, 274, 283, 284, 286–90, 292–95, 297, 299–301
United States of Central Africa, 260
Universal Declaration of Human Rights, 238, 246–47, 267
Universal Negro Improvement Association, 230
Upper Volta, 17, 33, 37, 53, 55, 56, 76, 97, 153, 177, 178, 186, 195, 233, 241, 260, 296, 299
urbanization, 22, 51–62, 74, 117
Usuman dan Fodio, 53, 98–99

Vansina, Jan, 30
Verwoerd, Hendrik Frensch, 112, 279
Vorster, Balthazar J., 112, 121, 129–31, 136, 145
Vy Vato movement, 71, 85

Wachuku, Jaja, 270
Waldheim, Kurt, 136, 251, 304
Warsaw Pact, 284
Welensky, Sir Roy, 138

West African Economic Community, 260
West African National Secretariat, 234, 260
West African Regional Group, 260
Whitehead, Sir Edgar, 138
William Ponty School, 44–45
Williams, Chief Rotimi, 262
Williams, H. Sylvester, 230
Wilson, Woodrow, 233
Winter, Edward, 19
Wolof, 11, 21, 75, 149, 153
Women, 179, 181
World Bank, 295, 299
World Federation of Trade Unions, 243, 291

Yao, 69
Yaya, Alfa, 71
Yoruba, 12, 32, 48, 62, 83–84, 88, 173–75, 261
Young Kikuyu Association, 79

Zaïre, 4, 25, 29, 31, 40, 51, 61, 88, 95, 103, 104, 143, 149, 153, 169, 170, 172, 177, 183, 185, 195, 196, 208, 238, 250, 253–55, 260, 264, 269, 272, 273, 290, 296, 303
Zambia, 11, 34, 37, 42, 52, 54–56, 61, 80, 86–87, 109, 128, 137, 138, 141, 143, 172, 175–77, 186, 207, 225, 236, 253, 254, 259, 260, 279, 280, 285, 288, 290, 295, 296, 303
Zanzibar, 5, 24, 34, 37, 102, 103, 236, 245, 295
Zimbabwe, see Rhodesia
Zimbabwe African National Union (ZANU), 128, 129, 139, 141
Zimbabwe African People's Union (ZAPU), 128, 138, 139, 141
Zolberg, Aristide, 194
Zulu, 16–17, 21, 26, 70, 114, 118, 120, 121, 165, 218

(212)-686-9137
Aimee —
    credit card.